D1607036

The Evolution of Mental Health Law

The LAW AND PUBLIC POLICY: PSYCHOLOGY AND THE
SOCIAL SCIENCES series includes books in three domains:

Legal Studies—writings by legal scholars about issues of relevance to
psychology and the other social sciences, or that employ social
science information to advance the legal analysis;

Social Science Studies—writings by scientists from psychology and
the other social sciences about issues of relevance to law and public
policy; and

Forensic Studies—writings by psychologists and other mental health
scientists and professionals about issues relevant to forensic mental
health science and practice.

The series is guided by its editor, Bruce D. Sales, PhD, JD, ScD(hc),
University of Arizona; and coeditors, Bruce J. Winick, JD, University of
Miami; Norman J. Finkel, PhD, Georgetown University; and Stephen J.
Ceci, PhD, Cornell University.

* * *

The Evolution of Mental Health Law

EDITED BY

Lynda E. Frost
Richard J. Bonnie

AMERICAN PSYCHOLOGICAL ASSOCIATION
WASHINGTON, DC

Copyright © 2001 by the American Psychological Association. All rights reserved. Except as permitted under the United States Copyright Act of 1976, no part of this publication may be reproduced or distributed in any form or by any means, or stored in a database or retrieval system, without the prior written permission of the publisher.

Published by
American Psychological Association
750 First Street, NE
Washington, DC 20002
www.apa.org

To order: Tel: (800) 374-2721, Direct: (202) 336-5510
APA Order Department   Fax: (202) 336-5502, TDD/TTY: (202) 336-6123
P.O. Box 92984   Online: www.apa.org/books/
Washington, DC 20090-2984   Email: order@apa.org

In the U.K., Europe, Africa, and the Middle East, copies may be ordered from
American Psychological Association
3 Henrietta Street
Covent Garden, London
WC2E 8LU England

Typeset in Goudy by EPS Group Inc., Easton, MD

Printer: Edwards Brothers, Inc., Ann Arbor, MI
Dust jacket designer: Berg Design, Albany, NY
Technical/Production Editor: Jennifer Powers

The opinions and statements published are the responsibility of the authors, and such opinions and statements do not necessarily represent the policies of the American Psychological Association.

Library of Congress Cataloging-in-Publication Data
The evolution of mental health law / edited by Lynda E. Frost and Richard J. Bonnie.
        p. cm.
    Includes bibliographical references and index.
    ISBN 1-55798-746-7 (alk. paper)
    1. Mental health laws—United States.   2. Insanity—Jurisprudence—United States.   3. Forensic psychiatry—United States.   I. Frost, Lynda E. II. Bonnie, Richard J.

    KF3828 .E94 2001
    344.73'044—dc21

                                                                                                    2001018897

British Library Cataloguing-in-Publication Data
A CIP record is available from the British Library.

Printed in the United States of America
First Edition

CONTENTS

CONTRIBUTORS

Joseph J. Bevilacqua, PhD, The Bazelon Center for Mental Health Law, Washington, DC

Richard J. Bonnie, LLB, University of Virginia School of Law, Charlottesville

Robert A. Burt, JD, Yale University Law School

Rebecca Dresser, MS, JD, Washington University Schools of Law and Medicine, St. Louis, Missouri

W. Lawrence Fitch, JD, Maryland Department of Health and Mental Hygiene, and University of Maryland Law School, Baltimore

Lynda E. Frost, JD, PhD, Institute of Law, Psychiatry, and Public Policy, University of Virginia, Charlottesville

Thomas Grisso, PhD, Law and Psychiatry Program, University of Massachusetts Medical School, Worcester

Seymour L. Halleck, MD, Department of Psychiatry, University of North Carolina, Chapel Hill

Gary Hawk, PhD, Institute of Law, Psychiatry, and Public Policy, University of Virginia, Charlottesville

John Monahan, PhD, University of Virginia School of Law, Charlottesville

Stephen J. Morse, JD, PhD, University of Pennsylvania Law School, Philadelphia

John Petrila, JD, LLM, Department of Mental Health Law and Policy, Florida Mental Health Institute, University of South Florida, Tampa

Svetlana V. Polubinskaya, Cand. Jur. Sci., Institute of State and Law, Russian Academy of Sciences, Moscow, Russia

Elyn R. Saks, MLitt, JD, University of Southern California Law School, Los Angeles

Christopher Slobogin, JD, LLM, University of Florida Levin College of Law, Gainesville

Henry J. Steadman, PhD, Policy Research Associates, Delmar, New York

David B. Wexler, JD, University of Arizona College of Law, Tucson, and University of Puerto Rico School of Law, San Juan

Bruce J. Winick, JD, University of Miami School of Law, Coral Gables, Florida

PREFACE

Three decades ago, mental health law did not exist as an identifiable field of specialized research or practice. Psychiatric hospitals and facilities for people with mental retardation carried on their activities without much guidance or limitation by the law, and the interests of people with mental disabilities had relatively skimpy legal protection. In the late 1960s and 1970s, however, innovative attorneys brought and won novel cases on behalf of people with mental disabilities. In the beginning, this litigation was understood as an effort to rein in the unchecked power of mental health professionals over institutionalized patients and residents. State legislatures drafted detailed mental health codes, and state departments of mental health found it necessary to craft policy according to emerging legal principles and requirements enunciated by courts and legislatures. More recently, a body of legal protections for people with mental disabilities outside institutions has begun to emerge.

In the academic world, a growing number of specialists in law, psychiatry, and psychology have generated the theoretical insights and empirical research needed to support a developing corpus of mental health law and policy. An early (and continuing) actor in this process was the Institute of Law, Psychiatry, and Public Policy at the University of Virginia. The institute was created in 1977 to pursue research, education, and policy development in mental health law and forensic psychiatry and psychology. (In this book, the phrase *mental health law* refers, comprehensively, to the bodies of law relating to people with mental disabilities and the activities of mental health professionals, as well as to the uses of mental health knowledge in adjudication and other legal contexts. In this broad sense the phrase encompasses what is often described as "law and psychology.") Through the expertise of the attorneys, psychiatrists, psychologists, and social workers on its faculty, the institute has pursued an integrated approach to interdisciplinary programs in mental health practice, social policy, and the law.

In celebration of the institute's 20th anniversary, the University of Virginia hosted a conference in October 1997 that brought together many of the most creative minds in the field to consider the history and future of this vibrant field of research and practice. The presenters at the two-day conference were asked to address significant developments in mental health law and policy over the preceding 25 years and to explore trends likely to influence the field in the future. Those presentations were the genesis of this book.

The chapters in this book explore cases and events that have shaped mental health law in these crucial, formative years. The authors will be familiar to most readers; many of them produced seminal books and articles in the early days of the field. All authors, whether their voices are familiar or new, bring unique and important perspectives to this developing discipline and have helped define and address the central questions in mental health law. We thank all of the authors for their insightful contributions and for their patience.

We also acknowledge the helpful contributions of Anne Woodworth, development editor of the American Psychological Association, and the useful comments of two anonymous reviewers. Brian Glass, Class of 2002, provided invaluable editorial assistance. We are also grateful to Robert E. Scott, dean of the School of Law, for his support for the institute, for its Anniversary Conference, and for the research support that enabled us to pursue this project.

The Evolution of Mental Health Law

INTRODUCTION

LYNDA E. FROST AND RICHARD J. BONNIE

This book is meant to be a retrospective view, a taking stock of the development of a field. It is therefore worth pausing at the outset to consider the point of departure. Obviously, most of the topics discussed here —the insanity defense for one—have deep historical roots, but we think that mental health law as a discernible field of specialized study began to emerge in the late 1960s and early 1970s. If we were to identify a particular year as a point of departure for historical reflection, we would pick 1972. In that year, the U.S. Supreme Court extended due process and equal protection doctrine to a criminal defendant with mental disabilities (*Jackson v. Indiana*, 1972), a federal district court in Wisconsin enunciated a list of constitutionally required procedural protections that must be followed before a state may civilly commit an individual (*Lessard v. Schmidt*, 1972), and another federal district court in Alabama issued a decree setting forth "minimum constitutional standards for adequate treatment" of hospitalized mental patients in Alabama (*Wyatt v. Stickney*, 1972).

Jackson involved a criminal defendant who was hearing impaired, mute, and mentally retarded and who had been civilly committed for an indeterminate period for restoration of competence to stand trial. Noting Indiana's lack of services for individuals like Jackson and the extent of his disabilities, the Supreme Court found that Jackson's commitment for competence restoration amounted to a life sentence imposed without the benefit of either a trial or a commitment hearing. The Court held that the due process clause permitted the state to institutionalize Jackson only for a reasonable period of time for the purpose of determining whether there was a substantial probability of restoring him to competence in the near future.

Lessard v. Schmidt was a class action on behalf of all individuals hospitalized under Wisconsin's commitment law, which allowed the state to commit individuals for up to 145 days without a hearing or even notice. The federal court delineated a list of constitutionally required protections (such as a right to an attorney and a jury trial) and procedures that the state must follow to restrict an individual's liberty through involuntary psychiatric hospitalization. The practical and policy implications of the stricter civil commitment standards constitutionally required in *Jackson* and *Lessard* opened a new path for constitutional litigation.

Although the constitutional grounding for the "right to treatment" enunciated in *Wyatt v. Stickney* has not yet been fully embraced by the United States Supreme Court, Judge Frank Johnson's decree served as a model for legislation and administrative action in many states designed to protect the rights of institutionalized patients and to monitor the conditions in public psychiatric hospitals. A new academic specialty emerged as practitioners, policymakers, and academics scrutinized and redefined the legal system's treatment of people with mental illness.

Many social changes have occurred since 1972, accompanied by dramatic changes in mental health law. Many individuals who in earlier years would have been confined in institutions are now living full lives in the community, whereas others are homeless or ensnared in the criminal justice system. The mental health system has become far more formalized in a procedural sense, although one may question whether the increase in procedural regularity has always been accompanied by enhanced justice. Oversight mechanisms for research and treatment are far more common than before, mandating more transparency in the provision and documentation of care, but repeated efforts to restructure public mental health services have left many gaps in care and in oversight.

The structure of mental health service delivery is also now radically different, with a long-term movement toward deinstitutionalization and a slow, inadequate transition to community-based services. Political and economic changes have led to increased privatization of public mental health services. Although states have adopted many different arrangements for delivering forensic evaluation services, the trend is toward providing them at the community level and requiring specialized training for evaluators. Forensic psychiatry and psychology are now recognized as subspecialties of their parent disciplines, thereby increasing the quality and sophistication of expert opinion, but also raising barriers to entry.

Research in the field has grown immensely since the early 1970s, as evidenced by the successful introduction of several journals devoted exclusively to the connections between psychiatry, clinical psychology, and the law, not to mention the many other topics and disciplines at the intersections of law and other subdisciplines within psychology. Examples of new North American journals include *Law and Human Behavior; The International Journal of Law and Psychiatry; Psychology, Public Policy, and Law; The Journal of the American Academy of Psychiatry and the Law;* and *The Journal of Psychiatry and Law.* Research initiatives such as those growing out of the MacArthur Foundation's multimillion-dollar support of the MacArthur Research Network on Mental Health and the Law have prompted dramatic advances in the knowledge base of the field.

This book aims to describe and reflect on these changes, presenting a developmental history of the field and drawing together specialists from its many domains. The chapters are organized in five sections. Part I includes two historical chapters addressing the values at the center of mental health law. In chapter 1, law professor Robert A. Burt, one of the early contributors to the effort to reform mental health care in this country, assesses developments in mental health law since 1972 by reaching even more deeply into the past. He compares the waxing and waning of legal protections for individuals with mental disabilities to the changing legal protections for racial groups in the United States. He concludes that although the courts once played a crucial role in guarding against the marginalization of socially vulnerable groups, other institutions are now needed to play this protective role. He thereby poses a challenge to academics and practitioners, lawyers and clinicians alike: How can we nurture and sustain a societal commitment to the well-being of people with mental illness and other stigmatized groups, displacing what has been a recurring cycle of broken promises? In chapter 2, editor Richard J. Bonnie identifies three strands in the fabric of mental health law—liberty, equal citizenship, and entitlement—and traces their development over the past three decades.

Part II addresses legal and ethical structures for protecting the rights of patients, including the provision of services that respond to their needs. In chapter 3, law professor Rebecca Dresser describes shifts in attitudes toward practices governing human participants in research, changing from concerns about lack of protections for research participants with mental disabilities to more recent allegations of unreasonable exclusion from promising research studies. Lawyer and health policy specialist John Petrila outlines in chapter 4 the statutory and regulatory framework that now undergirds public mental health services and questions whether this framework adequately protects patients' rights in an increasingly privatized service system. Drawing on a career of experience at the helm of public mental health service systems, Joseph J. Bevilacqua delineates in chapter 5 issues commonly overlooked as managed care absorbs mental health services, and he also raises concerns about the human costs of the privatization process. Chapter 6, by Russia's leading mental health law expert, Svetlana V. Polubinskaya, shows how the principles of mental health law in the United States have helped to shape newly developing international norms of human rights. She describes recent efforts to bring the Russian psychiatric system within reach of the rule of law and to eradicate the vestiges of Soviet psychiatry.

Part III considers the changing ideas and practices regarding conceptions of the criminal responsibility of defendants with mental impairments. In chapter 7, law professor Stephen J. Morse examines conceptions of free will and responsibility that underlie contemporary jurisprudence and presents a conceptual framework that explains why advancing knowledge regarding the "determinants" of human behavior does not undermine individual responsibility for criminal actions. The next two chapters address claims of diminished responsibility in two most controversial and unsettling domains of the law—punishment of juveniles and capital sentencing, each of which has been transformed over the past three decades. Forensic psychologist Thomas Grisso details in chapter 8 changes in the juvenile justice system bearing on the culpability of defendants whose judgment might be affected by age and immaturity. In chapter 9, psychiatrist Seymour L. Halleck describes legal and practical factors affecting forensic psychiatric testimony in mitigation in a capital case.

Part IV reviews advances in scientific understanding within the mental health disciplines and their impact on the practice of forensic mental health. Psychologist John Monahan and sociologist Henry J. Steadman, who have been working together for 20 years, analyze in chapter 10 the legal implications of research in risk assessment and argue that, in the future, actuarial risk assessment will be far more common than clinical risk assessment, minimizing reliance on clinical interpretation. In chapter 11, forensic psychologist Gary Hawk and state forensic services administrator and attorney W. Lawrence Fitch summarize the movement toward community-based forensic systems and suggest ways to support effective forensic subspecialization for clinicians in the community. Law professor Elyn R. Saks describes the contributions and limitations of psychoanalysis in a forensic context in chapter 12. Finally, in chapter 13 law professor Christopher Slobogin reviews judicial responses to novel syndrome testimony and proposes a means of improving the evidentiary analysis of expert psychiatric testimony.

Part V, the final section of the book, comprises two chapters describing and applying the perspectives of therapeutic jurisprudence by the co-founders of this new "school" of mental health law. David B. Wexler explains in chapter 14 how notions of therapeutic jurisprudence have begun to influence the behavior of judges and lawyers. In chapter 15, Bruce J. Winick proposes means by which judges, lawyers, and clinicians can proceed from a more therapeutic frame of reference in the context of civil commitment proceedings.

As readers will see, mental health law has changed dramatically in its first three decades as an identifiable field of academic discourse. However, as noted in the Afterword, the fundamental problems that lie at the center of the field (protecting the rights and needs of people with mental disabilities, defining the proper sphere of individualization in criminal justice, and drawing boundaries between science and morality in legal decision making) have remained the same. The challenge, as Professor Burt observes in chapter 1, is to address these problems while maintaining a commitment to the humanitarian values that inspired the field at its birth.

REFERENCES

Jackson v. Indiana, 406 U.S. 715 (1972).

Lessard v. Schmidt, 349 F. Supp. 1078 (E.D. Wisc. 1972).

Wyatt v. Stickney, 344 F. Supp. 373 (M.D. Ala. 1972).

I

MENTAL HEALTH LAW AND
AMERICAN SOCIETY

1

PROMISES TO KEEP, MILES TO GO: MENTAL HEALTH LAW SINCE 1972

ROBERT A. BURT

In June 1997 the U.S. Supreme Court rejected a constitutional challenge to a statute enacted by the Kansas legislature. This decision, *Kansas v. Hendricks* (1997), is not just important on its own terms; it is emblematic of the current difficult and dangerous moment in mental health law. Three years earlier, in 1994, the Kansas legislature had enacted what it vividly called the Sexually Violent Predator Act. The act provided indeterminate civil commitment for anyone found likely to engage in "predatory acts of sexual violence" due to "mental abnormality" or "personality disorder." In 1996, the Kansas state supreme court declared this statute unconstitutional on the grounds that substantive due process required a finding of "mental illness" and that the criteria set out in the statute constituted something less.

Beyond this somewhat formalistic and definitional holding, a deeper critique lay beneath the state supreme court's condemnation of the statute. The state court found that "treatment for sexually violent predators is all but nonexistent" and that, in enacting the statute, the state legislature had virtually conceded that "sexually violent predators are not amenable to treatment"; from these findings, the court held, "If there is nothing to treat

... then there is no mental illness" (p. 365). The state court found that the Kansas legislature had provided permanent incarceration without possibility of release but had disguised this imposition in a civil commitment statute that appeared to promise treatment and the possibility of ultimate release. As the state court observed with restrained understatement, this promise was "somewhat disingenuous" (p. 365).

The U.S. Supreme Court, however, disposed of the state court's objections in quick order. In an opinion by Justice Clarence Thomas, the Court ruled that the statutory criteria for commitment were adequate and that incapacitation of "sexually violent offenders" is a legitimate matter for civil as well as criminal law—especially, as Thomas wrote, when that concern is coupled with the state's goal "of providing treatment to those offenders, if such is possible" (p. 366).

This chapter begins with the Supreme Court's recent decision in *Kansas v. Hendricks* because the overriding goal of the chapter is to assess the progress of mental health law since 1972, and the striking fact is that the 1997 *Hendricks* ruling is, in the immortal words of Yogi Berra, "déjà vu all over again." In 1972 states confined various categories of people with mental disabilities and encircled these confinements with promises of beneficent treatment and ultimate restoration to the community. These promises, however, were dishonored in actual practice and were virtually fraudulent from the outset.

My personal involvement in litigation regarding people with mental disabilities began in 1972 with a case that raised the identical issue in *Hendricks* but reached the opposite result. This case was a successful constitutional challenge to a Michigan statute providing indefinite civil commitment for "criminal sexual psychopaths" (*Kaimowitz v. Michigan Department of Mental Health*, 1973). My client, Louis Smith, had been confined in the state maximum security mental institution for 18 years. When he was an adolescent, he had been charged but not convicted of rape and murder; as an alternative to criminal prosecution, his parents asked to have him committed under the civil statute because of its apparent promise of therapeutic treatment. Eighteen years later, when I was appointed to represent Smith, I tracked down the records of everyone who had been criminally convicted of first-degree murder around the time when Smith had been civilly committed as a "criminal sexual psychopath." As it turned out, none of those criminally convicted remained in prison, and the longest prison sentence served for any first-degree murder conviction in the state had been 16 years. (There was then, and still is, no death penalty in Michigan.)

Smith testified in a proceeding related to this constitutional challenge about his confinement in the special state mental institution for "the criminally insane." In the course of his testimony, I asked Smith how he felt about the state institution where he had been confined. He replied,

Well, Mr. Burt, overall, it is not a very good attitude. I must truthfully say that. The hospital was set up for detention, and as far as I am concerned, the attitude and the policies toward patients when I first went there were very nil. I have the feeling that when I was put there that it was just nothing but for detention and to get rid of me and, well, a place to stay. And this is the way it has been over the years. Of course, I have never been mistreated really physically, but the emotional treatment has been like—as far as I am concerned—it has been like a dog in a pen.

This testimony points to the underlying motivation that led the three-judge Michigan state court in 1973 to declare Smith's confinement and the state statute unconstitutional. Beyond this immediate impact, moreover, there was a large cultural significance to Smith's observations. His testimony expressively captured the social policy toward people with mental disabilities that had been dominant in this country for almost the entire 20th century until 1972: a policy of imposed invisibility.

The promise of medical treatment and beneficent paternalism was so patently false and so obviously disconnected to the true purpose and conditions of confinement that it was itself an imposition of invisibility. In truth, the promise was nothing more than a pretense of interaction and mutual recognition between the "normal public," as represented by state authorities, and "mentally abnormal" confinees, not just those who were labeled "criminal sexual psychopaths," but all manner of people identified as "mentally ill" or "mentally retarded" and confined in massive state institutions in remote rural areas hidden away from the general public. This fraudulent promise constituted a refusal to acknowledge the social reality between its maker and its recipient. The institutional confinement was a masked enterprise.

ENDING SOCIAL INVISIBILITY: EARLY 1970s VS. LATE 1990s

The new social phenomenon in 1972 was a stripping away of the masks. Judges were suddenly prepared to look behind the facade of these false promises and inside the mental illness and mental retardation institutions; they were ready to speak the truth that its inmates were treated not as patients, but as "dogs in a pen." The Michigan judges in Louis Smith's case were not, of course, acting alone in 1972. David Bazelon, in the U.S. Court of Appeals for the D.C. Circuit, had unmasked these conditions in a series of cases involving criminal insanity and ordinary civil commitments in the mid-1960s (*Lake v. Cameron*, 1966; *Rouse v. Cameron*, 1966). Frank Johnson in the U.S. District Court for Alabama had just declared a constitutional right to treatment for the brutalized residents of the state mental illness and mental retardation institutions (*Wyatt v. Stickney*, 1971).

Nor were these judges working alone. State legislatures responded, sometimes under the direct prod of litigation and sometimes simply in the face of the possibility of litigation, by repealing many of the most obviously punitive civil confinement laws. By the mid-1970s, some 15 states had repealed their confinement laws for "sexual psychopaths," "mentally defective delinquents," and others branded with similar nomenclature to delineate, as my former Chicago colleague Norval Morris aptly put it, a special category of the "mad *and* the bad," a category that would then be subjected to more brutal treatment than those considered only "mad" or only "bad" (Brakel, Parry, & Weiner, 1985, pp. 739–740; Morris, 1968, pp. 524–525).

Even more significantly, the U.S. Congress, in response to a ruling by just one federal court in Pennsylvania, enacted in 1975 the most sweeping reversal in the 20th century of the social policy of enforced invisibility regarding people with mental disabilities. Three years earlier, in the case of *Pennsylvania Association of Retarded Children (P.A.R.C.) v. Pennsylvania* (1972), a federal district court had ruled that the state's policy of excluding children with mental disabilities from public schools and providing resources for them only in massive, geographically isolated state institutions violated the children's rights to equal protection. The state of Pennsylvania itself, in this litigation, conceded the injustice of their exclusionary policy and agreed to a consent decree, which the district court then independently ratified.

This exclusionary policy was not unique to Pennsylvania; it was common throughout the United States (Burt, 1985, p. 329). In 1975, just three years after the Pennsylvania ruling, Congress enacted the Education for All Handicapped Children Act, imposing on every state an obligation—as a condition of receiving any federal educational funds—to provide a "free, appropriate public education" for all children no matter how severely disabled (either mentally or physically) they might be (*Board of Education v. Rowley*, 1982). This was a stunning reversal of the prior national policy, a reversal with great social significance and, not incidentally, quite impressive financial implications, amounting by today's standards to a commitment of some $6 billion in federal funds and much more in state educational funds.

These events clustered around 1972 shattered the enforced social invisibility of people with mental disabilities in judicial and in legislative proceedings. They give rise to the three questions I explore in this chapter: First, what might explain the sudden public visibility around 1972 of previously invisible, scorned, and excluded people with mental disabilities? Second, what might explain the current resurgence of the impulse to reimpose social invisibility—on people with mental disabilities, as represented by the Supreme Court's decision in *Kansas v. Hendricks*? And third, what kinds of strategies might best be pursued by people who remain passionately committed to honest social acknowledgment of and engagement with people with mental disabilities and to the truth as it was revealed in public forums around 1972?

These are large questions. The answers submitted in this chapter will therefore be both broadly sketched and, more importantly, quite speculative. I will not present substantial proof for the explanatory propositions or strategic courses offered here. The questions I have posed simply do not lend themselves to definitive resolutions. But the prospect of a return to the social policies that prevailed before 1972, and the harmfulness and indignities inherent in those policies, renders this kind of inquiry, speculative as it must be, of urgent concern. The Supreme Court's ruling in *Kansas v. Hendricks* is not an isolated event. The Kansas legislature did not act alone in 1994 when it resurrected the old, previously discredited policies of using civil commitment statutes and false promises of beneficent treatment as masks for indefinite incarceration of feared "sexual predators." At least five state legislatures had enacted similar statutes around the same time, and the Supreme Court's decision will undoubtedly provide the impetus for more such laws (Hansen, 1997, p. 43).

Beyond the laws targeted at so-called violent sexual predators, there are other indications of shifting social policies toward all categories of people with mental disabilities. The most striking indication is the inhospitality of federal courts today to litigation on behalf of members of this population. The courts, the principal public forums of the 1970s that gave visibility to these previously invisible people and the false promises and indignities inflicted on them, no longer act as a counterforce to the resurgent impulses of exclusion and invisibility that have already appeared and seem likely to intensify. It is against this urgent backdrop that I approach these questions: Why the new openness and honesty in the early 1970s? Why this falling away by 1997? What strategies might we follow to counteract this current trend?

PRECURSORS TO THE NEW OPENNESS

1950 marks one of the first modern breaches in the walls of social invisibility for people with mental disabilities. In that year, a group of parents of children with mental retardation banded together to form the National Association for Retarded Children (Burt, 1985, p. 328). The public self-identification of these parents represented an act of extraordinary boldness in ways that are hard to recapture today. Social hostility toward retardation was generalized and powerful, and parents bore a heavy load of shame, guilt, and self-mortification; they thus displayed enormous courage in "going public" and demanding social recognition and assistance for their children. That people with mental disabilities were invisible might suggest that the general public did not care much one way or the other about them, but that simply was not so, and it is important for the purposes of understanding the entire phenomenon addressed here to realize that the general public was actively hostile toward, and indeed in an imagined state of warfare with, people with mental disabilities.

The clearest evidence of this hostility can be found in an opinion of the U.S. Supreme Court written in 1927 by one of the great heroes of modern American law, Justice Oliver Wendell Holmes. In the now-notorious case of *Buck v. Bell* (1927), the Court upheld Virginia's compulsory sterilization law for so-called mental defectives:

> We have seen more than once that the public welfare may call upon the best citizens for their lives. It would be strange if it could not call upon those who already sap the strength of the State for these lesser sacrifices . . . in order to prevent our being swamped with incompetence. It is better for all the world, if instead of waiting to execute degenerate offspring for crime, or to let them starve for their imbecility, society can prevent those who are manifestly unfit from continuing their kind. . . . Three generations of imbeciles are enough. (p. 207)

This is a clear declaration of war—a war waged against those who "sap the strength of the State," against those who threaten to swamp the rest of us with incompetence, against those who will inevitably be executed for crimes or starve because of "their imbecility," whose very existence should therefore be met with a pre-emptive strike. To understand the social attitude toward mental disability in this light, not as apathy or even as aversion but as hostility so strong as to barely constrain violence, is to grasp the full significance of the geographic isolation and social invisibility imposed on people with mental disabilities. This imposition was in the psychological service of establishing a separation of hostile forces, an uneasy truce, and a kind of no man's land as an alternative to open and generally destructive warfare.

The aggression was, of course, not necessarily mutual. But when people with mental disabilities and those closest to them, such as the parents of children with mental retardation, perceived the depth and power of the hostility toward them from the self-proclaimed "normal community" (as represented by the redoubtable Justice Holmes), it is no wonder that they would choose to "lie low," "get out of the line of fire," and accept their isolation and invisibility in preference to the imposition of an even worse catastrophe.

This account does not, however, explain why the parents of children with mental retardation chose to challenge the regime of invisibility in 1950. It rather deepens the mystery: In the face of this kind of incipient warfare and threatened escalation, why would they ever have dared to go public? It is not enough to say that the accumulated burdens of indignities heaped on them finally became too much to tolerate; people with mental disabilities and those close to them had been carrying these burdens in shamed silence for generations before 1950. What emboldened them finally to speak out then? Two forces might explain this phenomenon.

The first was the force of an example: the example of Black Americans, who only recently, and almost equally as suddenly, had been openly protesting the indignities imposed on them for many generations past. The social impositions against which Black people protested were, moreover, remarkably similar to those imposed on people with mental disabilities. Not only did a spatial segregation separate Black from White Americans, just as institutionalization separated people with mental disabilities from "normal" people, but in both cases there was barely contained aggression on the part of the dominant party and a psychological sense of social invisibility imposed on the subjugated. In his novel *Invisible Man*, published in 1947, Ralph Ellison gave classic expression to this sense. Within the opening lines of the book, the narrator declares,

> I am an invisible man. No, I am not a spook . . . I am a man of substance, of flesh and bones, fiber and liquids—and I might even be said to possess a mind. I am invisible, understand, simply because people refuse to see me. (p. 7)

There is a direct linkage between Ellison's prologue and the less artful, less sophisticated, but nonetheless equally powerful testimony of my client, Louis Smith, in the 1972 Michigan trial.

Another parallel between these two accounts reveals the second force behind the challenge to social invisibility. Ellison's novel and Smith's testimony spoke to an audience from within the dominant segment of society that was, suddenly and unexpectedly, prepared to listen to them—to accept and even to cultivate the breach in the wall of invisibility that both of them so vividly described. The parents of children with mental retardation and other members of the mental disability community were emboldened to go public by an audience that was suddenly ready to listen to the voices of the oppressed and willing to look through the customary walls of invisibility that had masked the abuses inflicted on, and even the very existence of, Black people and those with mental disabilities.

But where did this new attentiveness come from, and what were the reasons for this unaccustomed receptivity within the general community? Large numbers of people, it seemed, suddenly came to believe that they had more in common with the oppressed, the excluded, and the invisible than they had previously recognized. Indeed, the very commonality that the general community suddenly recognized was precisely the status of being oppressed, excluded, and invisible. Regarding race issues, substantial numbers of White Americans suddenly looked at Blacks and found mirror images of their own newly vivid sense of victimization and vulnerability.

Ellison's depiction of Blacks as invisible men was emblematic of a sudden widespread sense among White Americans that they too had become "invisible" in crucially important aspects of their social and economic lives.

The publication in 1950 of David Reisman's book *The Lonely Crowd* and in 1956 of William Whyte's *The Organization Man* supports this claim. Both books were immensely popular among the general reading public; indeed, Reisman's book remains the all-time bestseller published by the Yale University Press. Both focused precisely on the themes that Ellison had portrayed for Black people—the sense of isolation and vulnerability, of nonrecognition and consequent pervasive powerlessness, in the social and working lives of White men. The old stereotypes of White men as dominant, self-possessed, and independent had been eroded in the post-Depression, post–World War II world; so too had the old images of White men confidently exercising authority over docile, subordinate Black people. We might say that Black people "rose up" into unaccustomed visibility because White men no longer felt confident about their capacity to keep them "in their place."

This same erosion of self-confident authority among White men was, it would seem, a crucial underlying element in the uprising of other subordinated and socially invisible groups in the 1960s and early 1970s. These groups were emboldened to speak up for themselves at the same time that the historically dominant group was newly receptive to hearing the voices of the oppressed, because those voices now spoke directly to them of their own unaccustomed sense of vulnerability and powerlessness. The new boldness of the subordinates was, to an important degree, a response to the new insecurities of the dominators. Whatever the underlying social and economic factors that produced this uncomfortable insecurity, its unaccustomed existence is the crucial element in explaining why public space suddenly opened for previously invisible groups, such as people with mental disabilities, to demand and obtain social recognition.

These shifting group self-images did not, of course, all move together in a smooth linear progression. Many White men, in particular, resisted these efforts to escape from invisibility, and many did so with a passionate intensity made all the more urgent by the very fact that their authority was being called into question by previously subordinate groups; these domineering men would not admit the existence of disturbing questions about themselves that were arising from deeper social forces.

HISTORICAL CYCLES OF PUBLIC ATTENTION

The post–World War II era was not the first time a dramatic shift had occurred in the relationships between previously dominant and subordinate groups. An examination of several previous historical instances of this shift offers an answer to the second question this chapter poses—that is, what might explain the current resurgence of the exclusionary impulse regarding people with mental disabilities. There have been, roughly speaking, three peak moments since the founding of the United States of intense, reform-minded, self-consciously benevolent and ameliorist public attention to people with mental disabilities.

The first moment was at the beginning of the Jacksonian era, around the mid-1820s—the moment, in Rothman's (1971) words, of the "discovery of the asylum," a period when specialized residential institutions were created to provide curative treatment for several different categories of socially "abnormal" people, not just those with mental illnesses, but also criminals and orphans. This period saw the invention of the penitentiary as well as the insane asylum and the orphanage, and all of them began with elaborate rationales to provide beneficent treatment to their inmates so as to cure their deviancies and return them safely to normal social life. By the end of the Civil War, all of these institutions had evolved into mockeries of their originally touted purposes. They had become almost exclusively custodial in practice. Even worse, the original promises of therapeutic treatment had been turned virtually upside down; the treatment of the inmates was patently brutal and antitherapeutic (Rothman, 1971, pp. 265–295).

The second moment of intensely reformist public attention came around the mid-1890s. The promises of therapeutic treatment were elaborately resurrected, and new and ambitious plans were formulated based on a new confidence in the curative powers of medical science and in the behavioral engineering possibilities of social scientists (Rothman, 1980). This was the era of Progressive reform in social and economic life generally (Rothman, 1980, p. 215). The distinctive innovation for the treatment and cure of social deviancy in this era was the invention of the juvenile court in 1899 and its rapid extension to almost every state by 1920 (Rothman, 1980, p. 215). The juvenile court philosophy (see Grisso, chapter 8, this volume) promised benevolent state paternalism to reform wayward children as a substitute for the prior social policy of punishing young criminals; this same philosophy reinfused state mental illness and retardation institutions with ambitious, publicly proclaimed therapeutic programs and promises.

But once again these promises were transformed into brutal mockeries. The mental disability institutions in particular grew exponentially in size while even the pretense of therapeutic programs virtually disappeared. By the end of World War II, life-term custody of large numbers of people with mental disabilities, in conditions of unspeakable brutality, had become the modal practice of these institutions in every state (Burt, 1985, pp. 326–327; Rothman, 1980, pp. 336–337, 374–375). The third moment of intense reform-minded public attention came in the late 1960s and early 1970s, the starting point of our era.

This chronology, of course, is deeply depressing. Like the regular progression of the celestial bodies, high moments of public attention and protestations of beneficent purpose are followed by public disregard for people with mental disabilities and by the reimposition of social invisibility and brutal treatment. If these cycles of boom and bust are simply recurrent natural events, then the Supreme Court's decision in *Kansas v. Hendricks* (1997) foretells another turn of the wheel, from promises of therapeutic assistance back toward Oliver Wendell Holmes's openly avowed warfare against people with mental disabilities. This quick historical account is, at the very least, a basis for concern. But a deeper examination of this recurrent cycle reveals some possibilities for self-conscious actions to break out of this terrible repetitive cycle.

Heightened Sense of Social Disorder

Each of the historical moments of public attention and professed benevolence toward people with mental disabilities was characterized by a heightened and generalized sense of social disorder. The mid-1820s marked the end of the comforting reign of the Founders' generation; James Monroe had been re-elected president in 1820 only one vote short of unanimity in the electoral college, and he lost that vote only because one elector decided that since George Washington had been unanimously elected, no one else should receive that high honor (Burt, 1992, p. 133). This so-called "era of good feeling" burst like the proverbial bubble when Monroe left the presidency. The succession of John Quincy Adams, the combative, provocative, and generally inept son of the second president (a genuine Founding Father), was a vivid symbol of our plunge into disturbing, unaccustomed social disorder (Burt, 1992, pp. 196–197; Wiebe, 1985, p. 150).

The 1890s had the same deeply unsettling general character. It was a time of sharp economic depression and of widespread violent disturbances between labor and capital. It was also a moment rife with the generalized fear that open civil war was about to erupt once again (Wiebe, 1967, p. 90). As for the late 1960s and early 1970s, vivid living memories remain of the ways in which customary expectations of social order were visibly dissolving: the turmoil of the Vietnam War, the stunning political assassinations, and the summer seasons of open race riots. The striking characteristic of all of these intense moments of social disorder is that they were not confined in their impact to some limited or self-contained segment of the population. This social disorder directly touched just about everybody's life; it was pervasively experienced and commonly shared.

Alternation With Issues of Race

A second characteristic of these high moments of attention to people with mental disabilities was that they each followed, by a generation or so (roughly 25–40 years), historical moments of intense public commitment to improve the status of Black people in society. There have also been three high moments of intense public attention and commitment to Black people. The first was at the very moment of the founding of the Republic, when the revolutionary fervor that had liberated the country from colonial servitude under Great Britain was immediately translated into significant ameliorative actions regarding Black slavery. Slavery was abolished in all of the northern states between 1776 and 1800, legislative changes in the states of the upper South considerably liberalized provisions for manumission of slaves and substantially increased the numbers of freed slaves, and Congress and state legislatures adopted extensive restrictions that virtually ended the transatlantic slave trade by 1790. All of these measures strongly suggested that the country was on its way toward a generalized abolition of slavery, even by 1787 when the new Constitution was drafted (Higham, 1997, pp. 52–56; Oakes, 1996, pp. 2027–2030).

Abolition, of course, did not happen; instead, following the same pattern experienced by people with mental disabilities, this moment of intense ameliorist attention was followed by an almost complete reversal of policy involving not only a retreat from the benevolent promises, but a regime of more brutal repression and imposed invisibility. By 1820 the dominant view in the South and in most of the North was that Black slavery was a permanent institution; the status of freed Blacks in the South, and only to a lesser degree in the North, was made increasingly intolerable (Burt, 1992, pp. 163–172). The most vivid symbol of the extrusion of Black people from the American polity—of their enforced social invisibility—was the founding of the American Colonization Society in 1817 with the avowed mission of returning all free Black people to Africa (Burt, 1992, p. 165), with Thomas Jefferson, James Madison, and John Marshall among the founding members.

The second high moment of ameliorative attention to Black people was midway through the Civil War with the promulgation of the Emancipation Proclamation, when total abolition of Black slavery became the war's central goal. The promises of this high moment were sustained, to some degree at least, during the decade of Reconstruction. After 1876, however, when Northern troops were withdrawn from the South, these promises were progressively abandoned until a new regime of disenfranchisement and racial segregation took hold in the 1890s and brought about a re-enslavement of Blacks that was probably more brutal in its violence than the old antebellum slavery regime (Williamson, 1986, pp. 117–151). Finally, in the 1950s and early 1960s came the third moment, our moment:

the abolition of legalized race segregation and the Second Reconstruction, followed by the falling away from these promises from the 1970s onward.

For the purpose of drawing lessons about the status of people with mental disabilities, there are two especially salient features of this similarly recurring cycle of ameliorative and then forgotten promises regarding the status of Black people. First, at each of the high moments of amelioration for Black people, there was a powerful and widespread conviction among White people that they had a common social identity with Black people: a fundamentally shared vulnerability. At the founding of the Republic, large numbers of White colonists explicitly described themselves as slaves in depicting their struggle and the injustice of their position in relation to Great Britain (Burt, 1996, p. 2058). Many Englishmen, of course, indicted the colonists for their hypocrisy in this self-depiction. As Samuel Johnson (cited in Ward et al., 1921) put it, "the loudest yelps for liberty [come] from the drivers of Negroes." The White colonists saw this hypocrisy themselves, and when their Revolution had succeeded, they acted to appease their consciences and assuage the shared vulnerability and common social identity that they had previously acknowledged with Black slaves.

During the Civil War, northern White people saw themselves, as they saw southern Black slaves, as the victims of aggression by southern White slaveowners. This common identity was a logical extension of the shared vulnerability that large numbers of northern White people had felt before the war, when they passionately opposed expansion of Black slavery into the western territories on the grounds that they too would become economically and socially subordinated if Black slave labor was put in direct competition with them (Foner, 1970).

Following World War II, Black and White people shared a sense of social invisibility and consequent oppressed vulnerability so vividly expressed by Ellison and Reisman in *Invisible Man* and *The Lonely Crowd*. The charge of hypocrisy also stung White people at this time, because they had just successfully fought Nazi racism in the name of liberty, and their own racist practices were forced into uncomfortably high visibility (Myrdal, 1944). Thus, as with the two prior moments of amelioration and liberation, large numbers of White people were pointedly aware of, and thus self-consciously acknowledged, a common social identity with Black people based on a sense of shared vulnerability.

The second salient feature in comparing these cycles of promise and repression is that the moments when ameliorative promises were made to people with mental disabilities almost precisely correspond to the moments when prior ameliorative promises made to Black people were abandoned. In the mid-1820s—the beginning of the Jacksonian era and the "discovery of the asylum"—Black slavery became viewed as a permanent fixture of Southern life, widely accepted as such by White northerners. The mid-1890s, during the resurgence of the Progressive Era promises for people with mental disabilities as epitomized by the invention of the juvenile court, also saw the legislative entrenchment of race segregation and Black disenfranchisement; *Plessy v. Ferguson* (1896) was decided in that decade. In our own time, the high point for social endorsement of a shared social identity with people with disabilities was the enactment of the Americans with Disabilities Act in 1990, a moment when widespread national commitment to ameliorated status for Black people had become an increasingly dim memory.

It is as if, in each of these instances, a publicly avowed commitment to improve the status of people with mental disabilities was an echo or a reiteration in a different key of an earlier but by then abandoned promise to Black people. This echo, however, had the same underlying and defining characteristic. The promise from the superior to the inferior was based on a new awareness and acknowledgment of a common social identity and equal status; the central component of that commonality or equality was shared vulnerability.

Empathy With People With Mental Disabilities

This review of the historical context of the high ameliorative moments for people with mental disabilities identifies the common social factor of a pervasive sense of communal disorder. In each of these moments, there was an unaccustomed and widespread public sense of social disorientation, of being cut adrift from traditional social moorings and stable landmarks. It is not hard to imagine how Americans in general may have experienced an unaccustomed fellow feeling for people who could not make sense of and who felt alienated from the customary, conventional, and stable social world—for people, that is, with mental disorders.

Although there is no way to substantiate this source of fellow feeling toward people with mental disabilities in these high moments, it is a plausible source of empathic connection and helps explain why the brutal conditions in mental illness and mental retardation institutions suddenly became publicly visible at specific moments in our social history and at other times remained invisible for long periods. The explanation for this sudden visibility must be found in the sudden receptivity of the general public to see these conditions. Some transformation in the viewer, not in the subject being viewed, must be responsible for this new capacity for sight. Whatever the transformative force might have been, acknowledgment of shared vulnerability is its consistent defining feature.

STRATEGIES FOR THE FUTURE

There is good news and bad news in this historical account. The good news is that the capacity and even the willingness of the powerful to acknowledge an empathic connection with the vulnerable appears to be an essentially consistent trait in our social history. The bad news is that this trait continuously shifts its focus: in the instances presented in this chapter, away from Black people and toward people with mental disabilities, then away from those with mental disabilities and toward Black people. Further, as this empathy moves away from one vulnerable group toward another, the disavowed group is subjected not simply to indifference but to brutal degradation. It is as though an empathic identification with any one vulnerable group cannot be sustained for too long without creating its own backlash; the identification becomes too close for comfort and engenders an impulse to sharply differentiate the powerful from the vulnerable as a way of reassuring the former that some other group is more wretched than they. From this perspective, there seems to be a natural psychological progression from, for example, the high point of sympathy for people with mental disabilities at the beginning of this century to the fears expressed by Justice Holmes in his opinion in *Buck v. Bell* (1927).

What then might we do to interrupt this historically recurring progression in our social psychology? What strategies might we pursue, those of us who see ourselves as advocates for, or as empathically connected to, any or all of these vulnerable groups? If the historical and psychological accounts presented here are correct, two warnings clearly follow. The first is that this progression, this cycle of promises made and promises broken, is a stubbornly persistent characteristic; we must not fool ourselves into thinking that it can be easily interrupted. We should accordingly be exceedingly suspicious of benevolent promises that offer nothing reliable and nothing enforceable.

The second clear warning is that those of us who think of ourselves as advocates for vulnerable groups should be exceedingly suspicious of our own motives and the reliability of our own commitment. There is a difference between conceiving of yourself as empathically connected to a group and seeing yourself as a full-fledged member: An empathic connection can be broken by an act of imagination in a way that full membership cannot. My historical account of the recurrent social pattern of empathy and distance, of benevolent impulses and actively hostile impulses, contains no exemption for the "truly sincere" or the "really and truly committed." The lesson to be drawn is that it is hard for anyone to sustain an identification with vulnerable or oppressed people unless one directly identifies oneself as one of them. But this is the fundamental strategic challenge. How can each of us sustain an intense personal identification with vulnerable or oppressed people? How can we transform this personal sense of connectedness into a vibrant and widely felt social force with deep strength and staying power?

The regular recurrence of this cycle of closeness and distance, of connection and rejection, suggests that neither position, neither empathic identification nor differentiation and rejection, is a psychologically stable posture. Put another way, each of these apparent polar opposites seems to stimulate its own contradiction; accordingly, neither close identification nor hostile differentiation can be successfully maintained without some persistent internal, psychological struggle against the opposing impulse.

This proposition is illustrated by a dispute that erupted in the early 1970s about the strategy for social approaches to people with mental disabilities. One side held that society should promise benevolent assistance to people with mental disabilities, and the other asserted that the existence of mental disabilities should be rigorously ignored and that all people, the so-called mentally normal and the so-called mentally disabled, should be treated identically, without special promises of benevolent assistance to anyone.

Advocates for "no more benevolent promises" came to this position from two different perspectives. Some, like Dr. Thomas Szasz (1970), maintained that there was no such thing as "mental illness," that the very construct was a social invention whose purpose was to degrade people. More moderate critics maintained that our social history of broken promises to people with mental disabilities was so strong that the promises themselves must be viewed as inherently fraudulent and inevitably harmful and avoided on this instrumental ground.

This position of "make no promises" to people with mental disabilities led to the advocacy of such positions as the abolition or at least the sharp curtailment of civil commitment laws, the closure of all large-scale geographically remote institutions for people with mental illnesses or mental retardation, a total reliance on community residence in small home environments, and the abandonment of the so-called rehabilitative ideal in all criminal correctional practices (Burt, 1992, pp. 269, 329–336; Burt, 1993). Since the 1970s, these positions have been extensively although not completely adopted in practice: Civil commitment laws have not been abolished, but they have been significantly limited in their reach; large institutions have not been altogether shut down, but they are now sharply disfavored as residential settings for people with mental illness and retardation; and in correctional practice, the rehabilitative ideal has been almost totally rejected. The old liberal vision—that most (or even some) criminal offenders are impaired by mental disability and deserve rehabilitation rather than punishment—has virtually disappeared.

The implementation of all of these policies have had practical consequences that, from the perspective of the 1970s, were both surprising and harsh. Take, for example, the rejection of the rehabilitative ideal. One of the most influential advocates for this position was the Goodell Commission, chaired by former New York Senator Charles Goodell and composed of a distinguished panel of political and academic leaders. The commission issued its report in 1976, and two of its members, psychiatrist Willard Gaylin and historian David Rothman, appended a concurring statement that included the following observation: "To abandon the rehabilitative model without a simultaneous gradation downward in prison sentences would be an unthinkable cruelty and a dangerous act" (Gaylin & Rothman, 1976, xxxix–xl). We now know, 20 years later, that prison sentences were not reduced at the same time that the rehabilitative model was abandoned. Quite the contrary, the numbers of people confined in our prisons have increased vastly since the mid-1970s. In 1974 there were just over 200,000 prisoners in state and federal correctional institutions; by the late 1990s there were more than 1.6 million prisoners (Bureau of Justice Statistics, 1996; Butterfield, 1997). We now have the highest rate of incarceration in the world.[1] And the lengths of U.S. prison sentences have themselves increased exponentially in the past 20 years (Burt, 1993, p. 362; Morris & Tonry, 1990, p. 48). This may be, as Gaylin and Rothman warned, "a dangerous act," but it has turned out not to be "unthinkable."

Similarly, we have dramatically reduced the long-term residential population of mental illness and mental retardation institutions since the 1970s. We now, however, have large numbers of homeless people, many of them with obvious and quite flamboyant mental disturbances, sleeping in parks and on sidewalk grates in all of our cities. To an extent that was unimaginable in the mid-1970s, mainstream American society has come to ignore the public presence of vulnerable and obviously disturbed people in our cities almost as vigorously as when they were locked away in unseen, geographically isolated institutions. Today's homeless people have freedom of mobility and individual liberty in ways that their earlier counterparts confined in institutions did not, and from their perspective this may well be an improved fate. But this is surely not what advocates on their behalf envisioned in the 1970s.

Nor is this is a stable situation. These street people, insistent beggars, and disheveled and sometimes obviously disturbed people are not now as invisible as they may soon become. We may be in the early moments of a renewed social impulse to sweep the streets clean of these disturbed and disturbing people, to return them to institutions but under conditions that are at least as harsh as the old terms of brutalized confinement. The Kansas legislature's enactment of civil commitment for violent sexual predators without even the pretense of benevolent treatment, so glibly approved by the Supreme Court in *Kansas v. Hendricks* (1997), is an early harbinger of this renewed but nastier policy.

The 1970s policy of "make no promises" seems in fact to be giving impetus to this repressive impulse. After the first step in the implementation of this policy—turning people with mental disabilities into the streets, essentially to fend for themselves—it was a natural subsequent step for the public to carry it forward by ignoring homeless people in the parks and on the sidewalk grates, by stepping over or around them while averting their eyes.

---

[1] In 1985, U.S. jails and prisons held an estimated 313 men and women per 100,000 residents; by June 30, 1996, this had increased to 615 inmates per 100,000 U.S. residents (Bureau of Justice Statistics, 1996).

This is an unstable social situation precisely because these homeless and vulnerable people cannot easily be ignored. There is only one alternative for the rest of us: either empathically identify with them or rigorously separate ourselves from them. But the make-no-promises approach gives no socially recognized framework, no acknowledged vocabulary, for acting on the impulse for empathic identification. The alternative impulse for rigorous separation is the only socially recognized framework and acknowledged vocabulary for framing a collective public response; to sustain its internal coherence, the make-no-promises framework requires increasingly harsh measures of social differentiation and distancing. This is the social psychology at the root of the exponential increase in imprisonment that has followed from the rejection of the rehabilitative ideal; this social psychology is also at the root of the contemporary threat, represented by *Kansas v. Hendricks*, to impose permanent custodial confinement on all manner of people with mental disabilities.

To promise beneficent treatment to people with mental disabilities obviously does not provide any guarantee that these promises will be kept. But viewed from the perspective developed here, these promises have a crucially important socially protective function. The promises serve as an acknowledgment of empathic connection and a socially recognized vocabulary of identification between the broader community and the more vulnerable members of that community. The promises serve as a counterweight to the impulses to differentiate the "strong" from the "weak" and to escalate the terms of this differentiation with ever-increasing rigidity.

There is, of course, a differentiation between the "strong" and the "weak" in any offer of assistance to a vulnerable person. The offer itself connotes a relationship of inequality and of differential strength. Those making this offer are obviously portraying themselves as stronger than the object of their beneficence, and that self-portrayal in itself can express an attitude of condescension, disrespect, and even worse. The refusal to offer assistance to a seemingly vulnerable person, however, does not solve this paradox, but in fact intensifies it, because the refusal is neither simply a neutral act nor an inattention to vulnerability, but rather an active turning away and aversion to vulnerability, which connotes greater weakness in the viewer. This sense of aversion and weakness in turn requires escalated effort by the viewer to maintain a desperately preferred belief in his or her own invulnerability.

It follows, then, that it is a safer course of action for everyone to explicitly admit that they are inextricably connected to one another and that the basis for that connection is acknowledged vulnerability, whether that vulnerability be directly or vicariously felt. For those who see themselves not as the "truly vulnerable," but as vicariously or empathically vulnerable, this is a safer, more self-protective course of action, because it protects them from imagining that they are obliged to distance themselves from the truly vulnerable. This explicit acknowledgment of vulnerability is a kind of psychic inoculation against a fear that they might be overwhelmed, that they might be "swamped with incompetence," or that they must constantly wage war to protect themselves, as Justice Holmes proclaimed in his fierce but implicitly frightened opinion. And for those who are prepared to see themselves as truly vulnerable, this mutual connection based on some shared sense of vulnerability offers protection against others' impulses toward escalated differentiation and brutalization.

The social history sketched in this chapter demonstrates, at least in a suggestive way, the truth of these psychological propositions, establishing the desirability on all sides of avowed promises of beneficent assistance for vulnerable people, whether one is "mentally ill" or "mentally normal," Black or White, or the giver or the recipient of the beneficence. The moments of greatest social brutality appear not when a breach of promise occurs but when society refuses to make such promises in an embattled effort to impose social invisibility on people rather than acknowledge empathic connections with them. The root problem, therefore, is not that promises have been made and repeatedly broken. The root problem is that the breach of promise has regularly been followed by an insistence that nothing has been promised at all, that there is no relationship between the strong and the weak—the normal community and the outcasts—and that each must be inaccessible and invisible to the other.

Solving this root problem does not require that the promises of beneficence actually be implemented. I do not mean to diminish the importance of implementing these promises, but actual implementation is, from my perspective, less important than public acknowledgment that promises have been made and broken. This acknowledgment in itself maintains the social connectedness that provides crucial protection against escalated brutality under the cloak of distanced, imposed social invisibility.

There is a public space where this kind of acknowledgment can occur. Courts are the places where anyone with a grievance should be able to say, "You may hate me, you may fear me, but you cannot ignore me; you cannot make me invisible." This was the great public service of the courts for Black people beginning in the late 1940s and reaching its highest point from the mid-50s through the mid-1960s, and for people with mental disabilities from the mid-60s through the highest point of the litigation of the 1970s. The great tragedy of the current moment is that American judges generally are now, especially in the higher reaches of the federal system, resolutely turning away from this socially protective role. And when judges acknowledge the promises that form the social linkages for our empathic connections, as the Kansas state supreme court did when it invalidated the Kansas sexual predator law, the U.S. Supreme Court rushes forward to suppress this understanding—to suppress it, with added irony, in an opinion written by the only Black member of the Court (*Kansas v. Hendricks*, 1997).

It has become fashionable these days to assess the worth of judicial interventions by hard outcome measurements, for example, how much actual integration of Black and White people has been accomplished, or how many therapists or community residences for people with mental disabilities have been provided (Rosenberg, 1991). By these measures, it is easy to discount the worth of judicial interventions. But these measures miss the true significance of judicial interventions: their basic socially protective function in providing a public judicial forum in these matters. Their basic function is to guard against the imposition of social invisibility on vulnerable people. If courts have turned away from this vital role today, then the task must be taken up elsewhere. As Robert Frost (1946) put it, in the poem that provided the title of this chapter, all of us "have promises to keep, and miles to go before [we] sleep" (p. 238).

REFERENCES

Americans with Disabilities Act, 42 U.S.C.A. § 12101 et seq. (West 1993).

Board of Education v. Rowley, 458 U.S. 176 (1982).

Brakel, S., Parry, J., & Weiner, B. (1985). *The mentally disabled and the law* (3rd ed.). Chicago: American Bar Association.

Buck v. Bell, 274 U.S. 200 (1927).

Bureau of Justice Statistics. (1996). *Prison and jail inmates at midyear 1996* (NCJ 162843). Washington, DC: U.S. Department of Justice.

Burt, R. (1985). Pennhurst: A parable. In R. H. Mnookin (Ed.), *In the interest of children: Advocacy, law reform and public policy* (pp. 326–364). New York: W. H. Freeman.

Burt, R. (1992). *The constitution in conflict.* Cambridge, MA: Harvard University Press.

Burt, R. (1993). Cruelty, hypocrisy, and the rehabilitative ideal in corrections. *International Journal of Law and Psychiatry 16*, 359–370.

Burt, R. (1996). Comments on James Oakes, "The compromising expedient." *Cardozo Law Review, 17*, 2057–2061.

Butterfield, F. (1997, January 20). Slower growth in the number of inmates. *New York Times*, p. A10.

Education for All Handicapped Children Act, 84 Stat. 175, 20 U.S.C. § 1401 et seq. (1975).

Ellison, R. (1952). *Invisible man.* New York: Signet Books.

Foner, E. (1970). *Free soil, free labor, free men: The ideology of the Republican Party before the Civil War.* New York: Oxford University Press.

Frost, R. (1946). Stopping by woods on a snowy evening. In R. Frost (Ed.), *The poems of Robert Frost.* New York: Modern Library.

Gaylin, W., & Rothman, D. (1976). Introduction. In A. Hirsch (Ed.), *Doing justice: The choice of punishments* (pp. xx–l). New York: Hill & Wang.

Hansen, M. (1997, August). Danger vs. due process. *American Bar Association Journal, 83*, 43.

Higham, J. (1997, November 6). America's three reconstructions. *New York Review, 44*, 52–56.

Kaimowitz v. Michigan Department of Mental Health, *Prison Law Reporter 2*, 433 (Circuit Ct., Wayne Co. Mich., 1973).

Kansas v. Hendricks, 521 U.S. 346 (1997).

Lake v. Cameron, 364 F.2d 657 (D.C. Cir. 1966).

Morris, N. (1968). Psychiatry and the dangerous criminal. *Southern California Law Review, 41*, 514–550.

Morris, N., & Tonry, M. (1990). *Between prison and probation: Intermediate punishments in a rational sentencing system.* New York: Oxford University Press.

Myrdal, G. (1944). *An American dilemma: The Negro problem and modern democracy.* New York: Harper.

Oakes, J. (1996). "The compromising expedient": Justifying a proslavery constitution. *Cardozo Law Review, 17*, 2023–2056.

Pennsylvania Association of Retarded Children (P.A.R.C.) v. Pennsylvania, 343 F. Supp. 279 (E.D. Pa. 1972).

Plessy v. Ferguson, 163 U.S. 537 (1896).

Reisman, D. (1950). *The lonely crowd.* New Haven, CT: Yale University Press.

Rosenberg, G. (1991). *The hollow hope: Can courts bring about social change?* Chicago: University of Chicago Press.

Rothman, D. (1971). *The discovery of the asylum: Social order and disorder in the new republic.* New York: Little Brown.

Rothman, D. (1980). *Conscience and convenience: The asylum and its alternatives in progressive America.* New York: Little Brown.

Rouse v. Cameron, 373 F.2d 451 (D.C. Cir. 1966).

Sexually Violent Predator Act. Kan. Stat. Ann. § 59–29-a-01 et seq. (1994).

Szasz, T. (1970). *The manufacture of madness.* New York: Harper & Row.

Ward, A. W., Waller, A. R., Trent, W. P., Erskine, J., Sherman, S. P., & Van Doren, C. (Eds.). (1921). *The Cambridge history of English and American literature* (Vol. X: The age of Johnson). New York: G. P. Putnam's Sons. Retrieved April 5, 2001, from the World Wide Web: http://www.bartleby.com/220/0823.html

Whyte, W. (1956). *The organization man.* New York: Simon & Schuster.

Wiebe, R. (1967). *The search for order, 1877–1920.* New York: Hill & Wang.

Wiebe, R. (1985). *The opening of American society: From the adoption of the Constitution to the eve of disunion.* New York: Vintage Books.

Williamson, J. (1986). *A rage for order: Black–white relations in the American south since emancipation.* New York: Oxford University Press.

Wyatt v. Stickney, 325 F. Supp. 781 (M.D. Ala. 1971).

2

THREE STRANDS OF
MENTAL HEALTH LAW:
DEVELOPMENTAL MILEPOSTS

RICHARD J. BONNIE

According to one of the most quoted aphorisms of Oliver Wendell Holmes, Jr., "The life of the law has not been logic; it has been experience." By experience, Holmes meant the realities of social life, the "felt necessities of the time" (Holmes, 1963, p. 5). In all aphorisms, however, the price for cleverness is some loss of accuracy. Law is, more precisely, a living tradition, shaped both by the internal logic of ideas embedded in the legal culture and by the changing social and technological circumstances. My goal in this chapter is to provide a broad overview of the fundamental principles of mental health law as they have evolved over the past three decades. By using certain U.S. Supreme Court decisions as markers or mileposts along the way, I hope to expose not only the internal logic of mental health law, but also the role of changing social circumstances.

Mental health law (including disability law) continues to be one of the most rapidly developing areas of public law. It often appears to be a seamless web, even to the experts. One way to make sense of this web is to focus on the three interwoven threads that give this area of law its distinctive color and character:

1. the individual's right to be free of unwarranted discrimination in the distribution of burdens and benefits (equality of citizenship)
2. the individual's right to be free of unwarranted coercion or state intervention (liberty)
3. the government's duty to provide needed services, a duty that may be rooted in the constitution or in statutory law (entitlement).

Equality of citizenship, in its thin form, refers to the right not to be legally disadvantaged on grounds of mental disability. In its thicker form, this idea encompasses affirmative government efforts to counteract the effects of private discrimination. *Liberty* refers to the right to be free of unwarranted government restraint or intervention. The need to regulate coercive treatment is what distinguishes mental health law from mainstream health law. In this respect, mental health law is analogous to the body of law governing infectious disease control and is analyzed within the same constitutional paradigm. The third strand of mental health law—*entitlement*—is much fainter than the other two and captures the idea that every person has a right to a minimum level of resources or necessary services in a just society. Despite the strong ethical basis for such a right, it is only weakly reflected in our law. As a result, the entitlement strand of mental health law is typically derived from the other two strands rather than standing on its own.

Sometimes these fundamental concepts tug against one another. For example, benefits or services may be provided to people who have mental disabilities on terms less generous than those provided to people with other problems or conditions—that is, entitlements may be unequally distributed. Restrictions on personal liberty may be justified in terms of the objecting person's need for services. Notwithstanding these tensions and ambiguities, the concepts of liberty, equality, and entitlement provide the basic premises from which the law continues to develop. Recent developments in each of these three areas also reflect an important common theme in the continuing evolution of mental health law—a gradual but substantial shift in the focus of legal attention from institutional to community settings.

THE EGALITARIAN STRAND

The egalitarian strand of mental health law is rooted historically in the same vision of equal opportunity that inspired the civil rights movement of the 1960s, but it has a more direct link to the evolving logic of gender equality. The core idea in race discrimination law is that there is no socially relevant difference between people of different races and that any differential treatment is therefore presumptively irrational and arbitrary. Up to a point, the law of gender discrimination rests on the same premise—but only up to a point. The difference in reproductive capacity between men and women leads to the possibility of rationally differentiated treatment. Employers, for example, who allow their employees to take leave for all sorts of medical reasons might nonetheless disallow maternity leave on the basis of its greater frequency and consequent disruptiveness to the enterprise. One could say that this policy differentiates not between women and men but rather between pregnant people and nonpregnant people (men and women both).

But this response really begs the underlying question: Do the differences between maternity leave and other medical leave justify a distinction in policy that forces pregnant women to choose between job and mothering but that excuses other workers from choosing between job and medical care? Workplace leave practices emerged when the reference point was a male worker whose wife was at home and therefore did not need maternity leave. The important question is whether employers should be required to adapt leave policies to new social realities.

The additional idea in gender discrimination law is that the significance of the real biological difference between men and women turns on how society is organized, not on any inherent characteristics of pregnancy, childbirth, or child rearing. And it goes a step further: Traditional workplace leave policies implicitly devalue the special demands of family life such as having a child or caring for a dying parent. Achievement of equal opportunity therefore requires changes in social practices that are rational but have the effect of reifying differences between men and women, or—in this context—between people with strong family obligations and people without them. The Family and Medical Leave Act of 1993 effectuates this principle.

The disability rights movement represents a continued elaboration of these ideas. A wheelchair-bound person is "disabled" only if buildings have been built without ramps or elevators. More pertinently, the disabling effects of mental disorders are often associated with the way people respond to unusual behaviors rather than with any functional impairment. Also, even if a person has functional impairments, the disabling effects of those impairments can be minimized by altering working conditions. The logic of these ideas culminated in the 1990 enactment of the Americans With Disabilities Act (ADA), a remarkable and far-reaching legislative achievement.

The importance of the ADA can hardly be exaggerated; I discuss its broad scope in more detail in the following sections. The historical significance of the act is made especially vivid by comparing the coverage of the act with the constitutional baseline established by the Supreme Court in 1985.

City of Cleburne and the Equal Protection Clause

In July 1980, a building on Featherston Street in Cleburne, Texas, was purchased for use as a group home for people with mental retardation. It was anticipated that the home, to be leased by an organization then called Cleburne Living Center (CLC), would house 13 retarded men and women who would be under the constant supervision of CLC staff members. It was also anticipated that the home would be operated as a private ICF–MR (Level 1 Intermediate Care Facility for the Mentally Retarded) and would be eligible for Medicaid reimbursement. The site of the proposed home was an area zoned R-3 (apartment house district). Under the applicable Cleburne city ordinance, the following uses are permitted in an R-3 district:

1. any use permitted in district R-2
2. apartment houses or multiple dwellings
3. boarding and lodging houses
4. fraternity or sorority houses and dormitories
5. apartment hotels
6. hospitals, sanitariums, nursing homes, or homes for convalescents or aged, other than for the insane or feeble-minded or alcoholics or drug addicts
7. private clubs or fraternal orders except those whose chief activity is carried on as a business
8. philanthropic or eleemosynary institutions, other than penal institutions
9. accessory uses customarily incident to any of the above uses.

Because the group home was not covered by the listed uses, Cleburne informed CLC that a special use permit would be required. The city had determined that the proposed group home should be classified as a "hospital for the feeble-minded." After holding a public hearing on CLC's application, the city council voted 3–1 to deny the special use permit.

CLC then filed suit in federal district court against the city, alleging that the zoning ordinance was invalid both on its face and as applied to CLC because it discriminated against people with mental retardation in violation of the equal protection clause of the Fourteenth Amendment. The District Court found that if the potential residents of the home did not have mental retardation "but the home was the same in all other respects, its use would be permitted under the city's zoning ordinance"; the city council's decision, therefore, "was motivated primarily by the fact that the residents of the home would be persons who are mentally retarded." Nonetheless, the District Court upheld the city's decision on the grounds that it was rationally related to several legitimate interests, including "the safety and fears of residents in the adjoining neighborhood."

The Court of Appeals for the Fifth Circuit reversed, concluding that the District Court had applied an unduly lenient standard in light of the fact that the city's decision discriminated against people with mental retardation. Applying a so-called intermediate standard of scrutiny, the Court of Appeals held that the ordinance was invalid because it did not "substantially further any important governmental interest."

The city then appealed to the Supreme Court. In *City of Cleburne v. Cleburne Living Center* (1985), the justices unanimously held that the city's refusal to issue the special use permit was unconstitutional, although the Court did not rule on the constitutionality of the ordinance itself. Three opinions were written, and many commentators characterized the decision as a defeat for people who have mental disabilities because six justices refused to apply the more demanding standard of review applied by the Fifth Circuit. Nevertheless, the Court's decision was a modest victory for the idea of equal citizenship, and it served as a valuable precedent in other cases challenging government decisions that unfairly discriminate against people who have mental disabilities. The fact that a majority of the Court refused to endorse the standard of review used by the Fifth Circuit was a troubling aspect of the decision; however, the majority actually used a higher standard than it said it was applying, and the debate carried on in the Court's three opinions had more to do with the unsettled nature of equal protection jurisprudence than it did with the constitutional rights of people with mental retardation.

The Court unanimously held the city's action unconstitutional. The justices saw the denial of the special use permit for the Featherston home for what it truly was—a reflection of the unfounded fears of the neighbors. "The short of it," said Justice White, "is that requiring the permit in this case appears to us to rest on an irrational prejudice against the mentally retarded, including those who would occupy the Featherston facility and who would live under the closely-supervised and highly-regulated conditions expressly provided for by state and federal law." Justice Stevens, who concurred in a separate opinion joined by the Chief Justice, noted that "the record convinces me that this permit was required because of the irrational fears of neighboring property owners, rather than for the protection of the mentally retarded persons who would reside in [the Featherston] home." Finally, Justice Marshall observed, in an opinion joined by Justices Brennan and Blackmun, that "Cleburne's ordinance sweeps too broadly to dispel the suspicion that it rests on a bare desire to treat the retarded as outsiders, pariahs who do not belong in the community." Thus, it can be seen that there was no controversy about the outcome in this case. Every member of the Court was willing to scrutinize and discount the arguments raised by the City of Cleburne.

To summarize the point of apparent dispute (using the Court's constitutional vocabulary), laws that draw lines based on "suspect" classifications—such as race or national origin—trigger "strict judicial scrutiny," and laws that classify on the basis of several other classifications—such as gender and legitimacy of birth—are "quasi-suspect" or "suspicious," subject to "heightened," though not "strict," scrutiny. If the classification is not "suspect" or "suspicious," the Court will not second-guess the legislative decision and will continue its review only as to whether the classification rests on a rational foundation—which is usually to say that it will be upheld.

The doctrinal issue raised in *City of Cleburne* was whether classifications based on mental retardation such as the one drawn in the Cleburne ordinance would be characterized as "suspect" or "suspicious" and therefore subject to heightened judicial scrutiny. In essence, the majority said, when classifications based on mental retardation are involved, as compared with classifications based on ethnicity or gender, there is less reason for judicial suspicion and correspondingly greater reason to defer to legislative and political judgments.

Justice Marshall questioned this conclusion, finding persuasive reasons for judicial suspicion in this context. He summarized the sorry history of prejudice against, and ostracism of, people with mental retardation ("the feeble-minded"). Indeed, the Cleburne ordinance itself, Justice Marshall emphasized, was enacted around the turn of the 20th century when discrimination against, and fear of, people with mental retardation were especially prevalent.

What is most interesting is that the majority's opinion never once explicitly mentioned this history of discrimination. Instead, Justice White took note of more recent legislation, especially at the federal level, designed to protect the interests of people with mental retardation. Justice Marshall was unpersuaded that recent federal legislation protecting the rights of people with mental retardation demonstrated that discriminatory attitudes had been erased. Regardless whether constitutional interpretation should turn on judgments about recent social history, it is clear that this was the articulated basis for the disagreement in the *City of Cleburne* case. Moreover, the community's fear of people with mental retardation was in fact the basis of the Cleburne ordinance and of its application to the Featherson home, and the Court knew it. Notwithstanding recent legislative willingness to promote equal citizenship, residual prejudice undoubtedly remains.

Broad Scope of the ADA

A more substantial victory for equal citizenship for people who have mental disabilities was achieved five years later with enactment of the ADA. In the landmark legislation, Congress made explicit what had been only implicit in *City of Cleburne* (the history of discrimination against people with disabilities, particularly those with mental disabilities), and the sweeping language of the act effectively displaces the equal protection clause as the source of federal protection for people with disabilities.

The ADA, which was enacted July 26, 1990, and in most respects became effective in January and July of 1992, provides broad antidiscrimination protection for people with physical or mental impairments that substantially limit one or more major life activities. The legislation builds on the Rehabilitation Act of 1973 and the Fair Housing Act Amendments of 1988. Rights and entitlements provided under federal laws predating the ADA are still in effect, but the ADA significantly extends the reach of those laws. For example, unlike § 504 of the Rehabilitation Act, the ADA's coverage is not limited to employers or public entities that receive federal funds. All but the smallest businesses and enterprises must comply with the ADA.

In the preamble to the act, Congress found that "historically, society has tended to isolate and segregate individuals with disabilities, and, despite some improvements, such forms of discrimination against individuals with disabilities continue to be a serious and pervasive social problem." Congress also found that people who have disabilities constitute a "discrete and insular minority" who have been subjected historically to purposefully unequal treatment and have been relegated to a position of political powerlessness based on characteristics beyond their control. These findings use the language of equal protection jurisprudence to justify heightened statutory protection for individuals with disabilities, embracing an understanding of history that a majority of the Supreme Court was unwilling to accept in *City of Cleburne*.

The ADA has three titles. Title I prohibits employers from discriminating against "a qualified individual with a disability" in employment, including the application process, hiring, advancement, and discharge. A "qualified individual with a disability" is defined as someone able to perform—with or without reasonable accommodations—the essential functions of a specific position.

Under Title II, no qualified individual may be excluded from the benefits of the services, programs, or activities of a public entity based on a disability. In this title, a "qualified individual with a disability" is defined as someone who, with or without reasonable accommodations, meets the essential eligibility requirements for a particular public service. In this context, reasonable accommodation means the modification of rules, policies, or practices; the removal of architectural, communication, or transportation barriers; or the provision of auxiliary aids and services a person with a disability needs to participate in a public service.

Finally, Title III prohibits discrimination that prevents an individual with a disability from fully and equally enjoying goods, services, facilities, privileges, advantages, or accommodations in privately run public services or enterprises that affect interstate commerce. Essentially, any private entity engaging in commerce between two states or between a state and a foreign nation is covered. In providing goods and services to individuals who have disabilities, public accommodations must provide those goods and services in the most integrated setting appropriate to each individual's needs. If a public accommodation provides separate or different programs or activities for people with disabilities, those people may not be denied the opportunity to participate in regular programs or activities. A person with a disability must be free to choose between a special and a normal public accommodation.

A decade after enactment, the impact of the ADA is hard to assess. Disability rights advocates have been disappointed by the low rate of success by employees under Title I, and have criticized what they regard as an unfriendly judicial attitude toward the employment provisions of the ADA (Diller, 2000; Krieger, 2000). However, it has been noted in response to such criticisms that the low rate of success by plaintiffs in litigation is not the best indicator of the ADA's impact on workplace practices; if employers are willing to accommodate meritorious requests, only the weakest cases will be litigated (Bell, 2000). The act's sponsors and supporters have applauded what they regard as a positive employer response to the principles and specific requirements of the ADA (Coelho, 2000). From the standpoint of mental disabilities, the ADA has already transformed job-related questionnaires and interviews, and has had a salutary effect on the availability of workplace accommodations—even the conceptualization and specification of accommodations for psychiatric disabilities represents a remarkable step forward (Hall, 1997). As David Mechanic (1998) has noted, "the ADA's real potential is less in the cases that are litigated and more in the establishment of an accepted community standard for fairness" (p. 20).

The employment provisions of the ADA have not been as useful for more severely disabled individuals—the ADA does not cast all the costs of employee disability on the employer, leaving the obligation to fund subsidized employment to the society at large. However, as Susan Stefan (2001) has shown, Title II of the act has become a powerful instrument for reforming public benefit and service programs, including mental health services, as will be described below. In summary, given its breathtaking scope, the ADA will be at the center of mental health law in the decades to come.

THE LIBERTARIAN STRAND

Mental health law as we know it has developed only over the past 30 years. The libertarian strand of mental health law was rooted in a distrust of discretionary power and a deepening skepticism about government intrusion into people's personal lives. It is in this sense tied to *In re Gault* (1967), which subjected the juvenile court to the rule of law (see Grisso, chapter 8, this volume), and *Roe v. Wade* (1973), which substantially restricted government interference with a woman's reproductive decision making. Both of these themes appear prominently in *O'Connor v. Donaldson* (1975), the libertarian font of mental health law. Kenneth Donaldson had been civilly committed to Florida State Hospital in Chattahoochee in January, 1957, and had been retained against his will for 15 years before he sued for his release and for damages under the federal civil rights laws. He claimed that he was not mentally ill or dangerous and that he has received no treatment for his supposed illness throughout his confinement. He was released before the case was tried, and a jury assessed compensatory and punitive damages against the hospital superintendent. The judgment was affirmed by the Court of Appeals and by the Supreme Court. Justice Stewart's opinion for the Supreme Court is at once a ringing endorsement of what has been called a "right to be different" (Kittrie, 1971) and a warning about the excesses of the "Therapeutic State":

> May the state confine the mentally ill merely to ensure them a living standard superior to that they enjoy in the private community? ... May the state fence in the harmless mentally ill solely to save its citizens from exposure to those whose ways are different? One might as well ask if the state, to avoid public unease, could incarcerate all who are physically unattractive or socially eccentric. Mere public intolerance or animosity cannot constitutionally justify the deprivation of a person's physical liberty. (p. 575)

With *O'Connor* establishing the constitutional boundary, the ongoing debate about the proper grounds for civil commitment has focused on the reach of the "harm principle"—the justifications for coercion derived from the police power (to protect society) and the parens patriae power (to protect the person him or herself).

Criteria for Police Power Commitment

Although the rate of violent crime turned downward during the final years of the 20th century, mental health law has been definitively shaped by the substantial escalating violence that characterized the 1970s and 1980s. All varieties of violence increased during this period—senseless unprovoked violence, drug-related violence, political and religiously inspired violence, and domestic violence. Further, this violence infiltrated almost all segments of society: the streets, the home, the workplace. Fear also increased, evident in the phenomenal growth of the private security industry. The impact of violence, and fear of violence, on mental health law can be seen in many domains:

1. The imposition of liability on mental health professionals for failure to protect victims of patient violence in outpatient contexts is the most controversial manifestation of this deep-rooted concern.
2. The salience of social concern about dangerous mental patients has been evident in periodic efforts to abolish the insanity defense and in the adoption and implementation of tightened procedures for postverdict confinement and release of insanity acquittees.
3. Over the past decade, many states have adopted an incapacitative strategy toward juveniles who have committed violent offenses (see Grisso, chapter 8, this volume).
4. During the 1990s, many state legislatures enhanced preventive confinement of dangerous sex offenders and "psychopaths."
5. An incapacitative ("mad dog") concept of the death penalty is increasingly evident. In 1993 the South Carolina supreme court upheld a death sentence against a defendant who had been found "guilty but mentally ill" (*South Carolina v. Wilson*, 1993).

These legal developments respond primarily to the violence of strangers. The tragic experience of battered spouses and children has also called increasing attention to violence within families. And something new surfaced over the last two decades of the 20th century—the recognition that we are all at risk of being victimized by an acquaintance in school or on the job. Violence in the workplace is now described as a public health problem, one within the regulatory purview of the Occupational Safety and Health Administration (VandenBos & Bulatao, 1996). In taking precautionary action, however, employers and administrators may run afoul of the ADA (Campbell & Kaufmann, 1997).

In the present context, the ADA has a paradoxical quality in that it draws an explicit legal link between mental disorder and violence: a person with a mental disability who is "otherwise qualified" may nonetheless be dismissed if he or she poses a "direct threat to the safety of others" (see generally Parry, 1994). Dangerousness assessments are becoming a feature of everyday institutional life. All of this is bound to affect the shape of mental health law, especially in relation to the scope of the state's coercive authority—its police power. How will the courts and legislatures respond? How will these developments alter the libertarian logic of mental health law?

Imagine the following hypothetical situation: Employee D.B. engages in hostile behavior toward coworkers, who become fearful and complain. D.B. is referred to the employee assistance program for evaluation. He is said to be depressed, hostile, and impulsive but has no diagnosable disorder. Psychotherapy is recommended, but he refuses to participate. The next time he behaves in a threatening and hostile manner, the employer reprimands him, D.B. gets angry, and the employer fires him and calls the police. D.B. does not have a mental illness, nor has he engaged in any criminal conduct. He has never actually hurt anyone. But he is is committed to a local detention facility for a week of "custodial restraint."

Is this scenario legally plausible? In broad terms, there are two jurisprudential predicates for confinement in our legal system: (a) arrest and conviction for criminal conduct and (b) therapeutic commitment under the mental health system based on findings of mental illness and imminent dangerousness and on the presumed connection between the two. Thus, even though D.B. may not be able to keep his job, he may not lawfully be restrained; with few exceptions, our law has not traditionally permitted purely preventive confinement unless the person is properly being detained by the criminal justice system. These are the foundational building blocks of our jurisprudence. But can we be so sure that they will not be shaken by the "felt necessities of the time"? In this connection, consider the Supreme Court's decisions in *Foucha v. Louisiana* (1992) and *Kansas v. Hendricks* (1997).

Foucha was found not guilty by reason of insanity (NGRI) for aggravated burglary and was committed. Taking the appellate record at face value, it appears that Foucha was experiencing the symptoms of a drug-induced psychosis at the time of the offense but that these symptoms had cleared by the time he was committed, meaning that he did not have a mental illness. (The staff apparently concluded that he had an antisocial personality but insisted that this condition was not a mental disease and was not treatable. These assertions were taken as given in the subsequent litigation.)

Four years later, after a multilayered review process, the staff recommended conditional discharge, but neither member of the court-appointed "sanity commission" was willing to certify that Foucha would not be a danger to himself or to other people if he were released. The trial court then ruled that Foucha had not carried his burden of proving that he was not dangerous and refused to discharge him. The Louisiana appellate courts affirmed. The case thus came to the Supreme Court raising, quite starkly, the question of whether an NGRI commitment could be based on dangerousness alone.

In a 5–4 decision, the Supreme Court said no. In the course of his opinion for the Court, Justice White reaffirmed what I have characterized as the libertarian foundation of mental health jurisprudence:

> A State, pursuant to its police power, may of course imprison convicted criminals for the purposes of deterrence and retribution. . . . Here, the

State has no such punitive interest. As Foucha was not convicted, he may not be punished. The State may also confine a mentally ill person if it shows "by clear and convincing evidence that the individual is mentally ill and dangerous." Here, the State has not carried that burden; indeed, the State does not claim that Foucha is now mentally ill. (p. 80)

Thus, neither of the two traditional jurisprudential bases of confinement could be invoked in Foucha's case.

But Louisiana had argued that preventive confinement could be constitutionally imposed outside the framework of criminal punishment and therapeutic commitment. In support of this argument, the state invoked *United States v. Salerno* (1987), in which the Supreme Court had upheld short-term preventive detention of dangerous offenders who were awaiting a criminal trial. Justice White responded as follows:

In our society liberty is the norm, and detention prior to trial or without trial is the carefully limited exception. The narrowly focused pretrial detention of arrestees permitted by the Bail Reform Act was found to be one of those carefully limited exceptions permitted by the Due Process Clause. We decline to take a similar view of a law like Louisiana's, which permits the indefinite detention of insanity acquittees who are not mentally ill but who do not prove they would not be dangerous to others. (p. 755)

If Louisiana had prevailed in *Foucha*, the constitutional impediments to preventive detention would have been greatly weakened. If a person acquitted by reason of insanity can be preventively detained when he or she is no longer mentally ill, there is no apparent reason why a person who has served a criminal sentence could not be preventively detained based on dangerousness alone. Further, such a ruling is only a short step away from a new version of civil commitment that does not require proof of mental illness and would permit preventive restraint of D.B. for custodial restraint in the absence of any criminal offense.

Foucha reaffirmed the prevailing logic of mental health law, but will it stand in the face of society's escalating fear of violence? As previously mentioned, it was only a 5–4 decision. Justices Kennedy and Thomas wrote separate dissenting opinions. Justice Kennedy argued, in effect, that an NGRI commitment is really a parallel track of criminal confinement and may be based solely on an incapacitative rationale. This view at least has the virtue of being limited to people found beyond a reasonable doubt to have committed a criminal offense. Justice Thomas's dissent was not so restrained. He denied the very premise of the libertarian strand of mental health law—that freedom from coerced confinement is a fundamental right—and implied that any scheme of preventive detention should be upheld as long as it is "reasonable." If this view were to prevail, it would wipe away the libertarian jurisprudence of mental health law set forth in *O'Connor v. Donaldson* (1975), *Addington v. Texas* (1979), and *Jackson v. Indiana* (1972), to mention only a few.

On its face, *Kansas v. Hendricks* (1997) does not contradict *Foucha*. The Supreme Court upheld Kansas's sexually violent predator commitment law against a number of constitutional challenges. The Kansas statute (identical to those enacted first in Washington, in 1990, and in many other states during the next decade) authorizes lifetime confinement of a person convicted of a violent sex crime who has already served his sentence if the person is found to have a "mental abnormality" or "personality disorder" that "makes the person likely to engage in predatory acts of sexual violence." Laws of this kind had first appeared as a response to the therapeutic optimism of the 1950s but had been largely repealed and disavowed in the 1970s. The American Bar Association Criminal Justice Mental Health Standards (American Bar Association, 1984) condemned them. Now they are back in a more virulent form.

Technically the Kansas sexually violent predator statute is distinguishable from the Louisiana NGRI statute struck down in *Foucha* because it requires proof of a predicate "mental abnormality" or "personality disorder"; it is therefore not based on "dangerousness" alone. However, its purpose and effect, if not its form, are purely incapacitative; the state makes very little pretense of treatment. Moreover, the predicate condition is little more than a conclusory label that could be attached to any person who has committed a sexual offense or, indeed, any assaultive offense. So what is to prevent a state from "civilly committing" any prisoner upon the expiration of his prison term based on a finding of "mental abnormality" and "dangerousness"?

It is possible that the Supreme Court will step back from the abyss. It may say that civil commitment may not be used in the absence of a severe disorder that substantially impairs cognitive or volitional capacity. The key to the decision in *Hendricks* from this standpoint is that Hendricks was a pedophile whom the Court believed to be "compelled" by his mental abnormality to commit his crimes. Also, it is possible that the Court will say that some meaningful opportunity for treatment must be provided by the state to vindicate the purpose of commitment under the due process clause; mere custodial care would not be enough. Nonetheless, the result in *Hendricks*, as well as Justice Thomas's reasoning, for the court, is fundamentally incompatible with the ringing endorsement of liberty embraced by the majority in *Foucha*.

Coercion in the Community

One of the most divisive and fiercely debated issues in mental health law has been the reach of the paternalistic justification for involuntary psychiatric hospitalization. The U.S. Supreme Court sketched the boundaries of the state's authority to confine a person against his or her will in *O'Connor v. Donaldson* (1975), and libertarians and paternalists continue to fight about the permissible scope of the *parens patriae* basis for commitment. The tightening of statutory commitment criteria has occurred simultaneously with the well-known trend toward deinstitutionalization. It is not surprising, then, that commitment to outpatient treatment is now receiving considerable attention. When viewed from a wider frame of reference, the question now being addressed is the permissible scope of legally coerced treatment in noninstitutional settings (see generally Dennis & Monahan, 1996).

A procedure authorizing "direct" commitment to outpatient treatment at the "front end" of the commitment process has been on the books in most states for many years, but it has not often been used, mainly because the criteria are the same as for inpatient commitment and patients who meet these criteria almost always need to be stabilized in an inpatient setting. Many states also have coercive devices after hospital discharge, such as conditional discharge to facilitate rehospitalization of patients who are deteriorating and who fail to comply with conditions of outpatient treatment, but these statutes are not typically used for civil patients, and when they are, the period of outpatient care usually has already been authorized by the judge at the time of the initial commitment. However, several states have enacted a new type of statute, the distinctive feature of which is outpatient commitment at the "front end" based on criteria of deterioration that would not be sufficient for inpatient commitment. The basic idea is that these patients are on a clinical course that predictably would lead to "dangerousness."

Many difficult issues concerning commitment to outpatient treatment must be addressed, including the following:

1. From a libertarian standpoint, is outpatient commitment a less restrictive or a more restrictive alternative? That is, is the procedure likely to be invoked mainly in cases in which patients would otherwise be hospitalized (eventually), thereby reducing the aggregate restrictiveness of coerced treatment? Or does it expand the net of coercive intervention to people who would otherwise be left alone?
2. From a clinical standpoint, is coerced outpatient treatment efficacious? Does outpatient treatment reduce the likelihood of hospitalization (or rehospitalization) as compared with nonintervention? To the extent that the procedure is used for people who would otherwise have been hospitalized initially, does it offer equivalent clinical benefits?
3. From a legal standpoint, how should these plans be imple-

mented? What procedures should be used to report or respond to noncompliance with the conditions specified in the commitment order? Should the clinicians responsible for providing treatment have the authority to forcibly administer medication?

A body of empirical literature on these issues is beginning to develop (Gerbasi, Bonnie, & Binder, 2000). Randomized trials have been conducted in North Carolina and New York, and the MacArthur Foundation has established a new research initiative to pursue research on outpatient commitment and other tools of therapeutic leverage.

At best, commitment to outpatient treatment can be a preferable alternative to involuntary hospitalization for a subgroup of patients who meet carefully drawn criteria—for example, those with psychotic illnesses whose condition responds well to antipsychotic medication and who have a demonstrated pattern of noncompliance with medication and subsequent deterioration after discharge from inpatient treatment. However, any outpatient commitment order must be predicated on a specific treatment plan prepared by the program to which the patient would be committed. This is necessary not only to guarantee clarity of expectations and procedures but also to ensure that the procedure is used only for those patients the program is willing to accept; a judge should not be able to commit someone to clinically inappropriate outpatient treatment simply because the person's condition is believed to be deteriorating. However the debate over outpatient commitment is resolved, it demonstrates that coercion in the community is the new battleground for libertarians and paternalists in mental health law and ethics.

THE ENTITLEMENT STRAND

The third strand of mental health law springs out of the egalitarian and libertarian strands. From an ethical standpoint, the underlying idea behind the "right to services" or entitlement strand is that vulnerable people have a moral claim on society for adequate health care (as they do for education, shelter, and so forth), including mental health care. How that moral claim is operationalized obviously depends on the resources and institutional structure of a particular society. In legal terms, U.S. society has not yet embraced a basic entitlement to health care (or, in the language of international human rights, a "positive right" to a minimum level of services in absolute terms). However, a relative or qualified right springs out of the libertarian and egalitarian strands of the fabric of mental health law. Some level of service entitlement arises, for example, whenever the state deprives a person of liberty or otherwise takes custodial control. Moreover, a right to equal treatment in health care insurance and financing is increasingly understood to require equivalent coverage of mental and physical diseases or disabilities. Ultimately, the contours of enforceable service entitlements very much depend on statutory context and factual circumstances.

Youngberg v. Romeo: *The Libertarian Basis for the Duty to Treat*

It goes almost without saying that the public mental health and mental retardation services system does not have the resources necessary to provide adequate care and support for its clientele. The annual appropriations process continues, unfortunately, to be almost a zero-sum game, as the effort is made to shift dollars from institutional budgets to community care without unduly compromising the adequacy of institutional care. Census reduction is, of course, the critical variable in this process; the major flaw of deinstitutionalization, however, has been the failure to provide adequate funding for treatment and support services in the community.

For the most part, inadequacy of services (within institutions or in communities) is a political issue rather than a legal one. However, in the right-to-treatment suits of the 1970s, an activist federal judiciary measured the adequacy of institutional conditions against judicially articulated standards and, in effect, ordered the state legislatures to put up the money. Some courts were more aggressive than others, but the underlying supposition was that the state's obligation was derived from libertarian premises, not from a freestanding obligation to provide needed services. Using the principle derived from *Jackson v. Indiana* (1972), the courts reasoned that when the state involuntarily hospitalizes a person for the purpose of treatment, it is obligated to make good on that promise to justify the deprivation of liberty. In short, from a constitutional standpoint, involuntarily committed patients, but not voluntary ones, had a constitutionally enforceable right to treatment derived from the due process clause.

It was against the backdrop of this decade of right-to-treatment litigation that the Supreme Court decided *Youngberg v. Romeo* (1982). Although the Court took a very narrow view of the scope of the state's obligation, it did adopt the basic thrust of the jurisprudence that had emerged in the lower courts. The Court began with the observation that "as a general matter, a state is under no constitutional duty to provide substantive services for those within its borders." It emphasized, however, that the state of Pennsylvania had conceded "that a duty to provide certain services and care does exist" when "a person is institutionalized—and wholly dependent on the State." The Court then went on to hold that the state's duty to Romeo encompassed sufficient training to prevent unnecessarily restrictive conditions of confinement.

Entitlement to Adequate Community Service: Thomas S. v. Morrow

Romeo says nothing about the state's duty to a person who is, practically speaking, dependent on the state but who is not institutionalized (or who is institutionalized but does not need to be). In short, does the state violate a person's constitutional rights when it discharges him or her without providing clinically adequate community services? Does the state violate a person's constitutional rights when it keeps him or her in an institution because less restrictive services are not available elsewhere?

The U.S. Court of Appeals for the Fourth Circuit answered yes to these questions in a truly remarkable decision in *Thomas S. v. Morrow* (1986). Thomas S. was placed for adoption by his mother at birth and became a ward of the social services department of Gaston County, North Carolina. Thomas was never adopted or placed in a home that could meet his special needs; rather, he was moved in and out of 40 foster homes and institutions. When community placements were unsuccessful, he was returned to the state hospital, but each time the staff insisted that hospitalization was not an appropriate placement.

In 1981, at age 17, he was placed at Gerald's Lazy Acres Rest Home for the elderly. When Thomas turned 18, he was, while living at Gerald's, declared incompetent. According to the social and psychological evaluations conducted in connection with the guardianship proceedings, Thomas's mental functioning was on the border between normal and mildly retarded, but his social functioning was at a much lower level—in the moderately retarded range. In light of his chaotic placement pattern and the absence of "consistent significant persons in his life," the evaluation team concluded that Thomas "needs a stable, very structured environment for three to six years," one that would give him "consistency in social contacts" so that he could "develop trust in interpersonal relationships." In summary, the team concluded, Thomas' "psychosocial maladjustment is the critical issue that must be addressed."

After Thomas was declared incompetent, his guardian—a regional adult mental health specialist with the North Carolina Department of Human Resources—concluded, unsurprisingly, that Gerald's Lazy Acres Rest Home was not an appropriate placement and had him transferred to the mental retardation unit at the state hospital while efforts were undertaken to find an appropriate placement and to identify the necessary support services. That was in April 1982, when Thomas was 19.

The hospital staff prepared a treatment plan and, 6 weeks after his admission, advised the community mental health agency of Thomas's needs upon his anticipated discharge on June 17, including community-based living either in a group home or in an adult foster care home. The Gaston County agency advised the hospital and Thomas's guardian that no residential placement was available. Thomas was not discharged as planned.

Finally, in late 1982, suit was filed on Thomas's behalf against the North Carolina Department of Human Resources, against his guardian, and against the Gaston County mental health and social services agencies. (Although the Court's opinion does not say so, the suit was, in all likelihood, inspired by the state hospital staff.) The plaintiff sought an order directing the defendants to place Thomas in an appropriate group home and to provide the other services recommended by the professionals who had evaluated and worked with him. (During the months after the suit was filed, several additional evaluations were conducted by the state hospital staff elaborating on his needs.) About a year after the suit was filed, the district court entered a consent order permitting the Gaston County mental health and social service agencies to contract with an independent nonprofit organization for foster care and treatment for the next year.

Pursuant to this consent decree, Thomas was released from the state hospital on March 3, 1983. He was placed with a foster family in Cleveland County. Although the arrangement was a positive one in many respects, Thomas decided to leave after 9 months. He was recommitted to the state hospital and, after 2 weeks, placed in a home for developmentally disabled adults. When he ran away, he was placed in a rest home for elderly and emotionally ill adults. Three months later, in August 1984, he was moved to the Gaston County detoxification and night care facility.

On December 7, 1984, the district court entered summary judgment in Thomas's favor, directing the secretary of human resources and the guardian to develop a clinically tailored treatment plan and appoint a case manager for him. In accordance with the recommendations, the order specified that Thomas should be placed in a "stable suitable supervised community residential placement such as: (1) a non-institutional specialized adult foster care situation . . . or (2) a group home with adults of average intelligence." Adhering to the clinical recommendation of the state hospital evaluation team, the court also suggested that Thomas be provided nonresidential services such as mental health counseling, adult basic education and vocational training, and "opportunities for community interaction." The secretary and the guardian appealed.

The Fourth Circuit affirmed the district court's order, ruling that Thomas was constitutionally entitled "to treatment and training based on the recommendations" of the professionals on the state hospital evaluation team. This included placement in an appropriate community residential setting. The court was unimpressed with the state's arguments that state law made local governments rather than state governments responsible for community services and that the order imposed an obligation on the state to establish new services.

The Fourth Circuit's decision in *Thomas S. v. Morrow* was virtually unprecedented, and its promise remains unfulfilled. It could be read as imposing an affirmative constitutional duty on the state to ensure that adequate community resources are provided to implement treatment or habilitation plans for people with mental illnesses or mental retardation where a failure to do so would constitute a "substantial departure from accepted professional judgment, practice or standards." In other words, the case seems to establish and apply a "right to appropriate community services" for patients who otherwise would be unnecessarily hospitalized.

This is a long step from *Youngberg v. Romeo*, as the Fourth Circuit must surely have recognized. What is the constitutional predicate for the affirmative duty imposed on North Carolina in *Thomas S.*? Apparently, the Court thought it was constitutionally significant that Thomas "remains a legally incompetent adult who is a ward of a guardian appointed by the state." This would imply that the right to appropriate services recognized in *Thomas S.* applies to any person who is a ward of the state but does not apply to a person who has not been adjudicated incompetent and who therefore remains legally free to make his or her own choices about where or how to live his or her life. Does this imply that Thomas would not have been constitutionally entitled to appropriate services if the state had not sought guardianship when Thomas had turned 18? Can a state avoid any constitutional obligations to its citizens with mental illnesses and mental retardation simply by abandoning them?

The Fourth Circuit also tried to link the duty imposed in Thomas's case to the liberty interests mentioned in Romeo's case. The Court emphasized that the treatment plan was designed to deal with Thomas's suicidal and aggressive behavior and therefore implicated his liberty interest in personal safety. Moreover, Thomas's interest in "freedom from undue restraint," the Court said, was implicated by any placement that was more restrictive than warranted by his needs.

It seems clear, however, that this rationale is much broader than the analysis undertaken in *Romeo*, where the Supreme Court was dealing with the conditions inside the institution. The Court reasoned that the state was obligated to provide training to reduce Romeo's self-destructive and aggressive behavior to reduce the need to resort to seclusion and restraint.

Entitlement to Adequate Community Service: Olmstead v. L.C.

Given the fragile reasoning in *Thomas S.*, it is unlikely that *constitutional* litigation would have generated much pressure for community mental health services. Once again, however, the ADA has provided a *statutory* grounding for a new developmental milepost in mental health law. The groundbreaking case under the ADA, decided in 1999, was *Olmstead v. L.C.*

The plaintiffs in *Olmstead* were L.C. and E.W., two dually diagnosed women with substantial histories of institutional care. L.C.'s most recent admission was in May 1992, when she was voluntarily admitted to the psychiatric unit of Georgia Regional Hospital (GRH). Although she was ready for discharge a year later in the opinion of her treatment team, she remained institutionalized until February 1996, when a community placement was finally arranged. E.W. was voluntarily admitted to a psychiatric unit of GRH in February 1995 and remained institutionalized until the *Olmstead* litigation was under way.

Plaintiffs in *Olmstead*, supported by the Justice Department, argued that Georgia's failure to place them in community-based programs, once treating professionals concluded that such placements were appropriate, unnecessarily segregated them based on their disability and therefore violated Title II of the ADA. Georgia argued, in response, that L.C. and E.W. encountered no discrimination "by reason of" their disabilities because they had been denied community services only because of shortage of funds. A 6–3 majority of the Supreme Court rejected the state's position, noting that "Congress had a more comprehensive view of the concept of discrimination advanced by the ADA." However, the Court also emphasized that the state was not obligated to provide a community placement if doing so would contribute an "undue burden."

Accordingly, the Court held that the ADA requires states

> to provide community-based treatment for persons with mental disabilities when the state's treatment professionals determine that such placement is appropriate, the affected persons do not oppose such treatment, and the placement can be reasonably accommodated, taking into account the resources available to the state and the needs of others with mental disabilities.

Specifically, the Court remanded *Olmstead* to the lower courts to "consider, in view of the resources available to the state, not only the cost of providing community-based care to the plaintiffs but also the range of services the state provides others with mental disabilities, and the state's obligation to mete out those services equitably."

As Susan Stefan (1999) has observed, *Olmstead* represents an "enormous achievement on behalf of citizens with disabilities" because it embraces the fundamental premise that "unjustified placement or retention of persons in institutions . . . constitutes a form of discrimination based on disability" (p. 142). As a result, the ADA now provides a powerful tool to press states and localities to create community alternatives for people with disabilities who do not need to be in institutions, and to erase unwarranted distinctions between mental disability and other disabilities or medical conditions in the financing of public services. These issues, she points out "are at the heart of the evolution of mental health law from an almost complete focus on the rights of mental patients vis-a-vis the state, to a concentration on integrating people with psychiatric diagnoses . . . into the communities that they choose to join" (p. 188). *Olmstead* strengthens the entitlement strand of mental health law but without embracing an underlying right to services. The ADA has intensified the involvement of the Justice Department and the federal courts in the organization and funding of public mental health and mental retardation services, precisely the institutional tangle that brought transformational right-to-treatment and deinstitutionalization litigation to a halt in the 1980s.

Need and Responsibility

The constitutional logic of mental health law has thus far prevented the Supreme Court from embracing a principle of entitlement in public mental health services. This resistance is fully understandable in a society that has so far failed to embrace the principle of universal access to health care. Even in the private sector, then, the tension between access and cost is strongly evident.

Health care reform is likely to have a far-reaching impact on mental health law (see chapters 4 and 5, this volume). Eventually, it is likely that the public-private distinction that has been so fundamental to mental health policy and law will be eroded or eliminated. Federal and state responsibilities will be realigned. Decisions about which mental health services are included in the "basic package" for health insurance will have a reverberating impact on virtually all features of the law relating to treatment and entitlement, including workers' compensation, social security, disability insurance, and the ADA.

An important issue lies beneath the emerging reform of health care financing, one that has implications for how we think about mental disorders and distributive justice. In any system of distributing scarce resources, there are several possible allocative principles or criteria. Two of the more common are "need" and "desert" (or responsibility). We must carefully observe how these considerations play out in the emerging system of mental health care and social services.

Obviously, the dominant distributive principle in a universal health care system will be need. In a capitalistic society, a secondary principle will inevitably be wealth. People who can afford to do so will be able to buy more comprehensive coverage than that to which everyone is entitled. Ordinarily, in a need-based distributive system, we do not ask how the need arose. Thus, we do not ask how a sick person got heart disease or cancer. We do not ration care according to whether the person was a smoker or not or, more generally, whether the person was in some way responsible for his or her own disease. Similarly, we do not ration care according to whether a person with AIDS became infected through voluntary sexual intercourse or through a transfusion of bad blood.

This is not to say, however, that notions of responsibility are irrelevant. Under workers' compensation laws, for example, the allocative criterion is need as long as the injury or illness was incurred in the course of employment. But these laws routinely make an exception for injuries incurred in the course of intentional misconduct (e.g., a head injury sustained in a crash resulting from driving at excessive speed or while intoxicated, even if on company business).

Intuitions about responsibility also shape our ideas about what "need" means in the context of mental disorder. Perhaps the biggest issue to be addressed when mental health benefit plans are structured is determining what "counts" as a covered condition. The developing law under the Rehabilitation Act and the ADA reflects a deep belief that a person with a substance abuse disorder is to some extent responsible for his or her own condition—if not for its onset, at least for failing to do something about it or for failing to comply with treatment conditions. Thus, accommodations are required for an alcoholic under the ADA only if he or she is under treatment. There is also case law under the ADA holding that people with severe mental disorders such as schizophrenia and bipolar disorder who are denied employment or government services are not being discriminated against on the grounds of disability if their conduct is attributable to refusal to take their medication.

CONCLUSION

As Holmes said, the life of the law has not been logic alone, for it is inevitably shaped by the "felt necessities of the time." And so it has been in the context of mental health law. First, the libertarian logic of mental health law has been powerfully reinforced by constraints on state mental health budgets, which have given states an incentive to move people out of public hospitals and to keep them out. Deinstitutionalization would have occurred even without libertarian developments in constitutional law. Second, stigmatization and social intolerance are powerful counterforces to the egalitarian vision of antidiscrimination law, and concerns about the costs of compliance will inevitably shape judicial practice under the ADA.

Many of the most important innovations in mental health and disability law during the past two decades were animated by a common ambition—to shift the locus of care to communities and to the least restrictive modalities of service. Legal mechanisms have been used to make it harder to place people in institutions and to keep them there. As these ambitions have been realized, the law has crossed new frontiers. Now that the locus of care has been shifted, new and puzzling problems are being presented, because the ideals of liberty, equality, and entitlement overlap and require redefinition. The goals of mental health law also come more clearly in conflict with competing social values. The path that the law will follow cannot confidently be predicted. What is clear, however, is that those who wish to shape the changing legal landscape will confront continuing challenges in the years ahead.

REFERENCES

Addington v. Texas, 441 U.S. 418 (1979).

American Bar Association (1984). Criminal justice mental health standards. *ABA Standards for Criminal Justice*, Chapter 7. Boston: Little Brown.

Americans With Disabilities Act, Pub. L. No. 101-336, 104 Stat. 327, 42 U.S.C. §§ 12101–12213 (1990).

Bell, C. (2000). Voluntary compliance key to ADA's success. *U.S. Law Week, 69*, 2084.

Campbell, J., & Kaufmann, C. (1997). Equality and difference in the ADA: Unintended consequences for employment of people with mental health disabilities. In R. Bonnie & J. Monahan (Eds.), *Mental disorder, work disability and the law* (pp. 221–240). Chicago: University of Chicago Press.

City of Cleburne v. Cleburne Living Center, 473 U.S. 432 (1985).

Coelho, T. (2000). Opened minds, greater accessibility illustrate progress of ADA after 10 years. *U. S. Law Week, 69*, 2083.

Dennis, D., & Monahan, J. (1996). *Coercion and aggressive community treatment.* Chicago: University of Chicago Press.

Diller, M. (2000). Judicial backlash, the ADA, and the civil rights model. *Berkeley Journal of Employment and Labor Law, 21*, 19–52.

Fair Housing Act Amendments, 42 U.S.C. §§ 3601–3619 (1988).

Family and Medical Leave Act. 29 U.S.C. §§ 2611 et seq. (1993).

Foucha v. Louisiana, 504 U.S. 71 (1992).

Gerbasi, J., Bonnie, R., & Binder, R. (2000). Resource document on mandatory outpatient treatment. *Journal of the American Academy of Psychiatry and the Law, 28*, 127–144.

Hall, L. L. (1997). Making the ADA work for people with mental disabilities. In R. Bonnie & J. Monahan (Eds.), *Mental disorder, work disability, and the law* (pp. 241–280). Chicago: University of Chicago Press.

Holmes, O. W., Jr. (1963). *The common law.* Boston: Little Brown.

In re Gault, 387 U.S. 1 (1967).

Jackson v. Indiana, 406 U.S. 715 (1972).

Kansas v. Hendricks, 117 S. Ct. 2072 (1997).

Kittrie, N. (1971). *The right to be different: Deviance and enforced therapy.* Baltimore, MD: Johns Hopkins University Press.

Krieger, L. H. (2000). Foreword—backlash against the ADA: Interdisciplinary perspectives and implications for social justice strategies. *Berkeley Journal of Employment and Labor Law, 21*, 1–18.

Mechanic, D. (1998). Cultural and organizational aspects of application of the Americans With Disabilities Act to persons with psychiatric disabilities. *The Milbank Quarterly, 76*, 5–23.

O'Connor v. Donaldson, 422 U.S. 563 (1975).

Olmstead v. L.C., 119 S. Ct. 2176 (1999).

Parry, J. (1994). *Mental disabilities and the Americans with Disabilities Act.* Washington, DC: American Bar Association.

Rehabilitation Act, 29 U.S.C. §§ 791–794 (1973).

Roe v. Wade, 410 U.S. 113 (1973).

South Carolina v. Wilson, 413 S.E.2d 19, cert. denied, 113 S. Ct. 137 (1993).

Stefan, S. (1999). The Americans With Disabilities Act and mental health law: Issues for the twenty-first century. *The Journal of Contemporary Legal Issues, 10*, 131–188.

Stefan, S. (2001). *Unequal rights: Discrimination against people with mental disabilities and the Americans With Disabilities Act.* Washington, DC: American Psychological Association.

Thomas S. v. Morrow, 781 F.2d 367 (4th Cir. 1986).

United States v. Salerno, 481 U.S. 739 (1987).

VandenBos, G. R., & Bulatao, E. Q. (1996). *Violence on the job.* Washington, DC: American Psychological Association.

Youngberg v. Romeo, 457 U.S. 307 (1982).

II

LAW AND ETHICS IN MENTAL HEALTH CARE

3

RESEARCH PARTICIPANTS WITH MENTAL DISABILITIES: THE MORE THINGS CHANGE . . .

REBECCA DRESSER

In the early 1970s, the U.S. government had just begun to give serious policy attention to how scientists treated human participants in biomedical research. Until that time, biomedical researchers had enjoyed almost complete freedom in conducting research on human participants. In the first federal policy initiative in 1966, the U.S. Public Health Service issued a statement requiring grant recipients to have their proposals reviewed by a committee of "institutional associates." The statement directed committees to consider each study's informed consent process, risks, and potential benefits. In the end, though, a proposal's ethical acceptability was determined by the researcher's peers (Veatch, 1975).

Today, this total reliance on scientific self-regulation seems quaint and naive. After that first initiative, numerous research "scandals" led the public and government officials to question scientists' commitment to observing basic ethical principles governing research on human participants. By the early 1970s, discussions of research ethics and policy focused on the need to protect people from being exposed to dangerous experimental interventions without their knowledge or consent. At that time, federal funding agencies moved to impose oversight systems in which officials and the public would join scientists in evaluating research proposals for conformity to basic ethical principles.

By the early 1980s, general regulations concerning human research had been adopted, as well as additional provisions governing studies involving some groups deemed especially vulnerable to unwarranted research practices. A federal effort to devise specific provisions on research involving institutionalized people with mental disabilities failed, however, apparently because various interest groups could not agree on a single approach (Bonnie, 1997). Currently we are seeing a renewed effort to formulate policy on research involving people with mental disabilities. The crucial question is whether old suspicions and hostilities will again block policy development, or whether more constructive dialogue is possible at this time.

This chapter reviews the origins of U.S. policy on the protection of human participants in research, including certain problematic research studies that influenced policy development. The chapter examines existing research policy and its failure to attend to many important ethical questions relevant to research involving individuals with mental disabilities. The chapter describes demands made by AIDS and other patient advocacy groups for expanded access to participation in clinical trials and discusses whether this shift in emphasis from participant protection to expanded access has occurred in the context of research involving people with mental disabilities. The chapter concludes by describing current efforts to develop improved policy for research on this population and considering whether progress is likely at this point.

EARLY ETHICAL CONSTRAINTS ON RESEARCH INVOLVING PARTICIPANTS WITH MENTAL DISABILITIES

The earliest international research ethics code emerged after World War II. German physicians were prosecuted at the Nazi war crimes trials for forcible and brutal "experiments" conducted on concentration camp prisoners. In the judgment convicting the Nazi doctors, members of the Nuremberg tribunal set forth 10 principles to govern future research involving human beings (Katz, 1972). The Nuremberg Code became the foundation for later national and international research ethics documents.

The Nuremberg Code contains several provisions relevant to research involving people with mental disorders and disabilities. Most prominent (and problematic) is its first principle: "The voluntary consent of the human subject is absolutely essential" (Nuremberg Code, 1949, pp. 181). The code explicitly approves only research involving people with the legal capacity to consent who freely agree to enter a study based on an adequate understanding of its purpose, length, procedures, inconveniences, and possible physical effects. As such, the code appears to rule out studies involving individuals who are cognitively or emotionally incapable of independent decision making about research participation. If the code's provisions controlled research, many studies on mental disorders and developmental disabilities could not be conducted. Although vulnerable individuals would be protected, people with these conditions would be denied the treatment benefits that research can produce.

The creators of the next international research ethics code took a less restrictive approach than the Nuremberg judges. In 1964 the World Medical Association adopted the Declaration of Helsinki, which confers limited approval on studies involving decisionally incapable individuals. The declaration allows research with the informed consent of an incompetent participant's legal guardian or responsible relative "in accordance with national legislation" (World Medical Association, 1997, p. 926). The declaration appears to approve only clinical research for participants lacking decisional capacity, however. According to the declaration, research conducted purely to advance knowledge should involve only volunteers— "either healthy persons or patients for whom the experimental design is not related to the patient's illness" (p. 926). Adherence to this restriction would rule out many studies on the biological dimensions of mental disabilities.

U.S. RESEARCH: EARLY PROBLEM CASES

During the late 1960s and early 1970s, a series of revelations indicated that many U.S. biomedical researchers were ignoring the Nuremberg and Helsinki provisions. In 1966, the *New England Journal of Medicine* published an article entitled "Ethics and Clinical Research" written by physician-investigator Henry Beecher (1966). Beecher described 22 examples of unethical or questionably ethical studies conducted by U.S. researchers between the late 1940s and mid-1960s. The studies had been published in major medical journals by researchers at leading institutions such as the Harvard Medical School, the University of Pennsylvania, and the National Institutes of Health (NIH; Rothman, 1987).

Most of the studies Beecher described were conducted on adult hospital patients or servicemen who were neither told of their research involvement nor given the opportunity to refuse participation. Two studies that involved participants with mental disabilities were particularly disturbing. One was a hepatitis study conducted at the Willowbrook State School for the Retarded (Krugman & Giles, 1970). In this study, children arriving at the institution purposely were exposed to hepatitis through injection or oral administration of the virus. The investigators wanted to learn more about the disease in hopes of facilitating the search for an effective vaccine.

Researchers believed the study was justified because it imposed relatively little harm on participants and was conducted with parental consent. Most of the children in the study were expected to contract a mild version of the disease, which would leave them immune from future infection. Moreover, researchers noted, because many Willowbrook residents were already infected with hepatitis, newly admitted children would be exposed whether or not they were part of the study. But critics argued that because effective alternative measures such as gamma globulin inoculation were available to prevent infection, the children were being used purely for the benefit of others. Critics also questioned the adequacy of information provided to parents and reported that some parents had been told that their children could be admitted to the facility only if the children were enrolled in the study (Beauchamp & Childress, 1994). Although the Willowbrook research became the target of media and scholarly criticism, the study was defended by the editor of *The New England Journal of Medicine* (Ingelfinger, 1972), and the investigator was later awarded the Lasker Prize for his research achievements (Rothman, 1991).

Beecher described another study involving participants with mental disabilities. This study was conducted by Chester Southam, a Cornell University Medical School professor on staff at the Sloan-Kettering Institute for Cancer Research. In this research, elderly patients at the Jewish Chronic Disease Hospital who were affected by dementia and other mentally debilitating conditions were injected with cancer cells to determine immune system response. No benefit to the participants was expected. The participants were of questionable capacity; moreover, they were told only that they were receiving "cells." The investigator claimed he was trying to prevent the participants from becoming frightened at undergoing a procedure that posed no risk to them. But according to historian David Rothman (1991), "When Southam was later asked why, if the procedure was so harmless, had he not injected the cancer cells into his own skin, he replied that there were too few skilled cancer researchers around" (p. 81).

The Jewish Chronic Disease Hospital study became the focus of two legal proceedings. A hospital board member brought action to ascertain whether improper experimentation had occurred, but he was denied access to participants' medical records. The New York Court of Appeals ruled in the board member's favor, citing his responsibility for the hospital's activities (*Hyman v. Jewish Chronic Disease Hospital*, 1965). The other legal proceeding resulted in a decision by the Board of Regents of the State University of New York to suspend the medical licenses of Dr. Southam and of the hospital's director of medicine, who had permitted the research to go forward over the opposition of several staff physicians (Katz, 1972, p. 63). Many researchers and physicians remained supportive of Southam's conduct, however. His study was published in the prestigious journal *Science* (Southam, Moore, & Rhoads, 1957), and he was elected president of the American Association of Cancer Research 3 years after the Board of Regents's action (Rothman, 1991).

FEDERAL RESPONSE TO ETHICAL VIOLATIONS

Beecher's (1966) report was the first of a series of disclosures of ethically problematic conduct by U.S. researchers. In 1972 the nation learned of serious ethical violations in the U.S. Public Health Service's syphilis study at Tuskegee. In the study, effective treatment was withheld from poorly educated, low-income African American men so that researchers could document the natural course of the disease (Jones, 1993; Rothman, 1991). The announcement of yet another troubling human study led Congress to conclude that a better oversight system was needed. It established the National Commission for the Protection of Human Subjects of Biomedical and Behavioral Research and directed the commission to review and make recommendations on research involving human participants (National Research Act, 1974).

Besides considering general principles and procedures governing research, the National Commission was instructed to make recommendations on certain vulnerable groups. One such group included "individuals who are mentally ill, mentally retarded, emotionally disturbed, psychotic, or senile, or who have other impairments of a similar nature and who reside as patients in an institution." The Willowbrook and the Jewish Chronic Disease Hospital studies became part of the backdrop for the commission's deliberations on this participant population.

In its *Report and Recommendations on Research Involving Those Institutionalized as Mentally Infirm*, the National Commission (1978) sought to balance the desire for research advancements against the need for safeguards to protect a vulnerable participant group. It suggested an oversight framework in which study interventions would be classified according to their expected harms and benefits. All studies would be examined by an institutional review board (IRB), an interdisciplinary committee composed of institutional employees and at least one individual not affiliated with the research facility. Study interventions presenting relatively high risk and no direct benefit to participants would undergo additional scrutiny at the national level. Investigators proposing research involving institutionalized people would also be required to justify why the desired information could not be obtained by studying a less vulnerable group. In addition, the clinician responsible for a patient would have to determine that research participation would not interfere with the patient's health care.

According to the National Commission's report, research interventions presenting no more than minimal risk[1] would be permitted with the consent of a decisionally capable individual or the assent[2] or failure to object of a decisionally incapable individual. If a study intervention presented higher risk, but also a reasonable chance of direct participant benefit, research would be permitted with the consent of a capable individual or the assent (and guardian's permission if required by state law) of an incapable individual. Investigators seeking to enroll people incapable of assent in research involving interventions with higher risk but possible direct benefit would have to obtain the consent of the participant's legal guardian or a court. Research interventions presenting this ratio of risk to expected benefit could be performed on objecting incapable individuals if potential direct benefit was available solely in the research context and a court specifically authorized participation. The commission recommended that IRBs be given discretion to appoint a "consent auditor"[3] for studies involving interventions presenting minimal risk or higher risk but possible direct benefit.

The highest moral concern is raised by research interventions presenting more than minimal risk and no prospect of direct benefit to participants in vulnerable groups. The National Commission's (1978) recommendations took a more permissive position on this form of research than either the Nuremberg Code or the Helsinki Declaration. The commission described two kinds of research interventions in this category. First, to approve interventions presenting a minor increment over minimal risk[4] and no prospect of direct benefit to participants, the IRB would be required to appoint a consent auditor to ensure compliance with the same consent and assent provisions applicable to the previous research categories. In

[1]The National Commission (1978) defined *minimal risk* as "the risk (probability and magnitude of physical or psychological harm or discomfort) that is normally encountered in the daily lives, or in the routine medical or psychological examination, of normal persons" (p. 8). Current regulations contain a similar definition, except they omit the phrase "of normal persons" (Federal Policy for the Protection of Human Subjects, 1991, pp. 28013–28014). As a result, minimal research risks are those that are comparable to the risks ordinarily encountered by an individual participant.
[2]To fulfill the assent requirement, the participant must "know what procedures will be performed in the research, choose freely to undergo those procedures, communicate this choice unambiguously, and be aware that subjects may withdraw from participation" (National Commission, 1978, p. 9).
[3]According to the National Commission (1978), the consent auditor "should observe the consent process and determine on behalf of the Institutional Review Board whether each prospective subject consents, or being incapable of consenting, assents, or objects to participation in the research" (pp. 10–11). The commission suggested that the auditor also could observe ongoing research to ensure continuing assent by incapable participants. According to the commission, the consent auditor should be someone not otherwise affiliated with the research and familiar with the physical, psychological, and social needs of the class of prospective subjects.
[4]In determining whether a study meets this criterion, the National Commission (1978) instructed the IRB to consider the degree of risk in light of "a common-sense estimate of the risk; an estimation based upon investigators' experience with similar interventions or procedures; any statistical information that is available regarding such interventions or procedures; and the situation of the proposed subjects" (p. 18).

addition, the IRB would have to find that the intervention had a reasonable chance of benefiting future participants or the research was "of vital importance for the understanding or amelioration" of the participants' condition (p. 17).

Studies that could not be approved under any of these provisions could still be approved through a national review process. First, an IRB would have to find that the study offered an opportunity to advance knowledge or to remedy a serious health or welfare concern involving institutionalized people with mental disabilities. Second, a national ethical review committee and the head of the federal department or agency sponsoring the research would have to find (after public notice and opportunity for comment) that the study would be conducted "in accord with the basic ethical principles that should underlie the conduct of research involving human subjects" (National Commission, 1978, p. 20), and would include adequate arrangements for obtaining participant consent or participant assent and guardian consent.

The National Commission's recommendations never became federal policy, however. In proposed regulations issued soon after the commission's recommendations, officials in the Department of Health, Education and Welfare (HEW, 1978) endorsed preferences for more stringent protections for participants in this population. First, the HEW proposal indicated that consent auditors might be mandatory in all studies involving this participant group. Second, HEW officials suggested that they might also require the authorization of an advocate assigned to protect the best interests of prospective participants incapable of consent. Third, the HEW proposal noted that officials were considering a requirement for national ethical review of all studies with interventions presenting greater than minimal risk and offering no prospect of direct benefit to participants. Finally, the proposed regulations revealed that HEW was considering prohibiting the involvement of any nonassenting, incapable participant in studies with intervention presenting greater than minimal risk and no prospect of direct benefit. Thus, HEW's proposed modifications were more protective than the National Commission's recommendations.

The position of the American Bar Association (ABA) Commission on the Mentally Disabled (1976) also may have been influential in blocking the National Commission's recommendations. This group contended that "the proposed subject should be represented at all stages by an independent attorney" (p. 157). The ABA group also favored a prohibition on research interventions presenting greater than minimal risk and no direct benefit to institutionalized participants. Disability advocates and others who attributed high significance to participant protection believed that such requirements were justifiable for research in this morally controversial category. However, researchers reacted negatively to HEW's proposed regulations, deeming the restrictions and procedural requirements unnecessarily severe. Researchers and others who focused on the need for improved treatment saw the requirements as impediments to progress (Bonnie, 1997).

The government's response to this lack of agreement was inaction. No regulations governing research involving participants with mental disabilities were ever issued. In 1983, the secretary of the Department of Health and Human Services (HHS) attributed the omission to the "lack of consensus" on the proper regulatory stance. He also wrote that the agency believed that its general provisions on human research adequately incorporated the National Commission's recommendations (President's Commission for the Study of Ethical Problems in Medicine and Biomedical and Behavioral Research, 1983).

The result of these events was a federal research policy that gives little attention to the special ethical concerns raised by research involving people with mental disabilities. U.S. regulations include only a few vague provisions addressing this form of research. "Mentally disabled persons" are identified as a vulnerable population, and IRBs are directed to include "additional [but unspecified] safeguards . . . to protect the rights and welfare" of research participants with mental disabilities (Federal Policy for the Protection of Human Subjects, 1991, p. 28016). Federal policy also instructs IRBs to ensure that "subject selection is equitable" (p. 28016) and that people with mental disabilities are not involved in studies that could be conducted with a less vulnerable participant population. The policy also suggests that IRBs that frequently review research involving participants with mental disabilities consider appointing as members "one or more individuals who are knowledgeable about and experienced in working with these subjects" (p. 28015).

The lack of clear guidance in the existing federal policy leaves to IRBs the task of resolving numerous ethical considerations, among them

- the standards and procedures for evaluating prospective participants' decisional capacity
- the identification of a "legally authorized representative" for people determined to be decisionally incapable
- the substantive standards governing surrogate decision making about research
- the permissibility of research involving incapable participants who object or fail to assent to participation
- the appropriate standards and procedures governing research interventions presenting greater than minimal risk to incapable participants.

How have IRBs coped with this responsibility? The available evidence is partial and largely anecdotal. It suggests, however, that IRB review has been inadequate in at least some cases.

RESEARCH ETHICS IN RESPONSE TO AIDS

In the late 1980s, a shift of emphasis became evident in general research ethics discussions. People with AIDS began to criticize research policy for being too protective and paternalistic. Given the life-threatening nature of their disease, many AIDS patients were willing to expose themselves to relatively high risks to gain access to even a remote chance of benefit from a newly developed drug. Existing research rules, they contended, interfered with their autonomous choice to accept such risks. These individuals, many of whom were young, well educated, and politically sophisticated, eventually convinced the Food and Drug Administration (FDA) to revise its rules to allow earlier and wider access to experimental AIDS medications. Such drugs became more available to HIV-infected individuals before the final stage of clinical trials (Epstein, 1996).

This change in access to research participation was accompanied by widespread criticism of other research policies and practices that were based in part on the desire to protect participants from harm. The media and members of Congress publicized researchers' failure to include adequate numbers of women and people of color in research studies. Some scientists and officials argued that this exclusionary practice was justified to protect pregnant women from research interventions that could harm their children and to avoid imposing disproportionate research burdens on traditionally disadvantaged groups.

Yet the result of this protective approach was a lack of knowledge about whether women and people of color would benefit from drugs and other interventions tested solely on White men. Those in the excluded groups thus were receiving a disproportionately small share of the health benefits generated through research (Dresser, 1992). In response to this criticism, the NIH (1994) and the FDA (1993) adopted provisions designed to produce a more inclusive approach to the selection of research participants.

Access to research has now become a common theme, evident for example in advocacy efforts on behalf of women with breast cancer and people with "orphan" (relatively rare but serious) diseases. Indeed, some observers are concerned that the pendulum has swung too far in this direction. They argue that "the current tendency to see research as largely beneficial and benign is just as wrong-headed as the earlier tendency to view it as primarily dangerous and exploitative" (Levine, 1994, p. 95). Have the demands for expanded access also begun to overshadow the concern for protection of research participants with mental disabilities? Recent inquiries addressing studies involving people with mental disabilities bear on this question.

RESEARCH INVOLVING PARTICIPANTS WITH MENTAL DISABILITIES: RECENT DEVELOPMENTS

In 1991, a federally funded schizophrenia study became the focus of an inquiry by the U.S. Office for Protection from Research Risks (OPRR). In the study, conducted by the University of California Los Angeles (UCLA), participants with recent-onset schizophrenia were given a fixed dose of antipsychotic medication. After 1 year, the medication was withdrawn to determine which participants were able to function without medication. The drug washout study was based on evidence that some individuals who have recently developed schizophrenia are able to function without medication and thus can be spared the short- and long-term side effects associated with the drugs (OPRR, 1994).

The OPRR inquiry began after officials received reports that the UCLA investigators had failed to obtain informed consent from participants and had exposed them to unnecessary risks by failing to implement adequate safety monitoring. The OPRR (1994) determined that the study's disclosure documents "omitted certain basic elements required for legally effective informed consent as defined under [HHS] regulations" (pp. 16–17). More specifically, the documents omitted adequate descriptions of research procedures and reasonably foreseeable risks (including the probability and magnitude of risks associated with medication withdrawal and with receiving a fixed dose, as opposed to the individualized doses available in the clinical setting). The documents also failed to include an adequate discussion of available clinical alternatives to research participation. Finally, OPRR determined that the documents should have alerted participants to the fact that UCLA treating psychiatrists were also acting as members of the research team and thus in some circumstances would be guided by the study's requirements as opposed to the individual participant's best interests.

The OPRR required UCLA to undertake remedial actions. Investigators were directed to develop written descriptions of the study, the family's role in decision making, and other relevant information for distribution to participants' families. Concerned that the UCLA IRB's monitoring was inadequate in this case, the OPRR (1994) directed the IRB to appoint one or more consumer representatives as members and to "establish one or more independent Data and Safety Monitoring Boards . . . to oversee HHS-supported protocols involving subjects with severe psychiatric disorders in which research investigators or coinvestigators are also responsible for the clinical management of subjects" (p. 22).

Several years later, other questionable studies involving participants with mental disabilities came to light. In 1994, President Clinton appointed a committee to review human radiation experiments conducted during the Cold War period and to make recommendations to guard against a recurrence of unethical behavior in government-sponsored research. To evaluate how well the contemporary oversight system was working, the Advisory Committee on Human Radiation Experiments (1995) reviewed selected research projects conducted during the early 1990s. The committee examined IRB reviews and other documents associated with eight federally funded studies involving adults with questionable decisional capacity. Four studies required participants to undergo diagnostic imaging that offered them no prospect of direct benefit, and two studies appeared to present more than minimal risk.

After reviewing the imaging study materials, the committee (1995) noted that the studies "required that the subjects' movements be restricted, yet there was no discussion in the documents or consent form of the implications for the subjects of these potentially anxiety-provoking conditions" (p. 706). The committee also found no evidence that participant capacity assessment or surrogate permission for research participation had been considered. Based on its review, the committee recommended that government officials formulate guidelines for research involving adult participants of questionable competence. It identified as an "issue of research policy deserving public debate and resolution" the matter of "whether and under what conditions adults of questionable capacity can be used as subjects in research that puts them at more than minimal risk of harm and from which they cannot realize direct medical benefit" (p. 822).

The lack of a clear resolution to these policy questions also caused problems in New York. In 1996, a state appellate court invalidated regulations adopted by the New York State Office of Mental Health (OMH) to govern non-federally funded research involving residents of facilities operated or licensed by OMH. In the case of *T.D. v. N.Y. State Office of Mental Health* (1996), the court determined that OMH lacked the statutory authority to regulate research and found that some of the regulations violated the prospective participants' common law and constitutional due process rights. Notably, the New York regulations in many respects demonstrated greater concern for participants' rights and welfare than current federal policy. Nevertheless, the court cited several problems in the OMH provisions on research interventions presenting more than minimal risk and little or no benefit to participants.

First, citing New York and U.S. Supreme Court case law addressing the forced administration of antipsychotic drugs, the court held that potential participants must be given notice when their capacity for research decision making will be assessed. Participants must also have an opportunity to seek "appropriate administrative and judicial review" of such capacity determinations (*T.D. v. N.Y. State Office of Mental Health*, 1996, p. 187). In addition, the court noted that the regulations should establish qualifications for those assessing prospective participants' capacity and should specify a procedure for assessment. The opinion also criticized the rules for failing to specify when such assessments should be conducted by people unaffiliated with the research.

Second, relying on New York decisions on cessation of life-sustaining treatment, the court stated that incapable adults may not be enrolled in research with interventions presenting more than minimal risk and no prospect of direct benefit unless evidence exists that the individual consented to participation while competent or designated a proxy to make research decisions. Moreover, parents or guardians may not authorize their children's participation in research with this ratio of risk to expected benefit. This determination was made in light of New York case law limiting parental authority to refuse treatment that offers a reasonable chance of protecting a child's health and welfare.

Finally, the court criticized a provision allowing research to proceed over an incapable participant's objection or the objections of a participant's authorized representative. Under this provision, such objections could be overridden if (a) a psychiatrist not involved in the study found that participation could provide an important direct benefit not otherwise available to the participant and (b) a court approved the individual's participation. The appellate court found fault with the provision's failure to require notice to participants or their representatives of the psychiatrist's determination and with the lack of a mechanism to challenge the determination. The judges also implied that the nature of the benefit in such cases must be directly linked to the research procedures and related to the participant's psychiatric condition.

Though OMH did not appeal the case, the plaintiffs appealed, asking the court to extend the ruling to federally funded research and to studies presenting greater than minimal risk and the possibility of direct benefit. In December 1997, the New York Court of Appeals dismissed the appeal on technical grounds, stating that the plaintiffs had already been granted everything they requested in their initial suit. (*T.D. v. N.Y. State Office of Mental Health*, 1997). The court also noted that the lower court had invalidated the regulations because OMH lacked the statutory authority to promulgate them, and any further analysis by the court was dicta and not binding precedent.

Public and professional reactions to these events reveal that the general calls for expanded access to research have not diminished concern for the protection of participants with mental disabilities. News reports on the UCLA schizophrenia study criticized the investigators' conduct and the IRB's performance. A *New York Times* editorial ("Medical Ethics," 1994) is representative:

A troubling ethics case at the University of California at Los Angeles has cast doubt on the elaborate protective devices set up to guard the subjects of medical research from unjustified harm. The case suggests the "informed consent" documents signed by patients can be a charade —and that review boards set up to monitor the projects can be rubber stamps. (p. A12)

Similarly, *Time Magazine* published a report questioning whether researchers were too slow to respond to signs of relapse in at least one participant (Willwerth, 1993).

The UCLA incident also triggered a negative response from advocacy groups ordinarily sympathetic to the research endeavor. The California Alliance for the Mentally Ill (1994) dedicated a full issue of its journal to the case and its ethical implications. Dan Weisburd, publisher of the journal, dramatically recounted his disappointment:

Just when we thought we were poised on the brink of making . . . big discovery leaps, armed with PET scans and MRIs, and faith in a new generation of brilliant multi-degreed researchers who show daring determination, willingness and that special sense of commitment that almost sings a sure song of impending success . . . lo and behold . . . in our face is a bleak vision; a foreboding spector of deception and betrayal, and maybe worst of all, the clear undeniable fact that our structure of rules is insufficient to the task of protecting our loved ones with serious illness—without whose participation in research—victory over their horrid, life altering afflictions is impossible. (Weisburd, 1994, p. 1)

Strong concern for participant protection is evident in the opinion and commentary concerning the *T.D. v. N.Y. State Office of Mental Health* (1996) outcome as well. The appellate division opinion referred to the emergence of new, more powerful psychiatric medications and to the pharmaceutical companies' eagerness to test and to obtain approval for marketing these drugs. Instead of justifying fewer restrictions on access to drug studies, "These developments serve to highlight the importance of safeguarding the rights of incapable adults and minors, who may be potential subjects of greater than minimal risk studies involving psychiatric medications" (p. 194).

Commentary on *T.D. v. N.Y. State Office of Mental Health* also revealed persisting tensions between advocates for participants and researchers. Many advocates and medical ethicists welcomed the decision and voiced hope that it would trigger action to address policy gaps at the federal level (Capron, 1997; Hilts, 1996). Yet researchers expressed fears that "vital experiments" would be blocked by the court ruling (Hilts, 1996). They predicted that the *T.D.* decision would have a "major, detrimental impact upon the prevention and treatment of mental illness" and "devastating" effects on pediatric research as well (Barnes, 1997, pp. 25–26).

AN END TO POLICY PARALYSIS?

The comments noted above suggest the continued existence of what Bonnie (1997) called "a classic fault line in psychiatric ethics and mental health law" (p. 108). Furthermore, they point to the mixed attitudes of the families of people with mental disabilities. Although many family members have a strong desire to promote the search for more effective treatments, they will not countenance the imposition of material harm on research participants to advance the cause. Even the Alzheimer's Association (*Ethical issues in dementia research*, 1997), which has been among the most vocal groups on the need for research advancements, issued a position paper counseling family surrogates to enroll incapable relatives in research only if participation is in the individual's best interests. The document also states that studies involving more than minimal risk and no direct benefit should be reserved for capable people who consent to participate and for incapable participants who previously executed a research advance directive consenting to participate or authorizing another person to consent on their behalf.

The important policy question today is whether the positions of researchers and advocacy groups remain sufficiently polarized to block regulatory reform. This question will be answered in the next few years as policymakers and interest groups respond to recent proposals from three advisory groups. One, the National Bioethics Advisory Commission (NBAC), was established in 1995 to provide guidance on protection of research participants. In late 1998, NBAC issued its *Report and Recommendations on Research Involving Persons with Mental Disorders That May Affect Decisionmaking Capacity*. The second proposal came from a group the New York Commissioner of Health appointed in response to the *T.D. v. N.Y. State Office of Mental Health* (1996) decision. The Advisory Work Group on Human Subject Research Involving the Protected Classes (1998) formulated proposed rules to govern research involving people with mental disabilities. The third proposal came from a working group organized by the Office of the Maryland Attorney General (1998) to draft legislation on the research involvement of individuals with decisional impairment. Although the three groups adopted similar positions on certain points, they differed on others. Moreover, it remains to be seen whether any of the recommendations will become part of state or federal research policy.

The recommendations address a number of substantive and procedural issues in need of policy attention. One such issue involves identifying the appropriate criteria for assessing a prospective participant's capacity for research decision making. Another issue concerns the proper identity, qualifications, and authority of surrogate decision makers for individuals found to lack decision-making capacity. Other contested issues include the role of participant assent and whether research should ever proceed despite a participant's verbal or physical resistance. Also debated is whether policy should authorize people to give advance consent to future research participation. Another central question is whether to limit the research risks to which incapable participants may be exposed. Moreover, if risk limits are adopted, should exceptions exist for participants with advance directives who agreed while capable to participate in higher-risk research?

A final general set of issues concerns the extent to which independent monitors should be involved in the research process. The overriding question is whether and, if so, in what situations a person with no other role in the research project should be assigned to evaluate compliance with policy requirements. One potential answer would be to mandate consent auditors or educators to evaluate participants' and surrogates' decisional capacity and understanding of the information relevant to study participation. Independent monitors could also be assigned to evaluate compliance with the requirements for ongoing participant or surrogate consent. In addition, they could evaluate initial and ongoing assent or lack of objection by decisionally incapable participants. Finally, such individuals could be given the responsibility to ensure that surrogates are appointed for participants who lose decisional capacity during the research process.

These unresolved substantive and procedural issues are ripe for policy clarification. Reflecting on my experiences as a consultant to NBAC and as a member of the New York advisory work group, I am unsure whether it will be possible to move beyond the impasse created by the conflicting views of researchers and advocates for people with mental disabilities. The testimony and discussions I have observed indicate that at least some participants in the debate appear to retain the uncompromising attitudes that prevented federal policy action in the 1970s. The possibility of continued stalemate is suggested by a recent exchange over the NBAC (1998) *Report and Recommendations*. A mental health researcher, Robert Michels (1999), claimed that many of the NBAC recommendations are unnecessary for participant protection and would impede progress in treating mental disorders. In turn, a member of NBAC argued that recent reports of ethics problems in psychiatric research indicate that the current oversight system is inadequate (Capron, 1999). Nonetheless, agreement may be possible on some important components of a revised policy. For example, Dr. Michels voiced support for NBAC's recommendation that IRBs reviewing research involving participants with mental disorders appoint as members representatives of the participant population.

My hope is that the various interest groups can put aside old hostilities and reach a policy compromise. Policy progress is unlikely if scientists oppose all measures that would add to the cost or complexity of conducting research. Such a stance could in the long run impede research progress by reducing public and consumer support for the research endeavor. In turn, if advocacy groups insist on substantial procedural safeguards and substantive restrictions on research, they could thwart current efforts at policy formation. The result would be a return to a problematic status quo—a policy that fails to address important ethical questions raised by research involving people with mental disabilities. An adversarial approach will further no one's interests, least of all prospective research participants and others living with the burdens of psychiatric disorders, dementia, and other mental disabilities.

REFERENCES

Advisory Committee on Human Radiation Experiments. (1995). *Final report.* Washington, DC: U.S. Government Printing Office.

Advisory Work Group on Human Subject Research Involving the Protected Classes. (1998). *Recommendations on the oversight of human subject research involving the protected classes.* Albany, NY: State of New York Department of Health.

American Bar Association Commission on the Mentally Disabled. (1976, September–October). Statement of ABA Commission on the Mentally Disabled before national human experimentation group. *Mental Disability Law Reporter,* pp. 155–159.

Barnes, P. G. (1997, March). Beyond Nuremberg: Fifty years later, the debate continues on informed consent. *ABA Journal,* pp. 24–27.

Beauchamp, T. L., & Childress, J. F. (1994). *Principles of biomedical ethics.* New York: Oxford University Press.

Beecher, H. K. (1966). Ethics and clinical research. *New England Journal of Medicine, 274,* 1354–1360.

Bonnie, R. J. (1997). Research with cognitively impaired subjects: Unfinished business in the regulation of human research. *Archives of General Psychiatry, 54,* 105–111.

California Alliance for the Mentally Ill. (1994). Ethics in neurobiological research with human subjects. *Journal of the California Alliance for the Mentally Ill, 5,* 1–70.

Capron, A. M. (1997, March–April). Incapacitated research. *Hastings Center Report,* pp. 25–27.

Capron, A. M. (1999). Ethical and human-rights issues in research on mental disorders that may affect decision-making capacity. *New England Journal of Medicine, 340,* 1430–1434.

Department of Health, Education, and Welfare. (1978). Proposed regulations on research involving those institutionalized as mentally disabled. *Federal Register, 43,* 53950–53956.

Dresser, R. (1992, January–February). Wanted: Single, white male for medical research. *Hastings Center Report,* pp. 24–29.

Epstein, S. (1996). *Impure science: AIDS, activism, and the politics of knowledge.* Berkeley: University of California Press.

Ethical issues in dementia research. (1997, May). Chicago, IL: Alzheimer's Association. Retrieved January 25, 2001, from the World Wide Web: http://www.alz.org/aboutus/overview/statements.htm

Federal policy for the protection of human subjects. (1991). *Federal Register, 56,* 28012–28018.

Food and Drug Administration. (1993). Guideline for the study and evaluation of gender differences in the clinical evaluation of drugs. *Federal Register, 58,* 39406–39416.

Hilts, P. J. (1996, December 27). New York court strikes down rules on psychiatric studies, halting some tests. *New York Times,* p. B28.

Hyman v. Jewish Chronic Disease Hospital, 15 N.Y.2d 317, 206 N.E.2d 338 (1965).

Ingelfinger, F. J. (1972). Ethics of experimentation on children. *New England Journal of Medicine, 288,* 791–792.

Jones, J. (1993). *Bad blood: The Tuskegee syphilis experiment.* New York: Free Press.

Katz, J. (1972). *Experimentation with human beings.* New York: Russell Sage Foundation.

Krugman, S., & Giles, J. P. (1970). Viral hepatitis—New light on an old disease. *Journal of the American Medical Association, 212,* 1019–1029.

Levine, R. S. (1994). The impact of HIV infection on society's perception of clinical trials. *Kennedy Institute of Ethics Journal, 4,* 93–98.

Medical ethics in the dock [Editorial]. (1994, March 14). *New York Times,* p. A12.

Michels, R. (1999). Are research ethics bad for our mental health? *New England Journal of Medicine, 340,* 1427–1430.

National Bioethics Advisory Commission. (1998). *Report and recommendations on research involving persons with mental disorders that may affect decisionmaking capacity.* Rockville, MD: Author.

National Commission for the Protection of Human Subjects of Biomedical and Behavioral Research. (1978). *Report and recommendations on research involving those institutionalized as mentally infirm.* Washington, DC: U.S. Government Printing Office.

National Institutes of Health. (1994). Guidelines on the inclusion of women and minorities as subjects in clinical research. *Federal Register, 59,* 14508–14513.

National Research Act, Pub. L. No. 93–348, 88 Stat. 342 (1974).

Nuremberg Code. (1949). In *Trials of war criminals before the Nuremberg Military Tribunals under control council law no. 10* (Vol. 2, pp. 181–182). Washington, DC: U.S. Government Printing Office.

Office for Protection from Research Risks. (1994). *Evaluation of human subject protections in schizophrenia research conducted by the University of California Los Angeles.* Bethesda, MD: Author.

Office of the Maryland Attorney General. (1998, July 12). *Final report of the Attorney General's research working group.* Baltimore, MD: Author.

President's Commission for the Study of Ethical Problems in Medicine and Biomedical and Behavioral Research. (1983). *Implementing human research regulations*. Washington, DC: U.S. Government Printing Office.

Rothman, D. S. (1987). Ethics and human experimentation: Henry Beecher revisited. *New England Journal of Medicine, 317,* 1195–1199.

Rothman, D. S. (1991). *Strangers at the bedside: A history of how law and bioethics transformed medical decisionmaking*. New York: Basic Books.

Southam, C. M., Moore, A. E., & Rhoads, C. R. (1957). Homotransplantation of human cell lines. *Science, 125,* 158–160.

T.D. v. N.Y. State Office of Mental Health, 650 N.Y.S.2d 173, 228 A.D.2d 95 (App. Div. 1996).

T.D. v. N.Y. State Office of Mental Health, 91 N.Y.2d 860, 690 N.E.2d 1259, 668 N.Y.S.2d 153 (1997).

Veatch, R. M. (1975, October). Human experimentation committees: Professional or representative? *Hastings Center Report, 5,* 31–40.

Weisburd, D. E. (1994). Publisher's note. *Journal of the California Alliance for the Mentally Ill, 5,* 1–2.

Willwerth, J. (1993, August 30). Tinkering with madness. *Time,* pp. 40–42.

World Medical Association. (1997). Declaration of Helsinki. *Journal of the American Medical Association, 277,* 925–926.

4

FROM CONSTITUTION TO CONTRACTS: MENTAL DISABILITY LAW AT THE TURN OF THE CENTURY

JOHN PETRILA

The treatment of people with serious mental illness has changed profoundly in the United States since 1970. There have been new ideas regarding what constitutes adequate services, transformations in the types of providers that deliver those services, and, most dramatically, acute modifications in financing services. The role of the government has changed as well. Many services formerly provided directly by the government have been privatized, and the notion that the government should provide a "safety net" for people with the most serious needs has come under attack.

As a result, the public mental health system has been transformed in many states. People with serious mental illness are treated in many settings, but the management of care is increasingly the responsibility of for-profit, national corporations operating under contract with state, local, or federal agencies. The freestanding state mental health agency no longer exists in a growing number of states (Glover & Petrila, 1994), and the Medicaid agency often effectively controls state mental health policy as states move to contain the rate of inflation in their Medicaid programs in both general and behavioral health (Rosenbaum et al., 1997).

The role of law has changed as well. In the 1970s, three major issues dominated mental disability law: challenges to civil commitment procedures and criteria, the right to treatment, and the right to refuse treatment. Each issue rested on federal constitutional theories, and each challenged the manner in which the state determined who would become subject to the public mental health system and under what conditions. Because plaintiffs generally believed that the care provided by public mental health systems was grossly inadequate, much mental disability litigation sought to create barriers between the state as provider and the individual in the role of patient.

These constitutional issues, combined with litigation occasioned by the "duty to protect" announced in *Tarasoff v. Regents of the University of California* (1976), largely defined mental disability law. However, federal statutory and regulatory law also had an important impact on mental health systems. For example, amendments to Medicaid and to social security laws created a financial base for expanding services provided in the community. These changes enabled many people formerly treated in state psychiatric hospitals to be treated elsewhere and, in many states, became the basis for providing services such as housing that were traditionally unavailable to people with serious mental illnesses.

Today, in contrast, the core issue for many people with a serious mental illness is obtaining access to services. The impact of civil commitment laws is still a very important question, as are questions regarding institutional conditions (see Burt, chapter 1, this volume). However, most people with serious mental illness are treated in community settings, and increasingly many are enrolled, often by default, in managed care plans designed in large measure to control cost inflation. New networks of providers have emerged, and health maintenance organizations (HMOs) have become significant factors in those networks, sometimes at the expense of traditional community mental health centers.

These developments have raised important questions regarding legal advocacy on behalf of people with mental disabilities. Constitutional doctrine is often less important in this new environment than contract law and the application of federal statutes regulating payment plans. Although judicial and legislative responses to changes in health and behavioral health care services have lagged behind the changes stimulated by the market, the skeleton of a legal framework for dealing with this dramatically changed landscape has begun to emerge.

This chapter examines the changes in the legal and policy framework that shaped mental health services over the past 30 years and discusses emerging legal strategies for addressing the problems that people with serious mental illnesses face today. The chapter begins with a discussion of changes in the public mental health system, including changes in financing and treatment. It then summarizes the emergence of managed care and privatization and discusses the impact of those developments on the public mental health system. The chapter then examines legal advocacy on behalf of people with mental illness in today's environment, focusing on provider and payer liability, as well as government's responsibility as a regulator of services provided through contract. It briefly summarizes legislative responses to issues arising from managed care and privatization and concludes with some predictions regarding legal issues of likely import in the near future. By necessity many of these developments are covered with broad strokes, but a unifying theme is the assumption that law, policy, and services for people with mental disabilities are inextricably connected and that mental disability law must be considered in the context of how and where people with mental disabilities receive services.

THE PUBLIC MENTAL HEALTH SYSTEM

In 1970, the public mental health system in many states consisted primarily of state-operated psychiatric hospitals and federally financed community mental health centers. Often little integration occurred between these two types of providers,[1] and other health care providers had little interest in the patients treated by the public mental health system. In the commercial market, people with health insurance typically had little coverage for mental health and substance use treatment, particularly compared to coverage in the same policies for physical illnesses.

This status quo eventually began to change, in part because of constitutional challenges to state practices. However, equally important were changes in federal financing statutes creating a fiscal underpinning for community programs. In addition, advances were made in the conceptual framework for providing treatment for people with the most serious mental illnesses. These developments led to great changes in the late 1970s and 1980s in both the private and the public sectors.

Changes in Financing

Until the 1970s, the provision of psychiatric inpatient care was considered the responsibility of the states. In 1972, however, Congress enacted legislation making psychiatric inpatient care provided in a psychiatric unit within a general hospital eligible for Medicaid reimbursement (Social Se-

---

[1] A central tenet of federal community mental health centers legislation was that the centers were funded directly by the federal government, giving the state mental health agency no direct role regarding the centers. This meant that many states encountered problems in integrating the activities of the community mental health centers with state-operated hospitals. It also in some states led to significant disagreement between the centers and the state regarding the mission of such centers and the degree to which the centers should allocate their resources to people with the most serious illnesses.

curity Act Amendments, 1972). Medicaid reimbursement also became available for inpatient psychiatric services provided to individuals younger than age 22 and older than age 64 regardless of setting. Congress also expanded the coverage of social security disability benefits for people with mental disabilities.

These statutory changes, combined with the expansion of the Medicare program, had two effects relevant here. First, general hospitals with psychiatric units found that the provision of psychiatric care to people with a serious mental illness could be an attractive financial proposition, and non-state hospitals began to assume greater responsibility for acute psychiatric hospitalization (Kiesler & Sibulkin, 1987). This shift included striking increases in the rate of hospitalization of adolescents, with consequences noted below in the discussion of managed care. Second, the availability of social security disability benefits provided the financial underpinnings for certain types of community services, such as community residences, which relied on the financial contributions of people cared for in such residences for at least part of their funding.

Changes in the Conceptual Framework of Treatment

Serious challenges to the primacy of the medical model as the mode of treating mental illness arose in the 1980s, leading ultimately to a redefinition of what constituted adequate treatment of serious mental illness. Three developments were particularly significant.

The first development was the elaboration of the community support model. This approach viewed "treatment" as a broad concept, incorporating nearly anything that would stabilize or improve the individual's functioning. Proponents of this model argued with great success that housing, employment, case management, and other supports traditionally viewed as the province of the social welfare system were integral to, and in many cases the most important part of, treating serious mental illness and increasing community tenure (Stein & Test, 1978).

The second major development, stimulated by William Anthony and his colleagues at Boston University (Anthony & Liberman, 1986) and Robert Liberman and his colleagues at the University of California Los Angeles (Liberman, 1988) was the emergence of "psychosocial rehabilitation" (also referred to as "psychiatric rehabilitation"). This approach assumed that maximizing client control of treatment choices would lead to the best outcomes. Like the community support approach, it viewed treatment broadly and holistically; even more than the community support approach, it challenged professional hegemony over treatment by insisting that the client and not the staff was the principle decision maker regarding treatment.

The third development was the emergence of the primary consumer and family movements. The primary consumer movement,[2] in particular, challenged traditional notions of treatment and flatly rejected many approaches, including clinically developed approaches to housing (Tanzman, 1993) and employment (McDonald-Wilson & Mancuso, 1989). The family movement insisted that families be given more access to the treatment process and be treated more respectfully by providers and administrators. Both movements expressed dissatisfaction with the mental health system; however, on the issue of coercion, they often disagreed. The family-oriented National Alliance for the Mentally Ill advocated the expansion of state commitment laws, whereas consumer groups advocated stricter limits on, and in some cases the abolition of, coercion.

These changes in financing and in the conceptual framework of care had important ramifications for where and how care was delivered. With government accounting for approximately half of specialty mental health spending in 1990, the availability of Medicaid and other entitlement funding resulted in an increase in the aggregate amount of resources devoted to the care of people with mental illness and an expansion of overall service capacity (Frank & McGuire, 1996). Although community services grew in many jurisdictions, state mental health agencies often continued to serve as the primary point in state government for the establishment of state mental health policy. At the same time, insurance coverage for mental health services, although failing to achieve parity with physical illness coverage, became more generally available in the 1980s.

It is conceivable, although not subject to proof, that the innovations in treatment developed in the late 1970s and 1980s, combined with the availability of public and private financing for services, might have resulted over time in the creation of integrated community-based mental health services for people with serious mental illness. By the late 1980s, however, many state governments were experiencing financial difficulties. In addition, a consensus began to emerge that the United States spent "too much" on health care. In at least partial response, two trends emerged that radically altered the organization and financing of behavioral health services under both commercial and public auspices. The first trend was the emergence of a set of strategies for containing costs in the health care system, labeled "managed care." The second trend was increased willingness by government to shed its role as a provider of services through privatization.

---

[2]The issue of nomenclature has been important in the primary consumer movement. Some individuals and groups use the term *consumer*, whereas others use the term *consumer/survivors*. Still others prefer terminology that expresses the idea of being liberated from unjust or punitive confinement, for example, *ex-psychiatric prisoners*. Good discussions of the effect of labeling can be found in many places, including Chamberlin (1994), Deegan (1990), and Reidy (1993).

EMERGENCE OF MANAGED CARE AND PRIVATIZATION

Managed Care

Conservatively, at least 10% of personal health care spending in the United States is for mental health and substance abuse services (Frank & McGuire, 1996). These expenditures increased rapidly during the 1970s and 1980s; one commentator estimated that expenditures on inpatient psychiatric care increased from $3 billion in 1969 to $21.4 billion in 1986 (Ellis, 1991). Health care costs in general rose dramatically through the same period, but two developments triggered the first application of managed care strategies to behavioral health care services, initially in the context of commercial insurance.

The first was a rapid rise in the rate of psychiatric hospitalization of children and adolescents, often in response to newly generous reimbursement plans (Schwartz, 1989; Weithorn, 1988). The second was claims that mental health and substance abuse costs were increasing at two to three times the rate of inflation for general health care costs (Bracken & Anderson, 1990). Employers began contracting with specialty managed care companies for the administration of mental health and substance abuse benefits, and in 1999, managed care became a $4.4 billion industry, costing Americans more than $176 million (Findlay, 1999).

The adoption of managed care in publicly financed systems began somewhat later but was also a response to rising costs, particularly in the Medicaid program. Combined federal and state spending on Medicaid, for example, rose 13% in 1989, 18% in 1990, 27% in 1991, and 30% in 1992 (Kaiser Commission, 1993). Because Medicaid is the financial responsibility of both federal and state government, the enactment by Congress of new Medicaid-mandated benefits, combined with expanded eligibility, resulted in increased expenditures in state spending as well. By the late 1980s, inflation in Medicaid spending had become a central political issue.

Many states, in response, incorporated managed care techniques in the administration of their Medicaid programs. Although cost containment was the primary goal, administrators also assumed that access could be improved through better administration of public funds. Because Medicaid had been used by state mental health agencies to expand community-based programs, such expenditures became an early target for managed care efforts. By June 1996, nearly 40% of Medicaid recipients nationally (approximately 13 million out of 33 million recipients) were enrolled in a managed care plan (American Academy of Pediatrics, 1997), whereas approximately 5 million Medicaid recipients received behavioral benefits through a managed care plan (Coughlin, 1998).

Managed care, in both publicly and privately financed plans, has several distinguishing characteristics. First, people are enrolled in the plan and, with certain exceptions not relevant here, the plan is under no obligation to provide services to non-enrollees. This is a fundamental change from traditional delivery systems, particularly in public sector mental health, where the notion of enrolled individuals was rarely used.[3] Second, nearly all managed care plans use prior approval of services, either through a physician or other health care professional acting as a gatekeeper, or through other prior approval mechanisms, in an effort to control and direct the utilization of services. Generally, such reviews apply to individual cases a definition of "medical necessity" that is included in the contract establishing the managed care plan. Third, plans usually seek to establish a provider network, which has the practical effect of limiting the numbers and types of providers eligible to provide services under the plan. Fourth, payment mechanisms often result in the assumption of partial or full financial risk by providers.

Fifth, and perhaps most important, contracts create and define the structure of the managed care plan, clarify the relationships between and duties of payers and providers, establish enrollee rights, define available benefits, and establish both reimbursement rates and payment mechanisms. The overarching importance of the contract in this environment cannot be exaggerated (Rosenbaum et al., 1997). As will be discussed below, many of the emerging judicial and legislative responses to problems that have arisen in managed care settings have been dictated by the fact that the health care system today is largely a product of and bound by contract terms.

Finally, behavioral health has often been "carved out" of general health for purposes of managed care, meaning that the behavioral health benefit is managed separately from the physical health benefit. The majority of behavioral health benefits currently are "carved out" for management. The application of managed care to behavioral health care services has had an impact on cost and on some types of utilization. Recent reports suggest that despite the expansion of insurance coverage for behavioral health disorders, inpatient utilization has decreased, and the percentage of health plan costs attributed to mental health and substance abuse services dropped by 50% between 1989 and 1995 (Buck & Umland, 1997; National Association of Psychiatric Health Systems, 1997).

Privatization

Although managed care has dominated the discussion of health and behavioral health care over the past 10 years, it is only part of the larger

---

[3]It should be noted that beginning in the mid-1980s mental health systems increasingly used analyses of expenditure data to identify those who used the largest quantity or most costly services. This "heavy user" analysis created the framework for targeting services more precisely to individuals (Surles & McGurrin, 1987).

trend of privatization that has marked the government's response to the delivery of human services in the last decade (Astrachan, 1993; Kettner & Martin, 1993; Mirin & Sederer, 1994). Until the 1980s, government was the presumptive provider of last resort for many services, including mental health, corrections, and social welfare. Although at least some of those government-provided services were delivered by nongovernment agencies through contract, such agencies usually were local, not-for-profit entities presumed to share a common set of values with the responsible government agency. In recent years, however, government at all levels has moved to divest itself of its responsibilities as a service provider, and the movement toward contracting for the provision of services in all spheres has accelerated.

As privatization has become an article of faith for many government officials, the vendors with whom government contracts have changed markedly as well. Many companies engaged in "government work" today are large, for-profit companies with contracts in many states. This development mirrors trends in the health care industry generally, where health care delivery and reimbursement are increasingly the province of multistate, for-profit corporations (Greene & Lutz, 1995; Kleinke, 1998; Reinhardt, 1998; Vladeck, 1998).

Privatization appears to reflect a larger philosophical shift in thinking about the role of government. Many government officials elected in the 1980s and 1990s were hostile to or at least ambivalent about the role of government as the provider of last resort, and they believed that competitive market forces were the best antidote to social problems. In addition, since the Reagan administration, aspects of political campaigns that often appear to be exercises in the creative stereotyping of individuals who receive government assistance have eased the shift to privatization. If government is assumed to be an inefficient provider and an overly intrusive regulator, and if it is believed that those who rely on government could best improve their lives by finding work, then giving private companies control over the expenditure of taxpayer-generated revenues may appear to some as the most logical route to increased efficiencies and reduced inflation in costs.

TODAY'S PUBLIC MENTAL HEALTH SYSTEM

As a result of the changes in behavioral health financing and organization, the public mental health system in a number of places has lost many of its distinguishing characteristics. First, most episodes of treatment for people with serious mental illness occur in settings other than state-operated facilities, and most episodes of treatment occur in non-inpatient settings (Iglehart, 1996). In many jurisdictions, even people who enter services through involuntary civil commitment are hospitalized in a state hospital only after assessment and treatment in another setting. In Florida, for example, there are more than 60,000 petitions for civil commitment in a year, and each person is assessed and initially treated in a community hospital or similar setting (Department of Mental Health Law and Policy, 1998).

The de facto monopolies of providers that characterized the public mental health system as recently as a decade ago have also begun to erode. During the 1970s, but particularly in the 1980s, service providers in the traditional public mental health system might have included state hospitals, which provided long-term and in some states acute psychiatric care; community hospitals with psychiatric units, which increasingly provided acute care to people with serious mental illness; community mental health centers, which were usually not-for-profit organizations providing services within a locality or region; private, freestanding psychiatric hospitals, often specializing in adolescent care; and providers of housing and other social supports, sometimes through community mental health centers and sometimes through stand-alone not-for-profit agencies. The late 1980s and early 1990s also saw the emergence of services operated by primary consumers, such as drop-in centers.

The state mental health agency was a major purchaser of services it did not provide (they were generally provided by community mental health providers) and often used sole-source contracting in making those purchases. In some states, certificate of need laws provided further insulation from competition.[4] Finally, the "commodity" at stake (the "public patient") was not particularly attractive to other types of providers. The result in many states was a series of quasi monopolies, with each type of provider able to survive economically with its own share of the "market," often assisted financially by the state mental health agency that relied on these providers for services.

The landscape in many states looks quite different today in both behavioral and general health care. The one- and two-physician office, the mainstay of the medical profession for the better part of this century, is becoming less common as physicians create integrated groups and as those groups are purchased by or affiliate contractually with health maintenance organizations, hospitals, and other provider networks. HMOs, hospitals,

---

[4]In 1974, Congress enacted the National Health Planning and Resources Development Act (Pub. L. No. 93-641), which required states to implement a certificate of need process. In general, such a process requires providers wishing to expand services to persuade the state that such services are needed. States were expected to create a plan that anticipated necessary changes in capacity, and the "needs methodology" that anchored that plan also usually was the frame of reference used by applicants as well as the government in implementing the certificate of need process. Congress repealed the requirement that states have a certificate of need process in 1986, and many states abandoned the process, further permitting market forces to determine the types and quantity of health care services that would be developed.

ambulatory care clinics, and other providers are forming networks with varying degrees of corporate integration to compete for contracts. The managed care market in behavioral health care is dominated by a handful of national companies, and integration in that market is proceeding as well.

Because caring for people with mental illness is perceived by some as an attractive investment opportunity, there is competition, often on a national basis, for contracts in both the privately and publicly funded sectors. As a result, the near monopoly formerly enjoyed in many states by community mental health centers is in danger of dissolution as their clients are enrolled in managed care plans that may not rely on the centers. In some places, community mental health centers, state hospitals, and other traditional providers have had difficulty competing. Some lack the necessary infrastructure (information systems, financial reserves) to be credible bidders for managed care contracts, whereas others simply do not know how to shift from a noncompetitive to a competitive environment.

The role of government, and the locus of policy making, has also changed markedly in many states. States that have adopted managed care have done so initially in their Medicaid programs, and about 20 have implemented some form of managed behavioral health care (National Health Lawyers Association [NHLA] & American Association of Hospital Attorneys [AAHA], 1998). Consequently, the state Medicaid agency, which under federal law has responsibility as the "sole state agency" for administration of the Medicaid program, has taken on a central role. In adopting managed behavioral health care, the Medicaid office has often assumed a policy-making role regarding at least that portion of the state mental health program paid for by Medicaid. The state mental health department continues to play an important and sometimes primary role where it is able, but it has lost political standing in many states, often being merged with other state departments such as the social welfare and public health departments (National Association of State Mental Health Program Directors Research Institute, 1997).

Government also increasingly pays for or regulates services rather than providing them directly. This shift has not been particularly easy for some states. A number of reports suggest that state efforts to monitor contracts have been uneven at best (U.S. General Accounting Office, 1997; Horvath & Snow, 1997; Rosenbaum et al., 1997). Also, the process of contract bidding and the selection of vendors in some states have been subject to litigation that has delayed state efforts to move to managed care (*Medco Behavioral Care Corporation v. State Department of Human Services*, 1996; *Value Behavioral Health Care, Inc. v. Ohio Department of Mental Health*, 1997).

In short, the financing and delivery of mental health services are very different from what they were at the beginning of the mental disability law movement. Core legal issues affecting providers and practitioners have also changed; a physician or hospital employing counsel today is as likely to have questions regarding contract law, antitrust law, or tax law as malpractice or privileging issues. Constitutional questions have continuing resonance because of the continued use of civil commitment and because individuals continue to be confined in state institutions. Prevailing in such litigation may, however, be more difficult than it was 20 years ago,[5] and the impact of such litigation may be diminished simply because most people with mental illness, even serious mental illness, spend little if any time in state institutions. Given these changes, a question of great significance is what, if any, judicial or legislative theories might prove useful in advocating on behalf of people with mental disabilities in this new environment.

LEGAL ADVOCACY IN THE ERA OF MANAGED CARE

Twenty years ago, the primary tool of advocates responding to abuses in the public mental health system was federal court litigation based on constitutional theories. The era of constitutional litigation and its consequences have been analyzed by a number of commentators, with the analyses by Appelbaum (1994) and by LaFond and Durham (1992) having particular value. Even a decade ago, civil rights litigation, particularly that brought under the Civil Rights for Institutionalized Persons Act (1980), played a significant role in shaping the responsibilities of states. In the past decade, however, changes in the health care market have far outstripped judicial, legislative, and regulatory responses to problems engendered by those changes.

One reason for this lag in response time may be the redefinition of the role of government noted earlier. The assumption that government should play a major regulatory role has been sharply challenged in the past few years, and the popular characterization of the Clinton health care reform proposals as a bureaucrat's dream did little to build a consensus that government should adopt an aggressive regulatory stance toward the changes sweeping the health care field. In addition, the political consensus

---

[5]In one of the most recent fully litigated cases alleging unconstitutional conditions in Pennsylvania's mental health facilities, brought by the Department of Justice (DOJ) under the Civil Rights for Institutionalized Persons Act (1980), a federal district court found against DOJ on nearly every count (*United States v. Pennsylvania*, 1995). This is not to suggest that such efforts have lost all utility. When safety issues exist, a DOJ inquiry may prove effective in raising the standard of care. However, in facilities in which a pattern and practice of unsafe conditions cannot be proved, state defendants have an excellent chance of prevailing if they go to trial. At the same time, a recent decision by the U.S. Supreme Court may reinvigorate institutional litigation (*Olmstead v. L.C.*, 1999). The court ruled that continued state institutionalization of people with mental disabilities who according to treatment staff could live in the community with proper support violated the provisions of the Americans with Disabilities Act (1990) barring discrimination on the basis of disability.

in the late 1980s and 1990s held that inflation in health care spending needed to be brought under control and that managed care, however defined, was the best strategy to achieve that goal.

Significant barriers to legal advocacy exist in this environment. Some have been political: for example, congressional cuts in the funding and jurisdiction of legal service groups. Other barriers, however, flow from the complexities of finding effective legal theories that go beyond individual claims in today's health care settings. A constitutional claim on behalf of individuals confined in a state-operated hospital was conceptually a comparatively easy claim to prepare and advance—the "class" was readily identifiable, conditions were often demonstrably unsafe, and the courts, at least for a few years, were ready to grant relief and to continue to monitor the facility long after the case had been decided. However, the service environment today is more complex, and the legal barriers, most notably the Employee Retirement Income Security Act (ERISA, 1974; discussed in more detail below), make the pursuit of successful litigation difficult. As a result, the task for advocates today is to identify legal theories that might prove useful in an environment in which government provides little care while divesting itself of many of its regulatory responsibilities, and in which contracts with for-profit companies are the primary vehicle for the organization, financing, delivery, and oversight of care.

Despite these difficulties, a number of judicial and legislative developments in the past few years make it possible to discern the outlines of strategies that advocates may rely on in the near future. These strategies depend in large measure on contract law and the concept of fiduciary responsibility. The remainder of this chapter discusses these developments in more detail, focusing in turn on the responsibilities of providers, payers, and government.

Provider Liability

A central tenet of the American Medical Association's code of ethics is the following statement: "A physician has a duty to do all that he or she can for the benefit of the individual patient. . ." (Seward, 1999). The courts have reified this principle in both traditional and managed care environments. For example, in *Muse v. Charter Hospital* (1996), the North Carolina supreme court upheld a jury award against a hospital that had discharged a 16-year-old 1 day before the results of blood work ordered by his physician were returned. The patient had been admitted for depression and suicidal thoughts and had a previous psychiatric history. He was discharged on the day his insurance expired, despite a promissory note signed by his parents assuring payment of future charges. He killed himself shortly thereafter. The court, in upholding the jury's award, emphasized the importance of preventing the financial contamination of clinical judgment.

The court found to be reasonable the jury's finding that the hospital had "a policy or practice which required physicians to discharge patients when their insurance expired and that this policy interfered with the exercise of medical judgment" (p. 474).

Courts have also rejected provider claims that managed care practices would force them to engage in unethical practice. In *Varol v. Blue Cross* (1989), for example, a district court, refusing to intervene in a decision by General Motors (GM) to contract out its behavioral health care program, commented that

> the purpose of the Pilot Program is to determine in advance whether the GM plan will pay for the proposed treatment. Whether or not the proposed treatment is approved, the physician retains the right and indeed the ethical and legal obligation to provide appropriate treatment to the patient. (p. 833)

This is not to say that courts have been insensitive to the potential for some types of cost containment measures and financial incentives to contaminate clinical judgment. As the discussion below suggests, such contamination is increasingly a major concern both judicially and legislatively. What does seem apparent, however, is that the fiduciary responsibilities of health care professionals continue to be a preeminent value ethically and legally, and that providers must recognize that financial discomfort will not provide a good defense to claims of bad practice.

Payer Liability

The earliest efforts to hold payers responsible for malpractice occurred in California. In *Wickline v. State of California* (1986), an appeals court rejected a claim by a patient that the state of California as payer and its fiscal intermediaries should be liable for injuries, including a leg amputation, suffered after she was released from hospital care. The intermediary had approved 4 additional days of hospitalization rather than the 8 requested by the treating physician. The court, in rejecting the claim, noted the physician's role as advocate, observing that "a physician who complies without protest . . . when his medical judgment dictates otherwise cannot avoid his ultimate responsibility for his patient's care" (p. 1643). Although the court later characterized as dicta this "duty to appeal," the *Wickline* court reinforced the notion of a wall between treatment (for which the provider bore responsibility) and payment (for which the payer bore responsibility).

This wall was tentatively breached by the same court a few years later in *Wilson v. Blue Cross* (1990). This was a psychiatric case in which the physician of a patient admitted for depression and suicidal thoughts sought approval for 3 weeks of treatment but was granted reimbursement for 10 days of care. The patient was discharged after 10 days and killed himself. Here the court found that a payer could be found partially liable for injuries suffered by a patient if the payer's conduct was both negligent and a substantial factor in bringing about the suicide.

Although this case appeared to signal the beginning of an era of litigation against payers on quasi-malpractice theories of liability, that era never really began (Petrila, 1996). Multiple reasons for this may exist; one that undoubtedly has been a major factor is the barrier created by ERISA (1974). ERISA, intended to create a uniform national standard to govern qualified employer-based insurance plans, preempts other laws that "relate to any employee benefit plan" (p. 1144). In addition, ERISA grants the federal courts exclusive jurisdiction over civil actions brought under it (p. 1132). As a result, the courts traditionally have removed cases brought in state court against ERISA-qualified plans to federal court, where a plaintiff can recover only the amount available under the benefit that is being contested. As a practical matter, this has meant that malpractice claims have been extraordinarily difficult to pursue against ERISA-qualified plans, for once the case is removed to federal court it is essentially transformed into a breach of contract case. Because most commercial health insurance is purchased through ERISA-qualified plans, malpractice claims largely have been unavailable in such settings (Blum, 1989).

However, some recent cases suggest that this may be changing following a 1995 U.S. Supreme Court opinion indicating a willingness to approach ERISA preemption with somewhat more flexibility. In *New York State Conference of Blue Cross and Blue Shield Plans v. Travelers Insurance* (1995), the Supreme Court upheld against a preemption challenge a New York statute that imposed a variety of surcharges on HMOs and other insurers. In addition, at least two federal circuit courts have ruled that cases seeking to hold payers responsible for substandard care would not be preempted by ERISA. In *Pacificare of Oklahoma v. Burrage* (1995), the Tenth Circuit ruled that

> when an HMO elects to provide medical services or leads a participant to reasonably believe that it has, rather than simply arranging and paying for treatment, a vicarious liability medical malpractice claim based on substandard treatment by an agent of the HMO is not preempted. (p. 155)

The Third Circuit reached a similar conclusion, finding that "quality control of benefits . . . is a field traditionally occupied by state regulation and we interpret the silence of Congress as reflecting an intent that it remain as such" (*Dukes v. U.S. Healthcare, Inc.*, 1995, p. 357). More recently, a federal district court held that a liability claim against a hospital, a physician, and a payer stemming from the death of an infant after discharge from the hospital could proceed in state court (*Bauman v. U.S. Healthcare, Inc.*, 1998).

These cases do not suggest that managed care companies are now routinely available as defendants in state court malpractice claims. As the court in *Pacificare* made clear, the HMO in that case could be sued under such a claim because the plaintiff was alleging reliance on the HMO as a care provider. This suggests that a claim brought against an HMO acting purely as a payer or plan administrator might have been rejected. However, these cases indicate more willingness on the part of the courts to exempt some types of claims against payers from automatic removal to federal court.

Payers are also vulnerable to claims that allege that the process by which a claim was reviewed was inadequate. For example, in *Crocco v. Xerox* (1997), a court required the employer to complete an additional review of a claim for reimbursement for psychiatric hospital care that had been denied. The claim had been rejected for periods during which the patient was hospitalized but had been given grounds passes, on the theory that if the patient was well enough for grounds passes then inpatient care was not medically necessary. The court did not substitute its judgment for the employer's decision but ordered the employer to conduct another review. The court characterized the initial review as "cursory and one-sided" because the reviewer failed to speak to the patient or the therapist, review the clinical records, or ask for another opinion on the matter. Courts have also overturned the application of a medical necessity standard when it appeared that reviewers were denying claims in the face of overwhelming evidence of need. In *Hughes v. Blue Cross of Northern California* (1989), another psychiatric case, the court found that "good faith demands a construction of medical necessity consistent with community medical standards that will minimize the patient's uncertainty of coverage in accepting his physicians' recommended treatment" (p. 857).

Each of these cases turns at least in part on the fiduciary responsibility of plan administrators. It appeared at one point as if this fiduciary responsibility might eventually result in an expansion of the application of informed consent doctrine to payers. The Eighth Circuit, for example, ruled that ERISA-qualified plans had an obligation to disclose to enrollees financial incentives that might affect a physician's clinical judgment (*Shea v. Esensten*, 1997). In *Shea*, a patient complained to his family physician of chest pains and dizziness and had a family history of heart problems. His physician persuaded him that he did not need to see a specialist, and the patient died of cardiac arrest shortly thereafter. His estate brought suit in state court alleging that the plan had violated its fiduciary duties by not disclosing to enrollees that financial incentives existed for primary care physicians not to refer patients to specialists. The Court of Appeals ruled that the case was properly removed to federal court, but on the substantive issue found that "when an HMO's financial incentives discourage a treating doctor from providing essential health care referrals for conditions covered under the plan benefit structure, the incentives must be disclosed and the failure to do so is a breach of ERISA's fiduciary duties" (p. 629).

Not all courts agreed with this conclusion (see, for example, *Weiss v. CIGNA*, 1997), and the U.S. Supreme Court in its spring 2000 term rejected the principle that treatment decisions made by physicians in an ERISA plan were subject to the fiduciary requirements of ERISA (*Pegram v. Herdrich*, 2000). This suggests that the trend toward increased payer and provider liability may be weakened, though that will depend on how the federal courts apply the Supreme Court's most recent decision. Although ERISA is generally not an issue in publicly financed plans, the application of theories of fiduciary responsibility to the parties to managed care contracts may have relevance for individuals enrolled in public sector plans. As the concluding section of this chapter suggests, these theories are beginning to find their way into legislative and regulatory responses to managed care as well.

Government Responsibilities as a Regulator

Both federal and state governments are responsible for the administrative oversight of publicly financed programs. In addition, most states codify bills of rights for individuals receiving mental health care. As states (and the federal government in the Medicare program) enter into managed care contracts, however, the question of government oversight becomes critical. The problem may be particularly pressing in some state mental health systems where both the political status of the state mental health agency and its staffing have been diminished.

A recent study of the oversight provided by four states that had entered managed care contracts concluded that the states should improve their methodologies for collecting and analyzing data, their clinical studies and medical record audits, their review of grievance data, and their beneficiary satisfaction surveys (General Accounting Office, 1997, p. 24; see also Horvath & Snow, 1997). Other commentaries, by primary consumer (National Health Law Program, Inc. & Cecil B. Sheps Center for Health Services Research, 1996) and family (Huskamp, 1996) groups have urged states to involve consumers and families in contract development and oversight as a mechanism for improving accountability. In addition, industry groups have attempted to develop standards to evaluate the performance of managed behavioral health care companies (American Managed Behavioral Healthcare Association, 1999).

Although government may divest itself of operational responsibilities in many situations, it cannot legally divest itself of all of its duties. In *Grijalva v. Shalala* (1998), for example, Medicare recipients alleged that the

Secretary of Health and Human Services had inadequately monitored the performance of HMOs providing Medicare services. The court of appeals affirmed a district court ruling rejecting the secretary's argument that she had only limited oversight authority over private HMOs. The district court had found that the claims denial process was inadequate, noting that 52% of adverse notices to enrollees were illegible, 74% provided only vague reasons for the denial, and 59% failed to notify the claimant of his or her personal liability for care pursued after the denial of Medicare reimbursement. The court had also rejected the argument that the right of enrollees dissatisfied with services to disenroll and seek care elsewhere made federal oversight less critical. In short, the federal government retained the responsibility to ensure that the providers with which it contracted met Medicare provisions establishing due process protections for people whose claims for coverage were denied.

LEGISLATIVE AND REGULATORY RESPONSES

As managed care has evolved, a number of complaints have become the focus of legislators and administrative agencies. Their responses have included attempts to ensure that consumers are fully informed about their choices, to ensure that consumers have access to some types of care either within or outside of the managed care plan, to provide for reviews of claims denials by an entity independent of the plan, and to create quasi-malpractice liability against payers.

Texas became the first state to address the liability issue, enacting legislation in 1996 that imposes a "duty to exercise ordinary care" on HMOs, managed care organizations, and insurers in treatment decisions (Texas Senate Bill 386, 1998). These organizations are held responsible for the actions of their employees, agents, and representatives. In addition, the statute requires that contractual definitions of "appropriate and medically necessary" services be in accord with "prevailing practices and standards of the medical profession and community." In 1999, at least 36 states introduced similar legislation (Stauffer & Levy, 2000), and 7 states have adopted legislation that bars "hold harmless" clauses used by insurers in contracts to prevent a provider from shifting liability to an insurer (NHLA & AAHA, 1998). The provisions of the Texas statute permitting pursuit of a lawsuit against a payer in state court was upheld against a challenge that it violated the ERISA preemption clause, though the court struck down a provision mandating independent review of an adverse benefit determination (*Corporate Health Insurers, Inc. v. Texas Department of Insurance*, 1998).

There have also been a number of federal proposals introduced in Congress from the mid-1990s to the present that address various access, consent, and procedural issues in managed care. These proposals have covered various issues, including

- mandating reimbursement for emergency services
- providing for access to ob-gyn and other specialty care
- establishing a state health insurance ombudsman program
- creating explicit liability for clinically or medically inappropriate decisions resulting from cost containment measures (much like the Texas legislation)
- requiring payers to indemnify their providers
- banning gag rules (contractual provisions that prohibited providers from disclosing certain information regarding plan provisions; at least 41 states already ban such provisions, NHLA & AAHA, 1998)
- providing due process rights for providers denied access to or removed from provider panels.

The federal government has also taken steps in its administration of the Medicare program and in its role as payer in the Medicaid program to achieve some of these goals, such as banning gag rules and prohibiting the use of financial bonuses to create incentives for physicians to reduce utilization (Balanced Budget Act of 1997).

On another front, a panel appointed by President Clinton endorsed a model patient "bill of rights" to be incorporated into all insurance plans. The recommendations include a right to appeal a denial of care, initially within the plan but in the case of major expenses to an outside panel; the provision of vastly increased information from payers and providers to consumers regarding financial incentives within the plan, malpractice history of the provider, and related issues; a "reasonable person" standard in determining whether emergency room care would be compensated; and barriers to the use of financial incentives that would contaminate professional decision making ("Panel of Experts," 1997).

The panel, however, was unable to agree on a set of fundamental issues, including

- the elimination of lifetime caps within plans
- a right for patients to participate in clinical trials, which would address the common refusal of managed care companies to pay for treatment that is part of an experimental program
- establishment of an ombudsman program for health care consumers
- the practice of many payers of refusing to enroll particular types of individuals based on health status, a practice that some have argued results in overly broad exclusion of racial minorities and people living in poverty.

Perhaps most importantly, the panel voted against incorporating these suggested "rights" into federal legislation, preferring voluntary adoption by affected parties ("Health Panel Declines," 1998). This failure to recommend legislative action suggests continuing ambivalence regarding the role of government in mandating the features of health care plans and may also suggest continuing fallout from the unsuccessful effort of the Clinton administration to legislate a number of guarantees as part of its comprehensive health care reform proposal.

As this brief summary suggests, a number of theories are emerging that may inform advocacy on behalf of people with mental disabilities in the next few years. These theories are grounded in traditional tort and contract law and are anchored in the fiduciary responsibilities of providers, payers, and government. At the same time, it is wise to be realistic about the potential reach of these theories. First, even if malpractice litigation becomes routinely available against payers, it seems unlikely to have more than the modest effect on practice attributed to such litigation when the conduct of practitioners is at issue (Furrow et al., 1997).

A more significant limitation may be that little of this litigation and legislation affects the benefit plan itself; rather, any redress they provide is available only after the contracts defining available benefits and coverage are in place. In other words, it is difficult to affect benefit design through litigation. In the private sector, employers, particularly those with ERISA-qualified plans, have almost unlimited discretion in benefit design.[6] Legislators do sometimes amend benefit plans, by providing, for example, for an extra day of hospital coverage after birth, or by providing access to certain types of specialists. These are, however, piecemeal amendments, often in response to an issue that has captured public imagination or in response to pressure from professional groups.

Even when a plan provides good physical health coverage, incentives may exist to keep people with serious mental disabilities from enrolling (Frank, McGuire, Bae, & Rupp, 1997). In the public sector individuals are often subject to processes that are idiosyncratic, perhaps controlled by officials who know little about behavioral health and who are disproportionately influenced by legislative budgeting decisions. Although there have been efforts to use the Americans with Disabilities Act to address disparities between mental health and health care coverage, those efforts have

---

[6]The amount of freedom employers have in benefit design is perhaps best illustrated by the case of *McGann v. H & H Music Company* (1991). In this case, McGann sued his employer, alleging a violation of ERISA's anti-discrimination provisions. McGann, after discovering he had AIDS, notified his employer. At the time of notification, McGann was covered by a policy providing $1 million in lifetime medical benefits. The employer reduced the lifetime benefit for AIDS-related illnesses to $5,000. The Court of Appeals rejected McGann's claim, concluding that the case was resolved by the "well-settled principle that Congress did not intend that ERISA circumscribe employers' control over the content of benefit plans they offered to their employers" (p. 407). The Court also noted that "there is nothing to indicate that defendants ever promised that the $1,000,000 coverage limit was permanent" (p. 405).

not been particularly successful (*Parker v. Metropolitan Life Insurance Company*, 1997).

Difficulties in influencing benefit design are of particular consequence in behavioral health, where very important services such as housing, some types of social supports, and employment are not mandated services within the Medicaid program. No good legal theory exists at this point that can force their inclusion in a managed care plan; in this environment, political advocacy by consumers, families, and providers thus assumes a critical role.

In addition, many of the proposed remedies noted above rely on providing more information to enrollees as a core principle. Others expand procedural rights for providers who wish to become part of a payer's provider panel and for enrollees denied care. These proposals may or may not prove effective remedies. The fact that an individual has a right to appeal a claims denial, for example, is important because the limited amount of data available suggests that claimants prevail in a significant number of cases in which appeals are made (Hall, 1994). The right to an appeal, however, begs the questions of whether an appeal will actually be pursued in either commercial or publicly funded plans and whether people will have the resources or the knowledge necessary to pursue such appeals in numbers significant enough to have an impact in practice. In addition, although providing additional information to individuals is generally assumed to be a positive development, many of the remedies proposed to date do not address questions of competency for at least some individuals with serious mental illnesses who will be expected to enroll (or who will be enrolled by default) in a health care plan.

Finally, cases arising in this new environment may not be susceptible to class action litigation, a favored and often very effective technique of mental health advocacy in the 1970s and 1980s. Some types of cases, such as an inadequate process for reviewing claims, may lend themselves to such relief. In contrast, substantive denials of claims almost by definition must be pursued on a case-by-case basis,[7] a factor that may limit the effectiveness of litigation as a strategy for broad relief. This is not to argue that such claims are of no value; it should not, however, be anticipated that class action litigation will in the future be the hallmark of mental health litigation that it was in the past, at least in the noninstitutional settings in which most people with serious mental illness now reside.

As these new litigation and legislative theories are implemented, a number of issues are worth considering by policy makers, researchers, and advocates. These include the following:

---

[7]There may be exceptions. For example, if a particular type of benefit is routinely denied, and a court finds that the denial violates a nonambiguous contract provision, the relief granted may be functionally equivalent to class relief, because any individual with the disputed condition will benefit. However, as a general rule, the question of whether reimbursement should have been available in a particular case will depend on facts peculiar to that case.

1. Will the reliance on expanded provision of information that is at the heart of many of these theories make individuals better consumers of behavioral health services? What if information is provided about alternative treatments that are inaccessible to the individual? What is the practical effect on individuals of receiving information regarding treatments and services that they cannot afford? Many of the proposals pending before legislatures will provide more detailed information than previously has been available to enrollees of private and public plans regarding benefits and their limits. Among the many significant contributions of the MacArthur Foundation's Research Network on Mental Health and the Law is a vastly increased understanding of clinical and legal issues related to competence to consent to treatment (Grisso & Appelbaum, 1998). However, less is known about the impact of disclosing information that cannot be acted on by the recipient. Research exploring the therapeutic or antitherapeutic impact of these emerging legal principles would be useful (Wexler & Winick, 1996; see Wexler, chapter 14, and Winick, chapter 15, this volume).

2. Further evaluation of the impact of the vast changes in the financing and organization of behavioral health care services is needed. A number of evaluations of the impact of managed care on people with mental disabilities have been performed (Mechanic, 1995), and the federal government has funded more than a dozen evaluations of public sector behavioral health managed care plans being conducted in the late 1990s. At this point, however, there is insufficient outcome data to provide detailed guidance to policy makers on the real consequences of the changes that have occurred.

3. Advocacy, including litigation that focuses on government's oversight responsibilities, may become increasingly important. It is unlikely, outside of the context of forensic services, that government will again serve as the core provider of mental health services. Rather, government for the foreseeable future will continue to contract for services, often with private, for-profit vendors. Early evidence suggests that government has struggled with its oversight role, and litigation designed to ensure that government meets its continuing responsibilities in this sphere could become as important as litigation directed at government as a service provider was two decades ago.

4. Those who teach and study mental disability law must rec-

ognize that the changes in payment and the role of government noted throughout this chapter have changed the legal landscape as well. Advocacy in this new environment is difficult and often demands the development of theories not traditionally considered integral to mental disability law. Today, however, it is as important for those representing people with mental disabilities to understand how managed care contracts are negotiated and implemented as it is to understand the Supreme Court's ruling in *Youngberg v. Romeo* (1982). It is not enough to understand the nuances of civil commitment law; it is increasingly necessary to understand the nuances of Medicaid as well. This development has ramifications for the education and training of students and professionals interested in mental disability law issues in the future.

CONCLUSION

Dramatic changes have occurred in the health and behavioral health care industries in the past three decades. The recent shift to managed care and the movement to contracts as the primary vehicle by which services are organized, financed, and delivered have outstripped judicial and legislative responses to the problems that have emerged in this new environment. This result is in part due to ambivalence on the part of many government officials about the role of government in protecting the disenfranchised and in part due to legal barriers to certain types of litigation. In recent years, theories for addressing problems encountered by people enrolled in managed care plans have begun to emerge, theories grounded in the fiduciary duties of various parties within the health care industry. Over time, these theories, combined with recent legislative and regulatory responses, may resolve some of the more pressing issues noted in this chapter. Given, however, the limitations inherent in the theories advanced to date, it seems likely that litigation will be adjunctive to political advocacy. This development is a stark change from the initial days of disability law, when little political advocacy on behalf of people with serious mental illness took place, and constitutional litigation was the primary tool to redress the grievous injuries that many people with serious disabilities suffered.

REFERENCES

American Academy of Pediatrics. (1997). *Medicaid managed care statistics* [Statistics posted on the World Wide Web]. Elk Grove Village, IL: Author. Retrieved

December 5, 2000 from the World Wide Web: http://www.aap.org/advocacy/stenroll.htm#numperc

American Managed Behavioral Healthcare Association. (1999). *Code of Conduct.* Washington, DC: Author. Retrieved December 19, 2000 from the World Wide Web: http://www.ambha.org/codeofconduct/index.htm

Americans With Disabilities Act. (1990). 42 USC § 12101 et seq.

Anthony, W. A., & Liberman, R. P. (1986). The practice of psychiatric rehabilitation: Historical, conceptual, and research base. *Schizophrenia Bulletin, 12,* 542–559.

Appelbaum, P. S. (1994). *Almost a revolution: Mental health law and the limits of change.* New York: Oxford University Press.

Astrachan, B. (1993). Administration and policy in mental health: Twenty years after. *Administration and Policy in Mental Health, 21,* 75–77.

Balanced Budget Act of 1997, 42 USC § 1395a.

Bauman v. U.S. Healthcare, Inc., 1 F. Supp.2d 420 (D. N.J. 1998).

Blum, J. D. (1989). An analysis of legal liability in health care utilization review and case management. *Houston Law Review, 26,* 191–243.

Bracken, B., & Anderson, S. (1990). Psychiatric care: An evolving industry. *HMO/PPO Trends, 3,* 2.

Buck, J. A., & Umland, B. (1997). Covering mental health and substance abuse services. *Health Affairs, 16,* 120–126.

Chamberlin, J. (1994). A psychiatric survivor speaks out. *Feminism and Psychology, 4,* 284–287.

Civil Rights for Institutionalized Persons Act. (1980). 42 USC § 1997.

Corporate Health Insurers, Inc. v. Texas Department of Insurance, 12 F. Supp.2d 597 (S.D. Tex. 1998).

Coughlin, K. (Ed.). (1998). *1998 Medicaid managed behavioral care sourcebook.* New York: Faulkner and Gray.

Crocco v. Xerox, 956 F. Supp. 129 (D. Conn. 1997).

Deegan, P. (1990). Spirit breaking: When the helping professions hurt. *Humanistic Psychologist, 18,* 301–313.

Department of Mental Health Law and Policy. (1998). *The Florida mental health act (the Baker act), annual report.* Tampa, FL: Louis de la Parte Florida Mental Health Institute, University of South Florida.

Dukes v. U.S. Healthcare, Inc., 57 F.3d 350 (3rd Cir. 1995).

Ellis, R. P. (1991). Reimbursement systems and the behavior of mental health providers. *International Journal of Law and Psychiatry, 14,* 347–362.

Employee Retirement Income Security Act. (1974). 29 USC § 1001 et seq.

Findlay, S. (1999). Managed behavioral health care in 1999: An industry at a crossroads. *Health Affairs, 18,* 116–124.

Frank, R. G., & McGuire, T. G. (1996). Introduction to the economics of mental health payment systems. In B. L. Levin & J. Petrila (Eds.), *Mental health* services: A public health perspective (pp. 23–37). New York: Oxford University Press.

Frank, R. G., McGuire, T. G., Bae, J. P., & Rupp, A. (1997). Solutions for adverse selection in behavioral health care. *Health Care Financing Review, 18,* 109–122.

Furrow, B. R., Greaney, T. L., Johnson, S. H., Jost, T. S., & Schwartz, R. L. (1997). *Health law: Cases, materials and problems* (3rd ed.). Minneapolis: West.

General Accounting Office. (1997). *Medicaid managed care: Challenge of holding plans accountable requires greater state effort. Report to ranking minority member, Committee on Commerce, House of Representatives* (Report No. GAO/HEHS-97-86). Washington, DC: General Accounting Office.

Glover, R., & Petrila, J. (1994). Perspectives: Can state mental health agencies survive health care reform? *Hospital and Community Psychiatry, 45,* 911–913.

Greene, J., & Lutz, S. (1995, May 22). A down year at not-for-profits; for-profits soar. *Modern Healthcare,* p. 43.

Grijalva v. Shalala, 152 F.3d 1115 (9th Cir. 1998).

Grisso, T., & Appelbaum, P. S. (1998). *Assessing competence to consent to treatment: A guide for physicians and other health professionals.* New York: Oxford University Press.

Hall, M. A. (1994). Managed competition and integrated health care delivery systems. *Wake Forest Law Review, 29,* 1–13.

Health panel declines to endorse laws for patients' bill of rights. (1998, March 13). *New York Times,* p. 1.

Horvath, J., & Snow, K. (1997). Emerging challenges in the state regulation of managed care: Report on a survey of state agency regulation of prepaid managed care entities [Report posted on the World Wide Web]. Princeton, NJ: Center for Health Care Strategies, Inc. Retrieved December 19, 2000 from the World Wide Web: http://www.chcs.org/resource_ctr/mmcp/misclink/horvath.htm

Hughes v. Blue Cross of Northern California, 215 Cal. App.3d 832 (1989).

Huskamp, H. A. (1996). *State requirements for managed behavioral health care carve-outs and what they mean for people with severe mental illness.* Washington, DC: National Alliance for the Mentally Ill.

Iglehart, J. K. (1996). Health policy report: Managed care and mental health. *New England Journal of Medicine, 334,* 131–135.

Kaiser Commission. (1993). *The Kaiser Commission on the future of Medicaid, the Medicaid cost explosion: Causes and consequences.* Washington, DC: Author.

Kettner, P. M., & Martin, L. I. (1993). Purchase of service contracting in the 1990's: Have expectations been met? *Journal of Sociology and Social Welfare, 20,* 89–103.

Kiesler, C. A., & Sibulkin, A. E. (1987). *Mental hospitalization: Myths and facts about a national crisis.* Newbury Park, CA: Sage.

Kleinke, J. D. (1998). Deconstructing the Columbia/HCA investigation. *Health Affairs, 17*, 7–28.

LaFond, J. Q., & Durham, M. L. (1992). *Back to the asylum: The future of mental health law and policy in the United States*. New York: Oxford University Press.

Liberman, R. P. (Ed.). (1988). *Psychiatric rehabilitation of chronic mental patients*. Washington, DC: American Psychiatric Press.

McDonald-Wilson, K., & Mancuso, L. (1989). Supported employment for people with psychiatric disability. *Journal of Applied Rehabilitation Counseling, 20*, 50–57.

McGann v. H & H Music Company, 946 F.2d 401 (5th Cir. 1991), cert. den. 113 S. Ct. 482 (1992).

Mechanic, D. (1995). Management of mental health and substance abuse services: State of the art and early results. *Milbank Quarterly, 73*, 316.

Medco Behavioral Care Corporation v. State Department of Human Services, 553 N.W.2d 556, Iowa S. Ct. (1996).

Mirin, S., & Sederer, L. (1994). Mental health care: Current realities, future directions. *Psychiatric Quarterly, 65*, 161–175.

Muse v. Charter Hospital, 117 N.C. App. 468, 452 S.E.2d 589 (1996).

National Association of Psychiatric Health Systems. (1997). NAPHS 1997 annual survey reports trends. Washington, DC: Author.

National Association of State Mental Health Program Directors Research Institute. (1997). *Preliminary 1996 SMHA profiles information*. Alexandria, VA: Author.

National Health Law Program, Inc. & Cecil G. Sheps Center for Health Services Research. (1996). *Making the consumers' voice heard in Medicaid managed care: Increasing participation, protection, and satisfaction, report on required and voluntary mechanisms*. Los Angeles: National Health Law Program, Inc.

National Health Lawyers Association & American Association of Hospital Attorneys. (1998). *Annual report on state health issues: A comprehensive fifty-state survey of current healthcare legislation*. Washington, DC: Authors.

National Health Planning and Resources Development Act. (1974). Pub. L. No. 93-641 42 USC § 300K-1 et seq. (repealed).

New York State Conference of Blue Cross and Blue Shield Plans v. Travelers Insurance, 513 U.S. 1108 (1995).

Olmstead v. L.C., 119 S. Ct. 2176 (1999).

Pacificare of Oklahoma v. Burrage, 59 F.3d 151 (10th Cir. 1995).

Panel of experts urges broadening of patient rights. (1997, October 23). *New York Times*, p. 1.

Parker v. Metropolitan Life Insurance Company, 121 F.3d 1006 (6th Cir. 1997); cert. den. 118 S. Ct. 871 (1998).

Pegram v. Herdrich, 2000 U.S. LEXIS 3964 (2000).

Petrila, J. (1996). Ethics, money, and the problem of coercion in managed behavioral health care. *St. Louis University Law Journal, 40*, 359–405.

Reidy, D. E. (1993). Stigma is social death. In *Mental health consumers/survivors talk about stigma in their lives*. Unpublished manuscript, Education for Community Initiative (on file with author).

Reinhardt, U. E. (1998). Columbia/HCA: Villain or victim? *Health Affairs, 17*, 30–36.

Rosenbaum, S., Shin, P., Smith, B. M., Wehr, E., Borzi, P. C., Zakheim, M. H., Shaw, K., & Silver, K. (1997). *Negotiating the new health system: A nationwide study of Medicaid care contracts*. Washington, DC: George Washington Center for Health Policy Research.

Schwartz, I. M. (1989). Hospitalization of adolescents for psychiatric and substance abuse treatment. *Journal of Adolescent Health Care, 10*, 473–478.

Seward, P. J. (1999). Restoring the ethical balance in health care. *Health Affairs, 16*, 195–197.

Shea v. Esensten, 107 F.3d 625 (8th Cir. 1997).

Social Security Act Amendments of 1972, 42 USC § 1382e.

Stauffer, M., & Levy, D. R. (2000). *2000 state by state guide to managed care law*. New York: Panel Publishers.

Stein, L. K., & Test, M. A. (Eds.). (1978). *Alternatives to mental hospital treatment*. New York: Plenum Press.

Surles, R., & McGurrin, M. (1987). Increased use of psychiatric emergency services by young chronic mentally ill patients. *Hospital and Community Psychiatry, 38*, 401–405.

Tanzman, E. (1993). An overview of surveys of mental health consumers' preferences for housing and support services. *Hospital and Community Psychiatry, 44*, 450–455.

Tarasoff v. Regents of the University of California, 17 Cal.3d 425, 551 P.2d 334 (1976).

Texas Senate Bill 386, Texas Civil Practice & Rem. Code Annotated 88.002 (a) et seq. (West 1998).

United States v. Pennsylvania, 902 F. Supp. 565 (W.D. Pa. 1995).

Value Behavioral Health Care, Inc. v. Ohio Department of Mental Health, 966 F. Supp. 557 (S.D. Ohio 1997).

Varol v. Blue Cross, 708 F. Supp. 826 (E.D. Mich. 1989).

Vladeck, B. C. (1998). Market realities meet balanced government: Another look at Columbia/HCA. *Health Affairs, 17*, 37–39.

Weiss v. CIGNA, 972 F. Supp. 748 (S.D. N.Y. 1997).

Weithorn, L. A. (1988). Note, mental hospitalization of troublesome youth: An analysis of skyrocketing admission rates. *Stanford Law Review, 40*, 773–838.

Wexler, D. B., & Winick, B. J. (1996). *Law in a therapeutic key: Developments in therapeutic jurisprudence*. Durham, NC: Carolina Academic Press.

Wickline v. State of California, 192 Cal. App.3d 1630 (1986).

Wilson v. Blue Cross, 222 Cal. App.3d 660 (1990).

Youngberg v. Romeo, 457 U.S. 307 (1982).

5

FINANCING PUBLIC MENTAL HEALTH SERVICES: BEYOND MANAGED CARE

JOSEPH J. BEVILACQUA

Public mental health is caught up in the market forces that are transforming the U.S. health care system and challenging the role of government in the health and human services system. The market seems to have displaced society's ethical commitment to disadvantaged people as the foundation for public mental health services. This chapter highlights the deficiencies in market-driven mental health services, especially for the chronically mentally ill population. It also takes the view that this trend, epitomized by privatization and managed care, will not last. Eventually, our system will return to the legal and ethical principles that have emerged over the past quarter century.

The contemporary version of "newspeak"—George Orwell's term from his famous novel *1984*—reflects the major changes under way in the health and human services systems. This version of "newspeak" includes terms such as stop/loss ratio, market share, product line, gatekeeper, downsizing, carve in, carve out, waiver, benefits package, provider, payer, capitation, full or partial risk, and shared risk. One obvious pattern, of course, is the corporate or entrepreneurial nature of the words; of greater interest, however, is the quality of the language that emerges. The elements of competition and chance are curious attributes for a system that purports to provide care for ill and disabled people. The illness becomes the focus of marketable commodities such as drugs and various treatment protocols. Benefits are market driven, with emphasis on costs and efficiency rather than on the patient's needs. Quality of care is in constant tension with cost.

The rapid transformation currently under way has taken on aspects of the fashion culture. The nature of fashion is change. It is not permanent but looks to difference, style, and whim. It is unreliable and often unpredictable. In fact, when it becomes predictable and too often copied, it becomes unfashionable. The lists that we see each year of what is "in" and what is "out" are quite revealing. Is managed care a transient fashion? Are the changes we are going through simply reflective of a particular phase or era? Speed and immediacy are in vogue today. Illnesses that are chronic and long term, such as many mental disorders, do not lend themselves easily to the discipline of a free market.

As public mental health becomes encompassed by the managed care movement, and as the rush to privatize takes hold, certain basic and fundamental aspects of care are being ignored. Admittedly, some important benefits can and will accrue. The past system was hardly ideal or perfect. My concern is that in our preoccupation with the current fashion, we leave unattended important and transcendent substantive issues that have received far too little attention in journals, studies, and general public dialogue. Too often, the discussion and debates on managed care create a false polarization between the old "fee-for-service" public Medicaid system and the current market-driven system. This simplistic dichotomy misses the complexity of the current transformation.

Four issues are critical and generic to a sound mental health system, be it public or private, and transcend whatever the fashion of the moment might be. These are regulation, consumer advocacy, organization of services, and national standards. Of the four, only consumer advocacy has received considerable attention, but its impact on managed care planning and implementation has been minimal. Regulation, organization and access to services, and national standards often get grouped under the quality assurance umbrella, but their presence is weak and anemic. In the discussion that follows, the lack of a coherent and related set of national and state policies dealing with regulation, advocacy, organization of and access to services, and standards suggests an environment of health care that will continue to be fragmented and dominated by market forces. The use of managed care in this environment without attending to these issues creates an unbalanced system of health care that further polarizes the issues of mental illness treatment from the main stream of health care.

REGULATION

The first unattended substantive issue concerns the regulatory function of government at both the federal and state levels. Devolution of authority to the states has left the role and authority of regulatory bodies ambiguous. Regulation, unfortunately, has been politicized.

In my work at the Bazelon Center for Mental Health Law, we have discussed with the Health Care Financing Administration (HCFA) concerns we have had about certain managed care practices in several states. In these discussions, the upper-level administrators have been reluctant to take on issues that might incur the wrath of legislators or officials from the state in question. In one meeting with the HCFA director, we were reminded of the limited federal authority to oversee state activity other than in highly publicized and egregious instances, such as those in Tennessee.

In Tennessee, the state's managed care activities, called the Partners program, have been fraught with confusion and instability because of a short start-up time, inadequate planning, and excess ambition. The managed care plan originally was a comprehensive plan that included both general and behavioral health, but it was later changed to carve out mental health. It is fair to say that the Tennessee plan was flawed from the very beginning. Even in Tennessee, however, the chaos had to reach a critical mass of media exposure before federal agents conducted an audit in February 1997. Their findings included the following:

1. Access to mental health and substance abuse services has been impaired.
2. Quality of care issues need to be addressed.
3. The program may be underfunded.
4. Data to assess the program are not available.
5. Contract issues are significant.
6. The state's monitoring efforts must be improved.

The findings concluded with the following assessment: "The program change to a carve-in model will not be approved by HCFA until the State demonstrates that it can effectively administer the current mental health program" (Vladeck, 1997, p. 7).

The corrective actions required included the following:

1. For the SMI/SED [seriously mentally ill/seriously emotionally disturbed] populations, the funding for the project must be restored to the level prior to the Partners program implementation
2. Establish and immediately implement procedures to assure and monitor that beneficiaries have access to care. The procedures must include, at a minimum, medical record reviews

until the state can demonstrate that services are being provided and quality of care is maintained. The methodology
must be approved by HCFA in advance.

3. The state must assure that BHOs [behavioral health organi-
zations] are honoring their contracts, providing appropriate
care, and paying health care providers timely, consistent with
federal regulations for FFS [fee-for-service] payments . . . in
addition to reports on all services provided by each BHO and
CMHC [community mental health center], including the
number of SMI/SED clients seen and number and type of
services provided.

4. The state must modify its contracts with the BHO to forbid
the passing of all risk for the cost of patient care to providers.

5. The state must assure that all support systems are in place
for the project, including data, claims processing and payment.

6. The state must submit a plan showing actions that will be
taken to reduce the current high level of inpatient utilization
(Vladeck, 1997, p. 6).

What is remarkable is just how basic these issues are. The audit report
referred to a state legislative hearing where the acting commissioner of the
Tennessee Department of Mental Health and Mental Retardation was reported to have indicated that the state has "found no effective way to
make sure the BHOs honor their contracts, provide appropriate care, and
pay health care providers" (Vladeck, 1997, p. 4). In December of 1998, a
process that had included active participation of stakeholders from Tennessee, representatives from the governor's office, and the HCFA culminated in the resolution of a number of the audit concerns. No sanctions
were imposed.

A second example of the lack of responsive and effective regulatory
action concerns the unfortunate and egregious death of a patient at Virginia's Central State Hospital in 1996. It was only after more than a year
of agitation by the director of the state National Alliance for the Mentally
Ill (NAMI), and a crescendo of negative press stories, that the state's protection and advocacy organization, the Department of Justice, the Substance Abuse Mental Health Administration, the Federal Administration
of Developmental Disabilities, and the Joint Commission on the Accred-
itation of Health Care Organizations investigated the death and other suspicious situations. One result was the appointment of a Human Rights
Study Group by the State Mental Health, Mental Retardation and Substance Abuse Services Board. The study group's report (Human Rights
Study Group, 1997) was considered by many to be weak and inconsequen-
tial.

Unfortunately, these two examples are not unusual. What is of concern in our current climate of managed care is the lack of appropriate mechanisms to address serious violations of human rights and basic protocols of service for people with serious mental illness. Why should the organizational format of services or payment structures compromise access to needed care or violate an individual's basic civil rights? Too little thought has been given to the importance of regulation as managed care and government realignment take hold. Indeed, some people seem to assume that market forces and the competitive environment will take care of these kinds of problems. Little evidence exists that this is in fact the case. Although recommendations proposed by the president's Advisory Commission on Consumer Protection and Quality in the Health Care Industry (1997) would address some of these problems, congressional action has not been forthcoming.

Bill Goldman, psychiatrist, former commissioner of mental health in Massachusetts, and active participant in managed behavioral health care for the past 15 years, has written that the traditional fee-for-service system and the current privatization approach are both myths. He argued,

> The contemporary struggle over health reform in the United States pits two powerful myths against one another. The first established and entrenched myth reifies the illusion that the existing health care non-system allows broad freedom of choice and access to uniformly available, compassionate, competent health providers. The second reform myth posits a new illusion. It suggests that competing organized care systems, under economic pressures for cost containment, will assure broad freedom of choice and access to uniformly available, compassionate, competent health providers (Goldman, 1994, p. 51).

Goldman contended that the shared goals of access and choice can be achieved by using a "public or quasi-public structure" such as a public utility model. He equated the significance of health care provision for the economic well-being of society at large with that of water, power, and communications. Goldman pointed out that although it took 50 years, the U.S. public now assumes that when a faucet is opened, the water will flow clear and drinkable; that when a switch is flipped, electricity will power appliances consistently and safely; and that when a phone is picked up, worldwide communication is available. Goldman suggested that we should view health care from the same perspective.

Goldman concluded that only by developing "organized systems of care—monitored and overseen jointly by the public and professionals—can quality, cost-effectiveness and uniform access be reasonably assured, and perhaps even available, compassionate, and competent health providers be chosen" (p. 51). Another difficulty in strengthening regulation of the mental health system, however, is that the track record of public participation in the transformation of the health and welfare system is discouraging. In fact, the lack of strong consumerism and advocacy is an issue being overlooked in the current environment.

CONSUMER ADVOCACY

In two surveys of Medicaid-managed behavioral health care across the states, the Bazelon Center for Mental Health Law (1997b, 1998) found very little consumer representation at the planning table as states negotiated contracts with managed care companies. After the contracts were approved, consumers were often invited to serve on advisory committees with little influence or power. A number of private companies have made overtures to consumer organizations or individual consumers, but little evidence suggests that consumers had any meaningful input in the planning or in the operation of the organization. Co-optation is always a real fear.

Advocacy organizations such as NAMI and the National Mental Health Association (NMHA) have been active in training consumers across the country and in preparing reports critical of managed care. The effectiveness of these efforts, however, is difficult to determine. Both organizations make it clear that they do not oppose managed care; rather, they see it as neutral but criticize some of its practices.

Advocacy work with Congress has produced more visible success. The parity legislation provided by the Kassenbaum-Kennedy Health Care Reform Bill (1996) was aided by the work of national advocacy groups such as NAMI and NMHA. Political figures who have had personal experiences with mental illness have become identified with the national organizations, and several leaders have become active participants in national campaigns to counteract the stigma of mental illness.

The presence of families, consumers, and advocates is important, and their activities over the past 10 to 15 years have helped to achieve reforms in many states. For this kind of activism to sustain itself is very difficult. Money is always a serious problem. A disturbing trend in this regard is the financial support that a number of drug companies have provided to several of the national advocacy organizations. Genuine conflicts of interest must be closely monitored. Similar concerns, of course, have always plagued psychiatric professional association meetings.

Lack of solid consumer and advocacy presence and the diminishing role of government regulation leave the system without any credible oversight. How do we build into our systems of care a permanent, objective, and responsive oversight capacity? This issue has generally been ignored by the market. Few states, if any, have viable ombudsman systems. The *Consumers Bill of Rights and Responsibilities: Report to the President of the United States* (Advisory Commission on Consumer Protection and Quality in the Health Care Industry, 1997) neither recommended such an office nor permitted consumers to seek damages in court. The protection and advocacy system is uneven and must fear congressional write-off if too much notoriety develops. Long-term litigation is viewed as expensive and difficult to support given the reduced frequency of settlement decrees (*Wyatt v. Stickney*, 1971, 1972). Furthermore, advocacy work can be made more difficult as privatization challenges the accessibility of records and patient contact in private hospitals, unlike public hospitals, where access to records and client contact is usually permitted by statute.

Much work remains to be done. The president's Advisory Commission offers steps in the right direction, but its report is not specific enough to address the unique issues presented by serious mental illness. A critical mass of discontent has not yet emerged to challenge the transformation.

ORGANIZATION OF SERVICES

One of the most elusive issues in providing care for people with serious mental illness has been the need for a broad base of supportive services. Too often these services are either not available or receive a low priority in planning and budgeting. Housing, transportation, psychosocial rehabilitation, and other nonmedical services are rarely included in contracts with managed care companies. The phrase "medical necessity" is often used to constrain the services that will be made available in the contract (Bazelon Center for Mental Health Law, 1997a).

Perhaps these "nonmedical" services should be removed from a behavioral managed health care plan. It has often been suggested that the state should arrange for other agencies to assume this responsibility. We know, however, that integrating services and maintaining continuity of care has been successful in keeping people with serious mental illness out of the hospital. The Program in Assertive Community Treatment (PACT) has been consistently successful in using integrated social support mechanisms (Stein & Santos, 1998). There are no states, it seems, that include such mechanisms in their managed care contract, though NAMI has undertaken a major initiative to attempt to market PACT to managed care organizations. When this issue is discussed with private companies, they argue that the states are not willing to include this kind of service in the benefits package. This may be telling, because the long-term care issues of mental illness have yet to be fully and satisfactorily addressed.

Active discussions are under way in a number of states concerning the organization and governance of the state mental health authority. Recommended structures include the state's financing agency or a larger health and human services umbrella coupled with a diminished role for the mental health agency. The important question is who will assume the responsibility for managing and overseeing the system of care for people with serious mental disabilities. Will we define this system of care in its true magnitude, or simply as a question of managing finances and resources?

Reorganization could also erase a visible mental health presence within the bureaucracy. For governance of mental health services to be buried within the bowels of the bureaucracy—out of sight and out of mind —further stigmatizes mental illness (see Burt, chapter 1, this volume). A visible sense of identity within the organization provides a vehicle for representing mental health interests in the corridors of government and for preserving psychosocial rehabilitation and other support services.

State mental health agencies deserve considerable credit for broadening the base of services for people with serious mental illness (sometimes with pressure from the courts) and moving to a community-based system of care. Reorganizational changes that would minimize the influence of the mental health authority would seriously compromise the long-term needs of individuals with serious and persistent mental illness.

Changes in health care governance are clearly being planned and in some states have already occurred; too often, however, discussions of these changes have failed to recognize the important role that the mental health authority has played and should continue to play. New configurations will be developed, but the visible presence of a mental health interest at the state level is an important issue and requires full deliberation. To transfer this function to an umbrella agency or a finance office or to eliminate the office altogether would be a serious mistake.

Increasingly, planners and policy-makers praise the logical and common-sense aspects of integrating all health care, including mental health, into one health care system. Nonetheless, the recently enacted federal parity legislation did not grant full parity to mental illness coverage. Until such parity exists, it is premature to think of integration. Furthermore, given the stigma and marginality that continue to accompany mental illness, the need for a visible organizational presence continues to be important. Once mental illness achieves true and full parity with all health care, then integration can be fairly implemented.

NATIONAL STANDARDS

Quality of care and outcome measures only superficially address behavioral health. The Center for Mental Health Services recently developed, with consumer participation, a report card system to assess how states are doing in addressing the needs of people with serious mental illness (Mental Health Statistics Improvement Program Task Force on a Consumer Oriented Mental Health Report Card, 1996). In the absence of national standards reflecting a broad consensus of support, efforts to promote quality and outcome measurement too often address the self-interests of the various professional guilds and provider organizations.

In attempting to fill this breach, the Bazelon Center has organized several meetings with representatives from both the public and the private sectors, including managed care companies, Medicaid agencies, state mental health authorities, consumers, and family members. Future work will include broadening the base of participants beyond mental health interests to include political and corporate representatives who have an interest in general health care. The following list of areas needing standards reflects a general consensus by those attending the meetings:

- access
- member rights
- member responsibilities
- choice
- disenrollment and lock-in
- autoenrollment procedures
- consumer education and information
- benefits
- gag rules
- appropriate care
- quality measurement
- quality improvement
- evaluations
- financial issues
- public reporting
- audits
- single coordinated systems of care
- grievances and appeals
- incentives.

In the current environment, the development and implementation of such comprehensive standards smacks too much of big government. And yet, as Cassidy (1997) suggested,

> The last decade has witnessed an unprecedented wave of mergers in sectors as diverse as entertainment, medicine, defense, and financial services. At the same time, budget cuts and conservative court rulings have undermined the effectiveness of government regulatory agencies, such as the Federal Trade Commission. Unless these trends are reversed, the inevitable result will be more mergers, higher prices, and fewer choices for consumers. (para. 21)

Some balance between the forces of the market and the role of government seems a sensible solution, but such a balance has not yet been struck. Perhaps the health care system is one area of human endeavor where common sense will ultimately prevail. Whether the approach will be a public utility model, as Goldman suggested, or some other arrangement that engages both the public and private forces remains to be seen.

From the failed efforts of Clinton's health care reform to the emergence of managed care in the public sector, we have seen, in a short time, proposals at both ends of the continuum: heavy government control at one end and the emergence of privatization and market forces at the other. A report issued by the National Coalition on Health Care (1997) found that the corrective cost adjustments that managed care was to have provided have not yet been realized. *Washington Post* columnist David Broder (1997), commenting on this report, observed that:

> earlier this decade, when millions of Americans were being shifted by their employers from traditional fee-for-service medical insurance into managed care, the competition for market share among those managed care companies held down premiums—to the point that operating margins almost disappeared. Facing big losses, the companies are now raising their rates, while an aging population drives up health care costs.

Broder pointed out that

> by forcing insurers to take on high-risk customers, the government has raised the rates for everyone. The $115 billion Medicare "fix," which cuts reimbursements to hospitals, doctors, and other providers, saves the government money but shifts costs to private policy purchasers.

It is not difficult to anticipate what will happen to the contracts dealing with services for clients with serious mental illness when these shifts move from health to behavioral health, especially if the public infrastructure is weak and public mental health services budgets are reduced.

CONCLUSION

On each of our four major themes, regulation, advocacy, organization of and access to services, and standards, we have seen the failure of managed care to integrate these components of quality into their system of care. Indeed, the containment of costs, which has been the primary rationale for supporting managed care, is slipping badly and we are witnessing the departure of managed care from many public programs. The culture of fashion, predictably, is unpredictable and unreliable. Managed care as an expression of fashion is no exception.

The public mental health system requires a stable and firm foundation. The market is unable, by itself, to produce a stable system of care. The basics of sensible regulatory oversight, a strong and vocal consumer constituency, a comprehensive array of accessible supportive services, and specific national standards can be the foundation on which we build a strong and responsive service system for citizens with mental illness.

REFERENCES

Advisory Commission on Consumer Protection and Quality in the Health Care Industry. (1997, November). *Consumer bill of rights and responsibilities: Report to the president of the United States.* Washington, DC: Department of Health and Human Services.

Bazelon Center for Mental Health Law. (1997a, March). *Defining "medically necessary" services to protect plan members: A policy analysis series.* Washington, DC: Author.

Bazelon Center for Mental Health Law. (1997b). *Managed care survey 1996.* Washington, DC: Author.

Bazelon Center for Mental Health Law. (1998). *Managed care survey 1997.* Washington, DC: Author.

Broder, D. S. (1997, October 28). Health care: The problems persist. *Washington Post.*

Goldman, W. (1994). Point of view: Myths and potentials. *Managed Care Quarterly, 2,* 51–52.

Human Rights Study Group. (1997, November). *Report of the Human Rights Study Group on the human rights system in Virginia for people with mental disabilities.* Richmond, VA: Department of Mental Health, Mental Retardation Substance Abuse Services.

Kassenbaum-Kennedy Health Care Reform Bill (Domenici–Wellstone Amendment). (1996). Pub. L. 104–191.

Mental Health Statistics Improvement Program Task Force on a Consumer Oriented Mental Health Report Card. (1996, April). *The MHSIP consumer oriented mental health report card.* Rockville, MD: Center for Mental Health Services, SAMHSA.

National Coalition on Health Care. (1997, April). *Changes in the growth in health care spending: Implications for consumers.* Washington, DC: Author.

Orwell, G. (1949). *1984.* New York: Harcourt, Brace, Jovanovich.

Stein, L. I., & Santos, A. B. (1998). *Assertive community treatment of persons with severe mental illness.* New York: W.W. Norton.

Vladeck, B. C. (1997). Letter from Bruce C. Vladeck, administrator of the Health Care Financing Administration, Department of Health and Human Services, to Nancy Menke, commissioner of the Tennessee Department of Health, March 1997.

Wyatt v. Stickney, 325 F. Supp. 781 (M.D. Ala. 1971), 344 F. Supp. 1341 (M.D. Ala. 1971), 344 F. Supp. 373 (M.D. Ala. 1972), 344 F. Supp. 387 (M.D. Ala. 1972), aff'd in part sub nom Wyatt v. Aderholt, 503 F.2d 1305 (5th Cir. 1974).

6

LAW AND PSYCHIATRY IN RUSSIA: LOOKING BACKWARD AND FORWARD

SVETLANA V. POLUBINSKAYA

For more than two decades, beginning in the 1970s, the former Soviet Union was accused of using psychiatry for nonmedical purposes, such as suppressing political disagreement with Soviet ideology and the regime by putting dissidents in psychiatric hospitals (Bloch & Reddaway, 1977; Reich, 1980). In 1977 the World Psychiatric Association (WPA) condemned the repressive use of psychiatry in the USSR, and the Soviet All-Union Society of Psychiatrists and Neuropathologists resigned from the association in 1983 in the face of almost certain expulsion.

Over the next decade, the winds of reform began to blow, and Soviet mental health law was fundamentally transformed. These legal reforms were strongly shaped by the ideas and principles developing in the United

On behalf of Professor Stanislav Borodin and myself, I thank all our colleagues who supported and helped us over the long period during which the 1992 Russian Federation law was drafted. The list of people who gave us information, books, foreign laws, and time is very long. But I am especially grateful to three professionals who served as foreign advisors in all stages of the drafting process: Professor Loren Roth, Professor Richard Bonnie, and Dr. Saleem Shah, who, although not with us today, will be remembered always. Without their indispensable assistance, the path leading to the adoption of the 1992 Russian law would have been much longer.

States since the early 1970s, and they reflected the rapidly developing norms of international human rights. In an important respect, the recent histories of mental health law in the United States and in Russia and the other former Soviet republics have been intertwined: The experience of Soviet psychiatric abuse has helped to shape Western ideas about the risks of coercive psychiatry, and legislative reforms in the USSR and its successor states have been directly influenced by reforms previously embraced in the United States. This chapter describes the evolution of mental health law in Russia and its links to reformers in the United States.

PSYCHIATRY AND REPRESSION IN THE USSR

In the past, the freedom and rights of Soviet citizens were violated by psychiatric interventions in their lives. Specific instances of the abusive use of psychiatry in the Soviet Union were described in the report of a U.S. State Department delegation that visited the USSR from February 26 to March 12, 1989 ("U.S. Delegation to Assess Recent Changes in Soviet Psychiatry," 1989). For example, one of the patients the delegation interviewed had been involuntarily hospitalized with a diagnosis of schizophrenia following his involvement in human rights political activity, including an antinuclear power plant campaign and support of Ukrainian schools. The U.S. team did not find any evidence of mental disorder in this patient, who had been hospitalized without any legal procedure or criminal charge. This summary hospitalization was accomplished because his name had been placed in the so-called psychiatric register (for outpatient psychiatric observation) following discharge from a previous hospitalization for similar conduct (p. 18). In another case, a political activist and advocate for a two-party system in the USSR was hospitalized with a diagnosis of "manic behavior," even though he showed no evidence of dangerousness, a necessary requirement for such hospitalization under the applicable administrative regulations issued by the USSR Ministry of Health (U.S. Delegation, 1989, p. 33).

Very similar behavior was used in political and nonpolitical cases as clinical evidence of a mental disorder: for example, writing anti-Soviet books, being outspoken in opposition to the authorities, defending the human rights of oppressed groups in the population, and signing petitions to the authorities. Simple nonconforming behavior, even writing a letter to Gorbachev, constituted a symptom of mental disorder (a "delusion of reformism"), supporting a diagnosis of "sluggish schizophrenia" for dissidents and nonpolitical psychiatric patients alike ("U.S. Delegation," 1989, pp. 25–26). Although some cases of dissidents were well publicized in the West, they were far fewer in number than the nonpolitical victims of Soviet psychiatry.

In cases of political abuse, the psychiatrists did not act alone. Most dissidents were charged with various criminal acts and were criminally committed by courts under provisions of criminal and criminal procedure laws (Bonnie, 1990). By contrast, individuals in nonpolitical cases were typically committed by psychiatrists alone, acting without judicial oversight and governed only by various administrative regulations developed primarily by the USSR Ministry of Health. These regulations did not conform with, and in fact substantially limited, the rights ensured to Soviet citizens under the USSR Constitution, which included the same political and civil rights as the constitutions of Western democratic countries, with the addition of social and economic rights such as a right to work, a right to education, and a right to participate in trade unions or other nongovernmental associations. Moreover, because the administrative regulations were written both broadly and vaguely, varying interpretations of the language led to arbitrary implementation. In addition, these regulations were not sufficiently disseminated, so that even lawyers did not know much about them, to say nothing of mental patients and their families. For all these reasons, it is no surprise that deficiencies in the legal regulation of psychiatric care resulted in abuses in the provision of such care and pervasive violations of human rights.

REFORM AND THE DEVELOPMENT OF SOVIET MENTAL HEALTH LEGISLATION

After resigning from the World Psychiatric Association in 1983, the All-Union Society was permitted to rejoin the international professional community in 1989, when Gorbachev's reforms in the Soviet Union were taking place and after the U.S. Delegation visited the USSR. Although it found continuing evidence of abusive practices in Soviet psychiatry, the delegation also noted in its final report some positive changes. Among the changes noted was the adoption in January 1988 of the USSR Statute on Conditions and Procedures for the Provision of Psychiatric Care, which became the first Soviet legislation on mental health (*Vedomosty Verkhovnogo Soveta SSSR*, 1988).

The 1988 statute, which helped correct some of the deficiencies in the regulation of psychiatric care, resulted from years of effort. At the end of the 1970s, Dr. Serebryakova, the chief psychiatrist of the USSR Ministry of Health at that time, had asked my colleagues in the Department of Criminal Law of the Institute of State and Law of the USSR Academy of Sciences to draft a legal act concerning emergency psychiatric hospitalization. It was to be designed as a "decree" to be adopted by the Presidium of the USSR Supreme Soviet.[1] Professor Alexander M. Yakovlev, the head of the Department, and Dr. Georgy Zlobin agreed to undertake this task, and I served as their assistant. A short draft was prepared, but it was never adopted.

More than 10 years later, in 1987, Professor Stanislav Borodin and I published a proposed USSR Law on the Protection of Rights and Legitimate Interests of Persons Suffering from Mental Disorders (Borodin & Polubinskaya, 1991). No one had asked us to do so. Professor Borodin and I had been involved in the drafting of the Model Criminal Code (General Part) and a commentary to it. Among other things, we were responsible for drafting what was called "compulsory measures of a medical nature," a special chapter in the Russian Criminal Code pertaining to offenders with mental illnesses. After the Model Criminal Code and commentary were published (Kudriavtsev & Yakovlev, 1987), we discussed various problems of criminal commitment and agreed that offenders with mental illnesses were better protected by Soviet law than were other patients with such illnesses. Feeling that the situation was unsatisfactory from a legal point of view, we wondered, "why can't we do something about this?" In response, we undertook our research project without any specific intention at the beginning that it take the form of a law. We were pleased with our initial draft, though, and we decided to bring it to the state agencies. The more we studied problems of psychiatry in our country, the more our resolve was strengthened.

We did not consider there to be potential risks for ourselves and for the project. It was the time of Gorbachev's reforms (*perestroyka*), and there was much more freedom in Soviet society than before these reforms were initiated, in 1985. Many problems that had been off limits to public discussion were brought out into the open. A majority of political and religious dissidents were freed from labor camps, and a free press arose. Thus, we felt no political risk undertaking this project. To the contrary, it was exactly the right time to attract public and professional attention to the problems of people with mental disabilities in our society.

Furthermore, the Institute of State and Law of the USSR Academy of Sciences was not directly linked with any state agency (in contrast to the Research Institute of the USSR Ministry of Interior or the Institute of the General Procuracy, for example). Our Institute always had been fairly liberal and gave its scholars much more intellectual freedom to do their work than other research centers. The scholars at the Institute of State and Law were not burdened by a bureaucratic agenda and had much more autonomy in conducting their own research and in publishing their conclusions. The USSR Academy of Sciences itself was not (at least formally)

---

[1]As a decree, it would be not a "law" in a strong sense but rather another type of legal act issued by the state legislative power. In fact, years later the 1988 statute was adopted by decree.

a state institution. It was and still is (now as the Russian Academy of Sciences) a public organization, and the scholars working for the academy, Andrey Sakharov for example, had relatively progressive and liberal attitudes. So Professor Borodin and I faced no administrative impediments to our project. To the contrary, the director of the institute at that time, academician Vladimir N. Kudriavtsev, and the head of our department in the institute, Professor Alexander M. Yakovlev, gave us as much support for the project as they could provide. Later, when we decided to draft a law on psychiatric care and publicize our conclusions, they used their positions to help us.

Today I can see that our ideas were not sufficient to bring the rule of law, especially due process, to psychiatric practice in the former Soviet Union. Professor Borodin and I drew on principles of criminal law and criminal procedure that already existed in our country, but at that time we had little practical access to international documents and foreign legislation. All we had were the general U.N. documents concerning human rights (e.g., the Universal Declaration of Human Rights, 1948, and the Daes Report, which served as the basis for the U.N.'s Principles for the Protection of Persons with Mental Illness and the Improvement of Mental Health Care, 1991), the 1968 East German mental health law, and the portion of the 1974 Bulgarian health law relating to psychiatric care.

We sent our draft to numerous state agencies, from the Presidium of the Supreme Soviet to the Ministries of Justice and Health. We even made a special request to the Central Committee of the Communist Party. Our ideas received some attention. For example, we were invited to be members of the working group of the Ministry of Health that drafted the statute of 1988, and some of our proposals, although not the principal ones, were included in the statute. At that time, we proposed requiring approval by a local procurator (in the U.S., this position would be similar to a state's attorney) for involuntary examination and hospitalization and judicial review for extending the term of such hospitalizations. However, the other members of the working group did not accept either this proposal or other suggestions we made concerning the rights of people with mental disabilities and procedures to guarantee their realization. Still, the 1988 statute for the first time provided legislative control over the Soviet mental health system.

THE 1992 RUSSIAN FEDERATION LAW

The Drafting Process

Although Professor Borodin and I felt that our 1987 draft had had much impact on the 1988 statute, we continued to lobby state agencies after it was adopted. Fortunately, in early spring of 1989, the U.S. delegation came to visit the Soviet Union and gave us great support. It was only after this visit that our efforts moved ahead. A new working group was created by the Ministry of Health, and in November 1989 a draft law on psychiatric care was introduced before the Committee on Legislation, Legality and Legal Order of the Supreme Soviet.

However, the draft was not adopted at that time because the General Procuracy and the Supreme Court could not reach an agreement on whether a local procurator or a local court should be responsible for legal decisions on involuntary psychiatric care. At that time, Professor Borodin and I proposed a judicial procedure for all involuntary hospitalizations, retaining a local procurator's approval only for involuntary examinations. We were supported by the psychiatric members of the working group (Drs. Kotov, Gurovich, Yastrebov, and Tikhonenko) as well as the Ministry of Foreign Affairs. Although the draft was not adopted, it was nevertheless embraced by Mr. Andrey Sebenstsov, a Peoples Deputy of the Supreme Soviet and a member of the Committee on Legislation. From then on, the working group continued its efforts under the auspices of the Supreme Soviet.

In June 1991, a delegation of the World Psychiatric Association came to review developments in Soviet psychiatry as a follow-up to the readmission of the All-Union Society to the WPA in 1989. Members of the WPA delegation included Professor Loren H. Roth and Professor Richard J. Bonnie, who had been members of the U.S. State Department delegation in 1989, and Professor Jim Birley from the Royal College of Psychiatrists in Great Britain. They testified in support of the working group's mental health draft law in the Supreme Soviet before a joint meeting of the members of the Committee on Health and the Committee on Legality, Legislation and Legal Order. Again we received serious and indispensable help from our foreign colleagues.

The working group's draft was more congruent with international human rights documents and mental health laws from democratic countries than previous proposed laws. It contained special rules concerning the rights of people with mental disabilities both in society in general and during the provision of psychiatric care. It guaranteed legal procedures for the protection of such rights, such as the right to appeal medical decisions to a court and judicial procedures for all types of involuntary psychiatric care. At that time, we possessed the latest draft of the U.N.'s Principles for the Protection of Persons with Mental Illness and the Improvement of Mental Health Care (1991) and many foreign mental health laws. Additionally, we benefited from an opportunity I had in 1990 to travel to the United States. During my trip, I visited the Institute of Law, Psychiatry, and Public Policy at the University of Virginia. Institute faculty members facilitated my observations of the U.S. mental health system and my study of American mental health law. All these resources enabled the working group to produce a better draft.

We planned to introduce the draft law in the first fall session of the Supreme Soviet in September 1991. Yet, as "man proposes and God disposes," a coup d'état was attempted in August, and the ensuing disintegration of the Soviet Union brought us to the Russian Federation Supreme Soviet to continue our work. The same group of professionals, headed now by Dr. Leonid Kogan, the only psychiatrist among the Peoples Deputies of the Russian Federation Supreme Soviet, finished the draft in July 1992. With much anticipation, the Russian Federation Law on Psychiatric Care and Guarantees of Citizens' Rights in Its Provision came into force on January 1, 1993 (Bonnie, 1994).

Main Features

The 1992 law heralded a whole new era of Russian legislation governing psychiatric care and patients' rights protection that supplemented legislation on the protection of public health (Decree No. 2171 of the President of the Russian Federation, 1993). The law is in accordance with Article 71(c) of the 1993 Russian Federation Constitution. Therefore, the republics and regions of the Russian Federation can have their own mental health legislation, but such legislation cannot be in contradiction to the federal law.

The 1992 law consists of a preamble and six sections, including 50 articles. The preamble emphasizes the spirit of the law: to promote the health (particularly mental health) of every person and to respect the individual's dignity and human rights. The absence of adequate legal regulation is recognized in the preamble as one of the factors that permitted the practice of psychiatry for nonmedical purposes, thereby harming the health, dignity, and rights of citizens as well as the international prestige of the Russian Federation.

Section 1 of the law contains the principal provisions for mental health care and establishes the principle of voluntariness in psychiatric care. It specifies that involuntary care is impermissible except under conditions specifically authorized by the law. It also establishes medical confidentiality in the provision of care, the requirement of consent to treatment, and a right to refuse treatment. It lists rights for citizens with mental illnesses, including additional rights they have as a vulnerable group within the Russian population.

Section 2 addresses types of state-financed psychiatric care and social protection for people with mental disabilities. Section 3 introduces provisions for institutions and professionals who have a right to provide psychiatric care; licensing and certification procedures did not exist in the former Soviet Union and were established for the first time by the 1992 law.

Section 4 concerns criteria and procedures for the provision of different types of psychiatric care on both a voluntary and involuntary basis. It addresses three types of treatment: psychiatric examination, outpatient care including continuing medical (called "dispensary") observation, and inpatient psychiatric care (hospitalization). Under the law, an involuntary psychiatric examination may be conducted when a person's behavior suggests that he or she has a severe mental disorder involving (a) imminent danger to self or others, or (b) helplessness (i.e., an inability to cope with the basic needs of everyday living), or (c) a risk of substantial harm to that person's health as a result of deterioration of his or her mental condition if not given psychiatric care (Part 4, Article 23). Involuntary examination can be carried out only with the approval of a local court, except in emergency cases. Involuntary hospitalization is permissible if the examination or treatment needed can be achieved only under inpatient conditions (Article 29). The procedure for involuntary hospitalization is judicial (Articles 33 to 35). Periodic judicial review of all cases of involuntary hospitalization is required after the first 6 months of the hospitalization and thereafter on an annual basis (Article 36). But at least once a month for the first 6 months, a hospitalized person must also be examined by a commission of psychiatrists from the psychiatric facility, and if the hospitalization is continued beyond 6 months, the examination must be repeated at least once every 6 months.

Involuntary outpatient treatment (or continuing dispensary observation) is considered by the 1992 law to be a medical action, and it is therefore left to the discretion of a commission of psychiatrists appointed either by the administration of the psychiatric facility providing outpatient care or by a commission of psychiatrists appointed by the public health agency (Part 2, Article 27). Involuntary dispensary observation may be arranged for a person suffering from a chronic and protracted mental disorder with severe, persistent pathological symptoms or frequent exacerbations (Part 1, Article 27). In Soviet times, a person under mandatory dispensary observation (listed on the so-called psychiatric register) suffered an automatic and serious restriction in the exercise of his or her rights (e.g., to obtain a job or a university education or to possess a driver's license) (U.S. Delegation, 1989). Also, the register served as a vehicle for rapidly readmitting a person to a psychiatric hospital, for instance during state holidays. The 1992 law strictly prohibits any restriction of a person's rights and freedoms solely on the basis of their psychiatric diagnosis or their being under continuing dispensary observation or in a psychiatric hospital (Part 3, Article 5). Restrictions of citizens' rights and freedoms because of a mental disorder are allowed only in cases permitted by the federal laws of the Russian Federation (Part 1, Article 5). Thus, with legal restrictions and dispensary observation completely independent from one another, it became possible to regard this type of involuntary psychiatric care as a medical procedure akin to those for tuberculosis or cancer patients.

Section 4 of the law also establishes provisions concerning patients' rights during inpatient care, corresponding duties of a psychiatric facility's administration, and an advocacy service for hospitalized patients. Unfortunately, a patient advocacy service has not yet been implemented in Russia.

Section 5 addresses government and nongovernment control and procuratorial supervision of psychiatric care. Section 6 delineates complaint procedures for actions or omissions associated with psychiatric care. Such complaints can be brought directly to a court, a superior agency official, or a local procurator. Any medical decision, whether it involves an action or an omission, that infringes on the rights of a person under psychiatric care may be subject to a complaint (Article 47).

Thus, the 1992 Russian law on psychiatric care established (a) provisions subjecting psychiatric decision making to meaningful review by a court, especially in involuntary cases; (b) rules for periodic review of the necessity of involuntary hospitalization by a commission of psychiatrists in the hospital and a court; and (c) regulations protecting the rights of people with mental disorders, including patients' rights within a psychiatric institution. The principles of legality, humanity, and respect for human and citizens' rights are mentioned among general principles for the provision of psychiatric care in Russia (Part 2, Article 1). Generally speaking, the 1992 Russian law is modern and democratic. The majority of its provisions have their roots in the U.N.'s Principles for the Protection of Persons with Mental Illness and the Improvement of Mental Health Care (1991). All indications are that the law will be a positive force for changing mental health care in Russia.

Implementation: Context and Problems

In 1993, the first year the law was in effect, there were 13,019 psychiatrists in the Russian Federation working in 160 psychiatric dispensaries, 135 outpatient units in psychiatric hospitals, and 2,878 psychiatric and psychoneurological clinics (Gurovich, Preis, & Golland, 1995, pp. 8, 20). In the same year there were 284 psychiatric hospitals and 101 inpatient units in dispensaries (p. 266). The rate of involuntary examinations was 3.25 per 100,000, and the rate of involuntary hospitalizations was 15.3 per 100,000 (p. 236). That year, 66,399 people were hospitalized involuntarily, representing 3.4% of all psychiatric hospitalizations (pp. 251–252).

These figures require some clarification. Involuntary examination is a separate procedure under the 1992 law. It serves as a first step in the provision of psychiatric care and involves primarily people with no previous psychiatric history. An involuntary examination is conducted to determine whether the person suffers from a mental disorder, whether that person needs psychiatric care, and if so in what form (Article 23). For patients already receiving care in the form of consultation and treatment and continuing dispensary observation (Article 26), the psychiatric examination is encompassed within the provision of outpatient care. When involuntary commitment procedures are initiated against patients already "in the system," the examination is a part of their hospitalization procedure under Article 29, and therefore it is not counted as an involuntary examination for statistical purposes.

Not all people examined are diagnosed as having a mental illness. For example, in 1993, 73% of those involuntarily examined in the Russian Federation were recognized as having a mental illness; in 1994 the figure was 81.3% (Gurovich et al., 1995, pp. 236, 244). As a consequence of involuntary examinations, some people with mental illnesses were put under continuing dispensary observation, and others were placed in psychiatric hospitals (61.4% in 1993 and 52.8% in 1994) (pp. 240, 248). Unfortunately, the data do not indicate how many hospital placements resulted from involuntary examinations. It seems likely that the majority of involuntarily hospitalized patients were already receiving outpatient care, and therefore probably fewer cases of such hospitalization occurred immediately after an involuntary examination.

Data on involuntary examinations varied widely from region to region. Some reported no such examinations (e.g., Dagestan, Karelia, Rostov area, Kemerovo area), and 12 others had rates of less than 1 per 100,000 population. Other regions had higher rates than average (e.g., 68.5 in Moscow, 156.6 in Tyumen area) (pp. 232–236, 253–256).

In 1996, the rate of involuntary examinations increased to 5.24 per 100,000, and the rate of involuntary hospitalizations increased to 4.17% of all psychiatric hospitalizations (Gurovich, 1997). Although the number of psychiatric beds decreased by 17,000 from 1991 to 1996, inpatient care is still preferred by Russian psychiatrists (Gurovich, 1997). Also, wide variations in the provision of psychiatric care among the Russian regions continued to exist in 1996.[2]

There are several reasons for continued problems in the mental health system. First, the 1992 law is not a fact of everyday psychiatric practice in some regions of the Russian Federation because psychiatrists lack of adequate knowledge of legal provisions. No special training in the new law was conducted for mental health or legal professionals. Psychiatrists in continuing postgraduate training (*povyshenie kvalifikacii*) received some lectures, but generally psychiatrists were not given a thorough review of the law,

---

[2]The new Russian Criminal Code of 1996, which came into force on January 1, 1997, contains the special offense of "illegal admission to a psychiatric hospital" (Article 128).

which contains many new legal rules for Russian psychiatric practice.[3] Second, psychiatrists continue to pressure patients or use other forms of coercion to get consent. Some "consents" are obtained formally without giving any information to the patient. Thus, traditional practice has not changed significantly. Third, in some cases a psychiatrist has declined to intervene, leaving a patient without necessary care (Gurovich, 1994, p. 114).

Nonetheless, Russia has taken a crucial first step. It would be unrealistic to expect overnight improvements in the psychiatric care system. Evaluating how the 1992 law has influenced mental health services and the mental health of the Russian population will be possible only after a long period of implementation. And the law is only one of tools that must be used if sufficient changes are to be realized.

In addition, Russian psychiatry has inherited certain characteristics from its Soviet predecessor, and this inheritance creates serious obstacles for reforms in mental health care. First, funding for necessary medical equipment in the former Soviet Union was dramatically less than modern standards. Health care in Russia currently receives less than 2.6% of the gross national product, whereas industrialized nations spend 8% to 12%, and the World Health Organization recommends expenditures of at least 5%. As a result, there are practically no new psychiatric facilities with modern instruments and equipment. It is no surprise that people with mental illnesses often do not want to be hospitalized and that mental health professionals do not want to be on staff at such clinics, where they would be preoccupied with improving the facility's material resources and conditions for the patients rather than exercising their professional duties.

Another problematic inheritance is that psychiatry in the former Soviet Union was "a psychiatry largely without psychology, without social workers, and it has had a very strong institutional (hospital-based) focus" (Roth, 1994, p. 9). Only in 1996 did the Russian Ministry of Health officially recognize social workers and medical psychologists as mental health professionals who should participate on treatment teams together with psychiatrists. Positions for medical psychologists and social workers have been established in only a small proportion of Russia's regions, and many of these positions have not been filled, especially those for social workers, because of a lack of special training. And the Russian mental health service has not yet begun to change its hospital-based focus.

In addition, the quality of psychiatric training was and still is rather poor. The training is not comprehensive. Modern textbooks are scarce,

---

[3]Just after the 1992 law was adopted, the professionals involved in its drafting prepared and published a commentary to the law. Unfortunately, most of the copies were burned in the White House (the parliament building for the Russian Supreme Soviet at that time) during the tumultuous events of October 1993 in Moscow. The revised second edition of the commentary was published in 1997 and is currently available.

especially foreign ones. These poor professional standards to a large extent are rooted in the dominating influence of a single school of psychiatry in the former Soviet Union. In those days, Snezhnevsky's school possessed a monopoly on truth and occupied the key positions. This school is famous for its concept of "sluggish schizophrenia," which conceptualized an individual's deviations from social norms as the early stages of schizophrenia and permitted the unrestrained extension of the limits of the illness. Naturally, ideas of the Snezhnevsky school were behind the repressive practices against dissidents (1989, pp. 24–25). Becase any deviation from the norm prescribed by Soviet ideology was viewed as an early stage of mental illness, it was very easy to declare any person to be mentally ill.

Finally, the most serious impediment to reform in Russian psychiatry is the lack of professional ethics among the majority of psychiatrists. In the former Soviet Union, the health system, including psychiatry, was entirely a state institution. The state allocated funds, set up the system of professional training, and controlled psychiatrists' practices. Psychiatry in the Soviet era was not an independent profession with internal guarantees of autonomy and norms of professional ethics. Russian psychiatry is not significantly different from that pattern. In an important step to make psychiatry a truly independent profession, the Russian Society of Psychiatrists adopted the Code of Professional Ethics of the Russian Society of Psychiatrists in April 1994 (Polubinskaya & Bonnie, 1996), but the code seems to be more like a declaration of good intentions than an instrument to guide everyday psychiatric practice. It is hoped that the provisions of the code and the 1992 Russian law will be used as the main tools for reforming psychiatry, especially the attitudes and mentality of psychiatrists, and for bringing the ideas of human rights and professional duties concerning those rights into every psychiatric outpatient and inpatient facility.

It is clear that the task of creating a modern system of mental health care in the Russian Federation is unfinished business. Yet if we remember that our efforts started practically from nothing, we can be satisfied with our progress thus far. Now psychiatrists must do their part in helping to overcome the Soviet heritage by changing their attitudes about patients and treating them in the same way that they would wish to be treated. Psychiatrists also need to accept the vocabulary of the international psychiatric community, to embrace modern classifications of mental and behavioral disorders, and to improve the curricula for professional training. In doing so they will provide a positive context for modern Russian mental health law.

REFERENCES

Bloch, S., & Reddaway, P. (1977). *Russia's political hospitals: The abuse of psychiatry in the Soviet Union.* London: Victor Collancz.
Bonnie, R. J. (1990). Coercive psychiatry and human rights: An assessment of recent changes in the Soviet Union. *Criminal Law Forum, 1*(2), 319–346.

Bonnie, R. J. (1994). Introduction: The evolution of the 1992 Law of the Russian Federation on Psychiatric Care. *Journal of Russian and European Psychiatry, 27*, 69–96.

Borodin, S. V., & Polubinskaya, S. V. (1991). Kakoy zakon vedet k Pravu [Which legislative act leads to law]. In S. V. Borodin (Ed.), *Pravo i psikhiatria* [Law and psychiatry] (pp. 366–382). Moscow: Yuridischeskaya Literatura.

Cassidy, J. (1997). The return of Karl Marx. Retrieved April 5, 2001, from the World Wide Web: http://arts.deakin.edu.au/IR/articles/marx.html

Decree No. 2171 of the President of the Russian Federation. (1993, December 16). On general legal classification for fields of legislation. *Sobranie zakonodatelstva Rossiyskoy Federatsii* [Collection of legislation of the Russian Federation], No.7, Art. 679.

Gurovich, I. Y. (1994). Psikhiatricheskaya pomoshch v nedobrovol'nom poryadke: Pokazateli realizatsii zakona [Involuntary psychiatric care: Indicators of implementation of the law]. *Social and Clinical Psychiatry, 5*(1), 111–114.

Gurovich, I. Y. (1997). Psikhiatricheskaya pomoshch v Rossii: aktual'nye problemy [Psychiatric Care in Russia: Actual Problems]. In I. Y. Gurovich (Ed.), *Reformy slughby psikhicheskogo zdorov'ya: problemy i perspectivy* [Reforms of Mental Health Services: Problems and Perspectives] (pp. 14–23). Moscow: The Russian Academy of Medical Sciences.

Gurovich, I. Y., Preis, V. B., & Golland, V. B. (1995). Psikhiatricheskaya pomoshch naseleniyu Rossii (v pokazatelyakh deyatelnosty za 1986–1993 g.g.) [Psychiatric care available to the population of Russian (indicators of activity in 1986–1993)]. *Social and Clinical Psychiatry (Suppl.)*, Moscow: 677.

Kudriavtsev, V. N., & Yakovlev, A. M. (Eds.). (1987). *Criminal law: An experience of theoretical modeling.* Moscow: Nauka.

Polubinskaya, S. V., & Bonnie, R. J. (1996). The code of professional ethics of the Russian Society of Psychiatrists: Text and commentary. *International Journal of Law and Psychiatry, 19*(2), 143–172.

Principles for the Protection of Persons with Mental Illness and the Improvement of Mental Health Care. (1991). G.A. Res. 199, U.N. GAOR, 46th Sess., Supp. No. 49, Annex, pp. 188–192, U.N. Doc. A/46/49 (1991).

Reich, W. (1980). The case of General Grigorenko: A psychiatric reexamination of a Soviet dissident. *Psychiatry, 43*, 303–323.

Roth, L. H. (1994). Introduction: Access to and utilization of mental health services in the former Soviet Union. *Journal of Russian and East European Psychiatry, 27*(2), 6–18.

Universal Declaration of Human Rights. (1948). U.N.G.A. Res. 217A (III), U.N. Doc. A/810, at 71.

U.S. Delegation to Assess Recent Changes in Soviet Psychiatry. (1989). Report of the U.S. Delegation to Assess Recent Changes in Soviet Psychiatry. *Schizophrenia Bulletin, 15*(4) (Suppl.), 1–79.

Vedomosty Verkhovnogo Soveta SSSR [Current Digest of the Soviet Press]. (1988). No. 2, Art. 19.

III

RESPONSIBILITY AND PUNISHMENT

7

FROM *SIKORA* TO *HENDRICKS*: MENTAL DISORDER AND CRIMINAL RESPONSIBILITY

STEPHEN J. MORSE

In January 1962, Walter Sikora shot and killed Douglas Hooey in a tavern in Paterson, New Jersey. Charged with murder in the first degree, Sikora tried to use psychiatric testimony to claim that he lacked the capacity to premeditate, a criterion for first-degree murder. In brief, the psychiatric claim was that Sikora's unconscious psychodynamics impaired his free will. In an influential opinion, the New Jersey supreme court upheld the exclusion of the testimony (*State v. Sikora*, 1965). Also in 1962, the American Law Institute published the proposed official draft of the *Model Penal Code*. The section on responsibility excused a defendant if, as a result of mental disease or defect, the defendant lacked substantial capacity to appreciate the criminality of "his" conduct or to conform "his" conduct to the requirements of the law. The *Model Penal Code* was silent about the implications of determinism, but at least the second, "volitional" prong lent itself to deterministic worries and confusions. Finally, in that same year, Sir Peter Strawson, an Oxford philosopher, published a justly famous lecture, "Freedom and Resentment," which has had a profound influence on the contemporary philosophical debate about determinism and responsibility (P. F. Strawson, 1982).

Both the New Jersey supreme court and P. F. Strawson concluded that determinism did not undermine responsibility. The court thought that the reason was practical; P. F. Strawson thought that it was conceptual. Since then, much of the discussion concerning the criminal responsibility of people with mental disorders has proceeded as if determinism, abnormality, or unconscious motivation—as if lack of "free will," "intent," "free choice," "control," or the like—was the characteristic that both distinguished people with mental disorders and justified the special legal treatment accorded some of them (see Melton, Petrila, Poythress, & Slobogin, 1997). Most recently, for example, the U.S. Supreme Court upheld the constitutionality of Kansas's violent sexual predator commitment law on the ground that violent sexual predators could not control themselves because they were "abnormal" (*Kansas v. Hendricks*, 1997). For another example, a respected law professor at a 1997 conference proclaimed that people with mental disorders were treated specially because they were "automatons" and lacked free will ("You Know Who You Are," 1997).

In this chapter, I contend that P. F. Strawson was right and *Sikora* was wrong. Either determinism, causation, free will, lack of control, and like concepts are not the touchstones of responsibility, or they contain a grain of truth but are confusing and prove too much. I argue that the general capacity to grasp and be guided by reason is the touchstone of responsibility in all mental health law contexts and that forensic mental health professionals should be concerned more with agents' reasons for action than with diagnoses, causal explanations, and other variables that are rarely directly relevant to moral and legal decisions about responsibility. Indeed, the criteria for all mental health laws are concerned with the agent's capacity for reason in a particular context (Morse, 1999). Nonetheless, much of the discussion of responsibility and mental disorder has been confused and has led to misguided forensic practice. Although a more careful philosophical analysis of responsibility has been available in the legal literature since at least the mid-1980s (e.g., Moore, 1985), confusions and misconceptions still abound. As *Hendricks* demonstrates, the mischief is still afoot.

I begin by articulating the criteria for the fair ascription of responsibility that explain moral and legal practices and that do not depend on the truth or falsity of determinism or on any other of the characterizations that have bedeviled us. In particular, I propose that the general capacity to grasp and be guided by reason is the basic criterion for responsibility (this formulation is borrowed from Wallace, 1994). This standard best justifies why some people with mental disorders are appropriate subjects for the application of special mental health law rules, all of which presuppose that they are not responsible agents in the context in question. My focus and most of the examples concern criminal responsibility, but the analysis generalizes to civil mental health law. Then I turn to a close examination of the many false, confusing, and limited alternative explanations of why some people are not responsible, suggesting why each fails. Finally, I consider how my analysis would affect the rationality of criminal and civil forensic mental health practice.

CRITERIA FOR RESPONSIBILITY

The primary condition for responsible conduct is the general capacity to grasp and be guided by good reason, and the two conditions that undermine responsibility are the lack of this capacity and wrongly produced hard choice. These latter two conditions explain why most adults are considered responsible and why children and some adults, including a subset of those with mental disorders, are not. In this section I discuss the criteria for these conditions and argue that most "internal" hard choice cases, which are usually analyzed as control, volitional, or compulsion problems, are better understood as rationality deficiencies.

The law's concept of responsibility follows logically from its conception of the person as a practical reasoner and from the nature of law itself. Law is a system of rules that guides and governs human interaction. It tells citizens in various contexts what they may and may not do, what they must or must not do, what they are entitled to, and what the conditions are for the fair and efficient ascription of responsibility. Unless human beings were practical reasoning creatures capable of understanding the world around them and capable of using the rules as premises in practical reasoning to guide their conduct, the law would be powerless to affect human action, and it would be unfair or inefficient to hold agents accountable for their conduct. We do not expect small children and some people with mental disorders to understand the world around them and to be able fully to follow or to conform to the rules precisely, because they lack the capacity for normative competence.

Rationality or Normative Competence

A *legally responsible agent* is therefore a person who is generally capable of *rationality* or *normative competence* (terms I use interchangeably). What kind and how much capacity is required is a normative standard that is a matter of moral, political, and ultimately legal judgment, about which reasonable people can and do differ. Consequently, there cannot be an uncontroversial definition of rationality or normative competence. Whatever the criteria might be within a polity and its legal system, however, the debate is always about human action—intentional behavior guided by reasons. Mental health law concerns human action, not simply the movements of biophysical organisms.

General capacity for rationality or normative competence means that the agent is capable of understanding and being guided by the good reasons a particular context demands. This criterion is generalizable to all mental health law criteria. Consider, for example, criminal responsibility, competence to contract, competence to make treatment decisions, and competence to stand trial. In each case, one is considered fully accountable as an agent—one is held deserving of blame and punishment, one's contracts are enforced, one's treatment decisions are honored, and one is permitted to stand trial—if the agent is capable of grasping and being guided by the good reasons that apply in the context.

The capacity to understand what one is doing and the applicable moral and legal prohibitions against doing harm is a precondition for fair blame and punishment. The capacity to understand one's bargain is a precondition for rational contracting and holding the agent to the bargain. The capacity to appreciate the costs and benefits of a proffered treatment is a precondition for rational treatment decision making and for permitting the agent to decide without parentalistic intervention. The capacities to understand the proceedings and to assist counsel are preconditions for rational participation in one's own defense and for a criminal defendant's ability to receive a fair trial. The necessary capacity is always general. Many people make foolish deals, for example, that are nonetheless enforced because the agent was capable of understanding the contours of the bargain. Special mental health rules apply in all these legal domains precisely because crazy beliefs, perceptions, affective states, and the like may disable the person's general capacity for normative competence in the situation.[1]

Consider, for example, a defendant who kills in self-defense because she believes delusionally that either her life is in danger or that the otherwise applicable moral and legal rules do not apply to her because she is God's chosen agent and God has suspended the earthly laws. In such a case, the defendant is unable rationally to comprehend the most morally relevant facts bearing on her culpability—whether her life is genuinely threatened or what the rules are. She of course knows in either case that she is killing a human being and does so intentionally. And although in the abstract she probably knows and endorses the moral and legal prohibition against unjustified killing, in this case the rule against unjustifiable homicide will be ineffective because she delusionally believes that her action is justifiable. Although the delusional agent knows the rules in the abstract and is instrumentally rational, her conduct is a clear example of

---

[1] I use *crazy* here and elsewhere because I believe that for mental health law purposes it is the least question begging and most descriptively accurate word to characterize the behaviors regulated by mental health laws. No disrespect toward people with mental disorders or the people who try to help them is implied (Morse, 1978, 1999).

rationality-within-irrationality (Link & Stueve, 1994). The general incapacity for normative competence is what distinguishes the delusional agent from people who are simply mistaken but who have the ability to follow the rule. Lack of a general capacity for rationality is the more general theory of excuse that explains the so-called cognitive test for legal insanity. It also explains why the agent may be said to be unable "to conform" to the requirements of law, a standard often misconceived as some type of compulsion criterion.

A normative, moral, and political judgment concerning the content and degree of normative competence required for responsibility is ultimately necessary, but guidance is possible. I do not have an exalted or complicated notion of rationality; most generally it includes the ability, in Susan Wolf's (1990) words, "to be sensitive and responsive to relevant changes in one's situation and environment—that is, to be flexible" (p. 69). It is the ability to perceive accurately, to get the facts right, and to reason instrumentally, including weighing the facts appropriately and according to a minimally coherent preference ordering. Put yet another way, it is the ability to act for good reasons. For example, it is always a good reason not to act (or to act) if doing so (or not doing so) will be wrong. Notice that it is not necessary for responsibility that an agent acted for good, generalizable reasons at the time in question. Presumably, for example, few criminal defendants or foolish contracting agents did so, or they would not have offended or made bad deals. The general normative capacity to be able to grasp and be guided by reason is sufficient. Although I have presented the criteria as if normative capacity were a unitary ability, in fact it is a congeries of cognitive, perceptual, and affective attributes that vary according to the demands of the situation.

I have concluded that normative competence in the context of responsibility for wrongdoing should include the abilities to empathize and to feel guilt or some other reflexive reactive emotion. Unless an agent is able to put himself or herself affectively in another's shoes, to have a sense of what a potential victim will feel as a result of the agent's conduct, and unless he or she is able at least to feel the anticipation of unpleasant guilt for breach, he or she will lack the capacity to grasp and be guided by the primary rational reasons for complying with moral expectations. What could be a better reason not to breach a moral expectation than a full, emotional understanding of the harm one will cause another? People who lack such understanding are, in my opinion, "morally irrational," and it is moral responsibility that is in issue.

People who lack empathy and guilt can of course feel pain and understand that pain will be inflicted if they violate the criminal law and are caught and convicted. Now, fear of criminal sanction is a good reason not to offend, but it is not a virtuous reason grounded in moral understanding. It is a purely calculating reason that does not arise from an internalized moral sense. If a criminal prohibition is primarily "regulatory" and has no substantial moral component, then such instrumental rationality should be sufficient for blame and punishment (R. Bonnie, personal communication, 1998). But when criminal prohibitions contain genuinely moral content, moral irrationality should excuse. Finally, most of the time when the desire to do harm arises, a police officer is not at one's elbow. The cost of future official detection, conviction, and punishment for most crime is relatively slight compared to the immediate rewards of satisfying one's desires, especially if one is a dispositionally steep time discounter, as such people tend to be. For morally irrational people, fear of the criminal sanction, anyway a problematic deterrent, will be of especially limited salience because it lacks a moral component. Such agents have not internalized moral prohibitions and do not fear guilt or being stigmatized as an immoral agent or as a wrongdoer.

The suggestion that normative competence for moral and criminal responsibility includes the capacities for empathy and guilt may seem paradoxical, and the criminal law does not now excuse the classic psychopath (e.g., American Law Institute, 1962, sec. 4.01(2)). Perhaps people who lack these capacities should instead be considered, as the law considers them, particularly immoral and deserving of special condemnation, rather than excuse, but this does not seem fair. To the best of our knowledge, some wrongdoers simply lack these capacities, and they are not amenable to reason. They may be dangerous people, but they are not part of our moral community. Once again, it is not required that the defendant have actually empathized and felt guilt at the time of the crime. Most wrongdoers presumably do not experience such states at the time of the crime. A general capacity to feel these emotions is sufficient to render the agent normatively rational.

A highly controversial question is whether desires or preferences in themselves can be irrational (Nozick, 1993). It is of course true that having desires most people consider irrational is likely to get someone into trouble, especially if the desires and situations that tempt that person have illegal or immoral objects and are strong. Nonetheless, I have concluded that even if desires can be construed as irrational, irrational desires do not deprive the agent of normative competence unless they somehow disable the rational capacities or produce an internal hard choice distinguishable from the choices experienced by people with equally strong but rational desires. In other words, if the agent with irrational desires can comprehend the morally relevant features of his or her conduct, he or she can be held responsible if those irrational desires are the reasons for breaching an expectation we accept. For example, the desire to have sexual contact with children is often considered irrational and can be a predicate for a diagnosis of pedophilia. Nonetheless, most pedophiles are fully in touch with reality and morality, including the moral and legal rules governing their conduct, and they should be held responsible unless their condition undermines their general capacity to grasp and be guided by reason.

Severe mental disorder is a primary condition that may sometimes generally or situationally disable an agent's normative competence, but we should recognize that it is not the only one. Stress, fatigue, shock, intense provocation, and a host of other variables may have the same effect. Consequently, there is little reason to limit an irrationality defense or the application of special mental health law rules generally to cases in which mental disorder is present or to force defendants to shoehorn their situation into the Procrustean, medicalized bed of mental disorder. Some have argued that in the criminal law a more permissive regime, unmoored from a mental health criterion, would threaten to flood the courts with insupportable claims (R. Bonnie, personal communication, February 1999). In response to such fears, for example, some claim that the requirement of a mental disorder would provide an "objective" element of abnormality that would discipline the domain of excuses (e.g., *United States v. Moore*, 1973 [Leventhal, J. concurring]). But they are wrong about the objectivity of mental health evidence compared to other potentially normatively disabling variables. Furthermore, they were mostly descriptively wrong and entirely normatively wrong about the disciplinary effect. If responsibility requires normative competence, as I have argued, justice demands that agents should be allowed to demonstrate that they nonresponsively lacked this competence for any reason.

Absence of Compulsion

Responsibility also requires that the agent act without wrongful compulsion or coercion, even if the agent is fully rational, because it is also unfair to hold people accountable for behavior that is wrongly compelled. *Compulsion* involves a wrongful, threat-produced hard choice that a rational and otherwise responsible agent faces. If she yields to the threat, it will not be because she fails to understand the legal rule or what she is doing or because the threat turns her into an automaton. Such an agent acts intentionally precisely to avoid the threatened harm. Consider the example of a desperado who threatens to kill you unless you kill two innocent people. The balance of evils is clearly negative: You can save your own, single, innocent life only by taking two innocent lives, so the killings would not be justified. But they might be excused because they were compelled. Or consider an agent who precisely understands an undesirable deal, but who is "requested" to sign at gunpoint. The agent is a rational, intentional contractor, but the contract would be unenforceable because it was compelled.

Acting through its legal rules governing such cases, society might decide that some choices are too hard to hold fairly the agent accountable and that wrongfully threatened agents should be excused for making the wrong choice, even if the agent was rational and his or her conduct was intentional action. Deciding which choices are too hard, that is, which threats might cause a person of reasonable firmness to yield and to do wrong, is of course a normative matter. Once again, the subjective reaction of the threatened person is not the issue. The excuse obtains only if the agent's conduct meets normative expectations. If the hard choice renders the person incapable of rationality, however, then there is no need to resort to notions of compulsion to excuse.

As in all cases of excuse, the wrongly compelled agent has good reason not to comply with the threat. The criminal defendant did wrong; the contracting agent made a deal contrary to his or her best interests. In general, respect for liberty, autonomy, and the rights of all citizens requires that hard choice should overcome the good reason not to comply only in limited circumstances. Indeed, the common criminal law, still followed in many states, never permits the excuse of duress, no matter how serious the threat, if the defendant took innocent life. Minor threats of limited consequence will not render a contract avoidable. Thus, the law excuses only if a person of reasonable firmness would have yielded under the circumstances: Only then do we conclude that the choice was too hard to have expected the defendant to resist. What is required of the person of reasonable firmness will of course vary with the circumstances.

How might psychopathology compel conduct? Many people believe, for example, that a compulsion theory explains the control test for legal insanity. One metaphorical notion is that some abnormal mental or emotional states act like an internal gun to the head, even if these people seem otherwise rational. Consider, for example, the pedophile, whose allegedly abnormal desire for sexual contact with a child may make the temptation feel irresistible, but who is clearly rational in all respects except, perhaps, the content of the desire. Or consider an extreme coward who is threatened with a hard punch unless he or she kills someone. Although virtually everyone, including cowardly types, would choose to be the victim of a punch rather than to kill, some people might find the threat of a punch as subjectively terrifying and coercive as a death threat. An easy choice for most people may be subjectively very difficult for the coward.

Explaining why psychopathology arguably compels conduct is difficult. As I argue in the following section, talk of "irresistible impulses" or "volitional problems" is more confusing than helpful. Can the hard choice model be applied instead to one-party cases? How should such cases be analyzed? Remember, to begin, that the "person of reasonable firmness" standard does not mean that everyone who is not dispositionally of reasonable firmness will be excused. The standard is normative. Those who are fortunate enough to be especially brave and those who are of average braveness will be able to meet it quite readily. Those who are of less-than-average dispositional firmness will have more trouble resisting when they should.

Still, if we judge that an agent had the general capacity to comply with the reasonable firmness standard, even if it was harder for him than for most, then he will be held responsible if he yields when a person of reasonable firmness would have resisted. This is true of most objective standards in the law: People with less-than-average ability to meet them are still held to objective standards if they are generally capable of meeting them. The legal result comports with common sense and ordinary morality. When important moral expectations are involved—for example, do not harm others under weakly threatening conditions—we believe it is fair to expect fellow citizens capable of meeting reasonable standards to comply (Hart, 1968).

What should be done, however, with the person we believe may not be capable of complying, such as the pedophile with extremely strong desires or the extreme coward who is threatened with a punch through no fault of his or her own? Justice seems to demand an excuse. In these cases, the internal threat, the metaphorical gun to the head, that creates the hard choice is not physical harm itself; rather, it is the threat of such supremely dysphoric inner states—extreme anxiety or frustration, for example—that renders the choice so hard for this agent (for a full explanation of internal hard choice, see Morse, 1994, pp. 1619–1634). A model of hard choice created by the threat of internal dysphoria may be the best explanation of why we might want to excuse in an array of cases that are often thought to require a volitional or control excuse, such as the pedophile, pyromaniac, compulsive gambler, or drug addict. In all, the predisposition causes desires whose frustration threatens the agent with great dysphoria. Perhaps a person of reasonable firmness faced with sufficient dysphoria would yield.

Although the internal hard choice model is plausible, and although competing explanations that rely on so-called volitional problems are confused or lack empirical support (Morse, 1994), I prefer to analyze these cases in terms of the capacity for normative competence. The agent's psychological state may disable his or her general capacity for normative competence because it prevents the agent from having reasonable access to the good reasons that should guide conduct. For example, the coward's fear of bodily injury may be so morbid that any threat creates anxiety sufficient to block the person's capacity to grasp and be guided by good reason. For another example, consider a manic businessperson who makes a foolish deal that will almost surely lead to bankruptcy. The reason that this person cannot conform to the requirements of rational contracting is not, say, that the agent's grandiosity compels him or her to contract. Rather, the grandiosity disables the agent's capacity to recognize reasonably the risks and rewards of the bargain. Finally, consider the drug addict or pedophile. In extreme cases, perhaps—and in precisely those cases in which we might want to excuse—the intensity of the addict's or pedophile's desire and the fear of frustration might prevent the agent from having access to the good reasons not to take the drug or to molest a child that are usually available (Morse, 2000).

In addition to the conceptual reasons to prefer a normative competence explanation for so-called control problems, at the most practical level, it will often be too difficult to assess the degree of threatened dysphoria that creates the hard choice. Assessing the capacity for *rationality* —the capacity to have access to good reasons in a given situation—is not an easy task either, but it is a more commonsense assessment of the sort we make every day. Second, it is simply not clear that the fear of dysphoria would ever be sufficient to excuse the breach of important expectations or to exempt an agent from ordinary responsibility, except in precisely those cases in which we would assume naturally that the agent's capacity for normative competence was essentially disabled. For example, molesting children is such a dreadful invasion of the rights and interests of children that we would only excuse such conduct in extreme cases in which the molester is indeed not a rational agent. To take a civil law example, suppose an agent's desperate desire for approval leads him or her to make a foolish investment simply because he or she is afraid of offending the offerer. The interests of efficiency might dictate enforcing the bargain, except in those few cases when the desire for approval might be considered so pathological that the agent would no longer be considered rational.

Necessity for Normative Interpretation

Because I claim that irrationality or normative incompetence best explains why the law excuses and is the primary excusing condition, the concept of irrationality must do a great deal of work in the account presented. One might therefore desire a more precise, uncontroversial definition of irrationality, but such a desire would be unreasonable. The definition I am using, which is always open to normative revision, is grounded in our ordinary, everyday understanding of practical reason and its critical role in human interaction, including morality. We are, after all, the only creatures on earth who truly act for reasons. We all, everywhere and always, successfully use the imprecise definition I am using to evaluate the moral and nonmoral conduct of ourselves and others. Moreover, such soft criteria, which both admit and require normative interpretation, are a common feature of acceptable legal standards, such as "reasonableness." A decision concerning the capacity for rationality is a commonsense judgment that requires a normative interpretation in response to shifting morals and politics. The imprecision in the definition of the capacity is, paradoxically, a virtue, because it gives proper latitude for such interpretation. The stringency of the capacity standard is open to debate, and the criteria suggested furnish the terms for that debate. To require more is to demand the impossible and the unnecessary. Indeed, if one wishes to abandon irrationality as the core excusing condition, the burden is then on the agent rejecting irrationality to offer and to justify a morally compelling and more precise alternative. Most of the alternatives offered do not and cannot explain the excuses we have, and they are unworkable.

Thus, an agent is responsible for a particular action if he or she was capable of rationality and acted without compulsion in this context. If incapable of rationality or wrongfully compelled to perform the particular action, he or she will be excused (or considered incompetent legally to perform the action). These criteria have nothing to do with the truth or falsity of determinism, free will, or the like. It is simply true that some agents are normatively capable and some are not and that some agents are wrongly threatened with a hard choice and others are not. It is these criteria that explain our practices of holding people responsible.

ALTERNATIVE BUT UNSATISFACTORY EXPLANATIONS FOR EXCUSE

Many confusions about the premises of excusing or exempting from responsibility have hindered rational legal analysis and sound forensic practice. In this section I address the following alternative explanations: determinism, causation, abnormality, lack of free will or volition, lack of intent, lack of choice, lack of self-control, and unconscious psychodynamics. In each case, I try to show that the explanation is misguided or confused or that, even if it contains a grain of truth, it does not provide a general explanation for why mental disorder or other variables might excuse or exempt the agent from responsibility for conduct. These misguided, confusing, or limited explanations are still rampant.

Determinism or Universal Causation

Determinism or universal causation is a standard but confused general explanation for specific excuses. If the defendant's conduct was "determined" or "caused," the conduct should allegedly be excused. Such claims are often made in the idiom of "free will": Defendants who lack this desirable attribute should be excused. Although such locutions are indeed common, these alternatives do not explain the excuses we have, nor do they represent a coherent theory that could explain the practice of excusing.

The simplest reason why the theoretical truth of determinism or universal causation does not explain the excuses we have is that determinism is true or not, "all the way down." No consensually accepted meaning of determinism exists, but a typical understanding is that the laws of the universe and antecedent events together determine all future events. Many people assume that this (or something like it) is true, at least at levels higher than the explanation of subatomic particles, and it is certainly the background assumption of many working scientists.

If determinism is true, what agents do, like all other phenomena, is the determined outcome of the laws of the universe operating on antecedent events. At the least, however, any sensible analysis of the conditions of criminal liability demonstrates that this truth does not explain the excuses we have. Current rules and practices are not dependent on the truth of determinism in general and certainly not as it may apply to some cases and not to others. The excuses we have can be explained quite consistently and coherently by facts about agents, such as the capacity for rationality, and about situations, such as whether the agent faced a hard choice, that are then considered according to moral theories about fairness. We excuse only a subset of agents, and it is simply not the case that all agents are or were irrational or faced hard choices at any time relevant for responsibility and blame ascriptions. Determinism generalizes to all cases; irrationality and hard choice do not generalize to all agents and all situations. In doctrinal terms, all agents do not meet the criteria for legal insanity or for duress. It does not matter how much one widens the time frame.

Prior events for which agents had no responsibility are always part of the "causal chain" that led to the conduct in question, but so what? Whatever causal chain may have been operative, some agents are rational and some are not; some face hard choices and some do not. Thus, if there are good moral reasons to distinguish irrational agents and those who face hard choices—and these moral reasons are among those about which we are most confident and committed—it does not follow that we must therefore excuse everybody or be guilty of incoherence. It would be absurd to claim that irrational agents are determined but rational agents are not, or that agents in hard-choice situations are determined but those in easy-choice situations are not. This would make no more sense than saying that small children are determined but adults are not. It is metaphysically preposterous to believe that children are determined but that somehow determinism loosens its grasp on human beings as they mature. Determinism is no internal threat at all to the coherence and consistency of holding people responsible and blaming them.

If the truth of determinism were the defining characteristic of excusing conditions, then everyone or no one would be responsible. The genuine reason human beings are considered more responsible as they mature is that they become more rational. The behavior of legally crazy people is no more or less determined by the laws of the universe and antecedent events than the behavior of people without disorders. The former are simply less capable of rationality in some contexts. People who accede to a threat made at gunpoint are no more determined than the desperado making the threat; the former faces a choice too hard to bear; the latter does not.

Much of the debate about determinism and responsibility has been framed in terms of whether the agent "could have done otherwise" or whether "alternative possibilities" were open to the agent. The basic notion appears straightforward. If all events are the determined product of the laws of the universe operating on antecedent events, then only one outcome is ever possible, and there are never alternative possibilities. The agent could not have done otherwise and therefore cannot be responsible. But alternative possibilities thus cannot explain the excuses we have because determinism generalizes. People with mental disorders or small children, for example, do not lack alternative possibilities in the relevant way, but are able to call on them as disorder loosens its grip or as they reach the age of responsibility. If alternative possibilities are necessary for responsibility but inconsistent with determinism, then no one can be responsible if determinism is true. "Alternative possibilities" is not a sensible way to talk about why we do and do not excuse and why we should and should not excuse.

We do talk colloquially about people having no choice and sometimes mean that they could not have done otherwise (I discuss these issues in detail in the section on lack of choice). For now, however, we should recognize that it is important when using such locutions to distinguish between their metaphorical and literal meanings and that neither depends on the truth of determinism. A reflex movement, for example, is not a matter of choice: If the agent is neurologically intact and stimulated in the right way, the reflex simply occurs. The agent could not have done otherwise. Indeed, the agent did nothing at all, because a reflex does not qualify as a human action. In some cases, an agent faced with a very hard (or a very easy) choice may feel as if there is no choice, but this is metaphorical. If we excuse in the case of hard choices, the choice is hard because the agent faces unattractive alternatives, not because determinism is true. In any case, not all choices are hard. Or an agent who makes a delusional mistake about the facts, like the delusional self-defender, may think that only one possible course of conduct is a reasonable alternative. But such an agent does not lack alternative possibilities in the manner that determinism implies. If hard choice or mistake excused because determinism were true, all our choices would be hard or mistaken, and everyone would be excused. Once again, deterministic conceptualizations do not explain why we excuse, and what is worse, they are confused and confusing.

The Fundamental Psycholegal Error: Causation

An argument related to determinism, and subject to similar defects, is that if science or common sense identifies a cause for human action, including mental or physical disorders, then the conduct is necessarily excused. I refer to this mistaken belief as the *fundamental psycholegal error*: Causation is neither an excuse per se nor the equivalent of compulsion, which is an excusing condition (Morse, 1998a). For example, suppose that I politely ask the brown-haired members of an audience of mental health law specialists to raise their hands to assist me with a demonstration. As I know from experience, virtually all the brunettes will raise their hands, and I will thank them politely. These hand raisings are clearly caused by a variety of variables over which the brunettes have no control, including genetic endowment (being brown-haired is a genetically determined, but-for cause of the behavior) and, most proximately, my words. Equally clearly, this conduct is human action—intentional bodily movement—and not simply the movements of bodily parts in space, as if, for example, a neurological disorder produced a similar arm rising. Moreover, the conduct is entirely rational and uncompelled. The cooperating audience members reasonably desire that the particular lecture they are attending should be useful to them. They reasonably believe that cooperating with the invited lecturer at a professional meeting will help satisfy that desire. So, they form the intention to raise their hands, and they do so. It is hard to imagine more completely rational conduct, according to any normative notion of rationality. The hand raisings were not compelled, because the audience was not threatened with any untoward consequences whatsoever for failure to cooperate. In fact, the lecturer's request to participate was more like an offer, an opportunity to make oneself better off by improving the presentation's effectiveness, and offers provide easy choices and more freedom, rather than hard choices and less freedom (Wertheimer, 1987).

The cooperative audience members are clearly responsible for their hand raisings and fully deserve my "thank you," even though their conduct was perfectly predictable and every bit as caused as a neuropathologically induced arm rising. Although the conduct is caused, there is no reason consistent with existing moral and legal excuses that it should be excused.

If causation were an excuse, no one would be responsible for any conduct, and society would not be concerned with moral and legal responsibility and excuse. Indeed, eliminative materialists, among others, often make such assertions (Churchland, 1995; Skinner, 1971), but such a moral and legal world is not the one we have. Although neuropathologically induced arm risings and cooperative, intentional hand raisings are equally caused, they are distinguishable phenomena, and the difference is vital to our conception of ourselves as human beings. In a moral and legal world that encompasses both responsible and excused action, all of which is caused, the discrete excusing conditions that should and do negate responsibility are surely caused by something. Nevertheless, it is the nature of the excusing condition that is doing the work, not the fact that the excusing condition is caused.

The *causal reductio*—everyone or no one is responsible if causation underwrites responsibility—is often attacked by an argument that might be termed *selective causation* or *degree causation*. This argument asserts that only some behavior is caused or that different behaviors are caused to different degrees. The further claim is that only that subset of behavior that is caused or is caused to a sufficient degree should be excused (Morris, 1982). The metaphysics of selective or degree causation is wildly implausible, however. If this is a causal universe, then it strains the imagination also to believe that some human behavior somehow exits the "causal stream" or that some behavior is only "partially caused." All phenomena of the universe are presumably caused by the necessary and sufficient conditions that produce them. Moreover, just because we possess the scientific understanding to explain some events more fully than others, it does not follow that the former are more determined or caused. And comparative lack of causal knowledge about behavior is not an excusing condition in any case. The reason that we excuse children is not because we understand the causal antecedents of their conduct more thoroughly than the antecedents of adult behavior. To explain in detail why the argument that selective or degree causation should excuse is unconvincing and ultimately patronizing (Hollander, 1973) would require a lengthy digression from this chapter's primary purpose. I have made the argument in detail elsewhere (Morse, 1986) and shall simply assert here that good arguments do not support this position.

Abnormality

Abnormality per se, including psychopathological and pathophysiological variables, is not an excusing condition simply because it is part of the causal explanation for agent's conduct. Pathology can produce an excusing condition, such as irrationality. If so, the excusing condition pathology causes does the analytic work, not the existence of a pathological cause per se. Consider again the delusional self-defender, who kills in response to the delusionally mistaken belief that she is about to be killed. Such a killing is no more caused or determined than a killing motivated by any belief that one's life is endangered by a presumed unlawful aggressor. Crazy beliefs are no more compelling than noncrazy beliefs. A nondelusional but unreasonably mistaken self-defender who feels the same desire to save her own life would have no excuse for killing. Crazy beliefs may not be as easily rectifiable as mistaken beliefs, but this does not mean that they are more compelling. It means only that the agent is less capable of rationality. Talk of compulsion only confuses the issue. Once again, we excuse the former but not the latter because only the delusional self-defender is incapable of rational conduct. Finally, consider infancy as an excuse. There is nothing abnormal about normal childhood, yet normal children are not held fully responsible. What the delusional self-defender and the child have in common is not "pathological causation"; they have in common the absence of full capacity for rationality. Irrationality is the genuine excusing condition that is operative.

When agents behave inexplicably irrationally, we frequently believe that underlying pathology produces the irrationality, but it is the irrationality, not the pathology, that excuses. After all, pathology does not always produce an excusing condition, and when it does not, there is no reason to excuse the resultant conduct. To see why, imagine a case in which pathology is a but-for cause of rational behavior. Consider a person with paranoid fears for his personal safety, who is therefore hypervigilant to cues of impending danger. Suppose on a given occasion he accurately perceives such a cue and kills properly to save his life. If he had not been pathologically hypervigilant, he would have missed the cue and been killed. He is perfectly responsible for this rational, justifiable homicide. Or take the case of a hypomanic businessperson, whose manic energy and heightened powers are a but-for cause of making an extremely shrewd deal. Assume that business conditions later change unforeseeably and the deal is now a loser. The deal was surely rational and uncompelled when it was made, and no sensible legal system would later void it because the businessperson was incompetent to contract. Even when pathology or abnormal causation is uncontroversially a but-for cause of behavior, that conduct will be excused only if an independent excusing condition, such as irrationality or hard choice, is present. Even a highly abnormal cause will not excuse unless it produces an excusing condition.

The great danger of abnormality explanations is that they lead to question begging about responsibility. Once we believe that human action, such as molesting a child, is a sign or symptom of an alleged abnormality, such as pedophilia, it is too easy to assume further that the agent is not responsible. Intentional human conduct is assimilated to the purely anatomical or physiological signs and symptoms of diseases, such as involuntary movements, that are not human action and for which the agent is not responsible. The assimilation is a confusion, however, at least in a legal world that distinguishes human action from the other phenomena of the universe. For example, in *Kansas v. Hendricks* (1997) the Supreme Court simply assumed that a sexual predator could not control himself if sexual predation was the result of "mental abnormality." Even if *Kansas*'s definition of mental abnormality were not tautological and incoherent—and, alas, it was both (Morse, 1998b)—the presence of abnormality would not have resolved whether sexual predators are responsible. The general capacity for normative competence may be present or absent in the presence or absence of causal abnormality.

Lack of Free Will or Volition

Courts and commentators routinely claim that excused agents lacked free will or volition, but this is virtually always just a placeholder for the conclusion that the agent supposedly lacking this desirable attribute ought to be excused. To understand the argument better requires that we first examine the concept of will or volition.

Nonreductive theories of action uncontroversially posit that people act for reasons that are rationalized by desire-belief sets. Human action is based on practical reason, but it is notoriously true that practical syllogisms are not deductive. A person may have a desire-belief set that seemingly should ensue in a particular basic action, but the person may not act at all. When the person does act, how do desires, beliefs, and intentions lead to the bodily movements that we call voluntary acts? This is the mystery that the theory of the will or volition seeks to explain. In brief, an "operator" is necessary to get us from here (desires, beliefs, and intentions) to there (a bodily movement that we hope will satisfy our desires through action).

Theories of the will or volition have waxed and waned in recent philosophy. Under the influence of Gilbert Ryle (1949), for a short period the concept of the will was considered preposterous by the majority of action theorists, but in recent years, some such concept has become central to accounts of voluntary action. Some think that volitions are actions of the will (e.g., Ginet, 1990); some treat the will or volition as simply another type of intention or trying (e.g., Mele, 1992). Michael Moore (1993), a leading theorist of philosophy of action and its application to criminal law, has argued that the will or volition is a functional mental state that translates desires, beliefs, and more general intentions into "basic" actions, including resolving conflicts between intentions. This and similar functional accounts emphatically reject equating volitions with wants (G. Strawson, 1986). In sum, modern theories treat the will in one fashion or another as an executory function.

Once one understands the meaning of the will or volition, it becomes apparent that the excuses are not based on a defective will, understood as an executory functional state. The victim of a threat of death or a delusional self-defender who kills to save her own life are both able to execute the actions that will, respectively, save them from genuine or delusionally feared death (Fingarette & Hasse, 1979). People acting under duress or as a result of mental disorder and children are all able to execute their more general intentions. Even if an agent's body is literally forced to move despite his or her strong desire to remain still, there is no defect or problem of the will, there is simply no intention to execute and no act to excuse. Agents can be physically forced or psychologically compelled to act against their desires, or they can be irrational, but the executory state remains intact. Even in cases of so-called weakness of the will, the best explanation of an agent's acting contrary to his or her strongest desire, belief, or intention is that the agent's action is clearly the intentional product of a well-functioning will (Moore, 1993).

In some of these cases, of course, we say colloquially that the agent's will was overborne in the sense that either the agent was forced to move or felt that he or she "had to" act (whether or not contrary to his or her preferences), or that the will was operating in response to irrational reasons for action. But talk of the will being overborne is a misleading, metaphorical locution. As noted, volitions are not wants or desires: On the best theory they are a species of intention. Cases of no action and irrational and compelled action alike do not entail a problem with the will. Nonetheless, for various reasons some people undeniably seem to lack self-control, either more generally or in specific contexts. These people find it more difficult to behave themselves and are more disposed to offend than others who are better controlled. Still, the problem is not a defect in the will as an executory state of bare intention.

In almost all instances when lack of free will is given as the general explanation for the excuses, this assertion cannot correctly mean either that there is a defect in the agent's executory mental functioning or that action is irrational or compelled solely because it is determined or the product of universal causation. In a deterministic or universally caused world, some people are irrational and others are not; some face hard choices and others do not. Moreover, if determinism or causation is true and inconsistent with free will, then no one has this quality (or the opposite), and no one is responsible (or everyone is). Often, I believe, the "unfree" will claim is used rhetorically to buttress an insufficiently supported conclusion that the agent under consideration ought to be excused, because we all "know" that free will is a necessary component of, and perhaps sufficient for, moral and legal responsibility. This move creates a tautology, however, and a conclusory label, no matter how rhetorically powerful, does not provide justifications and criteria for excuse.

A more promising approach, although daunting, would be to enter the highly contested, technical literature on free will to see what can be made of the claim that lack of free will underwrites excusing. For example, one might say that only agents capable of rational self-reflection on their reasons for action possess free will (e.g., Clarke, 1992), and it is precisely this capacity that excused agents lack. Or one might say that agents acting under certain constraints, such as threats or strong, unwanted desires— just the types of conditions that often lead to claims for compulsion excuses —lack free will (Frankfurt, 1988). Note that such arguments are, once again, not addressed to defects in the agent's narrowly conceived executory functioning or to problems that the truth of determinism might create.

Rather, they are claims about the proper criteria for the moral responsibility of intentional agents—irrationality or compulsion, for example; they are decidedly not about automatons, mechanisms, or the lack of some desirable attribute or condition such as free will.

The most sophisticated attempt to rescue a volitional theory of responsibility uses hierarchical theories of motivation, such as those most famously deployed by Harry Frankfurt (1988). Properly understood, Frankfurt's account is really a theory of autonomy and thus does not address responsibility, unless the two notions are collapsed. Nonetheless, many legal writers have adopted Frankfurt's theory as a explanation of responsibility. The central notion is that we are responsible for actions only if they are produced by desires that we identify with or ratify by evaluating them according to higher-order desires. For example, some argue that agents lack the ability to act differently and do not choose to act unless they are identified with, assent to, or ratify their desires, as the hand washer, pedophile, and drug-dependent person presumably do not (Gardner, 1991). Although hierarchical accounts are attractive, the concept of identification is itself problematic and seems to do little work in the justification of excuse.

As Gary Watson (1987) has argued, higher-order volitions, understood as Frankfurt and he used the term, are just desires themselves, and there is no reason to make them the touchstone of deliberation or any other criterion for responsibility. Indeed, Moore (1993) and others reject the account of volitions as desires. Moreover, what seems to give higher-order volitions authority is that they are evaluative; they mark what we consider worthwhile. But one can fail to identify with what one values and behave in ways one does not value from a more general standpoint. Watson argues that defining an evaluational system just in terms of what one does without regret abandons an explanation of self-determination that is based on identification by evaluation. Watson concludes that the notion of identification is "elusive" and that defining it as a type of "brute self-assertion seems totally unsatisfactory" (Watson, 1987, p. 151).

Another difficulty with hierarchical theories of responsibility is that ratification or identification does not do the work for which it is designed. An intensely greedy person, who accepts greediness as part of himself or herself, may feel powerless in the face of temptation, even if we consider these desires normal (albeit undesirable). By contrast, a person with unwanted but weak pedophilic urges may have the ability to resist temptation, even if these urges are rightly called pathological. The identification criterion would condemn the former and excuse the latter, but this appears to be a perverse result that needs far more explanation. If we assume that the "identified" agent has the ability to resist, but the "unidentified" agent does not, then the ability to resist, not identification, is doing the work, and the empirical assumption about "resistance ability" needs further support (compare Mele, 1987).

It is not immediately apparent why identification is coterminous with the ability to resist, nor is it apparent that a person faced with even a dreadfully hard choice produced by his or her own wanted or unwanted desires is not choosing. For example, the American Psychiatric Association's (2000) definition of compulsive behavior defines it as purposeful and intentional (p. 462)—the agent is hardly an automaton. Finally, a person with unfortunate desires may have tried without avail to change and finally accepted his or her unpleasant fate because there is no alternative. Should this person become a candidate for enhanced moral appraisal because he or she has ratified those desires? After all, no "positive" evaluation occurs; there is simply "brute acceptance" because life provides no alternatives.

Perhaps most controversially, Nozick (1993) claimed that conflict between one's desires at different levels violates a formal rule of the rationality of desires. One can make conflicting first- and second-order desires consistent by modifying either. To use Nozick's example, if an agent whose first-order desire is to take drugs has a second-order desire not to have such a first-order desire, the agent can achieve consistency by abandoning either the desire for drugs or the desire not to have the desire. Indeed, it might be entirely rational to abandon the second-order desire if the agent believes that abandoning the desire for drugs would be far more difficult. Thus, hierarchical accounts of volitions do not provide independent reason to believe that agents suffering from untoward internal states should be excused.

Hierarchical accounts do not convincingly disprove the claim that the analogy of psychological compulsion to physical compulsion is metaphorical. Suggestions that the agent whose different orders of volition conflict has no choice beg the difficult empirical and moral questions concerning human abilities and what the law and morality can demand when choice is unjustifiably constrained.

In sum, trying to underpin excusing in terms of will or volitional problems or lack of free will is likely to be inaccurate, confusing, rhetorical, or in its best incarnation a placeholder for a fuller, more adequate theory of excusing conditions. The will and free will are not legal criteria, and agents in the criminal justice system would do well to dispense with using them in responsibility analysis and attribution.

Lack of Intent

Another claim is that excused agents lack intent. Once again, if *intent* is a conclusory term that means "responsibility," "blameworthiness," "culpability," or the like, it is unexceptionable, but the conclusion does no analytic work. But if intent is more properly treated as a mental state, the absence of which might excuse, then this claim is incorrect as a general explanation of excusing. Indeed, it is apparent that excused action is intentional, even in the most extreme cases in which morality and law alike hold that an excuse is fully justified. We are considering cases of action, not bodily movements resulting from irresistible mechanism or literal physical compulsion. Consider cases of duress in which the agent is threatened with death unless he or she does the wrong thing. The agent compelled to act by such threats clearly acts intentionally to do the alternative, rather than to face destruction. The agent's opportunity set is wrongfully and drastically limited in such conditions, and we would surely excuse him or her, but not because he or she lacked intent. The agent acted fully intentionally to save his or her life. For further support, consider the American Psychiatric Association's (2000) generic definition of compulsive behavior —for which morality and the law might wish to provide a compulsion excuse—as intentional and purposeful (p. 462). And consider again the delusional self-defender. She kills for irrational reasons, but she surely does so intentionally in the delusionally mistaken belief that she needs to do so to save her own life. Action is by definition intentional and is not excused because it is unintentional.

Lack of Choice

Some claim that responsibility resides in the ability to choose (Kadish, 1987) and that excuses are based generally on a lack of ability to choose or a lack of choice. Philosophers of mind and action dispute the precise contours of choosing, understood as an agent's mental act (compare Bratman, 1987, with Mele, 1992), but the technical intricacies of the concept are not central to the ordinary-language notion that might support excuse or exemption from responsibility. Nonetheless, even ordinary accounts of the concept of choice can be ambiguous. Understood as a mental act, sometimes it seems to refer to the act of deciding between (at least two) alternative courses of action (or nonaction); other times, choice as a mental act seems to be synonymous with acting intentionally (e.g., "I chose to go out for hominy grits").

Another concept of choice refers to a feature of the agent's world that might be described as the alternative courses of action, the opportunities to act differently, that are available. If you are in a jail cell, for example, you can choose among and act on many alternative courses of action open to you at most moments: You can sit on your bed, stand up, walk around, sing, listen to the radio, and so on, but you cannot choose to go out for ice cream. These ordinary uses of choice can help us understand why lack of choice or opportunity is an inaccurate or potentially confusing general justification for excusing. At the very least, the concept of choice cannot provide a general account of why mental disorder or other variables might excuse or exempt an agent from responsibility.

Neither mental act usage is promising as a general foundation. Virtually all agents seem unproblematically able to choose between alternatives. If there is a gun at one's head, one may find it exceedingly easy to choose to accede to the wrongful death threat. Similarly, the delusional self-defender could believe that killing is never right (her delusional beliefs may also include the belief that she is a saint) and choose not to kill, but if she is like most people, she will find it easy to choose to save her own life at the expense of a perceived wrongful aggressor.

In some cases, a nonculpably ignorant or irrational agent may not be aware that a choice is possible. One might then claim that, at least in this instance, the agent lacks the ability to make a choice. Although this is not an implausible claim, it is entirely dependent on other standard exculpatory conditions, such as ignorance and the excuse of irrationality, which are doing all the work. In other cases, the agent might claim that the irresistibility of a desire deprived him or her of the capacity to make a choice. Again, such a characterization is plausible. But assuming the validity of the claim about the strength of the desire, it seems more accurate to say, like the case of the agent acting under duress, that he or she was psychologically compelled to make the hard choice "threatened" by the strength of the desire. The agent did, after all, choose to yield to the desire. Indeed, the strength of the desire made the choice easy, and if he or she struggled with conflict about yielding, this underscores the presence of the capacity to choose. The American Psychiatric Association's (2000) generic definition of compulsive behavior as, *inter alia*, purposeful, intentional, and "designed to neutralize or to prevent discomfort or some dreaded event or situation" (p. 462) further supports the conclusion that the agent is able to exercise choice. Even if conflict remains unresolved, agents are able to exercise and implement choice (Levi, 1986). In cases of irresistible desire, then, some theory of psychological compulsion rather than lack of a capacity to choose is the possible justification for an excuse. If the terror of the choice or the intensity of the desire renders the agent unable to think such that no choice is possible, this is a rationality defect.

The other mental-action notion of choice uses lack of choice as a synonym for lack of intentional action, but this basis for excusing suffers from the same defects identified in the earlier discussions of the will and intention. Agents we excuse choose their acts in this sense—that is, they act intentionally—so they do not lack choice in the same sense. Thus, lack of mental capacity to make a choice will not furnish a general justification for the excuses.

Lack of choice as lack of alternatives or opportunity is more promising, but this meaning can be both literal and metaphorical: To avoid the ever-present lure of mechanism, one must distinguish the two. On occasion, literally no relevant alternative action is open to an agent, such as in cases of literally irresistible physical compulsion. But such genuine compulsion defeats the prima facie requirements of responsible action, which include a voluntary act. These are not the standard cases of excuse. For example, the bodily movements of people with mental disorders are not reflexes.

Those wishing to draw the analogy to examples of no literal choice claim that the agent had no "real" or reasonable choice. Indeed, we talk this way colloquially all the time. In brief, a hard choice is assimilated to no choice. For example, the person acting under sufficient duress has a choice—he or she might refuse to harm another, despite the awfulness of the threat—but he or she is a nonculpable victim of a wrongfully imposed hard choice, and we cannot fairly expect the person not to yield. For another example, the delusional self-defender had the option of doing nothing, but her mental disorder deprived her of the relevant information necessary rationally to understand her range of alternatives. After all, no homicidal person threatened to kill her. Even judged from her internal point of view, passively enduring the attack of a wrongful aggressor (all things being equal) is not a reasonable option that we can require of anyone. But once again, irrationality is the more fundamental excusing condition in this case. Even agents acting in dissociative conditions are excused primarily because they do not have full access to the reasons that bear on their conduct, which is a rationality defect rather than an inability to choose. Or if movements performed in dissociative states are not action, then there is a sense in which there may be no choice, but this is so because either the person has not acted at all and "choice" concerns action, or the person does not have access to the rational reasons for action.

Hard choice cases, independent of rationality defects, in which we cannot expect the agent to behave differently undeniably exist, but what does the excusing work is not a defect in the agent. Instead, we are making a moral judgment about when options are so wrongfully or nonculpably constrained that it is simply not fair to require the agent to behave otherwise. It is not that the agent literally was physically forced to do wrong and thus literally had no choice. Rather, as a moral matter, we might excuse because the choice the agent faced was too hard. Finally, even if hard choice situations explain why some agents might be excused, many agents we excuse, such as children and many people with severe mental disorders, are neither objectively nor subjectively in hard choice situations. Hard choice does not mean that the agent lacks the capacity to exercise choice, and lack of choice thus fails to furnish a general justification for excusing.

In conclusion, although colloquial talk about lack of choice is commonly used to characterize many cases of excuse and contains a grain of truth, it is often inaccurate and potentially misleading, as when the lure of mechanism leads to the conclusion that no difference exists between cases of no literal choice and cases of hard choice. Agents facing sufficiently hard choices should sometimes be excused, but not because they do not choose to do what they do. These cases are better analyzed directly in terms of ordinary justifications for excusing conditions, such as irrationality and compulsion.

Lack of Self-Control

Being out of control or lacking self-control is sometimes offered as the general theory that justifies excusing. Here, too, there is a grain of commonsense truth, but properly understood this explanation does not account for the excuses we have. It is certainly true that various intrapersonal and environmental variables make it easier for a person to behave well. If anger-provoking or evil-tempting situational variables never arise, one is both lucky and less likely to engage in wrongdoing. It will be easier to exert self-control and to be in control. All things being equal, the reverse is also true. Similarly, if an agent has an even temperament, moderate desires, lots of dispositional self-control mechanisms, plenty of empathy, and the like, he or she is more likely to be in control and to control himself or herself, even if provoked or tempted to do wrong. Nonetheless, these observations are almost tautologically true and tell us little about excusing in general. For even a combination of unfortunate dispositions and situational variables will not necessarily excuse. A hot-blooded person sorely provoked will not have an excuse if he kills the provoker, even if he both lacks self-control and appears out of control. If, alternatively, "lack of self-control" or "out of control" are synonymous with "lack of culpability," then we need to see why people might talk this way.

I have suggested that lack of normative competence and hard choice are the foundations of excuse. People who are normatively incompetent or face hard choice may, in a loose sense, be out of control or lacking self-control. That is, such people will surely find it particularly difficult to behave rightly. But not all variables that make it harder to behave rightly are prerequisites for responsibility. Morality and the law alike set a minimum standard for what is required for responsible action, and not everything that would help an agent to behave well is included in the standard. What this means, of course, is that if a person lacks protective predispositions and is exposed to an environment that increases the risk of undesirable behavior, it will, all else being equal, be considerably harder for this person to behave well than for a person who is more fortunately endowed and exposed to a more benign environment. Nonetheless, morality and current law do not excuse unless the agent is incapable of rationality or faced with a hard choice. Moreover, even if the agent is fully and rationally in control, as in the case of the agent acting under duress, an excuse will obtain if the agent faced a sufficiently hard choice according to our best normative theory about which choices are sufficiently hard.

Claims about so-called irresistible impulses, which are related to claims about volition or the will, are a subset of the self-control argument that appears to exert a hold on the popular mental health and legal imagination. For example, although an irresistible impulse or a volitional or control test is not a currently favored insanity defense criterion, it remains a test in some jurisdictions, and its intuitive appeal continues. But even if such a behavioral state as irresistible impulse exists in some cases, it is not generalizable to explain the excuses, and once again it is reducible to irrationality or hard choice claims.

Impulse control disorders are an established category of mental disorders (American Psychiatric Association, 2000, pp. 663–677), some of which, such as intermittent explosive disorder, kleptomania, pathological gambling, and pyromania, may produce behavior for which the agent will seek an excuse. Moreover, impulsive behavior is blamed for much criminal conduct and other antisocial behavior (Gottfredson & Hirschi, 1990). Thus, there is reason to believe that attention to problematic impulses and impulsivity should shed light on excusing. Once again, however, although the basic concepts appear clearly relevant, the potential for metaphor and confusion warrants caution.

Human beings incontrovertibly can be subject to momentary and apparently capricious passions that leave them feeling subjectively unfree and that seem to compromise their ability to control themselves. Such fleeting passions are often described as "impulses," which should be distinguished from dispositional impulses that are generally characteristic of the agent, which professionals usually describe as "impulsive" or "compulsive" (McCown & DeSimone, 1993). Both impulses and compulsions are often thought to have the potential for coercive motivational force (Ainslee, 1992). Such observations, however characterized, are within the domain of common sense. The question is how these commonplaces bear on the general justifications for excusing.

Impulses are desires, fleeting and unconsidered desires to be sure, but simply desires nonetheless. If an agent acts to satisfy such a desire, doing so will surely be an intentional act executed by an undeniably effective will, and there is no reason to believe that determinism or universal causation plays a special role in such cases. The agent may have a strongly felt need to satisfy the impulse, but why is this different from standard cases of people desiring to fulfill momentary strong desires? What would it mean to say that such a desire was literally irresistible? The lure of mechanism is clearly at work but should be resisted. After all, why should a powerful desire—really, really, really wanting something—be equated with the patellar reflex?

One possibility is that such impulses create a hard choice, but if so, hard choice analysis will do the analytical work. A more likely possibility is that unthinking action in response to thoughtless or ephemerally thoughtful momentary desires should be judged irrational in appropriate cases. But is such action better understood as irrational or as simply non-rational? In any case, rationality problems and not some supposed irresistible quality of the desire would be the ground for excuse when action is impulsive. Finally, it is famously the case that even if impulses do have coercive motivational force, it is impossible to differentiate irresistible impulses from those simply not resisted.

An analogy used to attempt to demonstrate that impulses can be literally irresistible involves a person hanging by the fingernails from a cliff over a very deep chasm. The hapless person is strong enough to hold on for a while, but not strong enough to save her life by pulling herself up. As time passes and gravity and muscle physiology do their work, she inevitably weakens, and it becomes increasingly hard to hold on. Finally, it becomes impossible, and she falls to her death. The analogy asks us to think that the operation of strong impulses is like the combined effect of gravity and muscle physiology. At first, the sufferer can resist, but inevitably she weakens and yields, acting as the impulse allegedly dictates.

Brief reflection demonstrates that the analogy is flawed as an explanation of why impulses are irresistible. Unlike action to satisfy a desire, the fall is a genuine mechanism. We know that holding on indefinitely is physically impossible and that the ultimate failure of strength is not intentional. To further heighten the distinction, imagine the following hypothetical situation: A vicious gunslinger follows around a person and tells him that if he yields to an impulse, the gunslinger will kill him instantly. Literally no one, no matter how strong the impulse may be, will yield to it. One simply needs sufficiently good reason not to yield. Conversely, no one hanging by the fingernails from a cliff will fail to fall, despite having the best reason not to. Indeed, even if the vicious gunslinger threatened to shoot the person immediately if she started to fall, she would fall every time.

Impulsivity is a disposition or tendency to act with less forethought or steeper time discounting than most people of similar ability and knowledge (Dickman, 1993). Despite the apparent consensus on this general definition, more specific criteria or descriptions have proved elusive (McCown & DeSimone, 1993; Parker & Bagby, 1997). It is reasonable to assume, however, that at least some people who meet the general definition dysfunctionally suffer generally negative consequences as a result of impulsivity (Dickman, 1990). This assumption, too, is a commonplace and once again raises questions about why a disposition to act impulsively, as well as acting on an individual impulse, should excuse. The dispositionally impulsive agent surely acts intentionally, with an effective will, and not under any particular influence of determinism or universal causation. Like the agent acting in response to an individual impulse, the dispositionally impulsive agent acting impulsively may experience a hard choice or act irrationally or nonrationally, but literal irresistibility will not be the operative variable to justify an excuse.

I believe that the general intuition supporting an argument for excusing the dispositionally impulsive agent is not that desires are irresistible or that hard choice or irrationality exists. It is, instead, that the agent has the misfortune to possess a character trait that makes behaving oneself more difficult. Character does not furnish the basis for a legal excuse, nor could it (Lelling, 1998; Moore, 1990). In a precise sense, all our behavior is a function of our characters. If character excused in general, everyone or no one would be responsible. The law assumes that people who are characterologically thoughtless, careless, pugnacious, excitable, cowardly, cruel, and the like have sufficient general capacity for rationality to be held accountable if they violate the law. True, it may be harder for such people to behave well, but the law assumes that they do not lack the ability to do so, if they are minimally capable of rationality and did not face a hard choice. Finally, if such characterological considerations were the basis for excusing, it would be because we decided as a normative matter that certain prophylactic personality qualities were necessary for responsibility, not because the desires of characterologically disadvantaged agents were uniquely irresistible.

In sum, being out of control is just a conclusory synonym for lack of culpability that requires analysis to determine if it can explain the excuses we have. It fails to provide a unifying theoretical explanation that explains all the excuses, except in an extremely loose, unhelpful sense, and either irrationality or hard choice will explain those cases, such as irresistible impulse, to which it seems particularly to apply.

Unconscious Psychodynamics

Adherents of psychodynamic psychological theories claim that much of human behavior is caused by psychological motives that are dynamically unconscious, that is, prevented from reaching awareness because recognition of them would provoke dreadful anxiety and other unpleasant feelings. An example of such motivation might be the bank robber who robs to pay gambling debts, but who executes his crimes in a manner that virtually ensures that he will be caught. A psychodynamic formulation of the causes of his action might include the hypothesis that the robber unconsciously feels both unworthy and guilty and desires, without being aware of it, to be punished. As a result, and again without being aware of it, he commits his robberies in an unnecessarily incompetent manner, guaranteeing capture, conviction, and punishment. According to the dynamicist, such motivation is ubiquitous; there is, so to speak, a shadow system of practical reasoning of varying rationality that accompanies and influences our conscious motivations.

Dynamicists often suggest that unconscious motivation robs us of free will or that we are deprived of free will to the extent that unconscious motivation is operative. Indeed, it was precisely this type of claim that Sikora's psychiatrist advanced (*State v. Sikora*, 1965). We have already seen that free-will talk in such contexts is conclusory. But assuming the validity of psychodynamic hypotheses (Bonnie & Slobogin, 1980; but see Morse, 1982), what is their genuine bearing on excuses?

Dynamically unconscious motivation does not negate intention or choice. The hapless bank robber may not have been aware of the "real" reason he robbed the bank, but he surely chose to rob it and did so intentionally. Moreover, he was fully conscious in the legal sense because he did not rob during a dissociative state. If psychodynamic motivation did produce a lack of intention in some hard-to-fathom manner or, more plausibly but rarely, caused a dissociative state, then the absence of *mens rea* or dissociation is doing the analytical work. Unconscious motivation does not negate *mens rea* per se, however. In virtually all cases, claims that particular dynamic motivation negated *mens rea* will be simply incredible. No story about unconscious motivation, no matter how clinically or scientifically credible it may be, could or should convince us that an armed person who walks into a bank and demands money from a teller at gunpoint lacked the *mens rea* for bank robbery.

Should dynamically unconscious motivation have excusing force? There are two theories that might support such an excuse. The first is that an agent who is unaware of the real reason for conduct is not rational or normatively competent; the second is that dynamic unconscious motivation somehow compels the agent to perform the conduct so motivated. Consider our bank robber again. He was quite consciously rational: He knew the relevant facts about the world, and his conscious reason for robbing the bank—to obtain needed money—was certainly rational, if not laudable. Moreover, his will translated his desires into action. Is knowing the entire set of causes for one's behavior necessary for responsibility? All of us always are not fully aware of the present variables causally influencing us, whether they are of the dynamic type or not (Nisbett & Ross, 1980). This type of argument proves far too much.

If the presence of dynamically unconscious or other unperceived causes negated responsibility, no one would ever be responsible because such causes are always operative. Only if dynamically unconscious motives were distinguishable for these purposes would this theory have plausibility. But because dynamic motivation is ubiquitous, we would then need a further theory and method for distinguishing unconscious motives that render the consciously rational agent actually irrational from unconscious motives that did not have this effect. We would also have to distinguish rational and irrational unconscious motivation. Even if this were possible, which is entirely a tooth fairy hypothesis, the excuse would be irrationality.

There is one more irrationality approach to excusing the robber. He performed the robbery in a way calculated to fail to satisfy his conscious desire for money. How could he have messed up so badly unless he formed conscious irrational beliefs, say based on inaccurate perceptions, about the circumstances of the robbery? Such an account is plausible, and psychodynamic psychological evidence might be used to buttress the claim that the robber was "unable" to form true beliefs. Assuming, as always, the validity of the entire account, we must face again the problem of distinguishing incompetence from an inability to perceive accurately, to form true beliefs, and to reason well—in brief, to behave rationally. If this were possible, the excuse would be classically conscious irrationality.

Compulsion theory also addresses unconscious motivations. How might dynamically unconscious causes compel conduct? Why are dynamically unconscious causes any more compelling than the other, myriad causes of behavior of which we are unaware? Causes, even if they are unconscious, are not excuses. Of course, it is arguable that self-awareness about one's motives, in addition to self-awareness about what one is consciously doing, makes it easier to control conduct. But no sound empirical research demonstrates that this is true, and much research indicates that it is other variables that help people to change. The argument is really about an attribute, self-awareness generally, that may be self-protective, rather than about compulsion. Assuming that awareness of one's motives is self-protective, should lack of such awareness excuse in general or in the case of (some? which?) dynamic motives? If so, it would excuse because we believe that the self-protective variable is so important that lacking it deprives the agent of normative competence. But there is no reason to believe this in general or in the case of dynamic motivation in particular. "Compulsion theory," if supportable at all, reduces to a standard "hard to behave well" theory, much akin to irrationality claims. As long as an agent is consciously rational and not constrained by a perceived, blameless hard choice, the presence of dynamic unconscious motivation per se does not justify excuse.

RATIONAL PRACTICE

The thesis of this chapter, that the general capacity for normative competence is the touchstone of responsibility, has important implications for forensic practice. It suggests that much of the information forensic consultants provide fails directly to inform decision makers about the central question that confronts them. All potentially relevant evidence should be subjected to the same analytic scrutiny: Does the evidence validly contribute to the fact finder's understanding of whether the agent was capable of rationality in the situation under consideration? Rather than addressing all the possible types of potentially relevant information, let us consider as exemplars diagnosis, organic findings, psychological test results, causal explanations for an agent's behavior generally, and evidence of volitional impairment.

Diagnosis

The threshold requirement in all mental health law cases is a finding of mental abnormality. In practice, a respectable diagnosis will be required to support a finding that a mental health law applies, but does diagnosis do any important work in decision making? The question is always whether the agent was capable of rationality in the context at issue, and I suggest that a diagnosis per se does nothing further to answer that question independent of the behavior upon which the diagnosis is based.

The conclusion that a diagnosis is appropriate does not per se determine whether the capacity for rationality was sufficiently compromised to warrant the application of a mental health law. Assuming the validity of a medical model, a diagnosis does convey that the person diagnosed is "sick," "ill," or "disordered," but the presence of illness does not mean that legal incapacity is also present (American Psychiatric Association, 2000, pp. xxxii–xxxiii). Reaching the latter conclusion requires a normative judgment based on a commonsense evaluation of the agent's behavior. The fact finder therefore needs the fullest possible description of what the agent was or is perceiving, thinking, and feeling. If this description is available, as it should be if the clinicians and other investigators have properly done their work, then the diagnosis adds nothing further. Even assuming the reliability of a particular diagnosis, diagnosis does not enrich the necessary description because, as the *DSM-IV-TR* admits, a very wide range of behavior is possible among people with the same diagnosis, and "specific" diagnostic criteria are too general to convey precise information about the agent (American Psychiatric Association, 2000, p. xxxi–xxxii). For example, whether an agent actually had delusional beliefs and, if so, how much they entirely captured the agent's perception of reality are questions that might be important; whether the agent suffered from schizophrenia would add no further legally relevant information.

In general diagnoses risk the erroneous confusion of sickness with incapacity, and disputes about the appropriate diagnosis in a given case risk confusing the fact finder. Given how little useful information diagnoses potentially can convey, the risk does not seem justified. I have therefore argued in the past (Morse, 1978) and still believe that diagnostic terms should not be permitted in the courtroom, but I recognize that this is unlikely to become the general rule. At this point, I would be satisfied, with lingering regret to be sure, if forensic consultants understood the extremely limited contribution of diagnosis and conducted their evaluations and testified accordingly.

Organic Findings

Organic findings, wrapped as they are in the mantle of hard science, have the greatest potential to mislead, even if they are completely reliable and valid. For example, suppose a criminal defendant is discovered to have a brain tumor or suffers from "softer" brain damage earlier head trauma produced. Suppose, further, that there is a coherent account that causally links the organic pathology to the criminal conduct. The link will surely not be direct, however; there is no portion of the brain that inhibits the specific conduct that violates discrete provisions of a jurisdiction's penal code (Morse, 1996). Rather, the brain damage will have a more general behavioral effect, such as increased impulsivity, that will in turn increase the agent's predisposition to impulsive and perhaps criminal conduct. Believing in such cases that causal brain damage resolves the question of responsibility is the fundamental psycholegal error. The real question is whether the behavioral effects of the damage sufficiently compromise the agent's normative competence. The brain damage may convince the fact finder that the agent is not malingering, and there may be research evidence providing detailed, relevant behavioral consequences of such pathology. But neither pathology per se nor related research evidence can completely substitute for behavioral description or resolve the legal question.

Psychological Test Results

Various psychological tests are surely reliable and valid for the purposes for which they were developed, but are they legally valid? That is, do they provide added value to the fact finder beyond the value of a rich behavioral description, especially in cases in which the description and the test results diverge? No unitary answer is possible, and a test-by-test evaluation is required. I contend, however, that in most cases psychological tests will add very little and risk the potential for prejudice and confusion, because the fact finder will not be able independently to assess the virtues of the test. Furthermore, it is a commonplace of clinical psychology that if test results and real-world behavior diverge, the latter is almost always the more valid indicator of the agent's true capacities.

Some tests may on occasion provide helpful information that is otherwise unavailable. For example, an intelligence test may provide hard data to help a fact finder decide whether a person with developmental disabilities has sufficient comprehension to avoid the application of a mental health law rule. For another example, tests developed specifically to provide data about legal questions, such as the competence of people to make their own decisions about medical or psychological treatment (e.g., Grisso & Appelbaum, 1998), may also be helpful. Once again, however, such test results cannot fully replace behavioral description or per se resolve legal questions. People with the same tested IQ, for example, may differ substantially in their ability to respond rationally to the demands of a particular context.

Causal Explanations or Formulations

Melton et al. (1997) recently suggested that even scientifically unvalidated explanations, which they refer to as "stories," should be admissible because mental health professionals "are trained and experienced in generating explanations of abnormal behavior" that "may provide plausible explanations that would otherwise be unavailable" (p. 19). I will assume *arguendo* that these premises are true, but they do not explain what legal question the causal story helps resolve. Consider again, for example, an agent caused to become more impulsive by brain damage who impulsively commits a crime. Why does the causal story matter? Suppose the impulsivity was the result of genetic predisposition, inadequate socialization, unfortunate psychodynamic conflicts, or persistent stress. What difference would it make? The question is always whether the behavioral effect—impulsivity, in this case—supports an excusing condition such as irrationality. The cause of the behavioral effect is irrelevant. Even if the causal determinants are not conscious, or are dynamically unconscious or overdetermining, it makes no difference, as we have seen. The issue is whether at the time in question the agent was capable of rationality, an issue the causal story does not resolve. Causal stories do have the potential, however, to encourage fact finders to commit the fundamental psycholegal error and to conclude that causes excuse per se or because they somehow compel the conduct they cause. Fact finders should not be so encouraged.

Evidence of Volitional or Control Impairment

Previous sections have argued that volitional or control problems are often misconceived and are best understood as irrationality claims. Nonetheless, control tests continue to exist in a minority of jurisdictions, and they still have strong supporters who argue that justice demands their availability (Robinson & Darley, 1995). Moreover, evidence about alleged volitional or control problems may seem independent of the type of evidence necessary to judge the capacity for rationality or normative competence. How, then, does one assess volitional or control claims? To begin, the law will need a coherent account of what a volitional impairment is, independent of an irrationality defect. Remember that even if such claims are coherent, the agent is not a mechanism or an automaton. The allegedly out-of-control behavior will be human action. I propose to use for analysis the internal hard choice model suggested earlier, but I believe that the analysis that follows would fit any plausible theory.

The issue will always be the agent's psychological phenomenology—his or her perceptions, thoughts, and feelings. Needless to say, we cannot directly "read" each others' minds or measure the strength of desires or feelings. Most people are quite good at assessing the capacity for rationality, because the ability to identify and evaluate the rationality of other agents' reasons for action is necessary for minimally workable human interaction. But judging the strength of another's desires and dysphoria or fear of it is a herculean endeavor. Unlike rationality cases, there is no relatively clear phenomenon to match against a roughly consensual normative standard. Indeed, this is a major difficulty with the empirical model of internal coercion: We cannot distinguish between irresistible impulses and those impulses simply not resisted. No established metric exists to determine the magnitude of impulses, desires, or feelings. That two independent observers trained in the same system of assessment would agree that a subject exhibits desires of a certain strength or is unable to refrain from acting does not entail that the system is valid, and I am unaware of any such measurement system with established validity.

Furthermore, it is difficult to disentangle the strength of desires, the strength of temptations, and the capacity for self-control. There are numerous studies of impulsiveness and self-control in the psychological and psychiatric literature (see Baumeister, Heatherton, & Tice, 1994; Logue, 1988), and people do note apparent individual differences in these traits. Moreover, we talk about will, volition, and self-control as if these are independent psychological entities that are well understood and reliably identifiable. But the studies often contradict each other, measures of supposedly the same variable correlate poorly, findings are often based on suspect self-reports, and, most importantly, the studies do not address—and folk psychology does not know—whether and to what degree people are unable to refrain from acting (McCown & DeSimone, 1993). Diagnoses do not answer these questions either, including diagnoses of impulse control disorders. There is no reasonably uncontroversial understanding of these matters in psychology, philosophy, or folk psychology. Finally, we do not know how mental disorder affects the capacity to control oneself in general, apart from its more clear role in affecting perception and belief, which are variables central to normative competence.

The strongest contrary claims in the literature fail both conceptually and empirically. For example, in an article about legal insanity that purports to demonstrate that volitional problems can be reliably identified, Rogers (1987) provided allegedly "representative criteria for assessing volitional capacity" (p. 848). But inspection of the criteria Rogers proposed discloses that they are firmly in the camp of folk psychology, and most describe failures not of volition or the will, which are anyway never defined, but of rationality in the face of strong desires, emotions, impulses, and the like. For instance, Rogers's criteria ask, What did the defendant perceive as his or her alternatives to the criminal behavior? and Did the criminal behavior include planning or preparation? One criterion begs the question by asking, "Was the *loss of control* caused by a strong emotional state (e.g., rage reaction) or intoxication, or both?" (italics added; p. 848).

Neither any of these criteria individually nor all of them taken together can demonstrate with acceptable scientific precision whether and to what degree a defendant lacked the capacity to behave lawfully under the circumstances. Virtually all are designed to uncover rationality defects rather than defects of volition. In a later article using only four forensic psychiatrists as subjects—a tiny sample—Rogers and colleagues claimed that they empirically established that volitional criteria are practically important and logically distinct from cognitive criteria (Wettstein, Rogers, & Mulvey, 1991). But the article shows only that four psychiatrists believe that they can distinguish and use volitional criteria. No evidence demonstrates that they in fact used volitional criteria that are independent of rationality. Furthermore, nothing in the study, contrary to its blithe assurance, supports the conceptual validity of independent volitional problems.

Proponents of an independent coercion or volitional excuse often try to justify its adoption in the face of conceptual and assessment problems by correctly arguing that our understanding of the causes of cognitive or rationality defects is as primitive as the understanding of the etiology of inner coercion. Although true, this argument is irrelevant to the differential difficulty of assessing existing irrationality and inner coercion. The law's concern is not why glitches occur. Rather, to evaluate responsibility the law needs to know only whether and to what degree glitches occur. Understanding the causal background may in some cases be probative about whether an excusing condition exists, but no particular cause is required to justify the excusing condition. For example, if we are convinced that a person was in the throes of nonculpable irrationality, we excuse the agent, even if we do not know what produced the abnormality. The causes of cognitive and volitional defects are equally obscure, but we can empirically identify and assess each others' reasons for action far better than we can empirically identify and assess each others' strength of desire or intensity of feeling.

I have argued that internal coercion assessment may collapse into rationality assessment. Virtually all cases of so-called control problems that plausibly raise a substantial question about the agent's responsibility will prove on close analysis to be instances of irrationality, especially if the law continues to require that an abnormality is present. Even the commonsense basis for judging volitional problems is often a disguised rationality criterion. For example, the "policeman at the elbow" test, which is usually understood as a volitional standard, is, I think, better interpreted as a rationality test. Those who offend in the face of certain capture have either rationally decided for political or other reasons that the offense is worth the punishment, as in cases of civil disobedience, or they are irrational. We generally tend to conclude that intense internal coercion was operative if conduct was so irrational that we cannot make any sense of it; otherwise, why would the person do it? Again, however, rationality is the real issue, and the way to assess it is with the richest possible description of the agent's behavior in order to understand the agent's reasons for action.

Still assuming, however, that cases of pure internal coercion exist, the best we can do is to ask the actor to tell us how he or she felt and to observe psychophysical signs, such as trembling or perspiring, that may also provide a clue. The moral test asks only for phenomenological description and then weighs it in the moral balance. By comparing the intensity of the threatened dysphoria to the conduct chosen to avoid it, we can make the moral and legal decision whether an internal coercion excuse is warranted. We can attempt this without believing that the pseudoscientific enterprise of assessing so-called volitional problems is an empirically valid inquiry.

Many arguments used to explain why some people with mental disorders are not responsible for some conduct are conceptually confused and misleading, thus producing misguided forensic practice. Sound forensic practice depends on understanding the law's rationale for treating some people as not responsible and the type of evidence that is relevant to that rationale. Diagnoses, organic tests, psychological tests, and blithe causal stories, no matter how persuasive they may seem, are mostly unacceptable and often irrelevant shortcuts that cannot substitute for full behavioral description that exposes the reasons for action of the person potentially subject to application of a mental health law. In possession of such description, the fact finder can most reasonably make the necessary normative judgments.

CONCLUSION

Mental health law has for decades been bedeviled by incorrect, confusing, and misleading explanations of the basic rationale for generic mental health law rules, of why some crazy people are treated differently. This chapter tries to exorcise the bedevilments and to suggest that a better analysis would clarify both conceptual confusion and unsound forensic practice. The key is the agent's general capacity to grasp and be guided by reason—what I have termed the general capacity for rationality or normative competence. If decision makers and forensic professionals used this capacity as their focus, mental health law and practice would be more sound and just.

REFERENCES

Ainslee, G. (1992). *Picoeconomics: The strategic interaction of successive emotional states within the person*. New York: Cambridge University Press.

American Law Institute. (1962). *Model penal code*. Philadelphia: American Law Institute.

American Psychiatric Association. (2000). *Diagnostic and statistical manual of mental disorders* (4th ed., text revised). Washington, DC: American Psychiatric Association.

Baumeister, R. F., Heatherton, T. F., & Tice, D. M. (1994). *Losing control: How and why people fail at self-regulation*. San Diego, CA: Academic Press.

Bonnie, R., & Slobogin, C. (1980). The role of mental health professionals in the criminal process: The case for informed speculation. *Virginia Law Review, 66*, 427–522.

Bratman, M. (1987). *Intentions, plans, and practical reason*. Cambridge, MA: Harvard University Press.

Churchland, P. (1995). *The engine of reason, the seat of the soul: A philosophical journey into the brain*. Cambridge, MA: MIT Press.

Clarke, R. (1992). Free will and the conditions of moral responsibility. *Philosophical Studies, 66*, 53–72.

Dickman, S. (1990). Functional and dysfunctional impulsivity. *Journal of Personality and Social Psychology, 58*, 95–102.

Dickman, S. (1993). Impulsivity and information processing. In W. G. McCown, J. L. Johnson, & M. B. Shure (Eds.), *The impulsive client: Theory, research, and practice* (pp. 151–184). Washington, DC: American Psychological Association.

Fingarette, H., & Hasse, A. F. (1979). *Mental disabilities and criminal responsibility*. Chicago: University of Chicago Press.

Frankfurt, H. (1988). *The importance of what we care about: Philosophical essays*. New York: Cambridge University Press.

Gardner, J. (1991). The activity condition in criminal law. In H. Jung, H. Muller-Dietz, & U. Neumann (Eds.), *Recht und moral* [Law and morality] (pp. 67–80). Baden-Baden: Nomos.

Ginet, C. (1990). *On action*. New York: Cambridge University Press.

Gottfredson, M., & Hirschi, T. (1990). *A general theory of crime*. Stanford, CA: Stanford University Press.

Grisso, T., & Appelbaum, P. S. (1998). *Assessing competence to consent to treatment:*

A guide for physicians and other health professionals. New York: Oxford University Press.

Hart, H. L. A. (1968). *Punishment and responsibility.* New York: Oxford University Press.

Hollander, P. (1973, November). Sociology, selective determinism, and the rise of expectation. *American Sociologist, 8,* 147–153.

Kadish, S. H. (1987). *Blame and punishment: Essays in the criminal law.* New York: Macmillan.

Kansas v. Hendricks, 521 U.S. 346 (1997).

Lelling, A. E. (1998). A psychological critique of character-based theories of criminal excuse. *Syracuse Law Review, 49,* 35–97.

Levi, I. (1986). *Hard choices: Decision making under unresolved conflict.* New York: Cambridge University Press.

Link, B., & Stueve, A. (1994). Psychotic symptoms and the violent/illegal behavior of mental patients compared to community controls. In J. Monahan & H. Steadman (Eds.), *Violence and mental disorder: Developments in risk assessment* (pp. 137–159). Chicago: University of Chicago Press.

Logue, A. W. (1988). Research on self-control: An integrating framework. *Behavioral and Brain Science, 11,* 665–678.

McCown, W. G., & DeSimone, P. A. (1993). Impulses, impulsivity, and impulsive behaviors: A historical review of contemporary issues. In W. G. McCown, J. L. Johnson, & M. B. Shure (Eds.), *The impulsive client: Theory, research and treatment* (pp. 3–22). Washington, DC: American Psychological Association.

Mele, A. (1987). *Irrationality: An essay on akrasia, self-deception and self-control.* New York: Oxford University Press.

Mele, A. (1992). *Springs of action: Understanding intentional behavior.* New York: Oxford University Press.

Melton, G., Petrila, J., Poythress, N., & Slobogin, C. (1997). *Psychological evaluation for the courts* (2nd ed.). New York: Guilford Press.

Moore, M. S. (1985). Causation and the excuses. *California Law Review, 73,* 1091–1149.

Moore, M. S. (1990). Choice, character, and excuse. *Social Policy and Philosophy, 7,* 29–58.

Moore, M. S. (1993). *Act and crime: The philosophy of action and its implications for criminal law.* Oxford: Clarendon.

Morris, N. (1982). *Madness and the criminal law.* Chicago: University of Chicago Press.

Morse, S. J. (1978). Crazy behavior, morals, and science: An analysis of mental health law. *Southern California Law Review, 51,* 527–654.

Morse, S. J. (1982). Failed explanations and criminal responsibility: Experts and the unconscious. *Virginia Law Review, 68,* 973–1084.

Morse, S. J. (1986). Psychology, determinism, and legal responsibility. In G. Melton (Ed.), *The law as a behavioral instrument: Nebraska symposium on motivation* (Vol. 33, pp. 35–85). Lincoln: University of Nebraska Press.

Morse, S. J. (1994). Culpability and control. *University of Pennsylvania Law Review, 142,* 1587–1660.

Morse, S. J. (1996). Brain and blame. *Georgetown Law Journal, 84,* 527–549.

Morse, S. J. (1998a). Excusing and the new excuse defenses: A legal and conceptual review. In M. Tonry (Ed.), *Crime and justice: A review of research* (Vol. 23, pp. 329–406). Chicago: University of Chicago Press.

Morse, S. J. (1998b). Fear of danger, flight from culpability. *Psychology, Public Policy, and Law, 4,* 250–267.

Morse, S. J. (1999). Crazy reasons. *Journal of Contemporary Legal Issues, 10,* 189–226.

Morse, S. J. (2000). Hooked on hype: Addiction and responsibility. *Law and Philosophy, 19,* 3–49.

Nisbett, R., & Ross, L. (1980). *Human inference: Strategies and shortcomings of social judgment.* Englewood Cliffs, NJ: Prentice Hall.

Nozick, R. (1993). *The nature of rationality.* Princeton, NJ: Princeton University Press.

Parker, J. D. A., & Bagby, R. M. (1997). Impulsivity in adults: A critical review of measurement approaches. In C. D. Webster & M. A. Jackson (Eds.), *Impulsivity: Theory, assessment, and treatment* (pp. 142–157). New York: Guilford Press.

Robinson, P. H., & Darley, J. M. (1995). *Justice, liability and blame.* Boulder, CO: Westview.

Rogers, R. (1987). APA's position on the insanity defense: Empiricism versus emotionalism. *American Psychologist, 42,* 840–848.

Ryle, G. (1949). *The concept of mind.* New York: Barnes & Noble.

Skinner, B. F. (1971). *Beyond freedom and dignity.* New York: Knopf.

State v. Sikora, 44 N.J. 453, 210 A.2d 193 (1965).

Strawson, G. (1986). *Freedom and belief.* Oxford: Clarendon.

Strawson, P. F. (1982). Freedom and resentment. In G. Watson (Ed.), *Free will* (pp. 59–80). New York: Oxford University Press. (Original work published 1962)

United States v. Moore, 486 F.2d 1139 (D.C. Cir. 1973).

Wallace, R. J. (1994). *Responsibility and the moral sentiments.* Cambridge, MA: Harvard University Press.

Watson, G. (1987). Free action and free will. *Mind, 96,* 145–172.

Wertheimer, A. (1987). *Coercion.* Princeton, NJ: Princeton University Press.

Wettstein, R., Rogers, R., & Mulvey, E. (1991). A prospective comparison of four insanity defense standards. *American Journal of Psychiatry, 148,* 21–27.

Wolf, S. (1990). *Freedom within reason.* New York: Oxford University Press.

8

WHY JUVENILE JUSTICE WILL SURVIVE ITS CENTENNIAL

THOMAS GRISSO

Recent years have seen a substantial reform in the way U.S. society and law respond to juvenile offenses. The full impact of this reform, however, has been felt only in the past few years in a wave of statutory revisions of juvenile law that fully embrace the notion of punishment as the primary response to juvenile offenders. One sometimes hears that these revisions have so eroded the foundation of the aging juvenile justice system that it may not survive its centennial. This chapter challenges that prediction, applying to juvenile justice a perspective drawn from Appelbaum's (1994) important book *Almost a Revolution*.

Appelbaum's work, which traces the course of legal reform during recent decades, is of great value as a chronicle of the times and has special importance because of its analysis of what was being said—while those reforms were in process—about the probable outcomes of legal change. Appelbaum pointed out that the most provocative voices greatly overstated the problems of the past and tended to overestimate the impact of the anticipated reforms. Advocates of change, for example, described extreme conditions of past injustice and offered idealized reforms that they promised would correct them. Opponents of reform matched their zeal and predicted

167

that proposed reforms would result in chaos from which it would be impossible to recover.

In the end, neither side was right. The consequences of the civil rights reforms of that era, although creating important changes in many ways, turned out to be much less utopian or devastating than either side had anticipated. Each side had failed to recognize factors that ultimately slowed or modified the original reforms as they were played out in the context of real legal institutions dealing with real people's lives.

This insight can be applied to the current ongoing reform of the juvenile justice system. As in the reforms that Appelbaum described, extreme images abound in the popular press and in political and professional pronouncements. Responding to fears about a future in which teenage "superpredators" run wild, legislatures in almost every state have placed serious offenses by juveniles as young as 12 or 14 under the jurisdiction of criminal rather than juvenile courts (Snyder & Sickmund, 1995; Torbet et al., 1996). Trying to stem the tide, opponents predict that the current trend will bring us to a 21st century in which we brutalize and abandon children, ignoring their special needs when their transgressions are in fact a product of their immaturity.

If Appelbaum's thesis is right, neither view of the future will be correct. Both positions describe a fiction, plotted on a trajectory that presumes a simple continuation of recent events and that ignores factors that could slow, modify, or reverse current trends. This chapter explores those factors and concludes that although the present punitive trend in juvenile justice reform will leave its mark, some type of juvenile justice system based on the notion of mitigation in the sentencing of adolescents is likely to survive. What type of system will evolve is difficult to discern, but the chapter concludes with suggestions on how to influence its current process of change.

1970s: THE RIGHT TO A DEFENSE IN JUVENILE COURT

A series of events led to the current national wave of legislative reform in society's response to juveniles charged with serious offenses. These events can be described in three stages: (a) the introduction of due process rights in delinquency proceedings in the 1970s, (b) the challenge to the notion of individualized discretion in juvenile justice in the 1980s, and (c) the criminalization of juvenile offenses in the 1990s.

For over half a century the juvenile justice system was allowed to respond to juvenile offenders with a great degree of judicial discretion, consistent with the objectives of the system's founders. The founders constructed a system in which juveniles' offenses were excluded by statute from criminal court jurisdiction to allow a special juvenile justice system to meet the individual needs of youths in the name of rehabilitation. Rights of criminal defendants and due process of criminal courts were not necessary in a system that sought to save youths rather than to punish them.

The first major reform in juvenile justice was marked by U.S. Supreme Court decisions in *Kent v. United States* (1966) and *In re Gault* (1967). Based on a presumption of the juvenile court's historical abuse of its discretion, the Court concluded that youths had the worst of both worlds: an absence of due process protections from the state's power, which had been set aside in the interest of rehabilitation, and an absence of the rehabilitation that the system had promised. As a consequence, the Court said, youths charged with delinquencies in juvenile court henceforth would be able to claim many of the same rights and protections that were routinely provided to adult criminal defendants. The Court made it very clear, however, that the juvenile court's fundamental purposes—of providing services that would meet youths' developmental needs and of diverting youths from further delinquency—did not change.

Juvenile advocates hailed the cases as victories that would finally protect youths from problems in the system chronicled by important late-1960s treatises (e.g., Cicourel, 1968). As the 1970s proceeded, however, the juvenile court system was disoriented and conflicted. Juvenile courts struggled with an apparent anomaly: the right of delinquent youths to defend themselves against a justice system that was required to work for them in their best interest. Opponents loudly protested, claiming that this so-called progressive reform spelled the end of rehabilitation for delinquent youths. They argued that by arming youths with the tools to resist the custody of juvenile courts, the U.S. Supreme Court had guaranteed that juvenile courts could not fulfill their rehabilitation mandate.

As the decade wound down, however, neither the advocates nor the opponents of juvenile court due process reform were proved prescient. Fifteen years after *Gault*, the reformers could not claim that delinquent youths had acquired the legal protections of adult defendants, and the traditionalists had not seen the demise of individualized justice and rehabilitative ideals that they had feared. Certainly the juvenile court was transformed, but not as either side had anticipated. Two main reasons explain the unexpected outcomes.

First, appellate courts dealing with residual issues raised by *Kent* and *Gault* could not deny the fact that juveniles were not adults and that juvenile courts were not criminal courts. Juveniles might, for example, have Fifth Amendment rights, but when the waiver of their rights during police interrogations was questioned, many courts decided that juveniles were too vulnerable to waive those rights without additional protections (Grisso, 1981). When the rush to due process reached the question of juries, the U.S. Supreme Court in *McKeiver v. Pennsylvania* (1971) decided that the juvenile court was at least in part civil in nature and did not require juries.

Second, by necessity, juvenile courts eventually did find a way to accommodate the U.S. Supreme Court's dual mandates. While following the form of due process through the adjudication phase of delinquency proceedings, they allowed the traditional judicial discretion at the disposition phase, as justified by the historical focus of juvenile courts on the individualized needs of the youth.

In most juvenile courts, however, even the switch to due process adjudication was more form than substance. For example, courts tolerated and often reinforced the ambivalence of the new juvenile defense attorneys. Many attorneys opted to advocate for youths by straddling the fence between the role of defender against the state's powers and the role of guardian who collaborated with the court to determine what was best for the child (Genden, 1976; Puritz, 1995; Stapleton & Teitelbaum, 1972).

As a consequence, most juvenile courts in the 1970s evolved to provide a "junior version" of procedural rights for delinquent youths. For this reason, many due process questions went unanswered. No one, for example, took seriously the question of youths' competence to stand trial, even though one-third of the states nominally addressed the concept in their juvenile statutes (Grisso, Miller, & Sales, 1987). The notion that juveniles needed to be competent to exercise their rights at trial seemed unnecessary in what was still seen essentially as a civil proceeding aimed at meeting the needs of immature youths.

The shock waves of *Kent* and *Gault* had another effect during the 1970s that set the stage for the next phase of reform in the 1980s. The Supreme Court's condemnation of the juvenile justice system's record put the spotlight on the custodial conditions of programs that had passed as treatment for so many years. In the early 1970s, for example, Massachusetts gave itself one year to close its large training schools and to build a system of rehabilitation based on community programs and a few small, secure, intensive treatment facilities (Miller, 1991). Later, the new system was found to be fairly effective in reducing recidivism. In the meantime, however, the consensus of scholarly reviews arising during the 1970s was that nothing worked in the world of juvenile rehabilitation programs (Martinson, 1974). Fifteen years after *Gault*, therefore, delinquent youths had at best a modicum of protection from arbitrary custody. Once their delinquency had been adjudicated, however, they were largely unprotected from the potential for arbitrary placement—under the guise of a concern for their individual needs—in programs for which there was little evidence of effectiveness in rehabilitation.

1980s: FROM INDIVIDUALIZED DISPOSITIONS TO DETERMINATE SENTENCING

The second phase in the modern reform of the juvenile court focused on reducing the remaining discretion of judges in the disposition stage of juvenile delinquency proceedings. Reformers argued that juvenile courts were meting out arbitrary and disproportionate sanctions, primarily punitive in nature, cloaked as decisions based on judges' notions of the individual rehabilitation needs of youths (Morse & Whitehead, 1982). Reformers said this decisional masquerade not only was a pretense, especially in light of the lack of rehabilitation that ensued, but also was rife with abuses that were played out along racial and socioeconomic lines. Moreover, the apparently capricious variations in dispositions did not reliably hold youths accountable for their offenses.

To remedy the situation, the task forces formed by the Twentieth Century Fund and the Juvenile Justice Standards Project of the Institute of Judicial Administration and American Bar Association Joint Commission on Juvenile Justice Standards (1980) both called for determinate sentencing of juveniles in providing punishment that was proportional to the seriousness of the offense. Opponents decried the potential effects of these proposals on the objectives of juvenile justice, fearing that these changes would produce a fundamental reorientation of the juvenile court toward punishment as its chief mandate (Moore, 1987). They feared that rehabilitative dispositions tailored to the nature of each youth would be abandoned or relegated to a low position in the court's priorities. The objections, however, were not very loud. Many clinicians, for example, construed the reform as potentially therapeutic because it could promote in youths the notion of personal responsibility and a sense of fairness in the system, which could actually further rehabilitative objectives.

Few immediate changes were wrought by the notion of fair punishment as a juvenile court objective. By the end of the 1980s, only a minority of states had taken the opportunity to restructure their juvenile laws to make punishment a formal priority of the juvenile court or to specify mandatory sentences for juvenile offenses. But the arguments for determinate sentencing had a significant impact in a broader sense by establishing what Feld (1988) called the "principle of offense." Even in states that did not change their statutes' purpose clauses, definitions of legal procedures and outcomes were increasingly based on the nature of the offense rather than on the needs of the young offender.

In addition, scholars of the 1980s used the mounting call for an offense-based system to emphasize the need for a fundamental change. The scholars claimed that the shift toward offense-based sentencing no longer provided juvenile courts a "best interests" rationale for a junior version of due process and underscored the need for full procedural justice. Feld (1984), for example, called for abolition of the juvenile court so that youths would receive the full procedural protections of criminal courts. Melton's (1989) proposed reform was less drastic but equally substantial, calling for a "new juvenile court" with a type of due process that would recognize and respect the maturing capacities of adolescents and not treat them paternalistically as immature children.

Neither Feld nor Melton were adverse to offense-based rules, as long as they were administered fairly. Nevertheless, both scholars retained the notion that sentences, even when offense based and determinate, should be mitigated. They believed in the viability of a logic of diminished culpability for crimes by adolescents that need not be based on a trade-off for rehabilitation. Zimring (1982) best captured this argument in his notion of a "jurisprudence of semi-autonomy" that treated the period of adolescence as a "learner's permit"—a time during which society should recognize a mitigated response to youths' inevitable errors while they are first trying out the decision-making abilities and social potentials that they have only recently acquired.

From the task forces at the beginning of the 1980s to calls for juvenile justice reform by the end of the decade, the common theme was an acceptance of two notions: (a) that youths' potential for rehabilitation was no longer a viable basis for a system of juvenile justice and (b) that adolescents in general were sufficiently mature to be held accountable for their illegal acts. Moreover, adolescents were perceived as worthy of the same procedural rights as adult defendants in recognition of their personhood and, according to many developmental psychologists, their capacities for autonomous decision making.

Before the 1980s closed, however, U.S. society experienced a wave of juvenile violence that spread across cities and the front pages of newspapers, a deluge that would turn these rational arguments into a very slippery slope and would become the context for the major juvenile justice reforms of the 1990s. The fine points in the arguments of the previous decade's juvenile advocates were reduced by law-and-order retributionists to a simpler message: Violent youths were responsible for their actions and had no claim to either rehabilitation or mitigation.

1990s: THE CRIMINALIZATION OF YOUTH VIOLENCE

Legal reforms of the juvenile justice system in the early 1990s were the most sweeping of any since *Gault* and far more swift. Public fear was fanned by media portrayals of juvenile "superpredators." Urged by the public to do something, legislatures opted for taking violent juvenile offenders out of the hands of juvenile courts. By the mid-1990s, reviewers of the reforms found that almost all states had recently modified their statutes to expedite the criminal court trial and sentencing of more youths, for more types of offenses, at increasingly younger ages (Singer, 1996; Snyder & Sickmund, 1995).

For judicial transfer to criminal court, offense-based criteria were broadened, age-based criteria were lowered, transfer hearings were mandated, relevant criteria were expanded, burdens of proof were shifted to the defense, and standards of proof for transfer were reduced. Even more dramatically, however, the reforms diminished the judicial discretion around youths' transfer to criminal court. Three-quarters of the states changed their laws to exclude many serious offenses by youths from juvenile court jurisdiction, sending them automatically to criminal court (Feld, 2000). About one-fifth of states decided to allow prosecutors the option of filing charges against youths in criminal court for serious offenses (Torbet et al., 1996).

Proponents claimed that putting youths in criminal court was the only way to respond to the wave of youth violence that threatened society. They argued that youths who committed "adult" offenses deserved "adult" penalties, that the public needed protection from dangerous youth offenders, and that youths would be deterred by the realization that they could no longer fall back on the weakness of the juvenile court's limited jurisdiction to rap their knuckles with a year or two in training school. Allowing criminal courts to sentence these youths as adults would, proponents said, ensure that they were held accountable. Opponents, on the other hand, foresaw the end of rehabilitative responses to juvenile offenders as a dissipation of energy in punishment at the expense of efforts for prevention. Many youths who would otherwise naturally desist from illegal activity near the end of adolescence would now be transformed into criminals. To opponents, this amounted to an act of abandonment at a time when youths most needed guidance. A society that abandons its youths, the argument went, cannot survive for very long.

An evaluation of these claims is premature at this point, considering that the changes toward criminalization of juvenile offenses have been in place for only a few years. Any research on the effects of these reforms would be misleading without an elapse of time sufficient to study the reforms in ways that could produce reliable follow-up data. When the story is told, however, we likely will find that both sides were wrong. On the one hand, the new statutory transfer schemes will not make the public feel safer and will not consistently punish young violent offenders. On the other hand, we will not see the end of rehabilitative efforts or mitigation in sentencing of youths, much less the demise of the juvenile court.

THE FUTURE OF JUVENILE JUSTICE REFORM

Whatever the outcome of the current reform, there will always be a juvenile court, because we will always need a special legal mechanism to respond to children in need of services, status offenders, and first-time property and minor assault charges. If these cases were placed under the jurisdiction of the criminal court, their sheer volume would inevitably create a special division of the criminal court and modifications in existing criminal law to deal with such cases—in effect producing a new juvenile court. What is in question, then, is whether habitual or serious violent offenses by juveniles will be part of the future juvenile court's responsibility. There are at least two reasons to believe that transfer schemes designed to punish youths as adults probably will not survive for the full range of offenses to which they now apply: the costs of transfer and public disaffection with harsh punishments.

Costs of Transfer

Large-scale transfer of youths to courts designed to punish them as adults will be frustrated by a number of predictable negative consequences associated with implementation. As courts begin to apply the new transfer laws, they encounter demands and costs that were not factored in during legislation, demands that will eventually threaten to outweigh the expected benefits. For example, the transfer of juveniles to criminal court obviously increases the processing caseload for criminal courts. In Florida, up to 7,000 youths were transferred in a recent year—nearly 10% of the police referrals for felonies by juveniles (Snyder & Sickmund, 1995). In such circumstances, courts are likely to find ways to reduce the caseload that eventually will counteract the legislative intent. Anecdotally, this shifting has occurred in at least some jurisdictions, where virtually all referrals to criminal court involving juveniles are reverse waived, or transferred back to juvenile court, an option that is available in many states but about which there are few statistics.

In some states transfer rates have either remained the same or decreased under new laws that were designed to increase them (U.S. General Accounting Office, 1995). This result may be explained partly by increases in prosecutorial discretion about transfer that have turned the transfer option into a negotiable item in plea agreements, allowing youths to avoid transfer by turning state's witness against cohorts or by pleading guilty in juvenile court to crimes that there is reason to doubt they ever committed.

For youths who reach criminal court and are not reverse waived, new issues are arising concerning 13- and 14-year-olds' competence to stand trial and the fact that existing criminal statutes typically do not have a procedure for dealing with incompetence due to immaturity. When youths are tried in criminal court, conviction rates vary across the states (U.S. General Accounting Office, 1995). In some states, they are as high as adult conviction rates, but in others, such as Missouri and New York, the reported conviction rates are 25% to 50%—lower than adult conviction rates and much lower than conviction rates in juvenile court for similar levels of offense. When youths are convicted in criminal court on serious violent charges, they are very likely to be incarcerated in some states, whereas only one in four will be incarcerated in other states (U.S. General Accounting Office, 1995).

The legislatures' criminal penalties for youths are not playing out uniformly in practice, as they were likely intended. This trend may be in part due to what Walker (1989) has dubbed the "law of criminal justice thermodynamics": An increase in the severity of a penalty will result in less frequent application of the penalty. In this case, to gain the appearance of "getting tougher on youths," legislatures may have ensured that a few youths will be held more accountable while, because of the burdens on the criminal court, many more youths will be held less accountable than they otherwise might have been. This result cannot produce a beneficial outcome for crime prevention, and future statistics that acknowledge this outcome would certainly not be well received by the public.

Public Disaffection With Harsh Punishments

There is reason to believe that the public's perception of the value of harsh punishment in the form of criminal sanctions for violent juvenile offenders will eventually go sour. At some point in the next few years, there will likely be a turning of the tide and a call for penalties that once again recognize the lesser maturity of adolescents. In his book *The Cycle of Juvenile Justice*, Bernard (1992) demonstrated a repetitive pattern of changes over the past two centuries in attempts to deal with juvenile offenders, alternating between harshly punitive responses and rehabilitation-based responses of various kinds. Because neither response tends to change the public's perception of the rate of juvenile violence, the response that has been predominant at any given time eventually has lost favor and has been repudiated in exchange for the alternative. This pattern, if correctly identified, suggests that we should prepare for another swing of the pendulum away from policy that focuses one-sidedly on harsh punishment for juvenile offenders.

One might expect that recent reports of decreases in violent offenses would maintain public satisfaction with the new "get-tough" laws for juvenile offenders, supporting claims that harsh punishment is working. Public opinion, however, usually is not as impressed with statistics as it is moved by cases. In the late 1990s, my local newspaper announced an extraordinary 10% decrease in the annual violent offense rate, including a dramatic decrease in juvenile murders in Boston. The article, however, appeared at the bottom of the page, beneath three other articles that formed a wall of words and pictures describing (a) a Boston jury's decision that Eddie O'Brian, a quiet, well-behaved altar boy arrested at age 15 and transferred to criminal court, was guilty of first-degree murder when he entered the home of some friends while they were out and stabbed their mother 98 times; (b) the arrest of a 16-year-old in Mississippi who opened fire on his girlfriend at school, killing her and another youth and wounding six others; and (c) the arrest of a disturbed 15-year-old for killing an 11-year-old who had come to his front door selling candy.

These cases are rare but obviously shocking. They evoke images that are more frightening for many people than those of the "superpredator": the images of the boy two doors down the street in the house with the white picket fence who never did anything wrong until he suddenly and inexplicably went berserk. No laws that claim to get tough with juveniles will ever have an impact on the occurrence of these cases, and the media will continue to report them sensationally and regularly. Citizens may have these cases in mind at the approach of the next cycle of change in juvenile justice, when they decide that the new get-tough laws are not working and that something else must be done. Public dissatisfaction, together with the justice system's own frustrations regarding the costs of handling large numbers of juvenile offenders as adults, is likely to create a context for reorienting society's response to juvenile offenders once again.

Despite the recent criminalization of juvenile justice, some evidence suggests that the public never completely abandoned the notion that the responses to juvenile offenders should be different than the treatment of adults. In most communities, an intuition persists that adolescents are different from adults and that their degree of maturity is insufficient to provide them the full decision-making status and criminal responsibility of adults. One study, for example, found that the public was quite willing to give very harsh sentences to 12- and 14-year-olds for serious offenses but was much less inclined to do so when given facts that recognized youths' dependency and vulnerability—for example, that the youths had been abused by parents (Stalans & Henry, 1994). A Boston public survey a few years ago indicated a majority belief that public safety demanded longer sentences than the juvenile court could give, extending well into the adult years. The same majority, however, felt that sentences for most juvenile violent offenses should not be the same as for adults and that those sentences should serve as a time for rehabilitative efforts that were not available to adult prisoners (DiNatale, 1994).

In fact, the most recent legislative efforts in juvenile justice reform seem to represent a movement in the direction of sentencing that Bonnie (1989) proposed a decade ago (see Frost & Bonnie, Introduction, this volume). Backing away from transfer as the only approach to modified sentencing for juveniles, some states have legislated special youthful offender sentences that extend into the youth's adult years but provide sentences that are shorter than adults would receive or mechanisms for discontinuing the sentence at age 21 if the youth has shown signs of reform. Some states have placed these sentencing options in the hands of juvenile court judges, whereas others have given them to criminal courts. A few states, like Massachusetts, have used these special sentencing schemes to do away with transfer to criminal court for everything except murder (Massachusetts General Laws, 1997). Youths for all other violent offenses are tried in juvenile court and, if found guilty, are sentenced by the juvenile court under either juvenile or criminal law. Those sentences can be modified when the youth reaches age 21, based on an analysis of the youth's record and progress up to that time.

PREPARING FOR THE NEXT REFORM

Assuming that the public will soon recognize that providing the same criminal sanctions for youths and adults is not a satisfactory solution to its concerns, what should we be preparing to do to capitalize on the opportunities for forging a better response to youths' violent offenses? Special violent youthful offender sentencing schemes probably present the best option on which to focus. An exploration of detailed specifications for these schemes is not possible here, but one concern is that they will evolve in ways that are not anchored in principles that recognize the special developmental status of adolescents. We can do some things to strengthen those anchoring principles.

First, we should be mustering arguments for diminished culpability (mitigation in sentencing) associated with adolescent status. Such arguments will be necessary to undergird a basic logic for special youthful offender sentencing schemes that are now more theoretical than empirical. It would, for example, help a great deal if we could in fact demonstrate developmental differences between adolescents and adults in the ways they make choices related to offending, as well as clearer developmental explanations for the phenomenon of desistence in offending for most delinquent youths during early adulthood.

Second, we should be ready to use the new sentencing schemes to ensure that youths who face the new extended youthful offender penalties receive full due process in legal proceedings against them. With the potential for punitive sentences that extend well into adulthood, no rational reason exists for anything less than the full protection associated with criminal adjudication, including the use of juries and the requirement that juvenile defendants must be competent to assist counsel (Grisso, 1997). Fulfilling this objective also requires a renewed commitment to the development of a competent bar for the defense of youths.

Finally, we should be ready to provide a model for special juvenile offender sentencing that leads to something other than junior correctional programs. These sentences should serve some developmental functions that adult correctional sentences do not. Getting into the programs may be offense based, but the process of getting through them should focus on the developmental tasks of late adolescence and early adulthood, and the process of getting out of them should be based on individual differences in development related to the desistence in offending that frequently accompanies maturation into adulthood.

The key is to forge a system that responds to the needs for public safety and the accountability of youths, while offering proper mitigation, due process, and rehabilitative services appropriate to the developmental characteristics of adolescents. The answer is not to return to a system of individualized justice based solely on a rehabilitative objective, but rather to capture the aspects of the present reform that have merit and modify them in pursuit of a system that recognizes the personhood and needs of youths.

REFERENCES

Appelbaum, P. (1994). *Almost a revolution: Mental health law and the limits of change*. New York: Oxford University Press.

Bernard, T. (1992). *The cycle of juvenile justice*. New York: Oxford University Press.

Bonnie, R. (1989). Juvenile homicide: A study in legal ambivalence. In E. Benedek & D. Cornell (Eds.), *Juvenile homicide* (pp. 185–217). Washington, DC: American Psychiatric Association.

Cicourel, A. (1968). *The social organization of juvenile justice*. New York: John Wiley.

DiNatale, L. (1994). *A survey of voter attitudes on juvenile crime in Massachusetts*. Unpublished manuscript, McCormack Institute, University of Massachusetts Boston.

Feld, B. (1984). Criminalizing juvenile justice: Rules of procedure for the juvenile court. *Minnesota Law Review, 69,* 141–276.

Feld, B. (1988). The juvenile court meets the principle of offense: Punishment, treatment, and the difference it makes. *Boston University Law Review, 68,* 821–915.

Feld, B. (2000). Legislative exclusion of offenses from juvenile court jurisdiction:

A history and critique. In J. Fagan & F. Zimring (Eds.), *The changing borders of juvenile justice: Waiver of adolescents to the criminal court* (pp. 83–144). Chicago: University of Chicago Press.

Genden, J. (1976). Separate legal representation for children: Protecting the rights and interests of minors in judicial proceedings. *Harvard Civil Rights–Civil Liberties Law Review, 11*, 565–595.

Grisso, T. (1981). *Juveniles' waiver of rights: Legal and psychological competence.* New York: Plenum Press.

Grisso, T. (1997). The competence of adolescents as trial defendants. *Psychology, Public Policy, and Law, 3*, 3–32.

Grisso, T., Miller, M., & Sales, B. (1987). Competency to stand trial in juvenile court. *International Journal of Law and Psychiatry, 10*, 1–20.

In re Gault, 387 U.S. 1 (1967).

Institute of Judicial Administration & American Bar Association Joint Commission on Juvenile Justice Standards. (1980). *Juvenile justice standards.* Cambridge, MA: Ballinger.

Kent v. United States, 383 U.S. 541 (1966).

Martinson, R. (1974). What works? *Public Interest, 35*, 22–54.

Massachusetts General Laws, ch. 119, §§ 54, 58, 74 (1997).

McKeiver v. Pennsylvania, 403 U.S. 538 (1971).

Melton, G. (1989). Taking *Gault* seriously: Toward a new juvenile court. *Nebraska Law Review, 68*, 146–181.

Miller, J. (1991). *Last one over the wall: The Massachusetts experiment in closing reform schools.* Columbus: Ohio State University Press.

Moore, M. (1987). *From children to citizens: The mandate for juvenile justice.* New York: Springer-Verlag.

Morse, S., & Whitehead, C. (1982). Mental health implications of the Juvenile Justice Standards. In G. Melton (Ed.), *Legal reforms affecting child and youth services* (pp. 5–27). New York: Haworth Press.

Puritz, P. (Ed.). (1995). *A call for justice: An assessment of access to counsel and quality of representation in delinquency proceedings.* Washington, DC: American Bar Association Juvenile Justice Center.

Singer, S. (1996). *Recriminalizing delinquency.* New York: Cambridge Press.

Snyder, H., & Sickmund, M. (1995). *Juvenile offenders and victims: A national report.* Washington, DC: Office of Juvenile Justice and Delinquency Prevention.

Stalans, L., & Henry, G. (1994). Societal views of justice for adolescents accused of murder: Inconsistency between community sentiment and automatic legislative transfers. *Law and Human Behavior, 18*, 675–696.

Stapleton, W., & Teitelbaum, L. (1972). *In defense of youth.* New York: Russell Sage.

Torbet, P., Gable, R., Hurst, H., Montgomery, I., Szymanski, L., & Thomas, D. (1996). *State responses to serious and violent juvenile crime: Research report.*

Washington, DC: Office of Juvenile Justice and Delinquency Prevention, National Center for Juvenile Justice.

Walker, S. (1989). *Sense and nonsense about crime*. Pacific Grove, CA: Brooks/Cole.

U.S. General Accounting Office. (1995). *Juveniles processed in criminal court and case dispositions*. Washington, DC: Author.

Zimring, F. (1982). *The changing legal world of adolescence*. New York: Free Press.

9

PSYCHIATRY AND THE DEATH PENALTY: A VIEW FROM THE FRONT LINES

SEYMOUR L. HALLECK

Participation by psychiatrists and other mental health professionals in capital sentencing has become indispensable under the new generation of death penalty statutes upheld by the U.S. Supreme Court in 1976 (Bonnie, 1980). As a result, providing testimony in the punishment phase of capital murder trials has become one of the more common forensic psychiatric functions in the criminal justice system. Because the role of the forensic psychiatrist over the past quarter-century has in many ways been determined primarily by forces that have reshaped the criminal justice system, rather than by internal changes within psychiatry or other mental health disciplines, this chapter begins with a brief discussion of the evolution of psychiatric criminology. I then focus on the practical aspects of using psychiatric testimony in death penalty litigation, drawing on my own experiences as a forensic psychiatrist.

EVOLUTION OF PSYCHIATRIC CRIMINOLOGY

Throughout the 1950s and 1960s, many psychiatrists believed that their contribution to the criminal justice system went beyond assisting the courts in determining mental capacities involving competence to proceed or criminal responsibility. They viewed themselves not as forensic psychiatrists but as psychiatric criminologists. These professionals believed that psychiatric treatment could be used to change the offender into a law-abiding citizen. Treatment of an individual whose mental disorder was manifested by criminal behavior was viewed not only as compassionate and just, but also as an effective method of protecting the public from violent behavior.

During those decades, psychiatric criminology had something of an evangelistic quality. Even forensic psychiatrists who did not directly treat criminals but rather confined their role to testifying about issues of criminal liability in the courtroom often had a therapeutic agenda. Many prominent psychiatrists of that era who testified for the defense in insanity trials hoped that finding offenders not guilty by reason of insanity would result in treatment and rehabilitation for the offenders. They recognized that the insanity plea was available to only a small number of offenders but believed that providing treatment for the most disturbed offenders in hospitals rather than in prisons could serve as a model for the rest of the criminal justice system and might eventually move it toward a therapeutic orientation.

A few psychiatrists during that time also sought to influence the manner in which the courts sentenced offenders. In some jurisdictions, psychiatric experts had enormous influence in helping determine the location, the conditions, and the degree of punishment for individual offenders. They often recommended specialized sentencing arrangements with the hope that those who could benefit from intensive psychiatric treatment would receive it.

Finally, there were practitioners, such as myself, who believed that offenders could be rehabilitated through psychiatric intervention. We chose to work in the prison environment, delivering treatment directly as opposed to trying to orchestrate it through testifying or making recommendations to judges. We sought to treat offenders under a mental illness model of management, based on restraint and rehabilitation rather than on desert and deterrence.

Our views led us to support indeterminate sentencing. Several indeterminate sentencing programs developed throughout the country during those decades. Even where pure indeterminacy did not exist, lenient parole provisions made it possible to release most offenders when there was evidence that they had been rehabilitated. These parole practices were a modified form of indeterminacy and encouraged mental health professionals enthusiastically to participate in the task of rehabilitation. Most of us who worked in indeterminate sentencing programs felt that they were quite effective. We were even able to produce some data to substantiate that belief (Pacht, Halleck, & Ehrmann, 1962).

The story of the demise of these programs is itself an interesting part of history, insofar as the programs were attacked both by liberals, especially civil libertarians who felt that they imposed too many infringements on the rights of offenders, and by conservatives, who felt that dangerous offenders were being released too soon (Group for the Advancement of Psychiatry, 1977). At any rate, by the 1970s, indeterminate sentencing programs based on the idea that offenders could be rehabilitated, and should be released as soon as they were, disappeared. (In the 1990s, new efforts to develop indeterminate sentencing programs for sex offenders have flourished, but these efforts focus almost entirely on restraint rather than on rehabilitation.)

To illustrate the enormity of the change that began taking place in the criminal justice system in the mid-1970s and that has continued to the present, it is useful to describe the correctional environment in the very late 1960s and early 1970s. At that time, although indeterminate sentencing was under attack, our correctional system still held to a belief in rehabilitation. Early parole was still an option, and professionals placed new emphasis on treating more criminals in the community. At that time, the majority of Americans were against the death penalty. Most strikingly, I was the only member of a governor's commission to plan for the future of criminology in 1971 who dissented from a recommendation that all prisons in Wisconsin be closed by the year 1990.

The situation has changed dramatically since that commission recommendation. Throughout the 1970s, commitment to the idea of rehabilitation diminished. Much attention was paid to the writings of Martinson (1974), who argued that rehabilitation in any form did not work. Both liberal and conservative criminologists began to advocate prioritizing retribution in the form of just deserts rather than of rehabilitation. The system moved gradually toward lengthy, fixed sentences, thus removing discretion from the judge and ultimately from the parole board. Commitment to rehabilitation can be sustained when sentences are fixed and short, but it is almost impossible to maintain when sentences are fixed and long. The idea that one can be psychologically helped by a year or two of treatment to function in the outside world does not mean very much when that change takes place in the first or second year of a 20-year sentence. Not only is the offender's motivation for seeking rehabilitation diminished, but the risk is also great that prolonged incarceration will undo the efforts of rehabilitation.

All of these trends were accelerated by society's fear of violent crime. The media has played a prominent role in fomenting this fear by repeatedly and increasingly focusing on violence and victimization. By the 1980s, the majority of Americans favored the death penalty. By the 1990s, public demands for more severe forms of punishment seemed to escalate on a yearly basis. As a result of these major changes in the criminal justice system, psychiatric criminology changed significantly in focus.

USE OF PSYCHIATRIC TESTIMONY IN DEATH PENALTY LITIGATION

Psychiatric testimony was used with increasing frequency in capital cases in the wake of the Supreme Court's decision upholding capital punishment under specified circumstances in *Gregg v. Georgia* (1976). In a series of decisions culminating in *Lockett v. Ohio* (1978), the Court ruled that, in accord with the Eighth Amendment, a sentence of death could be imposed only after an individualized sentencing hearing in which the defense was permitted to introduce evidence related to a wide variety of potentially mitigating circumstances. Psychiatric testimony can usually be helpful in elaborating the broad range of potentially mitigating factors in a given case. Furthermore, the use of psychiatrists to testify for the defense was undoubtedly influenced by the Supreme Court's decision in *Ake v. Oklahoma* (1985, pp. 83–84), which in part directed that funds be made available to the defense team to hire a psychiatric expert in a capital proceeding in which future dangerousness or mitigating circumstances were at issue. In addition, under most capital sentencing schemes, the prosecution must prove at least one aggravating circumstance in addition to the elements of murder. In states that define dangerousness as an aggravating circumstance, psychiatric testimony can be used to support a sentence of death (when such testimony for the prosecution is not prohibited by statute; Bonnie, 1980).

Psychiatrists who become involved in death penalty work, either for the defense or for the prosecution, may have strong opinions about the ethics of capital punishment. Certainly, Dr. James P. Grigson, who has testified for the prosecution in more than 100 death penalty cases in Texas, has been frank in viewing himself as a crusader helping to protect the public by ensuring that as many dangerous offenders as possible are executed. At the same time, psychiatrists who testify in mitigation are likely to have anti-death penalty views. My own view is that the presence of the death penalty fails to deter crime or to promote public safety. This utilitarian judgment is the main reason for my opposition, although I also have some moral objections to the death penalty and, perhaps due to my treatment-oriented medical background, believe that physicians should do everything in their power to relieve suffering and keep people alive without sacrificing public safety.

Professional and Personal Hazards of Death Penalty Work

It should not be surprising that those who participate in developing mitigation arguments for defendants should be motivated at least partly by ideological agendas. The work is tedious and unglamorous. It is conducted under difficult conditions; the defendants are usually housed in high-security settings with other violent inmates, and the interview frequently must be conducted in an uncomfortable cell or office. I have worked in a number of institutions in which I have not felt entirely safe. Prison officials are sometimes unsympathetic to those working for the defendant and may show their feelings by being somewhat cavalier about the expert's safety.

Testifying at trial has its own discomforts. Particularly when the defendant facing the death penalty has committed a heinous crime (and this is often the case), the expert can anticipate a vigorous cross-examination and a certain amount of unpopularity in the community. Although I have never received any direct threats related to capital mitigation work, the stares and expressions of the family members of the defendant's victims are sometimes disconcerting. The occasional publicity one receives from these cases may also have an adverse influence on other aspects of a forensic psychiatrist's practice. When a national newspaper reported that I had examined Timothy McVeigh, a defendant in the Oklahoma City bombing case, a local defense attorney for whom I was working on a civil case told me that if he had known about my role in McVeigh's case, he would not have hired me as an expert.

Finally, an expert working for the defense in a capital case lives with a foreboding that the defendant, who may come to seem more like a patient than a criminal, may die an unnatural death. In the course of working with capital defendants, I have found myself experiencing the same kinds of countertransference responses I would have toward ordinary patients. I am always surprised at how continued contact in a professional context generally makes any patient more understandable and ultimately more sympathetic. I have been on the losing side in a number of forensic cases involving other criminal and civil matters and usually respond with professional detachment. When death is the response to losing, however, it is hard to avoid a more visceral response. I have worked with three defendants who were executed (two of whom I knew only in the appellate phase of the proceedings), and I have felt a strong sense of loss in each of these cases.

For all of these reasons, many of the more prestigious forensic psychiatrists throughout the country avoid death penalty work. At one time, the reluctance to do capital case work might have been explained by the difficulty in receiving compensation commensurate with the forensic psychiatrist's usual fees. These days, however, many jurisdictions authorize reasonably generous hourly fees. The reluctance to participate in capital case evaluations can be attributed more aptly to the nature of the challenges presented by the work.

The attorneys for whom the forensic psychiatrist may consult also face serious hazards in doing capital case litigation. Typically, the defense attorneys who hire a psychiatrist to evaluate their client for mitigation purposes are already convinced that no other mental health defense, such as insanity or diminished capacity, will be available (although, of course, they will ask the psychiatrist to evaluate any potential defenses). I have found all of the lawyers with whom I have worked in capital cases to be conscientious and diligent. Some have strong anti-death penalty feelings. Others may support the death penalty but are committed to their client and to the right to a vigorous defense. All defense attorneys in death penalty cases know that if their client is sentenced to death, the appeals to that sentence may include an allegation that they provided ineffective assistance of counsel. Some attorneys, particularly those who oppose the death penalty, are quite sanguine in facing this probability; others are disturbed by it and may end up supporting the prosecution in the appeals process out of a sincere belief that they did the best they could. More significantly, I have often wondered how capital defense attorneys deal with frequent negative legal decisions that ultimately result in the deaths of clients with whom they have spent hundreds of hours through the trial and appeals process. Perhaps the heroic extent of their commitment as they move on to their next capital case shields them from overwhelming despair.

Practical Issues in Capital Mitigation Evaluations

The range of potentially mitigating factors within the expertise of a forensic psychiatrist is broad. Many state statutes list mitigating factors; in North Carolina, for example, statutory factors include the defendant being under the influence of a "mental or emotional disturbance" at the time of the crime or having impaired capacity to appreciate the criminality of his conduct or to conform his conduct to the requirements of the law, a variant of the American Law Institute's (1962) *Model Penal Code* insanity defense standard.[1] (See Gen. Stat. of North Carolina, Vol. 1B (Repl. 1981) §15A-2000.) Nonstatutory mitigating factors can be quite broad in scope but generally include issues such as abuse or learning disabilities in childhood or a past history of mental illness or deficiency or substance abuse. The Supreme Court has said that the sentencer must "not be precluded from considering, as a mitigating factor, any aspect of a defendant's character or record and any of the circumstances of the offense that the defendant proffers as a basis for a sentence less than death" (*Lockett v. Ohio*, 1978, p. 604). Defense attorneys generally tend to believe that their clients are much more emotionally disturbed than is accurate and sometimes have to be reminded that the mitigating factors present in their client are not exceptional.

One critical issue for the forensic psychiatrist is how much time to

---

[1] For ease of reading I refer to the defendant as "he," given that the vast majority of capital defendants are men.

spend with the client. There is a natural but regrettable tendency for the expert to devote more time to high-profile cases. Generally, 10 to 20 hours of face-to-face evaluation time is desirable. Less than 8 hours with the defendant is objectionable, although some defendants have little to say and are extremely difficult to interview. Although other mitigation specialists may interview family members and friends, it is always advisable for the forensic expert to interview close family members personally.

Attorneys who have done one or more death penalty cases before will generally be quite knowledgeable about what information to provide the psychiatric expert. Attorneys who are new to the process or who have done it rarely, however, may ask for guidance. Psychiatrists should insist that the attorney try to find through medical records or reports of others any evidence that indicates that the defendant has some type of mental illness. School and work records are important to provide a more objective version of the defendant's past history compared with information shared by friends and family members. All medical records as well as all previous records related to imprisonment are essential.

Most attorneys are willing to provide the psychiatrist with all of the information relevant to the crime and to the police investigation that followed it. A few attorneys, however, are quite reticent about revealing to the expert all of the details of the crime, including the defendant's statements regarding it, particularly when these details accentuate the heinousness of the offense. The attorneys are concerned that if the expert knows about incriminating details, he or she can be asked to testify about them on cross-examination. It is uncertain, however, that this outcome would be catastrophic for the defense. Generally, I have insisted on seeing all of the crime-related material that is available to the attorneys. Although most of it is not relevant to my opinion, the more I know about the details of the crime, the easier it is to hypothesize relationships between the defendant's mental condition and the criminal act.

In recent years, defense attorneys in capital cases have employed mitigation specialists who take detailed family histories and interview family members and other individuals who have been involved with the defendant throughout his life. The reports that these specialists prepare vary in their quality and utility. The forensic expert is wise to stay in close communication with the mitigation specialist, who is likely to have a more extensive and objective picture of the defendant's history. Often friends and relatives will be able to verify facets of the defendant's mental disorder that are not included in medical records and whose absence will almost certainly be attacked by the prosecution.

Psychological testing is almost always available in death penalty cases. Usually it consists of tests of personality functioning, such as the MMPI and one projective test such as the Rorschach Inkblot Test or Thematic Apperception Test (Murray, 1943). I have come to insist that all capital defendants also receive neuropsychological testing at as sophisticated a level as possible. Many capital defendants have histories of multiple head injuries, and many more have sustained brain damage as a result of substance abuse. A jury is more likely to be convinced that the defendant was organically impaired by hearing evidence of cognitive or perceptual damage that has been demonstrated by standardized testing.

Similar considerations apply to medical tests. In most cases, some type of imaging test of the brain is essential, such as an electroencephalogram. Juries are likely to be impressed by anatomical and electrophysiological evidences of impairment. Any serious physical disorder that could have affected the defendant's mental status should, of course, be documented.

Interview With the Defendant

A psychiatrist should begin the interview with the defendant by explaining the purpose of the examination and telling the defendant a little bit about himself or herself. Although psychiatrists should make clear that complete candor is highly desirable, they should also clarify that they will probably be testifying about the defendant under oath and that whatever he says may be revealed to the jury.

In actually conducting the examination, a psychiatrist should adopt a more therapeutic and empathic stance than he or she does in most of his or her other forensic work (I should acknowledge here that, unlike many forensic psychiatrists, I believe that it is possible to do a good forensic evaluation and be therapeutic while doing so). In facing death, these individuals often need support, and a good psychiatrist must be able to gain their trust. One factor that facilitates a somewhat therapeutic approach is a psychiatrist's awareness that he or she will have ample time to spend with the defendant. As a consequence, psychiatrists need not go through any ritualistic or organized pattern of history taking and mental status evaluation, but rather can let the interviews flow in a relatively free manner. There will be time available later to return to any loose ends. A highly verbal defendant should be permitted to talk with relatively little interruption for as long as several hours. The less structured, more therapeutic approach results in the defendant being more willing to reveal himself in ways that may ultimately be to his advantage. In the course of such a free-flowing interview, the relationship between defendant and psychiatrist takes on much more of a doctor-patient relationship than is usual in forensic work.

All of the individuals I have examined have had at least one Axis I or Axis II diagnosis from the *Diagnostic and Statistical Manual of Mental Disorders, Fourth Edition* (DSM-IV; American Psychiatric Association, 1994), even though there are instances when the only practical diagnosis is substance abuse. Quite often there is a history of mild to severe depression in the weeks or months preceding the crime. A few defendants I have evaluated have been, in my opinion, grossly psychotic, but there have also been individuals who were quite adept at covering up their psychosis for long periods of time and who appeared to function, at least marginally, at many of life's tasks. Some of these people appeared to be bipolar, and at least one met *DSM-IV* criteria for schizophrenia. A history of learning difficulties is common, as is a history of head injuries, usually accompanied by equivocal findings on neuropsychological testing. Severe emotional or physical abuse is present in the history of most capital defendants. Axis II diagnoses are often present. In one case, I testified that the only diagnosis I could make was that of an antisocial personality disorder. The defendant was spared the death penalty almost certainly not as a result of my testimony, but rather because the parents of the victim, who were Quakers, asked the jury to recommend life imprisonment.

Some defendants are extremely difficult to evaluate. Even when facing the death penalty, they cannot bring themselves to talk about abusive experiences or past episodes of emotional disturbance. It may take many hours of interviewing before the defendant reveals instances in his past life that are dystonic. I have sometimes felt, even after many hours of interviewing a defendant who truly did not wish to die, that he was still withholding information that might have been mitigating.

It is especially difficult to find mitigating circumstances in a defendant who proclaims his innocence. Little can be learned about a defendant's mental state at the time he was accused of committing an act of homicide if he denies ever having committed the crime. This problem can be complex, because frequently the capital mitigation expert will interview the defendant prior to the guilt phase of the trial, when the defendant may still hope to be acquitted of the offense. One female defendant whom I examined denied having committed the crime during the trial and in the penalty phase, in spite of overwhelming evidence of her guilt. I worked with her in the postconviction phase, when she continued to deny the crime or any evidence of mental illness. There was an unusual circumstance in this case; she was being treated by a psychiatrist during the time that she was poisoning one of her victims. The clinical notes, which were quite thorough, documented the existence of a moderately severe depression during the weeks and months when the crime was committed; at her insistence, however, the evidence was not offered in mitigation at trial. In the appeal of her sentence (which is still pending), the new attorneys argued that the failure to include the mitigating evidence constituted ineffective assistance of counsel.

A few defendants claim that they would rather be executed than spend their lives in prison. It is productive to discuss this issue with the defendant early in the evaluation process, because a preference for death might hinder the defendant's full cooperation. Sometimes it is useful to remind the defendant that if he were to change his mind after being sentenced to death, it is usually too late at that point to make a strong argument for mitigation.

Finally, a defendant who commits homicide for political reasons may have serious concerns that any testimony that leads to his being found mentally ill would diminish the perceived meaning of his political action. Attorneys have a difficult time knowing how forceful to be in urging these defendants to accept psychiatric testimony in mitigation. There is always a question as to how much of the defendant's reluctance is based on ideology and how much on mental illness.

Testimony in the Sentencing Phase

With regard to actual testimony, it is preferable to work with attorneys who allow psychiatrists to tell the defendant's story in as great a detail as possible—including a very thorough social history, a description of emotional issues involved in the criminal act, a thorough medical and psychiatric history, current mental status examination, and a diagnostic formulation—rather than those who stifle testimony. Jurors are unlikely to be impressed by a psychiatrist's descriptions only of a defendant's mental disorder. This is often true even when the illness is of psychotic proportions. Occasionally, attorneys have convinced me not to overemphasize the symptoms of a defendant's mental disorder for fear that descriptions of psychotic thinking and behavior may cause the jury to think of the individual as a dangerous person who should remain incarcerated, even when dangerousness is not a statutory aggravating circumstance.

Substance abuse seems to have almost no mitigating value when associated with a brutal crime, notwithstanding all the efforts of psychiatry to define substance abuse as a mental disorder. Some of the defendants with whom I have worked have had extraordinarily high blood levels of multiple legal and illegal drugs both during and preceding the crime. They would meet all of the medical criteria of substance abuse if they walked into a doctor's office. Even if the defendant has been repeatedly and unsuccessfully treated for substance abuse, I have seen no evidence that jurors consider a history of such abuse to be mitigating when arriving at their decision. Nor, in the past few years, has a history of physical or sexual abuse made much of a difference, unless the testimony comes from an abusing parent or relative during the penalty phase of the trial and speaks to the nature of the abuse.

It is hard to know how psychiatric testimony influences the jury's decision. In light of psychiatric testimony offered at trial, juries' decisions, whether for death or for life imprisonment, are often surprising. Undoubtedly, factors other than psychiatric testimony exert much more influence on the jury's decision, including the nature of the crime, evidence that the defendant was not the actual perpetrator of the crime (when there are multiple defendants), particular characteristics of the defendant that come across during the trial, and the skill of the defense attorneys (Sundby, 1997).

As many capital defense attorneys suggest, the most important task in avoiding the death penalty is to humanize the defendant. Psychiatrists effectively do this, not only because of their status as physicians, but also because of their skills in learning about the defendant's history, personality, and specific mental illness. Psychiatrists are also adept at presenting this information to others. The mitigating information should not be framed as an excuse, but rather as an acknowledgment that the defendant had an extremely difficult choice to make and ultimately succumbed to doing wrong.

If the defendant is sentenced to death, two other circumstances may require psychiatric evaluation. One arises when the attorneys who are handling the appeal wish to argue that counsel at trial was ineffective because of improper use of psychiatric testimony. The psychiatrist working with such attorneys may, by interviewing the client and culling through records, point out that there was ample evidence for the existence of mental illness that could have been presented as a mitigating factor but that was never described to the jury.

Psychiatrists may also work with defendants who have been sentenced to death and have waived their right to continue their appeals. Such a waiver puts the defendant in jeopardy of imminent death. Usually, attorneys are concerned about the defendant's competence to waive his appeals and ask the psychiatrist to do a competence evaluation. In two of the cases in which I have done such evaluations, both defendants quite rationally described the horrors and meaninglessness of their current existence as well as their depression and exhaustion from having to cope with living on death row. In both cases, I found the defendants competent to waive their appeals, and in both cases, the defendants were summarily executed.

CONCLUSION

Decades of work as a forensic psychiatrist in capital cases can take its toll. Still, death penalty cases provide professional challenges that are unique and demanding. Although the current criminal justice landscape is bleak for rehabilitation-oriented mental health professionals, opportunities still exist to relieve suffering and to keep people alive without sacrificing public safety in the process. The model of individualized sentencing still prevails in capital cases. Until the death penalty is abolished in this country, which is not likely to occur any time soon, evaluating capital defendants and testifying in capital sentencing proceedings will continue to provide the most important—and most trying—challenges faced by forensic psychiatrists and other mental health professionals.

REFERENCES

Ake v. Oklahoma, 470 U.S. 68 (1985).

American Law Institute. (1962). *Model penal code*. Philadelphia: Author.

American Psychiatric Association. (1994). *Diagnostic and statistical manual of mental disorders* (4th ed.). Washington, DC: American Psychiatric Association.

Bonnie, R. J. (1980). Psychiatry and the death penalty: Emerging problems in Virginia. *Virginia Law Review, 66*, 167–189.

Code of Virginia, § 19.2-264.3:1(F-G) (1999).

Gregg v. Georgia, 428 U.S. 153 (1976).

Group for the Advancement of Psychiatry. (1977). *Psychiatry and sex psychopath legislation: The 30s to the 80s* (Vol. 9, Publication No. 98). New York: Author.

Lockett v. Ohio, 438 U.S. 586 (1978).

Martinson, J. (1974). What works: Questions and answers about prison reform. *Public Interest, 35*, 22–45.

Murray, H. A. (1943). *The Thematic Apperception Test: Manual*. Cambridge, MA: Harvard University Press.

Pacht, A. R., Halleck, S. L., & Ehrmann, J. C. (1962). Diagnosis and treatment of the sexual offender: A nine year study. *American Journal of Psychiatry, 118*, 802–808.

Sundby, S. (1997). The jury as critic: An empirical look at how capital juries perceive expert and lay testimony. *Virginia Law Review, 83*, 1109–1188.

IV

ADVANCING KNOWLEDGE AND EXPERTISE

10

VIOLENCE RISK ASSESSMENT: A QUARTER CENTURY OF RESEARCH

JOHN MONAHAN AND HENRY J. STEADMAN

The field now known as "violence risk assessment" has developed during the past quarter century. In the early 1970s, the empirical study of what was then the "prediction of dangerousness" was getting under way. In 1970, Steadman and Cocozza (1974) completed a study of the Baxstrom cases, which centered on the degree of "dangerousness" of the 967 patients transferred from maximum-security correctional forensic hospitals to regular-security civil state mental health hospitals as a result of *Baxstrom v. Herold* (1966), the first case in mental health law decided on constitutional grounds. Embedded within Steadman and Cocozza's descriptive case study was the implicit question of the accuracy of the "predictions" made by the state psychiatrists who signed the court reports saying all 967 patients had mental illnesses and were dangerous. Later hospital and police reports, however, indicated that only about 20% of the patients were subsequently violent.

For our analysis in this chapter, it is the context of the Baxstrom research, rather than its results, that is important. The relevant context includes two essential components: (a) the state of empirical research on the prediction of dangerousness and (b) litigation from the mental health advocacy movement, whose beginning may best be identified with the landmark decision *Lessard v. Schmidt* (1972) in mental health law and the Willowbrook consent decree in the mental retardation field (*New York State Association for Retarded Children v. Carey*, 1983).

No one better captured the state of empirical research on these issues as the Baxstrom research was in full bloom than Halleck (1967) in his classic treatise *Psychiatry and the Dilemmas of Crime* (see also Halleck, chapter 9, this volume). Halleck observed,

> Research in the area of dangerous behavior (other than generalizations from case materials) is practically nonexistent. Predictive studies which have examined the probability of recidivism have not focused on the issue of dangerousness. If the psychiatrist or any other behavioral scientist were asked to show proof of his predictive skills, objective data could not be offered. (p. 11)

What helped make this empirical void so important from the law's standpoint was the spate of class action litigation successfully pursued by the young legal activists entering the mental health field in the late 1960s (see Brown, 1985). It is useful in tracing the evolution of violence risk assessment to realize how intertwined the law and research were at that time.

LEGAL APPROACHES TO RISK ASSESSMENT

Lessard v. Schmidt (1972) introduced "dangerousness" into civil commitment statutes as the sole basis for commitment. *Dangerousness* was defined as a high probability of inflicting imminent substantial physical harm based on a recent explicit act. This standard assumed that someone could make a connection between past and future behavior. In fact, to the contrary, the American Psychiatric Association concluded in its 1974 task force report *Clinical Aspects of the Violent Individual* that "psychiatric expertise in the prediction of 'dangerousness' is not established and clinicians should avoid 'conclusory' judgments in this regard" (p. 33). The main basis for the American Psychiatric Association's assertion was the Baxstrom research and the weak but consistent findings that the clinicians were wrong, at best, twice as often as they were right (Monahan, 1975). Thus, in the mid-1970s the mental health advocacy movement had established a legal criterion for civil commitment that it knew could not be met. It appears that this is exactly what the advocates of that time wanted; if no one could meet a legal standard of proof for dangerousness and if dangerousness was the only commitment standard, then no one could be committed.

This historical analysis highlights a linkage between empirical research and mental health law, and between constitutional law and mental health practice, that no longer exists. Concerns about whether predictions of violence make "good enough" predicates for detention now seem distant. During the decade that followed, courts across the country and, in particular, the U.S. Supreme Court answered with a consistent and thunderous no the question, Does a reliance upon clinical predictions of violence make an otherwise valid law unconstitutional? Two of the many cases relevant to this point—*Barefoot v. Estelle* (1983) and *Schall v. Martin* (1984)—serve as examples.

In 1978, Thomas Barefoot was convicted of the capital murder of a police officer. At a separate sentencing hearing, the same jury considered the two questions put to it under the Texas death penalty statute: (a) whether the conduct causing the death was "committed deliberately and with reasonable expectation that the death of the deceased or another would result" (p. 884) and (b) whether "there is a probability that the defendant would commit criminal acts of violence that would constitute a continuing threat to society" (p. 884). The jury's affirmative answer to both questions required the imposition of the death penalty. In *Barefoot v. Estelle* (1983), the Supreme Court considered the constitutionality of using clinical predictions of violence for the purpose of determining whom to execute. In an opinion upholding the Texas statute, Justice White wrote,

> [Barefoot argues] that his death sentence must be set aside because the Constitution of the United States barred the testimony of the two psychiatrists who testified against him at the punishment hearing. . . . [I]t is urged that psychiatrists, individually and as a group, are incompetent to predict with an acceptable degree of reliability that a particular criminal will commit other crimes in the future and so represent a danger to the community. . . . The suggestion that no psychiatrist's testimony may be presented with respect to a defendant's future dangerousness is somewhat like asking us to disinvent the wheel. In the first place, it is contrary to our cases. If the likelihood of a defendant committing further crimes is a constitutionally acceptable criterion for imposing the death penalty, which it is, Jurek v. Texas, 428 U.S. 262, 96 S. Ct. 2950, 49 L.Ed.2d 929 (1976), and if it is not impossible for even a lay person sensibly to arrive at that conclusion, it makes little sense, if any, to submit that psychiatrists, out of the entire universe of persons who might have an opinion on the issue, would know so little about the subject that they should not be permitted to testify. In *Jurek*, seven Justices rejected the claim that it was impossible to predict future behavior and that dangerousness was therefore an invalid consideration in imposing the death penalty. (pp. 896–897)

The Supreme Court thus upheld a process that relied on clinical risk prediction that contemporaneous research had asserted was inaccurate in two out of three cases.

The next year, in *Schall v. Martin* (1984), the Supreme Court upheld a New York statute that authorized pretrial detention, without probable cause, of an accused juvenile delinquent based on a finding that there was a "serious risk" that the juvenile "may before the return date commit an act which if committed by an adult would constitute a crime" (p. 255). The district court had invalidated the statute after reviewing the research literature and concluding that "no diagnostic tools have as yet been devised which enable even the most highly trained criminologists to predict reliably which juveniles will engage in violent crime," (p. 262) and the Second Circuit had affirmed. In reversing the Second Circuit, Justice Rehnquist, writing for six members of the court, stated,

> Appellees claim, and the district court agreed, that it is virtually impossible to predict future criminal conduct with any degree of accuracy. Moreover, they say, the statutory standard fails to channel the discretion of the Family Court judge by specifying the factors on which he should rely in making that prediction. The procedural protections are thus, in their view, unavailing because the ultimate decision is intrinsically arbitrary and uncontrolled.
>
> Our cases indicate, however, that from a legal point of view there is nothing inherently unattainable about a prediction of future criminal conduct. Such a judgment forms an important element in many decisions, and we have specifically rejected the contention, based on the same sort of sociological data relied upon by appellees and the district court, "that it is impossible to predict future behavior and that the question is so vague as to be meaningless." (pp. 278–279)

Again, the U.S. Supreme Court stated that despite research showing low accuracy rates, as a matter of law clinical risk prediction is an acceptable means of assessing dangerousness.

Little has changed since the 1980s. In *Kansas v. Hendricks* (1997), the Supreme Court, by a 5–4 vote, upheld a civil means of lengthening the detention of certain criminal offenders scheduled for release from prison. Kansas's Sexually Violent Predator Act established procedures for the civil commitment to mental hospitals of people who may not have a major mental disorder, but who have a "mental abnormality or personality disorder" (in Hendricks' case, pedophilia) that makes them "likely to engage in predatory acts of sexual violence" (*Kansas v. Hendricks*, 1997, p. 350). A *mental abnormality* was defined in the act as a "congenital or acquired condition affecting the emotional or volitional capacity which predisposes the person to commit sexually violent offenses in a degree constituting such person a menace to the health and safety of others" (p. 352). The language of the act implied the need for a violence risk assessment to determine which individuals meet the defined standards. In upholding Hendricks's civil commitment under the act, the Supreme Court emphasized two specific facts of the case: Hendricks's own admission of his uncontrollable urges and a risk assessment predicting high risk. The Court noted,

> Hendricks even conceded that, when he becomes "stressed out," he cannot "control the urge" to molest children. This admitted lack of volitional control, coupled with a prediction of future dangerousness, adequately distinguishes Hendricks from other dangerous persons who are perhaps more properly dealt with exclusively through criminal proceedings. (p. 360)

In *Hendricks*, the Supreme Court thus reiterated its approval of risk assessment as an acceptable determinant of civil commitment.

Like the courts, professional organizations have concluded that predictions of violence are here to stay. For example, the American Bar Association's (1989) *Criminal Justice Mental Health Standards* recommended that a person acquitted of a violent crime by reason of insanity be committed to a mental hospital if found currently to have a mental illness and to present "a substantial risk of serious bodily harm to others" (Standard 7-7.4). The American Psychiatric Association's (1983) model state law on civil commitment included the involuntary hospitalization of people with mental disorders who are "likely to cause harm to others." (p. 672). Likewise, the guidelines for involuntary civil commitment of the National Center for State Courts (1986) urged that

> particularly close attention be paid to predictions of future behavior, especially predictions of violence and assessments of dangerousness. Such predictions have been the bane of clinicians who admit limited competence to offer estimates of the future yet are mandated legally to do so. [However,] such predictions will continue to provide a basis for involuntary civil commitment, even amid controversy about the scientific and technological shortcomings and the ethical dilemmas that surround them. (p. 493)

The professional consensus is that predictions of future dangerousness will remain a significant element in legal decisions to restrict the liberty of individuals with mental disorders.

Now that the Supreme Court clearly has rejected constitutional challenges to risk assessment, tort law frames the legal questions asked of violence prediction (Monahan, 1993). *Tarasoff v. Regents of the University of California* (1976) is, of course, the landmark case in this area. Initially the subject of vilification by mental health professionals, the California Supreme Court's holding in *Tarasoff*, that psychotherapists who know or should know of their patient's likelihood to inflict injury on identifiable third parties have an obligation to take reasonable steps to protect the potential victim, has become a familiar part of the clinical landscape. Although a few state courts have rejected *Tarasoff* and others have limited its scope, most courts addressing the issue have accepted the essence of the "duty to protect," and several have even expanded that duty to include nonidentifiable victims (Appelbaum, 1988).

The duty to protect, in short, is now a fact of professional life for nearly all American clinicians and, potentially, for clinical researchers as well (Appelbaum & Rosenbaum, 1989; Monahan, Appelbaum, Mulvey, Robbins, & Lidz, 1994). One related unresolved legal issue is the development of professional standards for institutionalizing a potentially violent person or releasing that person from an institution (Poythress, 1990). Liability, rather than constitutionality, is the concern that motivates interest in the accurate prediction of violence in the mid-1990s.

SOCIAL SCIENCE APPROACHES TO RISK ASSESSMENT

Twenty-five years ago, only two published studies had addressed the accuracy of clinical predictions of violent behavior (Kozol, Boucher, & Garofalo, 1972; Steadman & Cocozza, 1974). Both studies looked at male forensic patients who had been institutionalized for lengthy periods of time. Both used long (four- to five-year) follow-up periods. Both used official records (arrest, rehospitalization, and ward reports) as the source of their criterion measure of violence. And both reported true-positive rates, or rates of accurate predictions of future violent events, in the 20% (Steadman & Cocozza, 1974) to 35% (Kozol et al., 1972) range.

Today, much more prediction research is available, and much of it involves both male and female civil patients who are subject to acute, rather than lengthy, hospitalization and about whom short-term, rather than long-term, predictions are made, with the predictions being validated by multiple-criterion measures. The conclusions reached by current researchers are somewhat more optimistic than those reached 20 years ago (e.g., Harris & Rice, 1997; Hart, Webster, & Menzies, 1993; Menzies, Webster, McMain, Staley, & Scaglione, 1994; Monahan, 1997; Mossman, 1994; Rice, 1997; but see Litwack, Kirschner, & Wack, 1993).

For example, Lidz, Mulvey, and Gardner (1993), in what is surely the most sophisticated study published on the clinical prediction of violence, took as their participants male and female patients being examined in the acute psychiatric emergency room of a large civil hospital. Psychiatrists and nurses were asked to assess potential patient violence toward others over the next 6-month period. Subsequent violence was measured using official records, patient self-reports, and the reports of a collateral informant in the community (e.g., a family member). Patients who elicited professional concern regarding future violence were found to be significantly more likely to be violent after release (53%) than were patients who had not elicited such concern (36%). The accuracy of clinical prediction did not vary as a function of the patient's age or race. The accuracy of clinicians' predictions did vary by gender, however. Their predictions of male violence substantially exceeded chance levels for patients both with and without a prior history of violent behavior. In contrast, the accuracy of clinicians' predictions of female violence did not differ from chance. Although the actual rate of violent incidents among released female patients (46%) was higher than the rate among released male patients (42%), the clinicians had predicted that only 22% of the women, compared with 45% of the men, would be violent.

A study by McNiel and Binder (1991) illustrates research predicting inpatient violence. They investigated clinical predictions that patients would be violent during the first week of hospitalization. Of the patients who nurses had estimated had a 0% to 33% probability of being violent on the ward, 10% were later rated by the nurses as having committed a violent act; of the patients who nurses had estimated had a 34% to 66% chance of being violent, 24% were later rated as having committed a violent act; and of the patients who nurses had estimated had a 67% to 100% chance of being violent, 40% were later rated as having acted violently. Although in both recent studies clinicians overpredicted the likelihood of future violent acts, they were far more accurate than their colleagues in the earliest studies.

Not only have research methods and findings changed during the past 20 years, but in important ways the research questions have changed as well. When the legal issue was the constitutionality of violence prediction, it made sense to focus on whether clinicians could accurately predict violence—that is, the validity of clinical prediction. However, after it became clear that courts, even when directly confronted with research findings of 20% to 35% accuracy (true-positive) rates, would uphold the constitutionality of laws that relied on clinical violence prediction, the research question began to shift from whether violence could be predicted to how violence prediction could be improved (Grisso & Appelbaum, 1992). Framed in this way, the answer for violence prediction has seemed to a number of researchers in recent years to lie in the same direction as the improvement of clinical prediction more generally—that is, in the use of actuarial methods. Borum (1996) pointed out that actuarial instruments have varying functions:

> At a minimum, these devices can serve as a checklist for clinicians to ensure that essential areas of inquiry are recalled and evaluated. At best, they may be able to provide hard actuarial data on the probability of violence among people (and environments) with a given set of characteristics, circumstances, or both. (p. 948)

Thus, over the years, changes in the focus of research on violence prediction have led to an emphasis on improving actuarial analysis.

A prime example of the use of actuarial data to predict violence on an acute inpatient ward is a study by McNiel and Binder (1994). They constructed an actuarial scale consisting of five variables, each scored yes or no, with one point given for each yes answer. The variables were

1. History of physical attack and/or fear-inducing behavior within two weeks before admission?
2. Absence of suicidal behavior (attempts, gestures, or threats within two weeks before admission)? (This item is checked if patient has *not* shown recent suicidal behavior).
3. Schizophrenic or manic diagnosis?
4. Male gender?
5. Currently married or living together? (p. 581)

Patients who scored three or above on this five-point actuarial scale were called "high risk," and patients who scored two or less were called "low risk." If "fear-inducing behavior" (i.e., "attacks on objects, threats to attack persons, or verbal attacks on persons") is included along with actual physical assault as "violence," 57% of the high-risk group were violent to others early in their hospitalization compared with 29% of the low-risk group (if one restricts the criterion to actual physical assault, the figures become 32% and 18%, respectively) (p. 581).

A noteworthy advance in the development of actuarial risk assessment to predict violence among forensic patients released into the community was reported by Harris, Rice, and Quinsey (1993; see also Webster, Harris, Rice, Cormier, & Quinsey, 1994). Participants included 618 men who were either treated or administered a pretrial assessment at a maximum-security forensic hospital in Canada. All had been charged with a serious criminal offense. A wide variety of predictive variables were coded from institutional files. The criterion variable was any new criminal charge for a violent offense or return to the institution for an act that would otherwise have resulted in such a charge. The average time at risk after release was almost 7 years. Twelve variables were identified for inclusion in the final statistical prediction instrument: (a) score on the Psychopathy Checklist (Hare, 1985), (b) separation from parents under age 16, (c) victim injury in index offense, (d) DSM-III schizophrenia, (e) never married, (f) elementary school maladjustment, (g) female victim in index offense, (h) failure on prior conditional release, (i) property offense history, (j) age at index offense, (k) alcohol abuse history, and (l) *DSM-III* personality disorder. For all variables except c, d, g, and j, the nature of the relationship to subsequent violence was positive. That is to say, participants who injured a victim in the index offense, who were diagnosed as schizophrenic, who chose a female victim for the index offense, or who were older were significantly less likely to be violent recidivists than other participants. If the scores on this instrument were dichotomized into high and low, the results indicated that 55% of the high-scoring participants committed violent recidivism, compared with 19% of the low-scoring group. The authors concluded,

> Clinical judgment can be improved ... through the use of actuarial information; this has been referred to as "structuring discretion." In this approach to decision making about an individual, an actuarial estimate of risk is used to anchor clinical judgment. More specifically, clinicians can use dynamic (changeable) information such as progress in treatment, change in procriminal attitudes, and the amount and quality of supervision in the postrelease environment to adjust the risk level computed by the actuarial prediction instrument. If adjustments are made conservatively and *only* when a clinician believes, on good evidence, that a factor is related to the likelihood of violent recidivism in an individual case, predictive accuracy may be improved. (p. 331; but see Quinsey, Harris, Rice, & Cormier, 1998)

As Harris et al. (1993, p. 331) noted, additional research is necessary to determine the degree to which the impressive validity of these actuarial predictions generalizes to other populations. Attempts at cross validating some other instruments have yielded negative results (Klassen & O'Connor, 1990).

Gardner, Lidz, Mulvey, and Shaw (1996) recently made an important methodological contribution to the use of actuarial information in predicting violence by civil patients in the community. They contrasted the usual regression equation model, in which points for various risk factors are summed to yield a prediction score to which cutoffs are applied (as in McNiel & Binder, 1994, and Harris et al., 1993), with newer "regression tree" methods:

> A regression tree is a structured sequence of yes/no questions that lead to the classification of a case. ... Statistical predictions requiring calculations may be infeasible in many clinical settings, while a decision procedure specified by a tree is easy to perform. A regression tree is also easy to grasp and explain because it generates a series of statements about a patient that provide reasons for the prediction. We therefore believe that clinicians will be more likely to accept regression trees than numerical formulas as methods for making actuarial predictions. (pp. 36–37)

The four yes/no questions contained in the Gardner et al. (1996) regression tree were (a) "Is BSI Hostility [score on the Hostility subscale of the Brief Symptom Inventory] greater than 2?" (b) "Is age less than 18?" (c) "Is the patient a heavy drug user?" and (d) "Are there more than 3 prior violent acts?" (p. 40). This regression tree identified a small group of patients (3% of the patient population) who committed violent acts at the high rate of 2.75 incidents per month.

As a final illustration of the use of actuarial approaches to improve the prediction of violence, the MacArthur Risk Assessment Study (Steadman et al., 1994) assessed a large sample of male and female acute civil patients at several facilities on a wide variety of variables believed to be related to the occurrence of violence. The risk factors fall into four domains. One domain consists of "dispositional" variables: the demographic factors of age, race, gender, and social class, as well as personality variables (e.g., impulsivity and anger control) and neurological factors (e.g., head injury). A second domain consists of "historical" variables, or significant events participants experienced in the past, such as family history, work history, mental hospitalization history, history of violence, and criminal and juvenile justice history. A third domain consists of "contextual" variables, which are indices of current social supports, social networks, and stress, as well as physical aspects of the environment, such as the presence of weapons. The final domain consists of "clinical" variables: types and symptoms of mental disorders, personality disorders, drug and alcohol abuse, and level of functioning. Community violence is measured during interviews with the patients and with a collateral that occur postdischarge in the community, as well as from official records.

The principal results of the MacArthur Violence Risk Assessment Study are reported in Steadman et al. (2000) and in Monahan et al. (2000). In brief, we were able to classify approximately three-quarters of the patients we assessed into one of two risk categories. "High violence risk" patients were defined as being at least twice as likely as the average patient to commit a violent act within the first 20 weeks following hospital discharge. "Low violence risk" patients were defined as being at most half as likely as the average patient to commit a violent act within the first 20 weeks following hospital discharge. Because 18.7% of all patients committed at least one violent act during this period, this meant that high violence risk patients had at least a 37% likelihood of being violent, and low violence risk patients had at most a 9% likelihood of being violent. Risk factors identified for the MacArthur instrument for given groups of patients included a screening version of the Hare Psychopathy Checklist (Hare, 1985), serious abuse as a child, and whether the patient was suicidal (which had a negative weight). Of the patients scoring in the low-risk category on this instrument, 4% committed a violent act during the follow-up, whereas of the patients scoring in the high-risk category, 44% committed a violent act. In the two most extreme low and high groups, the rates of violence were 0.0% and 58.5%, respectively. Even more dramatic results were reported in Monahan et al. (2001).

FUTURE ISSUES IN VIOLENCE RISK ASSESSMENT

The past 25 years—in particular, the past decade—have produced an enormous amount of research on what is now known as violence risk assessment. The field today, with its emphasis on actuarial assessment, bears little resemblance to the field dominated by clinical prediction in the early 1970s. Monahan and Steadman (1994), reflecting on recent developments in decision theory and in public health, suggested that research on violence prediction in the coming decades, if it is to advance the state of the science, must have seven characteristics:

1. "Dangerousness" must be disaggregated into its component parts, the factors used to predict violence ("risk factors"), the amount and type of violence being predicted ("harm"), and the likelihood that harm will occur ("risk").
2. A rich array of theoretically chosen risk factors in multiple domains must be chosen.
3. Harm must be scaled in terms of seriousness and assessed with multiple measures.
4. Risk must be treated as a probability or frequency estimate that changes over time and context.
5. Priority must be given to actuarial research that establishes a relationship between risk factors and harm.
6. Large and broadly representative samples of patients at multiple, coordinated sites must participate in the research.
7. Managing risk as well as assessing risk must be a goal of the research (Heilbrun, 1997, p. 347).

We would add one additional item to this list. Risk communication as an essential adjunct to risk assessment is an issue that we believe will become increasingly salient over the next two decades (Monahan & Steadman, 1996). After a clinician, perhaps with the assistance of an actuarial risk device, has estimated the likelihood of harm that a person represents, how is the clinician to communicate this information to decision makers? The National Research Council (1989) defined *risk communication* as

> an interactive process of exchange of information and opinion among individuals, groups, and institutions; often involves multiple messages about the nature of risk or expressing concerns, opinions, or reactions to risk messages or to legal and institutional arrangements for risk management. (p. 322)

Currently, the language used to assess and communicate risk varies widely. For example, most states have adopted the language of the California "dangerousness standard": that to be admitted to a mental hospital against his or her will, a person must have a mental disorder and be "dangerous to self or others" (Brakel, Parry, & Weiner, 1985). But some states refer to the "likelihood" that the individual will cause "serious harm" (Brakel et al., 1985, p. 34). The National Center for State Courts (1986) spoke of "predictions of violence" (p. 409), and the American Bar Association (1989) made reference to "a substantial risk of serious bodily harm to others" (p. 418). Finally, one influential court decision phrased the issue in terms of a "probability" of future harm (*Barefoot v. Estelle*, 1983).

"Dangerousness," "likelihood," "risk," and "probability," therefore, often have been used fungibly to refer to the level of uncertainty of undesirable outcomes that may occur if some people with mental disorders are left at liberty. However, the extensive literature in the area of risk perception and behavioral decision theory (e.g., Slovic, Fischhoff, & Lichtenstein, 1982) has uncovered many subtle and anomalous effects that suggest that these various terms may not be fungible. They may, in fact, have differential effects on the judgments rendered by clinicians and courts. For example, in Slovic and Monahan (1995), adults were shown hypothetical stimulus vignettes describing mental patients and were asked to judge (a) the probability that the patient would harm someone else, (b) whether the patient should be categorized as "dangerous," and (c) whether coercion should be used to ensure treatment. Probability and dangerousness judgments were systematically related and were predictive of the judged necessity for coercion. However, judged probability was strongly dependent on the form of the response scale, suggesting that probability was not represented consistently and quantitatively in the respondents' minds.

For example, one response scale for expressing the probability of harm went from 0% to 100% in 10% increments. Another response scale went from "less than 1 chance in 1,000" to "greater than 40%" (p. 51). Judgments about the probability of violence were much higher using the first response scale than using the second. In a second study, Slovic and Monahan (1995; see also Slovic, Monahan, & MacGregor, 2000) replicated these findings with experienced forensic clinicians as participants. How to communicate the results of clinical risk assessments to relevant audiences so as to facilitate effective risk management and risk reduction is an issue that the field will likely begin to confront over the next two decades.

CONCLUSION

If three federal reports are to be believed, the next two decades may see much more research on the prediction of violence than the past two. The first of these reports, the National Institute of Mental Health's *Caring for People with Severe Mental Disorders: A National Plan of Research to Improve Services* (1991), stated as follows:

> The practices of criminal and civil commitment rest on untested assumptions about violent behavior and about the ability of professionals to predict such violence. More study is needed on the extent of clinical accuracy in predicting violence by individuals with severe mental illness. Particularly informative would be investigations of the relation-

ship between violence and specific aspects of mental illness—for example, the nature, extent, and effect of delusions. (p. 44)

The second report, the National Research Council's *Understanding and Preventing Violence* (Reiss & Roth, 1993), recommended major increases in federal support for research on violent behavior. Prominent among the new research initiatives proposed by the Council to the Centers for Disease Control, the National Institute of Mental Health, the National Institute of Justice, and the National Science Foundation was the intensified study of risk factors for violent events.

Finally, the National Institutes of Health (NIH, 1994) released a *Report of the Panel on NIH Research on Antisocial, Aggressive, and Violence-Related Behaviors and Their Consequences* that included the following among its recommendations: "NIH should substantially increase its funding for research on antisocial, aggressive, and violence-related behaviors and their consequences. Focus on preventive intervention studies and on social, legal, and ethical issues is essential" (p. 18).

The context of research on violence risk assessment in the future may be quite different than the context of past research. We hope that the following are among the questions asked by researchers over the next 25 years:

1. How are issues of community violence being played out in the new world of "managed" care provision? For example, under managed care, are community members who are assessed to be at high risk for violence more likely than others to have access to care (because of the provider's fear of tort liability if care is denied), or more likely to be denied access to care (because of the higher costs of care for this difficult group of patients)? And can the use of formal risk assessment tools affect both access to services and the types of services to be reimbursed for (e.g., anger control training)?

2. What degree of legal restrictiveness will be placed on high-risk people receiving mental health care in the name of "community supervision" or "community monitoring" to ensure the public health and safety? Can the use of formal risk assessment tools by clinicians or courts affect these patterns of risk management?

3. In light of the strong relationship in many studies between violence and co-occurring substance abuse and mental disorder, how can the services systems be better integrated, or reconfigured, to better manage and ultimately to reduce the risk of violence?

If such questions are addressed in creative ways that capitalize on developments—particularly the use of actuarial instruments—already under way in the field, then the next 25 years will be an exhilarating time to be studying the risk assessment of violence.

REFERENCES

American Bar Association. (1989). *ABA criminal justice mental health standards.* Chicago: American Bar Association.

American Psychiatric Association. (1974). *Clinical aspects of the violent individual.* Washington, DC: Author.

American Psychiatric Association. (1983). Guidelines for legislation on the psychiatric hospitalization of adults. *American Journal of Psychiatry, 140,* 672–679.

Appelbaum, P. (1988). The new preventive detention: Psychiatry's problematic responsibility for the control of violence. *American Journal of Psychiatry, 145,* 779–785.

Appelbaum, P., & Rosenbaum, A. (1989). *Tarasoff* and the researcher: Does the duty to protect apply in the research setting? *American Psychologist, 44,* 885–894.

Barefoot v. Estelle, 463 U.S. 880 (1983).

Baxstrom v. Herold, 383 U.S. 107 (1966).

Borum, R. (1996). Improving the clinical practice of violence risk assessment: Technology, guidelines, and training. *American Psychologist, 51,* 945–956.

Brakel, S., Parry, J., & Weiner, B. (1985). *The mentally disabled and the law* (3rd ed.). Chicago: American Bar Association.

Brown, P. (1985). *Mental health care and social policy.* Boston: Routledge and Kegan Paul.

Gardner, W., Lidz, C., Mulvey, E., & Shaw, E. (1996). A comparison of actuarial methods for identifying repetitively-violent patients with mental illness. *Law and Human Behavior, 20,* 35–48.

Grisso, T., & Appelbaum, P. (1992). Is it unethical to offer predictions of future violence? *Law and Human Behavior, 16,* 621–633.

Halleck, S. (1967). *Psychiatry and the dilemmas of crime: A study of causes, punishment and treatment.* New York: Harper & Row.

Hare, R. (1985). *Manual for the Hare Psychopathy Checklist—Revised.* Toronto: Multi-Health Systems.

Harris, G., & Rice, M. (1997). Risk appraisal and management of violent behavior. *Psychiatric Services, 48,* 1168–1176.

Harris, G., Rice, M., & Quinsey, V. (1993). Violent recidivism of mentally disordered offenders: The development of a statistical prediction instrument. *Criminal Justice and Behavior, 20,* 315–335.

Hart, S., Webster, C., & Menzies, R. (1993). A note on portraying the accuracy of violence predictions. *Law and Human Behavior, 17,* 695–700.

Heilbrun, K. (1997). Prediction versus management models relevant to risk assessment: The importance of legal decision-making context. *Law and Human Behavior, 21*, 347–359.

Kansas v. Hendricks, 521 U.S. 346 (1997).

Klassen, D., & O'Connor, W. (1990). Assessing the risk of violence in released mental patients: A cross validation study. *Psychological Assessment, 1*, 75–81.

Kozol, H., Boucher, R., & Garofalo, R. (1972). The diagnosis and treatment of dangerousness. *Crime and Delinquency, 18*, 371–392.

Lessard v. Schmidt, 349 F. Supp. 1078 (E.D. Wisc. 1972).

Lidz, C., Mulvey, E., & Gardner, W. (1993). The accuracy of predictions of violence to others. *Journal of the American Medical Association, 269*, 1007–1011.

Litwack, T., Kirschner, S., & Wack, R. (1993). The assessment of dangerousness and predictions of violence: Recent research and future prospects. *Psychiatric Quarterly, 64*, 245–273.

McNiel, D., & Binder, R. (1991). Clinical assessment of the risk of violence among psychiatric inpatients. *American Journal of Psychiatry, 148*, 1317–1321.

McNiel, D., & Binder, R. (1994). Screening for risk of inpatient violence: Validation of an actuarial tool. *Law and Human Behavior, 18*, 579–586.

Menzies, R., Webster, C., McMain, S., Staley, S., & Scaglione, R. (1994). The dimensions of dangerousness revisited: Assessing predictions about violence. *Law and Human Behavior, 18*, 1–28.

Monahan, J. (1975). The prediction of violence. In D. Chappell & J. Monahan (Eds.), *Violence and criminal justice* (pp. 15–31). Lexington, MA: Lexington Books.

Monahan, J. (1993). Limiting therapist exposure to *Tarasoff* liability: Guidelines for risk containment. *American Psychologist, 48*, 242–250.

Monahan, J. (1997). Clinical and actuarial predictions of violence. In D. Faigman, D. Kaye, M. Saks, & J. Sanders (Eds.), *Modern scientific evidence: The law and science of expert testimony* (pp. 300–318). St. Paul, MN: West.

Monahan, J., Appelbaum, P., Mulvey, E., Robbins, P., & Lidz, C. (1994). Ethical and legal duties in conducting research on violence: Lessons from the MacArthur Risk Assessment Study. *Violence and Victims, 8*, 380–390.

Monahan, J., & Steadman, H. (1994). Toward the rejuvenation of risk research. In J. Monahan & H. Steadman (Eds.), *Violence and mental disorder: Developments in risk assessment* (pp. 1–17). Chicago: University of Chicago Press.

Monahan, J., & Steadman, H. (1996). Violent storms and violent people: How meteorology can inform risk communication in mental health law. *American Psychologist, 51*, 931–938.

Monahan, J., Steadman, H., Appelbaum, P., Robbins, P., Mulvey, E., Silver, E., Roth, L., & Grisso, T. (2000). Developing a clinically useful actuarial tool for assessing violence risk. *British Journal of Psychiatry, 176*, 312–319.

Monahan, J., Steadman, H., Silver, E., Appelbaum, A., Robbins, P., Mulvey, E., Roth, L., Grisso, T., & Banks, S. (2001). *Rethinking risk assessment: The Mac-*

Arthur Study of Mental Disorder and Violence. New York: Oxford University Press.

Mossman, D. (1994). Assessing predictions of violence: Being accurate about accuracy. *Journal of Consulting and Clinical Psychology, 62,* 783–792.

National Center for State Courts. (1986). Guidelines for involuntary commitment. *Mental and Physical Disability Law Reporter, 10,* 409–514.

National Institute of Mental Health. (1991). *Caring for people with severe mental disorders: A national plan of research to improve services.* Washington, DC: U.S. Government Printing Office.

National Institutes of Health. (1994). *Report of the panel on NIH research on antisocial, aggressive, and violence-related behaviors and their consequences.* Washington, DC: U.S. Government Printing Office.

National Research Council. (1989). *Improving risk communication.* Washington, DC: National Research Press.

New York State Association for Retarded Children v. Carey, 706 F.2d 956 (2d Cir. 1983).

Poythress, N. (1990). Avoiding negligent release: Contemporary clinical and risk management strategies. *American Journal of Psychiatry, 147,* 994–997.

Quinsey, V., Harris, G., Rice, M., & Cormier, C. (1998). *Violent offenders: Appraising and managing risk.* Washington, DC: American Psychological Association.

Reiss, A., & Roth, J. (1993). *Understanding and preventing violence.* Washington, DC: National Academy Press.

Rice, M. (1997). Violent offender research and implications for the criminal justice system. *American Psychologist, 52,* 414–423.

Schall v. Martin, 467 U.S. 253 (1984).

Slovic, P., Fischhoff, B., & Lichtenstein, S. (1982). Facts versus fears: Understanding perceived risk. In D. Kahneman, P. Slovic, & A. Tversky (Eds.), *Judgment under uncertainty: Heuristics and biases* (pp. 463–489). New York: Cambridge University Press.

Slovic, P., & Monahan, J. (1995). Danger and coercion: A study of risk perception and decision making in mental health law. *Law and Human Behavior, 19,* 49–65.

Slovic, P., Monahan, J., & MacGregor, D. (2000). Violence risk assessment and risk communication: The effects of using actual cases, providing instruction, and employing probability versus frequency formats. *Law and Human Behavior, 24,* 271–296.

Steadman, H., & Cocozza, J. (1974). *Careers of the criminally insane.* Lexington, MA: Lexington Press.

Steadman, H., Monahan, J., Appelbaum, P., Grisso, T., Mulvey, E., Roth, L., Robbins, P., & Klassen, D. (1994). Designing a new generation of risk assessment research. In J. Monahan & H. Steadman (Eds.), *Violence and mental disorder: Developments in risk assessment* (pp. 297–318). Chicago: University of Chicago Press.

Steadman, H., Silver, E., Monahan, J., Appelbaum, P., Robbins, P., Mulvey, E., Grisso, T., Roth, L., & Banks, S. (2000). A classification tree approach to the development of actuarial violence risk assessment tools. *Law and Human Behavior, 24*, 83–100.

Tarasoff v. Regents of the University of California, 551 P.2d 334 (1976).

Webster, C., Harris, G., Rice, M., Cormier, C., & Quinsey, V. (1994). *The violence prediction scheme: Assessing dangerousness in high risk men*. Toronto, Canada: Centre of Criminology, University of Toronto.

11

COMMUNITY FORENSIC EVALUATION: TRENDS AND REFLECTIONS ON THE VIRGINIA EXPERIENCE

GARY HAWK AND W. LAWRENCE FITCH

The provision of forensic mental health evaluation services in criminal and juvenile court cases has been the focus of extensive research and professional commentary from both practice and systems perspectives. This chapter describes the continuing need for such services, the factors that have intensified the demand for them, and the systems developed to meet the demand in various states. About 20 years ago, Virginia moved to a forensic evaluation system primarily based in community agencies; this experience of developing and maintaining a network of clinician–evaluators has provided important lessons for other states about how such a community-based system works and changes.

DEVELOPMENTS IN FORENSIC MENTAL HEALTH AND THE DEMAND FOR EVALUATION SERVICES

The field of forensic mental health has developed remarkably over the past three decades. Forensic psychology, forensic psychiatry, and forensic social work all have emerged as well-defined specialties. In each discipline, professional organizations have been established with a focus on forensic issues (e.g., the American Psychology–Law Society/Division 41 of the American Psychological Association, the American Academy of Psychiatry and the Law, and the National Association of Forensic Social Work). A burgeoning body of research has found outlets in new professional journals like *Behavioral Sciences and the Law*; *Psychology, Public Policy, and Law*; and *Law and Human Behavior*, and important ethical questions in the field have been explored in works such as *Who Is the Client?* (Monahan, 1980). A number of important reference volumes have appeared as well, including Grisso's (1986) volume on the structure and evaluation of trial competence (see Grisso, chapter 8, this volume), the influential forensic evaluation handbook of Melton, Petrila, Poythress, and Slobogin (1997), Roger's (1997) volume on malingering research, and the many publications on violence risk assessment by Monahan and his colleagues (e.g., Monahan, 1997; Monahan & Steadman, 1994; see Monahan and Steadman, chapter 10, this volume).

Grisso (1996) recently commented on developments in the psychological assessment of trial competence and criminal responsibility. He discussed changes in the law, research studies on innovative assessment techniques, the emergence of relevant professional standards, and evolving delivery systems for forensic evaluation services. He noted that the relatively well-articulated legal standard for competence to stand trial—a constitutional standard that applies uniformly in every state—has afforded the development of specialized competence assessment instruments whose ready acceptance nationally has brought an important degree of structure, quantifiability, and reliability to the assessment of trial competence. Although legal standards for criminal responsibility are more varied across jurisdictions (and, thus, may be less susceptible to quantifiable assessment), assessment protocols have emerged nonetheless, bringing a significant degree of consistency to the approach psychologists and others take to these cases.

The demand for forensic evaluations has been high for many years and is likely to remain high in the future. Individuals with mental disorders increasingly are represented in jail populations (Lamb & Weinberger, 1998), and consequently the criminal courts increasingly are looking to the mental health community for assistance. Whether the question is competence to stand trial, criminal responsibility, or need for treatment, the sheer volume of referrals in recent years has had a significant impact on the organization and delivery of mental health services nationwide. Forensic services have become a major component of the public mental health service delivery system in every state. Indeed, in some states forensic patients (individuals hospitalized as incompetent to stand trial, as not guilty by reason of insanity, or on transfer from jail or prison) represent more than

50% of the state psychiatric hospital population at any given time (Scott, 1999).

Forensic services also have a major presence in community mental health programs. Taking their lead from Oregon, Connecticut, and Maryland, nearly two-thirds of the states now have community-based conditional release programs for individuals who have been found not criminally responsible or not guilty by reason of insanity. Featuring specialized case management, ongoing risk assessment, and periodic court reporting, these programs keep the bench and bar apprised of an acquittee's suitability for community placement and, when necessary, need for rehospitalization.

Another expansion of the scope of forensic assessment has been in the juvenile justice system (see Grisso, chapter 8, this volume). Concerned as they are with the "best interests" of the child, the juvenile courts always have sought mental health input to aid in treatment planning and disposition. In recent decades, however, new issues have arisen. As states increasingly have permitted the trial of adolescents on adult criminal charges, the question of suitability for "transfer" (to adult court) or "waiver" (of juvenile court jurisdiction) has called for psychiatric or psychological assessment in many cases.

Even questions of trial competence and criminal responsibility—practically unheard of in juvenile court just a few years ago—are beginning to receive attention. As states have adopted "get-tough" laws regarding juvenile delinquency (e.g., laws that recognize retribution as a legitimate concern in juvenile court and that stiffen penalties for delinquent youth), the atmosphere in juvenile court has become more adversarial and the dispositions more punitive. Accordingly—and not surprisingly—concerns about competence to stand trial and criminal responsibility have become more pronounced (Showalter & Fitch, 1989). In many states, questions regarding trial competence or criminal responsibility may be raised with or without clear statutory authority or dispositional provisions (Fitch, 1989). Clinicians who are asked to conduct these evaluations will not find good instruments or age norms for competence-relevant functioning for teenage (or pre-teen) defendants (Grisso, 1998; Heilbrun, Hawk, & Tate, 1996).

Another type of forensic evaluation in great demand lately is the specialized assessment of sex offenders. Every state requires sex offenders released from confinement to register with law enforcement authorities. Many states condition registration requirements on a finding that the offender suffers from a "mental abnormality or personality disorder" that renders him or her dangerous. In these states, a forensic assessment invariably will be necessary. Additionally, sex offenders with a mental abnormality or personality disorder may, in many states, be branded "sexually violent predators" and subjected to indeterminate psychiatric hospitalization on release from jail or prison (Fitch, 1998; Fitch & Ortega, 2000). These laws, which received a qualified approval from the U.S. Supreme Court in *Kansas v.*

Hendricks (1997), make explicit provision for a mental health assessment of commitability.

In sum, the demand for pretrial, pre-sentence, and other forensic mental health evaluations is on the rise, if only because of the increasing numbers of individuals with mental illnesses having criminal court involvement. The scope of evaluation, moreover, has been broadened in recent years by (a) the emergence of new, evidence-based evaluation technologies; (b) the advent of new treatment and management systems for specialized populations (e.g., insanity acquittees on conditional release); (c) the new adversarial pressures in juvenile court; and (d) the new statutory provisions for the special treatment of sex offenders.

DEVELOPMENTS IN CRIMINAL PROCEDURE

As the professional disciplines have become more sophisticated in their understanding of forensic mental health, so too has the law. Courts and legislatures have clarified legal standards and reformed procedures for determining such issues as a criminal defendant's competence to stand trial and criminal responsibility (i.e., the insanity defense). The rights of the defendant have received particular attention. Calling "psychiatric assistance" a "basic tool of an adequate defense," the U.S. Supreme Court in 1985 guaranteed such defendants the right to an evaluation by a qualified expert and the right to expert assistance in the preparation and presentation of a mental state defense (*Ake v. Oklahoma*, 1985, p. 77). The Supreme Court also has recognized the applicability of the Fifth Amendment to information resulting from a forensic mental health evaluation, ruling that statements made by a defendant in an evaluation to determine competence to stand trial may not be used by the state as evidence of "dangerousness" in a death penalty proceeding when a finding of dangerousness may provide the basis for imposition of the death penalty (*Estelle v. Smith*, 1981). Similarly, courts in many states have ruled that the Fifth Amendment protects against the government's use, as evidence that the defendant committed an offense, of any disclosures the defendant may have made during the course of a pretrial evaluation or during treatment ordered by the court prior to trial. In at least one state, defendants in capital cases enjoy statutory protection against the government's use, as evidence in aggravation (to bolster the case for a death sentence), of any disclosures made by the defendant not only during a pretrial evaluation but also during a presentence evaluation to assess factors in mitigation (Va. Code §19.2-264.3:1 1996).

These and other protections have done much to enhance the rights of criminal defendants to meaningful mental health assistance. Equally important, however, has been the radical reconfiguration of states' systems for providing these services. Thirty years ago, criminal defendants requiring pretrial psychiatric or psychological evaluation routinely were exiled to remote, maximum-security facilities, where they would typically remain until the time of trial (or longer). The period of pretrial confinement for these defendants far exceeded that for defendants not requiring evaluation. With the development in recent years of specialty forensic assessment instruments and protocols, however, most states today are able to provide court-ordered evaluations on an outpatient basis in the community. In some states, laws require these evaluations to be performed on an outpatient basis whenever possible (Va. Code Ann. §19.2-169.1 1996). In states with community-based evaluation systems in place, cases move to trial more quickly, defendants are more accessible to their attorneys for trial preparation, opportunities for diversion to treatment in the community are enhanced, and scarce inpatient resources are preserved for individuals truly in need of hospital-level care (Fitch & Warren, 1988). Mental health professionals responsible for community-based evaluation in most states have received specialized training in forensic assessment and understand the legal parameters of the pretrial process. As a consequence, evaluation reports and expert testimony are more sharply focused and much more responsive to the needs of the bench and bar (Melton, Weithorn, & Slobogin, 1985).

Laws regulating the treatment and release of defendants found incompetent to stand trial or not criminally responsible have been refined as well. In keeping with the U.S. Supreme Court's 1972 decision in *Jackson v. Indiana* (1972), defendants found incompetent to stand trial no longer languish in psychiatric facilities for indeterminate periods but must be evaluated periodically for their restoration to competence and must be released or civilly committed if at any point it appears they will not attain competence in the "foreseeable future." Individuals found not criminally responsible may be committed indeterminately in most states, and the courts have permitted this commitment even when ordered pursuant to a different set of standards and procedures than apply for ordinary civil commitment; the U.S. Supreme Court has ruled, however, that commitment of such an individual on grounds of dangerousness alone violates the Constitution. The nature of confinement, the court declared, must be related to its purpose, and if its purpose is solely incapacitation (for dangerousness), then psychiatric hospitalization cannot be justified (*Foucha v. Louisiana*, 1990).

Thirty years ago, individuals found not criminally responsible looked forward to a life of confinement in a maximum security psychiatric facility. Today these individuals receive services at all levels of care. In many states, far more live and receive their care in the community, on an order of "conditional release," than are hospitalized. Reflecting the view that, like other consumers, these individuals should be served in the least-restrictive setting consistent with public safety, conditional release laws allow for a graduated transition back into the community and provide for close supervision and a mechanism of rapid rehospitalization should that transition fail. Recidivism (annual rearrest) rates for individuals on conditional release are very low, ranging from 2.1% in Maryland (Office of Forensic Services, 2001) to 7.8% in New York (Wiederanders, Bromley, & Choate, 1997).

Forensic mental health reform in many states has been patterned on the American Bar Association's (1989) *Criminal Justice Mental Health Standards*, developed in the early 1980s by an interdisciplinary work group of attorneys, judges, and mental health professionals. Reflecting not only the many developments in law from the 1970s and early 1980s, but also a growing professionalism among forensic mental health practitioners, researchers, and scholars, these standards have served as a blueprint for states interested in improving the delivery of services for individuals with court involvement. And, importantly, they have provided an impetus for further study in the field of forensic mental health.

EVOLVING FORENSIC EVALUATION SERVICES SYSTEMS

States have met the demand for forensic evaluation services in ways that have evolved significantly over the past three decades. Poythress, Otto, and Heilbrun (1991) identified models of pretrial evaluation systems that differ on the dimensions of centralized vs. community-based and inpatient vs. outpatient service delivery. Grisso, Cocozza, Steadman, Fisher, and Greer (1994) presented the results of a national survey of pretrial evaluation services in which they found a marked trend toward the use of outpatient evaluation approaches, with only 10 states continuing to maintain traditional, facility-based assessment systems. Grisso et al. identified five general evaluation system models but noted that systems varied greatly from state to state, even among states with the same model.

Melton, Weithorn, and Slobogin (1985) detailed the transition in Virginia from a centralized, hospital-based forensic evaluation system to one based in community mental health centers throughout the state. In 1988, Fitch and Warren described the effects of this change on the delivery of forensic services statewide. Both reports underscored the importance of specialized training and continuing education in the delivery of forensic services. They demonstrated a high level of satisfaction among the consumers of these services (judges and attorneys), a substantial savings in costs to the state, improved treatment services in the state's inpatient forensic units, and increased availability of knowledgeable mental health professionals to serve offenders with mental disabilities in the community.

LESSONS FROM THE VIRGINIA EXPERIENCE

Unhooking Forensic Evaluations From the Jail-to-Hospital Transfer Process

In many states, pre-trial evaluations historically have been used as a means—sometimes the exclusive means—of hospitalizing jail inmates for psychiatric care. Whether a court was concerned about a defendant's ability to stand trial or the jail was concerned about an inmate's need for treatment, a referral was made for a competence evaluation. Such evaluations often entailed weeks or months of hospitalization. Often, defendants would remain hospitalized until trial.

Studies show that a minority of individuals referred for evaluation are seen as incompetent to stand trial (Roesch & Golding, 1980, pp. 47–49). For the balance, hospitalization may be wasteful and inefficient. Jail inmates with mental disorders who are in need of inpatient care, moreover, may have their treatment delayed while they wait for an evaluation to be scheduled. For these individuals, what is needed is some means of rapid admission for treatment. In Virginia a jail-to-hospital transfer process independent of the pre-trial evaluation process has permitted a more timely response to psychiatric emergencies in the jail. In addition, it allows inmates charged with relatively minor offenses to receive the services they need and proceed to trial without the delays that so often attend the process of competence evaluation and adjudication.

Optimizing Facility Capacity to Back Up Community Forensic Services

Community-based forensic evaluators inevitably encounter cases that challenge the limits of their clinical expertise or that pose questions demanding inpatient observation and treatment. Having a readily accessible facility placement for such cases is a critical component of any state's forensic evaluation system. One common assessment question that may call for a period of inpatient observation is suspected malingering. Unusual medical issues or diagnostic questions may also require inpatient attention. Reserving these most intensive (and expensive) resources for the most challenging cases—and training the staff accordingly—increases the likelihood that this special expertise in fact will be available when it is needed.

Should hospitalization be indicated for evaluation or treatment, the question arises whether a maximum-security forensic facility must be used. Although many defendants will require such security, defendants with less serious charges or with special needs (e.g., geriatric patients) may not. Indeed, some may fare better in a non-forensic setting. In Virginia, only about half of the hospitalized forensic population resides in a designated forensic unit at any given time. In many states, the percentage is even smaller. Using ordinary, "civil" beds for some forensic patients permits a rational matching of the clinical needs of the referred individual with the services available in the state's system and may facilitate community transition for individuals who are candidates for diversion. Such an arrangement, however, requires that both clinical and administrative staff on non-forensic units be aware of the special needs of forensic patients. Such staff require appropriate training and perhaps enhanced supervision by forensic specialists.

Forensic Services Training for Generalists

Staff working in community mental health centers who do not formally participate in forensic evaluations may nonetheless be involved in activities that demand forensic knowledge and skill—for example, those working with insanity acquittees on conditional release or with convicted offenders on "mental health" probation (i.e., probation with mental health treatment as a condition). Facility staff on non-forensic units may have forensic patients on their case loads whose management calls for a grasp of relevant statutes and coordination with courts or jails. General mental health staff in both community and facility settings need to be aware of basic concepts of risk assessment and risk management. Providing clinicians with broad access to relevant forensic knowledge is increasingly important as responsibility for patients and clients with court involvement is diffused throughout facility and community settings.

In Virginia, training programs on a variety of legal and systems issues (e.g., civil commitment, guardianship, confidentiality, risk assessment, and management of insanity acquittees) are available to mental health professionals statewide. Like the more comprehensive training available for forensic specialists, these programs are provided by the University of Virginia's Institute of Law, Psychiatry, and Public Policy under a contract with the Virginia Department of Mental Health.

System Flexibility in the Delivery of Forensic Evaluation Services

It is probably an unattainable goal to have full forensic evaluation capacity at community mental health centers throughout a geographically diverse state. Rural areas, in particular, often do not have the professional resources (i.e., sufficient psychiatrists or clinical psychologists) to provide all of the evaluation services the courts may require. Other centers may experience high rates of staff turnover, limiting the availability of qualified evaluators at times. In rural areas of Virginia, the demand for evaluation services is typically very low (e.g., a handful of cases per year). The occasional referral may go to an inpatient facility (typically for an outpatient evaluation). Some rural areas in Virginia, however, have developed a regional evaluation network. The networks were not planned but rather evolved organically over time as community mental health centers with an active evaluation component, typically anchored by a psychiatrist or psychologist with a persistent interest in forensic work, began to accept referrals from courts beyond their catchment areas.

Increasingly in Virginia, clinicians in the private sector have become involved in forensic work as well. Many began their careers in state facilities and community mental health centers, where they received forensic training and gained valuable experience providing evaluations. Not wanting to give up forensic work, many have contracted with local mental health centers to handle their court referrals. These private practitioners tend to share the values of the public system, participate in ongoing training, and approach cases with the forensic methodology endorsed by the state's Department of Mental Health.

Court-appointed criminal cases in Virginia are not highly remunerative but represent an interesting practice subspecialty and keep the practitioner in contact with the legal community, where the occasional private-pay referral may represent a significant source of income. In the most recent directory of Virginia Psychological Association clinical psychologists, nearly 10% of the members listed forensic services as a practice specialty. Virtually all these psychologists had completed the state's forensic training program at some time in the past.

Continuing Forensic Education and Specialty Training

A program of basic training in forensic evaluation, as initially described in Melton et al. (1985), is essential if a state wishes to establish and maintain a community-based system of forensic evaluation services. And ongoing education and consultation are needed if a cohesive and functional system is to be maintained. Continuing forensic education in Virginia includes semi-annual symposia (with attendance in the 200+ range) featuring speakers, workshops, and legislative updates. By presenting national experts and showcasing programs devoted to research and practice issues, the state ensures that its cadre of evaluators keep abreast of developments in law and practice and maintain a current perspective on the field. These symposia also facilitate networking and promote a sense of personal investment in the community forensic services system.

Virginia also offers specialty training for alumni of its basic training program. Focused on advanced practice issues (e.g., evaluation of sex offenders, evaluations in capital cases), this training functions as an extension of the basic training program and typically features a smaller-group format to facilitate discussion. Participants may present cases to highlight legal, clinical, or ethical dimensions of their forensic practice; mock trial segments allow for critical analysis and assessment of the participants' expert testimony skills.

Maintaining Consultative Capacity and Coordinating Links

Forensic evaluators in Virginia are strongly encouraged during training to seek consultation as they take on challenging cases or encounter problems. Although many questions may be resolved through supervisory or collegial connections at the local level, a central consultative resource is available to provide advice and guidance statewide on the full range of legal, ethical, and practice issues that arise. Clinical and legal staff at the Institute of Law, Psychiatry, and Public Policy have long served this function, offering consultation as a natural extension of the training programs it conducts for the state. The institute also links courts and attorneys from around the state with experts who can provide evaluation and consultation services in criminal and juvenile court cases. An additional consultative and coordinating link has been the Office of the Forensic Director for the state Department of Mental Health. Such an office exists in nearly every state and plays a critical role in the allocation of resources, management of services, and direction of policy with regard to forensic matters statewide.

Encouraging a Team Approach to Evaluation

Forensic evaluations addressing such specialized issues as criminal responsibility typically may be performed only by professionals with doctoral-level clinical training (e.g., clinical psychologists or psychiatrists). Because such professionals are in short supply in many community mental health centers, it is often necessary for program staff to take a team approach to evaluation, relying, for example, on social work staff to collect background information and develop a psychosocial history of the referred individual before any interview is conducted by the statutorily designated lead evaluator. The use of evaluation teams both distributes the effort required for the assessment and brings a broader pool of clinical skill to the task. Team evaluations also naturally facilitate the training process and allow students and interns to get their feet wet in forensic work. Virginia recently enacted legislation permitting licensed social workers to conduct court-ordered trial competence evaluations in juvenile court cases. Although this is the first time that social workers in Virginia have been accorded statutory authority to perform court-ordered evaluations, many social workers in the state already have had significant evaluation experience as members of community-based evaluation teams.

Designating Forensically-Trained Clinicians for the Courts

It is important for the bench and bar to have confidence that the evaluators assigned to cases in fact have the expertise to provide adequate assistance. To qualify for court appointment as an expert in a criminal or juvenile court case under Virginia law, a mental health professional must have specialized training and experience in forensic evaluation. Clinicians who satisfy all the requirements of the basic forensic evaluation training program in Virginia and who are otherwise qualified by law to be appointed to conduct evaluations are listed in a directory of evaluators, copies of which are provided to judges and attorneys throughout the state. Only those clinicians who have completed the training program, passed a test of forensic knowledge, and submitted satisfactory work samples are listed in the directory. Judges and attorneys use the directory to identify clinicians in the community for assignment when a pretrial or presentence evaluation is needed.

Virginia has avoided certifying or otherwise formally qualifying individuals as experts for the courts. If a clinician is assigned, the courts retain the prerogative of deciding whether to qualify the clinician as an expert, and they do so on a case-by-case basis, considering the clinician's education, training, and experience. The traditional qualification process, coupled with the essential ethical obligation of competence that licensed clinicians must observe, serves to screen for evaluators who are properly trained and capable of serving as experts. The alternative of formal certification (i.e., awarding a credential of "forensic examiner" or "forensic specialist") requires a level of regulation—typically involving professional boards—that Virginia has chosen not to undertake. Psychiatrists or psychologists who engage in a significant level of forensic work may, of course, elect to pursue a forensic diplomate or board certification within their profession, thereby enhancing their credentials.

Keeping Evaluation Compensation at an Incentive Level

The method of compensation for a court-ordered forensic evaluation usually depends on the type of system a state uses to provide this service. Facility-based evaluation systems typically employ full-time, salaried staff who handle cases as they arrive. In contrast, community-based systems often pay by the case, with courts or public mental health authorities authorizing the evaluator's fee. Virginia's community forensic evaluations are paid out of state court funds as authorized by the trial court judge. Evaluations are paid on a set-fee basis, depending on the type of evaluation performed. Hourly fees ordinarily are not paid. This approach to compensation is meant to provide an incentive for community mental health centers to devote staff time (already partially underwritten by state grant funds) to forensic work, with a modest but dependable cost recovery. Private practitioners and private facilities may also bill for evaluations at the set rates, but state hospitals may receive no compensation from the courts. In addition to submitting documentation for reimbursement to the courts, mental health centers and others provide evaluation information essential to the maintenance of the state's forensic information system.

Assuring Special Expertise in Challenging Cases

Most psychologists and psychiatrists in Virginia's community forensic mental health system are not forensic specialists whose practice is devoted exclusively to court cases. Rather, they are generalists who have a sufficient interest in forensic work to pursue training and continuing education and thus qualify to serve the everyday evaluation and consultation needs of their local courts. Some evaluation cases, however, pose demands that may be too daunting for these clinicians. In these cases, a referral is made to a smaller pool of highly experienced clinicians who specialize in forensic assessment. Capital sentencing evaluations, for example, are almost always assigned to clinicians who have had extensive experience in homicide cases and are willing to devote the exceptional amount of time and energy these evaluations demand. The courts are permitted to authorize reasonable hourly fees in capital cases, and, as a consequence, a cadre of highly qualified capital case experts has materialized to serve these needs in Virginia.

CONCLUSION

Systems for delivering forensic evaluation services continue to evolve. Most today rely in large measure on mental health professionals working in community settings. Virginia's experiment in community-based forensic evaluation began in 1980. Twenty years later, it stands as a model for states interested in forensic services reform. Mental health professionals throughout Virginia are familiar with issues in mental health law. They understand and respect the needs of the courts and are available in almost every locality to serve those needs. Attorneys have ready access to experts, and individuals with mental disabilities who become involved with the courts are served by mental health professionals who understand their plight—who not only are equipped to perform competent forensic assessments, but who, by virtue of their experience, are also comfortable providing treatment and other services for offenders in jail, in corrections, and in the community.

REFERENCES

Ake v. Oklahoma, 470 U.S. 68 (1985).

American Bar Association. (1989). *ABA criminal justice mental health standards.* Chicago: American Bar Association.

Estelle v. Smith, 451 U.S. 454 (1981).

Fitch, W. L. (1989). Competency to stand trial and criminal responsibility in the juvenile court. In E. Benedek & D. Cornell (Eds.). *Juvenile homicide.* Washington, DC: American Psychiatric Press.

Fitch, W. L. (1998). Sex offender commitment in the United States. *Journal of Forensic Psychiatry, 9,* 237–240.

Fitch, W. L., & Ortega, R. (2000). Law and the confinement of psychopaths. *Behavioral Sciences and the Law, 18,* 663–678.

Fitch, W. L., & Warren, J. I. (1988). Community-based forensic evaluation. *International Journal of Law and Psychiatry, 11,* 359–370.

Foucha v. Louisiana, 504 U.S. 71 (1990).

Grisso, T. (1986). *Evaluating competencies: Forensic assessments and instruments.* New York: Plenum Press.

Grisso, T. (1996). Pretrial clinical evaluations in criminal cases: Past trends and future directions. *Criminal Justice and Behavior, 23,* 90–106.

Grisso, T. (1998). *Forensic evaluation of juveniles.* Sarasota, FL: Professional Resource Press.

Grisso, T., Cocozza, J. J., Steadman, H. J., Fisher, W. H., & Greer, A. (1994). The organization of pretrial forensic evaluation services: A national profile. *Law and Human Behavior, 18,* 377–393.

Heilbrun, K., Hawk, G., & Tate, D. C. (1996). Juvenile competence to stand trial: Research issues in practice. *Law and Human Behavior, 20,* 573–578.

Jackson v. Indiana, 406 U.S. 715 (1972).

Kansas v. Hendricks, 117 S. Ct. 2072 (1997).

Lamb, H. R., & Weinberger, L. E. (1998). Persons with severe mental illness in jails and prisons: A review. *Psychiatric Services, 49,* 483–492.

Melton, G. B., Petrila, J., Poythress, N. G., & Slobogin, C. (1997). *Psychological evaluations for the courts: A handbook for mental health professionals and lawyers* (2nd ed.). New York: Guilford Press.

Melton, G. B., Weithorn, L. A., & Slobogin, C. (1985). *Community mental health centers and the courts: An evaluation of community-based forensic services.* Lincoln, NE: University of Nebraska Press.

Monahan, J. (Ed.). (1980). *Who is the client? The ethics of psychological intervention in the criminal justice system.* Washington, DC: American Psychological Association.

Monahan, J. (1997). Clinical and actuarial predictions of violence. In D. Faigman, D. Kaye, M. Saks, & J. Sanders (Eds.), *Modern scientific evidence: The law and science of expert testimony* (Vol. 1, pp. 300–318). St. Paul, MN: West.

Monahan, J., & Steadman, H. J. (Eds.). (1994). *Violence and mental disorder: Developments in risk assessment.* Chicago: University of Chicago Press.

Office of Forensic Services. (2001). *Not criminally responsible in Maryland* [press release]. Baltimore, MD: Maryland Mental Hygiene Administration.

Poythress, N. G., Otto, R. K., & Heilbrun, K. (1991). Pretrial evaluations for criminal courts: Contemporary models of service delivery. *Journal of Mental Health Administration, 18*(3), 198–207.

Roesch, R., & Golding, S. (1980). *Competency to stand trial.* Urbana, IL: University of Illinois Press.

Rogers, R. (1997). (Ed.). *Clinical assessment of malingering and deception* (2nd ed.). New York: Guilford Press.

Scott, D. (1999). [National survey of forensic inpatient populations]. Unpublished survey.

Showalter, C. R., & Fitch, W. L. (1989). The psychiatrist in court. In A. Tasman, R. E. Hales, & A. J. Frances (Eds.), *American Psychiatric Press review of psychiatry* (Vol. 8, pp. 485–504). Washington, DC: American Psychiatric Press.

Weideranders, M. R., Bromley, D. L., & Choate, P. A. (1997). Forensic conditional release programs and outcomes in three states. *International Journal of Law and Psychiatry, 20*, 249–257.

12

PSYCHOANALYSIS: PAST, PRESENT, AND FUTURE CONTRIBUTIONS TO THE LAW

ELYN R. SAKS

As the millennium came to a close, no one could doubt that Freud was one of its most important figures. In a way we are all psychoanalysts; we think in terms of the unconscious. Most people, for example, have heard of a Freudian slip. And even the most cursory glance at popular culture demonstrates how pervasive psychoanalytic thinking has become. Television, magazines, and movies all show this influence. Think of Hitchcock's *Spellbound* or the television show *Dr. Katz*.

If psychoanalysis is this important in popular culture, it must have played an enormous role in the law. Indeed, as early as 1930, Jerome Frank, one of the founders of legal realism, spoke of judging in psychoanalytic terms. The first law and psychiatry casebook, by Katz, Goldstein, and Dershowitz (1967), brought together legal and psychoanalytic thought. Why has psychoanalysis been so important in the law? The law's aim is to influence people so that they might live together in harmony. Therefore, how a culture thinks about people will then influence the law. It could not be otherwise.

This chapter has three parts. In the first I examine the contributions

227

psychoanalysis has made to the law, focusing on three seminal contributions. In the second part I sketch the future directions for psychoanalysis and the law, and in the third I discuss limits to using psychoanalytic understandings in the law. In the end, I conclude that psychoanalysis has much to offer the law and will continue influencing legal thought and process well into the next millennium. My goal is to provide an overview of psychoanalytic contributions to legal practice and theory and to speculate on future contributions.

CONTRIBUTIONS OF PSYCHOANALYSIS
TO THE LAW

Three psychoanalytic contributions have fundamentally changed current ways of thinking about important legal problems, especially in the areas of family law, professional–client relationships, and legal responsibility.

Child Placement

The first contribution of psychoanalysis to the law was made by Joseph Goldstein, Anna Freud, and Albert Solnit (1973, 1975, 1986) in their trilogy addressing the best interests of children. The trilogy was reissued recently in one volume, *The Best Interests of the Child: The Least Detrimental Alternative* (1996), with Sonja Goldstein contributing as well. These authors' work rested on two fundamental convictions. First, the child's need for continuity of care means that generally parents should be entitled to raise their children as they think best, free of state intrusion; thus, the authors expressed a preference for minimum state intervention. Second, once a justification for state intervention has been established, the child's well-being must be paramount—not the parent's, not the family's, not the child welfare agency's.

Beyond the Best Interests of the Child (Goldstein et al., 1973) examined the permissible grounds for the state to intervene—for instance, when the parents request intervention or when they fail to provide adequate care (e.g., in cases of death, abandonment, or physical abuse). *Before the Best Interests of the Child* (Goldstein et al., 1975) suggested various guidelines that should be operative if the child has already been caught up in the legal process. For instance (and perhaps most important), placement decisions should safeguard the child's need for continuity in relationships and should reflect the child's sense of time. In addition, they should take into account the limits of the law and should provide the "least detrimental available alternative." *In the Best Interests of the Child* (Goldstein et al.,

1986) discussed the professional boundary issues that the various actors in the child placement process face if they are to do their job adequately.

In making their recommendations, Goldstein et al. brought psychoanalytic knowledge to bear on the child placement process. Psychoanalysis could be used to describe the nature of children and the nature of a child's relationship to a parent. Most important, psychoanalytic theory and research established the importance of the primary psychological parent–child relationship and of the child's being "wanted." Instead of automatically favoring the mother, or looking at all of the issues comprised under the rubric of best interests of the child—including such things as wealth and religion—these books called on courts to preserve the most important relationship a child has. They should preserve this relationship even if it means favoring nonparents over parents. This position gained considerable favor in the courts, and a number of courts came to speak in terms of the "psychological" parent, with some legislatures adopting "primary parent" statutes.

Goldstein et al. made other recommendations based on their focus on preserving and perhaps strengthening the psychological parent–child bond. For instance, they endorsed state intervention into the parent–child relationship only in the most exigent circumstances—a position justified in terms of the desire not to interrupt an ongoing relationship and of the bleakness of the alternatives. In addition, they vested complete authority in the custodial parent to decide on visitation and did not favor joint custody when tension existed between the parents. Psychoanalytic theory and practice have taught us, according to the authors, that children need their parents to be both powerful and loving—and to have full authority to care for them.

Another important psychoanalytically based contribution that Goldstein et al. made was to establish that children experience time very differently from adults. Psychoanalysis tells us that the urgency of children's needs, and their difficulty in anticipating the future, prolong time for them. Time simply moves much more slowly for children—the younger the child, the greater the urgency of his or her needs. Full appreciation of this insight would lead to substantial changes in the law surrounding child placement. For instance, bonds developed over short times can be very firm for children, whereas adults often do not find quickly formed bonds meaningful. In addition, protracted court proceedings on an issue important to children —such as with whom they will live—seem to take longer to children and are consequently more destructive of their well-being.

Goldstein et al. took the considerable body of knowledge about child development that psychoanalysis had to offer and, on the basis of that knowledge, made some important recommendations for the law. Their work has been extremely influential, although some of their recommendations remain controversial. For instance, the idea that the custodial parent should have final say on visitation with the noncustodial parent has caused quite a storm, although the authors attempt to answer the critics in their reissued volume (Goldstein et al., 1996). Others may not share the authors' preference for minimal state intervention and would want to intervene earlier if sexual or emotional abuse were occurring. Still, these works have been so influential that much of what they taught has become commonplace in child welfare circles and areas of the law that address such issues.

Doctor–Patient Relationships

The second major psychoanalytic contribution to the law was made by Katz (1984, 1987, 1994), who advanced the understanding of the doctor–patient relationship and how the nature of that relationship bears on the possibility of informed consent. Katz's exploration of the nature of this relationship was thoroughly psychoanalytic and raised questions about the power of transference within such relationships—a power that becomes all the more intense at times of stress. Is the patient making a voluntary, informed, and competent choice when he or she accedes to treatment under the influence of an image of the doctor as a powerful, Godlike, parent figure? Does the concept of informed consent make sense, and are doctors right to exploit the dependency of patients in the interests of cure, capitalizing on the placebo effect?

Katz believed that doctors often invoke their authority to make decisions for patients, enabled by patients' regression at times of illness. In addition, doctors, according to Katz, invoke the idea that their decisions are based on esoteric knowledge that patients cannot understand and on the idea that they are committed to altruism, which is an additional safeguard against abuses of their authority. But these very practices, according to Katz, reinforce patients' regression. Patients' autonomy interests, he maintained, should not be given short shrift. Autonomy is a central value in the doctor–patient relationship. Patients, after all, may not share the same values as their doctor, and they have to live with the consequences of their choices. Thus, he proposed an ideal of joint decision making in which doctors take measures to mitigate the effects of regression and engage their patients in genuine conversation.

One interesting facet of Katz's work is his effort to explore the roots of doctors' roles in reinforcing paternalistic behavior toward patients. He posited that the patient's needs are not the only ones being met in the relationship; the doctor's needs are met as well, both consciously and unconsciously. Doctors sometimes have an agenda, a need, to keep their relationship with the patient "silent."

Katz's work on the doctor-patient relationship explored the impact that transference and countertransference may have on consent. This concept, pivotal in psychoanalysis, has implications for all doctor–patient relationships—indeed, all professional–client relationships, including those between lawyer and client.

Katz touched on many more aspects of the doctor–patient relationship. For example, he discussed whether a "right to treatment" makes sense in light of the psychoanalytic dimensions of a right to treatment and a duty to be treated (Katz, 1969). He also extensively discussed issues concerning human experimentation, such as the conscious and unconscious conflicts that investigators may have and the particular need to heed the claims of autonomy (Katz, 1972, 1993a, 1993b). He brought a psychoanalytic understanding to bear on all of these issues. Others have also written on the nature of ambivalence in the doctor–patient relationship (e.g., Burt, 1979), showing that such relationships are far more complicated than previously thought. Their insights have extended in interesting directions—for example, to boundary violations (Gabbard & Lester, 1995) and confidentiality (Bollas, 1995).

The Unconscious and Responsibility

The third major contribution of psychoanalytic issues to the law is Moore's (1984) work on the unconscious and responsibility. This work is located in a tradition of concerns about legal responsibility, given the determinist slant of psychoanalysis. Moore addressed two issues. First, does the unconscious increase responsibility, given that what pass as accidents are really often unconsciously motivated? Second, does the unconscious decrease responsibility, given that often behavior is caused or motivated by forces outside one's awareness and control?

About the first issue Moore said no: Unconscious motivation does not generally render accidents acts, let alone intentional acts or attempts. When it does, we can restrict responsibility to behavior involving conscious knowledge. About the second issue he said that simply because a behavior is caused does not mean that we are not responsible for it. To make this case, he adopted the concept of "soft determinism," whereby only acts that are compelled or are based on irrational reasons are nonresponsible. Moore's soft determinism is an important effort to reconcile psychoanalytic ways of thinking about how the mind works with the free will premise of the law and of everyday life. What is distinctive about his book is the philosophical care with which he unpacked these issues and the effort with which he grappled with the problems posed by the unconscious and by psychoanalysis. Some authors, like Wallwork (1991) in the psychoanalytic context, have followed Moore in his soft determinism, whereas others have taken different positions on this fundamental issue. In the end, though, Moore's approach has come to be adopted by many other legal scholars.

Contributions in Areas Related to the Law

These three contributions brought psychoanalytic understandings to bear on the law and issues of concern to the law. Although psychoanalysis does not carry the panache it once did, many legal scholars still draw on psychoanalysis to understand law and particular legal issues such as responsibility. Psychoanalysis, for instance, has made and is making important contributions to such areas as trauma (Pynoos, 1990, 1994), psychoanalytically informed policing (Marans, 1996; Marans & Adnopoz, 1995), and unconscious racism (Hernandez, 1990; Lawrence, 1987). Many legal scholars in the tradition of critical theory use psychoanalytic insights, drawing in particular on Lacan (Caudill, 1991, 1995, 1997; Goodrich, 1995). Indeed, harking back to Jerome Frank (1930), a recent special issue of the *Cardozo Law Review* was entitled "Law and the Postmodern Mind" (1995). Other authors have written in other postmodern traditions—for example, exploring judging in psychoanalytic/hermeneutic terms (Goodrich, 1997; Hogan, 1996; Humble, 1997). No doubt exists that in recent decades, psychoanalysis has made significant contributions to law and legal theory.

PSYCHOANALYSIS AND FUTURE LEGAL PROBLEMS

Psychoanalysis, I believe, will continue to play a significant role in shedding light on legal problems. Three areas clearly merit further exploration from a psychoanalytic point of view: first, challenges to the soft determinist response to the problem of unconscious motivations; second, the impact of unconscious guilt and how the law should respond; and third, understandings of the self and their relevance to questions of interest to the law.

Unconscious Motivations

A first area meriting further exploration involves Moore's (1984) soft determinist solution to the problem of unconscious motivation. This solution may face severe problems. In particular, unconscious emotions may result in compulsion, and unconscious delusions may lead to irrationality. I am particularly interested in the question of unconscious delusions and their effect on competence and responsibility.

Competence assessments focus on a person's conscious awareness. Yet psychoanalytic thinking holds that people have all sorts of unconscious reasons for what they do. For example, very powerful transferences can be established in doctor–patient relationships. Consider a man who needs an operation. Suppose the patient has an unconscious belief that his doctor is omnipotent, that he is going to save him, and that he will therefore suffer no harm as a result of the surgery. If this were his conscious reason for his consent to the surgery, he would be found incompetent, because he is unable to assess the risks of this treatment. How would it affect his competence if he reasons this way unconsciously?

The same kind of phenomenon may occur in the criminal context: A man assaults his supervisor because for him, unconsciously, the boss *is* (not "is like") his father in an act of striking him. Are we only concerned about a person's conscious thought processes—a variant on the "don't ask, don't tell" way of doing things? But is this right? If this person's true reason for his act is this patently irrational unconscious belief, why should he not be held nonresponsible just as much as if the belief were conscious?

There are several potential responses to this problem. First, when both unconscious patently irrational reasons and conscious rational reasons exist, we can rely on the law's doctrine that in "mixed-reasons" situations, if there is a rational reason, it prevails. But the conscious rational reason may well be a pretext; people are often mistaken about their true reasons. In addition, the law's treatment of the mixed reasons situation may not always be right. Second, perhaps when a person has both delusional beliefs and nondelusional beliefs, he or she is in a position to decide. But the person may be mistaken that he or she truly believes the conscious nondelusional beliefs. In any case, he or she may actually not have the capacity to choose the correct belief.

Another response to the problem would state that there are no beliefs in the unconscious, that there are no delusional beliefs in the unconscious, or that there are no delusional beliefs that are one's reasons for one's decisions. But there is simply nothing in psychoanalytic theory that indicates that these statements are true. One can take the hermeneutic position that psychoanalytic interpretations do not reveal historical truth, but only narrative truth. Therefore, we cannot conclude that unconscious patently irrational reasons exist (this theory differs from the last in saying not that there are not such things, but simply that psychoanalysis does not commit us to believing them). But I have argued at length that this is a bankrupt theory of psychoanalysis (Saks, 1999).

Alternatively, we can assert that even if such patently irrational unconscious reasons for acts exist, psychoanalysts cannot reliably identify them. Although this point probably motivates legal practices today, it is not a satisfying theoretical answer to the problem of unconscious delusions.

The problem of unconscious delusions potentially extends beyond just the possibility that some who seem in intact states of mind are really incompetent. What if it should turn out that most people have unconscious delusions as the reasons for their decisions? If so, Moore's soft determinist response to the problem of the unconscious is unsatisfying; he would find incompetence only if there is irrationality (or compulsion), so most people would be incompetent. Given the current lack of capability to make reliable judgments about unconscious motivations, this problem may not be of much practical importance, but it is quite important theoretically and could become practically important. The problem of the unconscious and legal responsibility still has not gone away, and further research is needed on this issue.

Unconscious Guilt

The second area meriting further psychoanalytic exploration is that of unconscious guilt. People often do things because they feel guilt, but their guilt may bear no relationship to the legal matter at hand. As Goldstein (1968) pointed out in his description of a court case that takes account of the psychoanalytic point of view, someone may flee the scene of crime not because he or she has done anything wrong at that moment but because he or she feels guilt about something else; hence, flight does not necessarily represent guilty feelings, and guilty feelings do not necessarily represent actual guilt. In the same way, a person may confess to a crime he or she has not committed, refuse a favorable plea bargain, or not pursue an appeal, even in a capital case.

What should the law do in light of this possibility? At a minimum, the law should not instruct juries that there is a presumption that, for example, if one flees, one feels guilt, and if one feels guilt, one is guilty. Psychoanalysts may be able to help in improving the design of legal institutions and procedures to minimize the risk that people's guilt will lead them to accept legal responsibility for unrelated matters. For instance, perhaps certain forms of interrogation increase a person's sense of unconscious guilt. Psychoanalysts can also further study reliable ways to tell when someone is responding to unconscious guilt. When reliable judgments can be made, legal professionals and procedures should prospectively refuse and retrospectively repudiate an individual's unconsciously guilt-based decisions. Perhaps these judgments will never reach a sufficient level of reliability to enable this, or perhaps reliability could only be achieved after inordinate time with the person. Nonetheless, thinking about this issue and studying it are certainly necessary.

Understandings of the Self

A third area meriting exploration is that of psychoanalytic understandings of the self, which may inform a legal understanding of severe forms of dissociation such as multiple personality disorder (MPD). To understand MPD and what follows legally, it is important to comprehend the nature of alter personalities. Psychoanalytic views of the self may play a role in judging whether alters are really people according to psychoanalytic understandings of the self, a question that could have enormous implications for the law (Saks with Behnke, 1997). Alternatively, Kernberg (1975, 1984), for instance, made observations about splits in the psyche that may indicate that alters are simply fragments of a divided person. Psychoanalytic understandings of the self may have important additional payoffs in other areas of the law that depend on a concept of personhood, such as who is a person for purposes of the Fourteenth Amendment or for purposes of the law of homicide (think, for example, of feticide).

LIMITS OF PSYCHOANALYSIS IN THE LAW

Although psychoanalysis has proved useful to the law and promises to provide insights in the future, it has important limits. Goldstein (1968) noted some of these limitations, and I discuss four of them here: value judgments, fact judgments, the law as a blunt tool, and free will.

Value Judgments

The first limitation of psychoanalysis was noted by Goldstein (1968): Psychoanalysis cannot answer value questions. Psychoanalysis can provide invaluable pieces of information to the law; for example, it can explain how the mind of a child works and how a child may experience a particular decision about his or her custody. This information, however, explains nothing about how the law should balance the interests of the child against the rights of the parent. For Goldstein et al. (1996), the interests of the child should always be paramount, but that is a value choice that they themselves acknowledge. Another value question is whether that choice makes sense even when the detriment to the child's interests is minor and the harm to the adult's interests is great. Psychoanalysis cannot aid in answering these questions. Goldstein et al. clearly saw the limits of psychoanalytic expertise and stated their value preferences up front.

Such value questions are pervasive in the law. For instance, Katz (1984) described in great detail how the transferential aspects of the doctor–patient relationship often impair the patient's ability to make an informed choice regarding treatment. Katz valued autonomy and therefore made recommendations to minimize the risks of transference, both in the ordinary doctor–patient relationship and in the context of human experimentation. However, Katz's value of autonomy did not derive from his psychoanalytic expertise, and no amount of psychoanalytic training can help one choose between autonomy and paternalism.

In the same way, the issues Moore addressed are fraught with value questions. Should unconscious delusions vitiate consent? Should unconscious intentions increase responsibility? What about irresistible impulses? Moore dealt with these as value questions and engaged in careful philosophical analysis to address them. Psychoanalysis runs up against a wall if expected to answer these value questions.

To the extent that psychoanalysts are tempted to dress up value questions in psychoanalytic garb, they are overstepping the limits of their expertise. None of the theorists I have discussed does so, but others have yielded to the temptation. Indeed, many psychoanalytic judgments made in the course of everyday practice are inevitably value judgments, however much psychoanalysts attempt to maintain neutrality. The very concepts of mental health and pathology often import disguised value judgments (e.g., independence is healthy), as do judgments to intervene in self-destructive behavior. An inclination may arise to defer to psychoanalytic experts on other issues, such as "What is it to be a competent adult?" We must be careful to rein in psychoanalytic and psychiatric imperialism.

Fact Judgments

The second limit of psychoanalytical theory is that fact judgments of psychoanalysis may often be problematic. The problem may be put thus: Is psychoanalysis a science? And if psychoanalysis is a science, is the law in a position to determine which psychoanalytic views are right? The question about the scientific status of psychoanalysis has generated much debate. Some of this debate has been fruitless, and some of the debate has formulated the nature of psychoanalysis in a completely destructive way. The debate has been fruitless when the question posed was whether psychoanalysis is a natural science, like physics, for example. The answer is irrelevant. Even if psychoanalysis is a human science, a hermeneutic science, a social science, or a folk science, as long as it says true things, both as generalizations and in individual cases, it has relevance as a science. The debate has proved destructive to psychoanalysis when theorists, trying to be helpful, have suggested that psychoanalytic interpretations are merely fictitious stories. This view of psychoanalysis is completely bankrupt and self-destructing (Saks, 1999). If true, this view would indeed impose severe limits on the use of psychoanalysis to the law, because the law tries not to act on falsehoods.

The second question is whether, if psychoanalysis is a science in the relevant sense, the law is in a position to determine which of its theories and interpretations are true. The two questions are related, of course, inasmuch as one might be tempted to deny scientific status to psychoanalysis if there is no means of adjudicating among disputed psychoanalytic claims. For instance, when one psychoanalyst (or school of psychoanalysis) says that X is good for children and another says Y, how can the law decide who is right? Similarly, when one psychoanalyst says that transference in the ordinary doctor–patient relationship is profound and another says this is the case only in certain kinds of doctor–patient relationships or with patients with certain kinds or degrees of illness, who is to be believed? Or when one psychoanalyst says that unconscious delusions are pervasive and another says they are rare, how does the law decide who is right?

I have given examples of psychoanalytic generalizations here, but my claim also applies to psychoanalytic claims about individuals. One psycho-analyst says that the person who assaulted his supervisor unconsciously believed that the boss was his father about to assault him, whereas another says that the boss unconsciously reminded the man of his father's inatten-tion to him. Still another psychoanalyst says the man's unconscious was in synch with his conscious mind and the whole motivation was to vent his anger against his boss. How does the law decide among these conflicting views?

The inability to adjudicate among these views is similar to the un-certainty about every interpretation of someone else's mental state. One does not have direct access to other people's minds, so one never knows what they really are thinking and feeling, especially when trying to recreate someone's state of mind at an earlier point in time. The inability to know with certainty what is in another's mind applies no less to the conscious mind than to the unconscious mind. It applies as much to lay judgments as to expert judgments. Nonetheless, a profound difference exists between judgments about the unconscious mind and the conscious mind of another person. One assumes that the person's access to his or her own mind en-ables the honest person to definitively confirm or deny its contents. Of course, people can become self-deceived about what has been or is cur-rently in their conscious minds. At that point, or to that extent, the con-tents of their minds become unconscious. (I am speaking of the person who is aware of something in his or her mind and aware of being aware of it.) When one has reason to trust the individual, one becomes convinced of one's own judgments about his or her conscious mind.

To put this idea another way, statements about another's conscious thought processes are determinate in a way that statements about another's unconscious thought processes are not. It would be possible to play a parlor game of guessing what is in another's conscious mind and to know who won, but how would one know who won when the question was what was in a person's unconscious mind? People can "recover" unconscious thought processes, but the dangers of suggestion in this context are fairly severe. There is perhaps no real fact of the matter; the answer is not determinate.

Thus, an important potential limit of applying psychoanalytic under-standings to the law is that the law can never tell which are true. Naturally, if this is the case for individual psychoanalytic judgments, it is also the case for psychoanalytic generalizations, which must be based on a series of individual cases. I describe this as an important "potential" limit, because I think too much can be made of this difficulty. No definitive answer exists about whether psychoanalytic judgments are reliable enough, or able to be determined to be made reliably, so that they can be useful to the law. The law has difficulty with all sorts of social science evidence. Moreover, in most contexts, the conscious and unconscious mental states can be considered equivalent, as there are reasons to doubt the veracity of the person whose state is at issue. Psychoanalytic statements are no more suspect than any other statements about another person's mind.

In sum, a second potential limit of psychoanalysis is its lack of authority to make factual statements. Perhaps psychoanalytic claims are not scientific. Perhaps they cannot be sufficiently verified to be accepted in the law. This limit of psychoanalysis in the law should not be exaggerated, but critics who make these claims must be taken seriously.[1]

The Law as a Blunt Tool

The third potential limit of the use of psychoanalysis in the law derives from the fact that psychoanalysis is an enormously subtle instrument, whereas the law is a blunt tool. In some ways psychoanalysis is a laser beam and the law is the lights in a football stadium. Therefore, there may be very real limitations on the use of psychoanalytic ways of thinking in a legal context.

Psychoanalysis attempts to achieve a deep, subtle understanding of a person's ever-so-complex motivations, both conscious and unconscious. Doing so may take an inordinate amount of time from the law's perspective, for the law must often act quickly. A mismatch becomes evident because the law does not have the time to do the work necessary to make fine distinctions.

In addition, because everyone is different in both important and subtle ways, if one disregards the time issue and attempts to understand individuals psychoanalytically so that the law may respond to them in a particular way, the system would have to allow decision makers enormous discretion in taking account of the complex data a psychoanalytic understanding can generate. Given the immense complexity of individual psychology in general and human motivation in particular, the law could never specify in advance all the possible findings and outcomes. If legal decision makers are vested with enormous discretion, such a regime would encounter serious problems: potential abuse of power of the state, unrestrained bias in the individual decision maker, post hoc judgments, ineq-

---

[1] There is also a danger that a psychoanalyst's value preferences—again, not a psychoanalytic matter—will cause him or her unconsciously to see the facts in a certain way and to justify his or her vision in psychoanalytic terms. For instance, an analyst who favors an interventionist state may think that psychoanalysis justifies much state interference in the family on the grounds that children are relieved that there is a power superior to their parents, whom they would fear too much, both oedipally and pre-oedipally, if they were too powerful. If the factual statements are hard to verify or falsify, there is naturally even more danger of this happening.

uities in the treatment of like subjects of legal judgment—the antitheses of the rule-of-law virtues.

The need for enormous discretion exacerbates a limit mentioned earlier: It is hard to discern psychoanalytic truths. Vesting the individual decision maker with authority to determine the truth, given its frequent opacity, simply amplifies the threat to rule-of-law virtues. Thus, the law is a blunt instrument, because to be otherwise would vest too much discretion in the decision maker.

The claim that the law is a blunt tool while psychoanalysis is a subtle instrument is also a way of saying that the law needs to paint with broad strokes. The idea here is twofold. First, if it were possible to take account of complex individuality in formulating rules, the result would produce an enormous information overload on citizens, who would not be able to comprehend or keep in mind all the resulting legal information. Thus, the law must paint with broad strokes so it can provide people clear messages about appropriate behavior.

Second, even if people could process more detailed and subtle information about individuals, the information, being psychoanalytic, would necessarily advert to unconscious motivation. It is arguable that people must be able to rely on the gross features of people in their everyday interactions—that is, on what they say and what they do, not on what is in their unconscious minds.[2] Imagine the confusion and uncertainty of a world in which one could not rely on these things. The security of transactions would be threatened, and one's ability to exercise due care toward those to whom one has such a duty would be impaired; all aspects of one's interactions would become more onerous.

Does this limit on the use of psychoanalysis in the law apply to its use in both individual cases and generalizations, as with the fact judgment limitation? Goldstein (1968) argued that psychoanalysis ought not to be used in individual cases. His principal reason was that individual psychoanalytic judgments take substantial time to arrive at a reliable conclusion—time that the law does not have. Generalizations, on the other hand, can be based on individual cases studied in the psychoanalysis field in sufficient detail over sufficient time and can be of use to the law.

I am not persuaded by Goldstein's position, although I think it has some merit. His point about time constraints in the legal system is completely unassailable. On the other hand, the law must often make difficult decisions, and it does the best it can within the available constraints. It is not clear that simply not trying is the best answer. In addition, for certain

---

[2]Indeed, certain areas of law recognize this in a somewhat different context; consider the move toward objective indicators of intent in the contracts arena. See, e.g., Farnsworth, 1999, sec. 3.6. There, one need not even worry so much about what is in another's mind, let alone his or her unconscious mind, when one is making a contract; one need look only at the objective features of the transaction that serve as exclusive indicators of what he or she means.

inquiries it would be well to extend the time in which decisions are made so they can be based on good data.

Furthermore, it is unclear that, if individual inquiry is impermissible, the use of psychoanalytic generalizations is helpful. Psychoanalysis may indicate that children do better when placed with their primary parent. That is a generalization, but it is still necessary to make individual determinations about who the child's psychological parent is. Having a psychoanalyst attempt to gauge who that is is better than leaving it to the jury without expert input or basing a judgment on very gross features of the child's relationship to his or her parents. Similarly, what use is it to know that flight does not often represent guilt feelings and guilt feelings do not often represent actual guilt if this knowledge cannot be applied to the individual case? Someone must necessarily apply it. We are better off if a psychoanalyst or other expert makes his or her best judgment rather than leaving the fact finder to simply guess. In short, psychoanalytic generalizations are useless unless they can be used in individual cases. Sometimes it will be better to have expert judgments about how they apply to the individual cases rather than to leave the judgment to someone who is ill equipped to decide.

In contrast to Goldstein's assertion, I believe that the points discussed in this section apply equally to generalizations as well as to individual claims (with the exception of the time constraints involved in making psychoanalytic judgments, which affect individual cases more than generalizations). Given the enormous complexity of human nature, the law will turn to multiple generalizations, and decision makers will arguably need enormous discretion, with all its costs. In addition, the multitudinous generalizations will result in information overload for individuals trying to govern their behavior according to law. Some of the generalizations, inasmuch as they will refer to people's unconscious minds, will make it enormously difficult for people to rely on others. Thus, the limits that the bluntness of the law places on the use of psychoanalysis in individual cases would apply as well to psychoanalytic generalizations.

In conclusion, the problems I have sketched under the limit that the law is a blunt tool can be exaggerated. I do not think this limit is firm as it is in psychoanalysis's inability to answer value questions, but it does call for thought. A response to this limit would be to question whether complexity—if enough certainty can be achieved about enough things to lead to complexity—necessarily entails too much discretion and whether painting with fine strokes might not be compatible with the law's sending clear messages to people and allowing them sufficiently to rely on each other. After all, there can be rules that minimize the importance of hidden mental states insofar as an innocent third party is relying on someone. Even though the issues discussed as part of this limit do not provide a definitive limit, they suggest a need for caution in the use of psychoanalysis in the law.

Free Will

The fourth potential limit of psychoanalysis's use in the law is that the deterministic psychoanalytic worldview may be incompatible with the legal worldview, which sees individuals as possessing free will. Moore (1984) and many others have tried to address this problem, but some may not be persuaded by their solutions. They may believe that incompatibilism is the philosophically correct position, so that if psychoanalysis is right, no one is accountable for his or her actions. Or they may accept compatibilism —soft determinism—yet believe that psychoanalysis reveals that many, or perhaps all, people are still not legally responsible because of pervasive unconscious irrationality or compulsion.

If one accepts either of these positions, the law is faced with severe problems. For if no one is responsible, it is impermissible to punish anyone, because a precondition of punishment is that the person be blameworthy. Other alternatives—to reject a mixed theory of punishment that requires blameworthiness as a side constraint (Hart, 1968) or to cease to punish people and only to incapacitate or treat them—would radically alter the legal regime.

Indeed, if no one is responsible, there are bigger problems than what to do with the criminal law. The entire legal system depends on the premises that most agents are accountable and can fairly be made to accept the consequences of their choices; that praise and blame generally are appropriate, including noncriminal sanctions for behavior; and that threatened sanctions influence behavior. If nobody were accountable, people would have to cease making distinctions between the competent and incompetent in all walks of life. Everyone would be incompetent, including the people making the competence determination. Therefore, no one would be in a better position to make a choice for the "incompetent" person.

In short, the system's commitment to autonomy depends on a notion of free will. If psychoanalytic premises concerning psychic determinism are right, and if whatever determinism psychoanalysis finds is incompatible with free will, there is a serious mismatch in the regimes of these two disciplines. The law would either have to radically transform itself—and psychoanalysis would face a limit in its use to the law as we know it—or the law would simply have to reject psychoanalytic understandings, which would itself naturally provide a limit to the use of psychoanalysis in the law. Thinking about free will is an either–or proposition: Either one chooses a psychoanalytic way of thinking, or one chooses a way of thinking based on personal responsibility. In that sense, the determinism postulated by psychoanalysis creates a limiting factor.

This fourth limit, of course, is also just potential. Many people may embrace a concept of free will that is compatible with the kind of determinism that psychoanalysis finds compelling. For those who do not, or for those who are still struggling with this difficult issue, this potential limit can be quite threatening.

CONCLUSION

Despite these limits, psychoanalysis has much to offer the law. I believe that, with the exception of the value judgment limit, the other "limits" are more like soft edges than true limitations. I am not persuaded that they justify forgoing any reliance on psychoanalytic understandings, but they are food for thought. Progress is continually being made in the ability to understand things psychoanalytically, to understand how to verify psychoanalytic understandings, and to assess the scientific status of psychoanalytic claims. In the same way, progress is being made in grappling with the free will vs. determinism issues implicated by psychoanalysis. Considerable benefits have accrued from psychoanalytic ways of thinking in the law; it is specious to claim that psychoanalysis has nothing to offer.

It will be interesting to try to gauge the effects of psychoanalysis on the law over the next 25 years. Psychoanalysis is no longer in its heyday, but it seems to be reviving in mental health circles, it is alive and kicking in universities, and it has thoroughly permeated modern consciousness. Its influence, particularly on the law, may increase as a result of its frequent joining of hands in some circles with neuroscience (Pally, 1997a, 1997b; Schore, 1991, 1997). This union could make for increasing testability and reliability of psychoanalytic judgments. It could also raise more acute free will puzzles. In other words, some of the limits discussed above may become more tractable, whereas others become more firm. Furthermore, the joining with neuroscience may persuade some who say that psychoanalysis is obsolete to rethink their position and face some of the vexing problems psychoanalysis poses for the law. Psychoanalysis has been one of the most important influences on the millennium. I expect it to continue to profoundly affect our ways of thinking about ourselves and our world.

REFERENCES

Bollas, C. (1995). *The new informants: Betrayal of confidentiality in psychoanalysis and psychotherapy*. Northvale, NJ: Jason Aronson.

Burt, R. (1979). *Taking care of strangers: The rule of law in doctor–patient relations*. New York: Free Press.

Caudill, D. (1991). Freud and critical legal studies: Contours of a radical sociolegal psychoanalysis. *Indiana Law Journal, 66*, 651–697.

Caudill, D. (1995). Lacanian ethics and the desire for law. *Cardozo Law Review, 16*, 793–803.

Caudill, D. (1997). *Lacan and the subject of law: Toward a psychoanalytic critical legal theory.* Atlantic Highlands, NJ: Humanities Press.

Farnsworth, E. A. (1999). *Contracts* (3rd ed.). New York: Aspen Law & Business.

Frank, J. (1930). *Law and the modern mind.* New York: Brentanos.

Gabbard, G., & Lester, E. (1995). *Boundaries and boundary violations in psychoanalysis.* New York: Basic Books.

Goldstein, J. (1968). Psychoanalysis and jurisprudence. *Yale Law Journal, 77*, 1053–1077.

Goldstein, J., Freud, A., & Solnit, A. (1973). *Beyond the best interests of the child.* New York: Free Press.

Goldstein, J., Freud, A., & Solnit, A. (1975). *Before the best interests of the child.* New York: Free Press.

Goldstein, J., Freud, A., & Solnit, A. (1986). *In the best interests of the child.* New York: Free Press.

Goldstein, J., Freud, A., Solnit, A., & Goldstein, S. (1996). *The best interests of the child: The least detrimental alternative.* New York: Free Press.

Goodrich, P. (1995). *Oedipus lex: Psychoanalysis, history, law.* Berkeley: University of California Press.

Goodrich, P. (1997). Maladies of the legal soul: Psychoanalysis and interpretation in law. *Washington and Lee Law Review, 54*, 1035–1074.

Hart, H. L. A. (1968). *Punishment and responsibility: Essays in the philosophy of law.* New York: Oxford University Press.

Hernandez, T. K. (1990). Bias crimes: Unconscious racism in the prosecution of "racially motivated violence." *Yale Law Journal, 99*, 845–864.

Hogan, P. (1996). *On interpretation: Meaning and interference in law, psychoanalysis, and literature.* Athens: University of Georgia Press.

Humble, P. (1997). Review of "On interpretation: Meaning and interference in law, psychoanalysis, and literature." *British Journal of Aesthetics, 37*, 299–301.

Katz, J. (1969). The right to treatment—an enchanting legal fiction? *University of Chicago Law Review, 36*, 755–783.

Katz, J. (1972). *Human experimentation.* New York: Russell Sage Foundation.

Katz, J. (1984). *The silent world of doctor and patient.* New York: Free Press.

Katz, J. (1987). Physician–patient encounters "on a darkling plain." *Western New England Law Review, 9*, 207–226.

Katz, J. (1993a). "Ethics and clinical research" revisited: A tribute of Henry K. Beecher; tribute to a bioethicist. *Hastings Center Report, 23*, 31–39.

Katz, J. (1993b). Human experimentation and human rights. *St Louis Journal, 38*, 7–54.

Katz, J. (1994). Informed consent—must it remain a fairy tale? *Journal of Contemporary Law and Health Policy, 10*, 69–91.

Katz, J., Goldstein, J., & Dershowitz, A. (1967). *Psychoanalysis, psychiatry, and law.* New York: Free Press.

Kernberg, O. F. (1975). *Borderline conditions and pathological narcissism.* New York: Jason Aronson.

Kernberg, O. F. (1984). *Severe personality disorders: Psychotherapeutic strategies.* New Haven, CT: Yale University Press.

Law and the postmodern mind [Special issue]. (1995). *Cardozo Law Review, 16,* 699–1444.

Lawrence, C. (1987). The id, the ego, and equal protection: Reckoning with unconscious racism. *Stanford Law Review, 39,* 317–388.

Marans, S. (1996). Psychoanalysis on the beat: Children, police, and urban trauma. *Psychoanalytic Study of the Child, 51,* 522–541.

Marans, S., & Adnopoz, J. (1995). *The police–mental health partnership: A community-based response to urban violence.* New Haven, CT: Yale University Press.

Moore, M. (1984). *Law and psychiatry: Rethinking the relationship.* New York: Cambridge University Press.

Pally, R. (1997a). Developments in neuroscience: I. How brain development is shaped by genetic and environmental factors. *International Journal of Psychoanalysis, 78,* 587–593.

Pally, R. (1997b). Developments in neuroscience: II. How the brain actively constructs perceptions. *International Journal of Psychoanalysis, 78,* 1021–1030.

Pynoos, R. (1990). Children's exposure to violence and traumatic death. *Psychiatric Annals, 20,* 334–344.

Pynoos, R. (1994). Traumatic stress and developmental psychopathology in children and adolescents. In R. Pynoos (Ed.), *Posttraumatic stress disorder: A clinical review* (pp. 65–98). Lutherville, MD: Sidran Press.

Saks, E., with Behnke, S. (1997). *Jekyll on trial: Multiple personality disorder and criminal law.* New York: New York University Press.

Saks, E. (1999). *Interpreting interpretation: The limits of hermeneutic psychoanalysis.* New Haven, CT: Yale University Press.

Schore, A. (1991). Early superego development: The emergence of shame and narcissistic affect regulation in the practicing period. *Psychoanalysis and Contemporary Thought, 14,* 187–250.

Schore, A. (1997). A century after Freud's project: Is a rapprochement between psychoanalysis and neurobiology at hand? *Journal of the American Psychoanalytic Association, 45,* 807–840.

Wallwork, E. (1991). *Psychoanalysis and ethics.* New Haven, CT: Yale University Press.

13

PSYCHIATRIC EVIDENCE IN CRIMINAL TRIALS: A 25-YEAR RETROSPECTIVE

CHRISTOPHER SLOBOGIN

If the picture painted by the popular press is any indication, the public's current image of mental health professional testimony in criminal cases is not a pretty one (Goldberg, 1994; Price, 1994; Slade, 1994). Witnesses with medical and psychology degrees stand ready to make a "syndrome" out of any criminal behavior. Even in the average case, psychiatric diagnoses are a dime a dozen. "Experts" battle over conclusions about insanity and diminished responsibility that have very little scientific basis. A tabloid reader could be excused for thinking that spurious psychobabble will eventually swallow up the criminal justice system. Even a more temperate observer is likely to wonder whether opinion evidence about abuse excuses, rape trauma syndrome, abortion clinic mania, and the like is worthy of consideration in courts of law. That is the question this chapter seeks to address.

In keeping with the purpose of this book as a retrospective on mental health law, in the first three sections of this chapter I review the past quarter century of psychiatric and psychological testimony in criminal trials (henceforth referred to simply as "psychiatric testimony"). This review makes clear that, contrary to what the popular literature would have us believe, psychiatric innovation is neither at an all-time high nor the prevalent form of opinion testimony by mental health professionals. At the same time, nontraditional expert opinion from clinicians appears to have changed over the past few decades in both content and objective. Furthermore, the law governing the admissibility of psychiatric testimony has changed in recent times, at least on the surface.

The final two parts of the chapter consider the implications of these changes and ways of improving the evidentiary analysis. A good framework for the latter already exists: Under the *Federal Rules of Evidence*, the admissibility of any expert testimony hinges on its materiality, probative value, helpfulness, and the presence of countervailing reasons for exclusion. Courts could benefit from an elaboration of this framework as it applies to psychiatric testimony.

CHANGES IN THE CONTENT OF TESTIMONY

Probably the single biggest change in the nature of psychiatric testimony over the past 25 years has been the advent of "syndrome testimony." A quarter century ago forensic experts rarely spoke of syndromes in criminal court. Today, this type of testimony abounds. The battered-woman syndrome describes the state of "learned helplessness" allegedly suffered by women who have endured cyclical battering from their spouses or significant others (Dutton, 1993; Walker, 1979); it might be used to support an insanity, provocation, or self-defense defense. The child sexual abuse accommodation syndrome (Summit, 1983) and rape trauma syndrome (Burgess & Holmstrom, 1974) identify symptoms experienced by people subjected to sexual abuse; prosecutors rely on these syndromes to bolster testimony by victims whose injuries are otherwise hard to discern. The "Vietnam veteran syndrome," like the three syndromes just discussed, is an application of the posttraumatic stress disorder (PTSD) diagnosis, this time to those who experienced the trauma of war (Shatan, 1973); it is usually introduced in insanity cases. "Urban survival syndrome" posits that Black ghetto youths are in a war zone of their own, one that makes them particularly fearful of other Black youths; it has been advanced in at least one case to support a self-defense claim (Owens, 1995). Perhaps most controversial of all are prosecutions for decades-old child abuse (e.g., *Commonwealth v. Crawford*, 1996; *New Hampshire v. Morahan*, 1995), bolstered by psychiatric evidence that memories can be repressed and then "discovered" years later, and rebutted by what has been called the "false memory syndrome" (Ernsdorff & Loftus, 1993). With such a wide array of psychiatric claims finding their way into criminal trials, it is no wonder that a book like Hagen's (1997) *Whores of the Court* has become a popular bestseller.

But the more things change, the more they stay the same. Twenty-five years ago the psycholegal landscape was no less dotted with gaudy psychiatric claims. In the 1970s, defendants based exculpatory defenses on "television intoxication" (*Zamora v. State*, 1978), cultural upbringing (*People v. Poddar*, 1972), "brainwashing" (*United States v. Hearst*, 1976), "rotten social background" (*United States v. Alexander and Murdock*, 1973), and the possession of an extra Y chromosome ("Note," 1972). Going back even further, a number of criminal defendants in the 1960s relied on claims of multiple personality disorder (Anspacher, 1965), "psychic disintegration" (*People v. Gorshen*, 1959), and other manifestations of the unconscious (*United States v. Pollard*, 1960).

Furthermore, whether the focus is today or a quarter century ago, the bulk of criminal trials in which mental health professionals testify do not involve any of these dramatic claims. Rather, the typical expert psychiatric opinion is rather humdrum, usually concerning whether the defendant was exhibiting symptoms of schizophrenia, manic-depressive psychosis, antisocial personality, schizoid personality, or some other traditional diagnosis (see Melton, Petrila, Poythress, & Slobogin, 1997, pp. 216–217, regarding insanity defense testimony). In the training programs for veteran forensic mental health experts that I have conducted in Florida, Virginia, and elsewhere over the past 18 years, rare is the professional who has offered syndrome or other "novel" opinion testimony.

When such testimony is offered, however, it does seem to be changing at the margins. First, such testimony is more likely to be explicitly nomothetic, as opposed to idiopathic, in nature. Instead of individualized descriptions based on an intimate interview with the subject of the testimony, which was the usual fare 25 years ago, the newer brand of nontraditional evidence tends to rely on off-the-rack data or impressions about a group of people presented by an expert who may never have seen the defendant or witness to whom it is applied. Walker and Monahan (1987) called this testimony "social framework evidence" because it provides background information that must be tied into the case at hand by other submissions. For instance, nomothetic framework testimony in a child abuse case might describe the typical psychological characteristics of a child who has been abused. Other evidence is needed to link those characteristics to the child in question. Although all psychiatric testimony fits this pattern to some extent (e.g., testimony that the defendant was hearing voices bolstered by references to the typical symptoms of schizophrenia), the new syndrome testimony is often more explicit about focusing on "group character" (Taslitz, 1993) as distinguished from the character of the subject.

Another difference is that today's nontraditional testimony is more likely to be presented in a self-consciously scientific style. This is not to say that today's testimony is based on better science, but rather that it is more commonly framed in scientific terms. For instance, experts who testify about battered-woman syndrome or rape trauma syndrome often talk about studies purporting to show specific symptoms to be sequelae of battering and rape (e.g., *Ibn-Tamas v. United States*, 1979; *People v. Taylor*, 1990). In contrast, the testimony of yesteryear about unconscious conflicts, brainwashing, and rotten social background, as well as unusual defenses of the early 1980s, such as pathological gambling (*United States v. Lewellyn*, 1983) and premenstrual syndrome (*People v. Santos*, 1982), rarely referred to concerted scientific research; rather, the usual basis of opinion was experience and theory.

A third difference between psychiatric testimony today and that of a quarter century ago, or even that of 15 years ago, is the degree of reliance on the medical model of mental disability. Psychodynamic testimony and claims about extra Y chromosomes, premenstrual conditions, or pathological gambling attribute mental problems primarily to biological or intrapsychic causes. In contrast, claims based on urban psychosis, war-induced trauma, or cultural differences (the latter of which became frequent only in the 1980s and 1990s) place primary blame for mental disturbances on the environment. The "abuse excuse," a label encompassing a wide array of claims to the effect that previous abuse caused particular criminal behavior (Dershowitz, 1994), also focuses on exogenous etiological factors.

One should not make too much of these tendencies regarding psychiatric evidence at criminal trials. Certainly some nontraditional psychiatric testimony from a quarter century ago was nomothetic and explicitly research based (e.g., concerning the effects of watching television), and many of the individual defenses focused on environmental causes (e.g., television intoxication, rotten social background, and brainwashing testimony). Furthermore, individualized medical model testimony remains the norm today (*People v. Medina*, 1995; *Van Poyck v. State*, 1997). Nonetheless, these trends are worth noting; as developed below, they may bear some relationship to the judicial analysis of psychiatric evidence.

CHANGES IN THE OBJECTIVE OF TESTIMONY

Psychiatric testimony has experienced not only changes in content but also an expansion of purpose. In earlier days, such testimony was offered almost entirely in support of an insanity defense, with occasional attempts to prove lack of *mens rea* (the latter sometimes referred to as "diminished capacity"; Lewin, 1975). Today, psychiatric testimony is used to ground self-defense, provocation, duress, and entrapment claims, as well as insanity and absence-of-*mens rea* arguments (Melton et al., 1997, pp. 208–212). In each of these areas, the testimony takes advantage of, or tries to get the courts to adopt, relatively recent substantive reforms in the law that subjectify inquiries into the defendant's mental state at the time of the offense.

For instance, in some jurisdictions self-defense no longer depends on whether the force used by the defendant was reasonably necessary, but on whether the defendant honestly believed the force was necessary (e.g., American Law Institute, 1962, § 3.09(2); North Dakota Century Code, 1998, §§ 12.1-05-08). Similarly, in some jurisdictions, a manslaughter instruction must be given not only when a reasonable person would have been provoked but also when, to use the *Model Penal Code*'s much-copied formulation (American Law Institute, 1962, § 210.2(1)(b)), the provoked reaction was reasonable in light of the actor's situation under the circumstances as he or she believed them to be (*People v. Shelton*, 1986; *State v. Ott*, 1984). When blameworthiness is subjectified in this way, the door is opened wide to psychological speculations.

Psychiatric testimony in criminal cases has not been limited solely to assessments of mental state. Courts have also allowed such testimony in support of a claim that the defendant does not meet the act requirement of an offense. Usually, the testimony is framed in terms of the defendant's character; someone with the defendant's personality, the expert opinion suggests, could not have (or could have) committed the offense in question (e.g., *Kanaras v. State*, 1983; *State v. Treadaway*, 1977; *United States v. MacDonald*, 1981; *United States v. Powers*, 1994). Although the first reported appellate opinion sanctioning such testimony was handed down in the 1950s (*People v. Jones*, 1954), the phenomenon appears to have become much more prevalent in the past 20 years.

Another way in which innovative lawyers have used psychiatric testimony in recent years is in connection with the credibility of a witness. In a sense, this issue arises any time a mental health professional testifies in support of or against a psychiatric defense. An opinion that the defendant is insane suggests that the defendant's claim of insanity is true, whereas a contrary opinion suggests the opposite. The type of credibility testimony of concern here, however, is that which is explicitly framed in terms of whether a witness other than the defendant is telling the truth about some event. Perhaps the most famous example is the psychiatric testimony in the Alger Hiss trial that Whittaker Chambers, Hiss's prime accuser, was a psychopathic liar (*United States v. Hiss*, 1950). Although that trial took place in the 1950s, it seems to have been well ahead of its time. Most appellate cases dealing with expert testimony concerning the truthfulness of a witness have come in the past two decades, many of them in cases involving child abuse and rape (see *State v. Foret*, 1993; *State v. Kim*, 1982; *State v. Wilson*, 1982).

A related novel use of behavioral testimony in criminal trials is to help the trier of fact determine whether a witness is accurate, as opposed to truthful (a truthful witness is one who merely believes that his or her story is accurate). The most obvious example of this practice is expert testimony about the foibles of witnessing and remembering an event. The eyewitness expert points to phenomena that can affect one's registration of an event (e.g., a weapons focus), memory of an event (e.g., time), or recall of an event (e.g., suggestions by the police) (Loftus, 1979). The jury then considers this nomothetic information in deciding whether a particular eyewitness identification is correct. A variant is testimony about the theoretical basis for repressed memory, designed to support the validity of a sudden remembrance of an event that occurred years ago. In this case, however, the expert tends to provide information not only about the theory of repressed memory, but also about the accuracy of the particular memory in question (compare *Isely v. Capuchin Province*, 1995, p. 1067).

CHANGES IN EVIDENTIARY LAW GOVERNING ADMISSIBILITY

A third perspective on the history of psychiatric testimony over the past quarter century comes from looking at changes in the rules of evidence governing expert testimony. The biggest change in this connection is the advent of the *Federal Rules of Evidence* in 1975 (1997). To put those rules in context, a brief history of the law on expert evidence is useful.

For many years, the usual threshold requirement for opinion testimony was that it be based on specialized information "beyond the ken of the jury" (Weinstein & Berger, 1986, § 702[02]). In theory, opinions about something the typical layperson could grasp were not admissible. Testimony that met this threshold might also be subject to two further limitations. The testimony could not rely on information, such as hearsay, that was not independently admissible (Strong, 1992, § 15), and it could not address the ultimate legal issue in the case (Strong, 1992, § 12).

Coexisting with these rules, both at the federal level and in many states, was the so-called *Frye* test. This test came from *Frye v. United States* (1923), which held that the results of polygraph testing were inadmissible because the basis of the test was not "sufficiently established to have gained general acceptance in the particular field to which it belongs" (p. 1014). In many jurisdictions, the "general acceptance" test became the primary means of evaluating the admissibility of scientific evidence, especially novel scientific evidence in criminal cases (Moenssens, Starrs, Henderson, & Inbau, 1995, p. 8). Indeed, many courts evaluating such evidence relied entirely on *Frye*, without any explicit inquiry into whether evidence was beyond the ken of the jury (Strong, 1970, p. 14; see also *Commonwealth v. Fatalo*, 1963, p. 480; *Coppolino v. State*, 1969, p. 70).

Then, in 1975, the *Federal Rules of Evidence* went into effect. On their face, the new federal rules governing expert testimony—widely copied by the states—relaxed previous restrictions. Under Rule 702, opinions based on "scientific, technical or other specialized knowledge" need only "assist the trier of fact to understand the evidence or determine a fact in issue." Although the difference between evidence that "assists" and evidence that is "beyond the ken" may be subtle, the former language suggests a greater willingness to classify an opinion as expert, and courts have so held (*State v. Bednarz*, 1993, pp. 171–172; *United States v. Downing*, 1985, pp. 1226–1229). In more obvious contrast with the previous practice in many jurisdictions, Rule 703 permits opinions to be based on otherwise inadmissible information (such as hearsay) if "of a type reasonably relied upon by experts in the particular field." Finally, in contrast to the law in some jurisdictions at the time it went into effect, Rule 704 permitted qualified opinion testimony to "embrace an ultimate issue to be decided by the trier of fact" (p. 108).

Although Rule 703's reasonable reliance language resonated with *Frye*, the commentary to that rule and the other federal rules governing expert testimony made no reference to that case, and thus *Frye* was not directly acknowledged by the rules (Saltzburg & Redden, 1982, p. 452). Nonetheless, many courts continued to apply *Frye* to scientific evidence, with or without reference to the federal rules or the analogous state rules (Moenssens et al., 1995, p. 12; *United States v. Christopher*, 1987, p. 1299; *United States v. Two Bulls*, 1990, p. 60). Other courts developed their own separate screening tests for scientific testimony. For instance, one test looked at whether there is "substantial," as opposed to general, acceptance of the subject matter (*United States v. Gillis*, 1985, p. 558), and another focused on whether the opinion is the product of an "explicable and reliable" system of analysis (*State v. Kim*, 1982, p. 1336).

Other courts, supported by many commentators (Berger, 1987; Imwinkelreid, 1983; Louisell & Mueller, 1977; Strong, 1992, § 203), rejected a separate screening test for expert testimony (Strong, 1992, p. 872). Rather, they adhered to the federal rules' helpfulness analysis, supplemented by the balancing test applicable to any proffered evidence. Under this regime, any helpful specialized knowledge from a qualified expert is admissible unless its probative value is substantially outweighed by its potential for confusing the jury, thus prejudicing one of the parties or wasting time. This approach might be called the 401/403 balancing test, in reference to the federal rules that deal with the definition of relevance (401) and the delineation of countervailing factors (403).

In short, the scope and effect of Rule 702 were unclear for many years. Then came the U.S. Supreme Court's decision in *Daubert v. Merrell Dow Pharmaceuticals* (1993), which purported to clear up the confusion, at least at the federal level. In *Daubert*, the Court rejected the "austere" *Frye* standard as the sole test of admissibility in favor of the multifactor "liberal" regime of the federal rules (pp. 588–589). Under this approach, the Court explained, the admissibility of scientific evidence is to be judged by its helpfulness, which depends on "whether the reasoning or methodology underlying the testimony is scientifically valid and . . . whether that reasoning or methodology properly can be applied to facts in issue" (pp. 592–593). Validity, said the Court, can be determined by the "falsifiability" or "testability" of the theory and the methodology underlying it, the error rate associated with the theory or procedure, the extent to which it has been subject to peer review and publication, and the extent to which it has been generally accepted in the relevant field. Although the latter factor echoes *Frye*, the difference under *Daubert* is that general acceptance is now neither necessary nor sufficient for admissibility. Some states have followed the federal lead and adopted *Daubert* (*Jones v. State*, Arkansas, 1993, *State v. Cephas*, Delaware, 1994; *State v. Foret*, Louisiana, 1993), whereas others have adhered to *Frye* or its equivalent (*Flanagan v. State*, Florida, 1993; *People v. Leahy*, California, 1994; *State v. Bible*, Arizona, 1993).

IMPLICATIONS OF CHANGES FOR PSYCHIATRIC TESTIMONY

How has all of this evidentiary ferment affected psychiatric testimony? Not at all, if one focuses on traditional psychiatric opinion. Mental health professionals who testify in insanity cases relying on a typical Axis I or Axis II diagnosis (see American Psychiatric Association, 1994) have been able to say virtually anything they want, post-*Frye*, post-Rule 702, and post-*Daubert*. Most forensic mental health professionals (who, it will be remembered, rarely offer syndrome or another type of novel testimony) have never had their testimony challenged. For instance, one review of post-*Daubert* case law, which would be the most likely group of cases to view traditional testimony with skepticism, found that nearly all of the 30-plus opinions that applied *Daubert* to social science evidence involved nontraditional "syndrome" testimony (Richardson et al., 1995). The only significant limitation on traditional psychiatric opinion has been a new prohibition on ultimate testimony concerning mental state, introduced in the federal system in the wake of the Hinckley trial in 1984 (*Federal Rules of Evidence*, 1977, Rule 704(b)), and even that has had little practical effect (e.g., *United States v. Davis*, 1988; *United States v. Salamanca*, 1993).

In nontraditional contexts, however, the courts have been more willing to scrutinize the admissibility of psychiatric testimony. Thus, for instance, pathological gambling, XYY testimony, battered-woman syndrome, rape trauma syndrome, child sexual abuse accommodation syndrome, and eyewitness testimony have all been subjected to one of the screening tests mentioned above (see *United States v. Lewellyn*, 1983, pathological gambling; *State v. Roberts*, 1976, XYY; *Ibn-Tamas v. United States*, 1983, battered-woman syndrome; *State v. Black*, 1987, rape trauma syndrome; *State v. Kim*, 1982, child sexual abuse accommodation syndrome; *United States v. Fosher*, 1979, eyewitness identification testimony). The application of a screening test often means the testimony is excluded, although not always or for all purposes.

The first question one might ask in light of these facts is: Why has traditional testimony been exempted from any type of screening analysis? Although there are several possible answers to this question, the two answers that seem to predominate in the courts were neatly summarized by the California supreme court in the course of describing when to apply its version of the *Frye* test:

> First, *Kelly-Frye* only applies to that limited class of expert testimony which is based, in whole or in part, on a technique, process, or theory which is new to science and, even more so, the law. . . . The second theme in cases applying *Kelly-Frye* is that the unproven technique or procedure appears in both name and description to provide some definitive truth which the expert need only accurately recognize and relay to the jury. (*People v. Stoll*, 1989, p. 710)

In the current context, this reasoning suggests that traditional psychiatric testimony is not subject to judicial scrutiny because (a) it is traditional and, more persuasively, because (b) juries are not likely to consider it objective or infallible but rather will naturally treat it with skepticism.

Assuming that a particular type of psychiatric evidence is thought to be novel enough to require screening, a second question arises: How do courts apply the relevant screening test? This question is more difficult to answer because, as McCord (1987) demonstrated, in the psychiatric context application of the general acceptance test and similar screening tests seem to be placeholders for other concerns. Interestingly, to the extent they are explicitly mentioned or discernable from the cases, these concerns appear to parallel the previously discussed trends in nontraditional psychiatric testimony. As a general matter, the more nomothetic, scientific looking, nonmedically oriented, and doctrinally suspicious testimony is, the more likely it will be excluded.

A few examples illustrate this point. As social science testimony goes, testimony about the accuracy of eyewitness identification is highly reliable evidence (Penrod, 1995). Yet it is often excluded (Handberg, 1995, p. 1032). Some courts do so because expert testimony about eyewitnesses is general in nature (that is, it is social framework evidence par excellence) and is less likely to be based on the facts of the case or contact with the eyewitnesses involved (*Ex parte Williams*, 1993, p. 1227; *Lewis v. State*, 1990, p. 911; *State v. Gardiner*, 1994, pp. 713–714). Other courts worry about the jury being able to analyze the expert evidence about eyewitnesses (Handberg, 1995, pp. 1033–1041; *United States v. Kime*, 1996, p. 884). In other words, because eyewitness identification testimony is nomothetic and scientific in appearance, judges believe it is both less relevant and more likely to confuse or overawe the jury.

Expert opinions about poor living conditions, television intoxication, and urban survival syndrome have not fared well either (see Montgomery, 1994; *United States v. Alexander and Murdock*, 1973, pp. 959, 968; *Zamora v. State*, 1978, p. 780). Here, however, exclusion seems to be based not on the nomothetic nature of the evidence but on a fear that the claim is too far removed from the medical model. After all, the judges in these cases seem to be saying, almost everyone who commits a crime is subject to some type of traumatizing environmental condition; we cannot excuse them all. Even relatively liberal judges reflect this concern. In his dissent to the "rotten social background" case, Judge Bazelon, well known for his "radical" positions on criminal responsibility, gave several reasons why the law should recognize a combination rotten social background/Black rage defense. Ultimately, however, he conceded that

> it does not necessarily follow . . . that we should push the responsibility defense to its logical limits and abandon all of the trappings of the medical or disease model. However illogical and disingenuous, that model arguably serves important purposes. Primarily, by offering a rationale for detention of persons who are found not guilty by reason of "insanity," it offers us shelter from a downpour of troublesome questions. (*United States v. Alexander and Murdock*, 1973, p. 961)

Further commentary along these lines came from Judge McGowan, who wrote the majority opinion in the case:

> As courts, however, we administer a system of justice which is limited in its reach. We deal only with those formally accused under laws which define criminal accountability narrowly. [We uphold the trial court's instructions because they] remind the jury that *the issue* before them for decision *is not one of the shortcomings of society generally*, but rather that of appellant Murdock's criminal responsibility for the illegal acts of which he had earlier been found guilty. . . . (emphasis added; pp. 965, 968)

In *Zamora v. States* (1978), involving the television intoxication defense, the appellate court made a similar comment:

> In the concluding pages of defense counsel's lengthy brief the following language appears: "In the case at bar, television was on trial. . . ." Such was simply not the case. . . . Television was not on trial; Ronney Zamora was on trial. . . . Stated simply, this was a murder trial, and it is to the trial judge's credit that he confined the testimony and evidence to the relevant issues. (p. 784)

Finally, in some cases exclusion of novel psychiatric testimony seems to be based not on its nomothetic or nonmedical nature, but on the fact that it pushes the doctrinal envelope or creates entirely new doctrines. In these cases however, judges are not always as explicit about their reasoning; their skepticism about substance may be masked by evidentiary rulings. For instance, courts have rejected pathological gambling as a basis for an "irresistible impulse" insanity defense on *Frye* grounds, even though the diagnosis is in the *Diagnostic and Statistical Manual of Mental Disorders* (American Psychiatric Association, 1994; see e.g., *United States v. Lewellyn*, 1983). As Bonnie (1984) has argued, the real reason for this type of ruling is probably concern that permitting acquittal in such cases would open the floodgates to impulsive crime claims, which virtually any criminal could make. Substantive misgivings have also affected evidentiary analysis of clinical testimony concerning *mens rea*. Although diminished capacity evidence is clearly material and often not much different from insanity testimony in terms of content, it is limited in many irrational ways (Reisner & Slobogin, 1990, pp. 538–545). Courts also have rejected psychiatric testimony in self-defense cases on what appear to be substantive grounds, even though the ostensible reason for the decision is lack of expertise (e.g., *Jahnke v. State*, 1984).

The same type of reaction often occurs when judges are confronted by psychiatrically based claims about whether a criminal act occurred and whether a witness is truthful or accurate. Even if such claims have probative value, judges resist them, apparently because they believe that such testimony is more likely than traditional testimony to tread upon well-accepted lay functions or, as courts often put it, "usurp the jury" (*Commonwealth v. Seese*, 1986; *United States v. Azure*, 1986).

Perhaps the most interesting thing about the courts' approach to psychiatric evidence is the minimal role that reliability often plays in determining admissibility. The two reasons given by the California supreme court for exempting traditional testimony from special judicial scrutiny—precedent and the accessibility of the evidence—have nothing to do with reliability. Even more surprisingly, relative reliability does not seem to play much of a role in determining the admissibility of nontraditional psychiatric testimony, even when it is subjected to one of the screening tests. According to one mammoth study that looked at more than 100 syndrome cases decided since *Daubert*,

> Courts are not generally engaging in scientific reviews of the proffered syndrome. . . . Most typically, the focus is on general acceptance and the qualifications of the expert, and even then the judicial review tends to be cursory. (Richardson et al., 1998)

More concretely, consider the way the courts have handled claims based on some version of PTSD, such as the claims of Vietnam veterans, child abuse victims, rape victims, and battered women. If reliability were the test, one might speculate that because the same basic diagnosis is at issue, the admissibility analysis would be the same with respect to each claim. Yet it is not. Because Vietnam veterans almost always use PTSD evidence in support of an insanity defense (Erlinder, 1984), they have had no problem introducing such testimony (McCord, 1987, p. 66). In contrast, alleged rape victims have had some trouble doing so, and alleged child sex abuse victims have met much more judicial resistance (Moenssens et al., 1995, p. 1154), largely because the evidence is perceived as an effort to prove that a criminal act occurred or to bolster the victim's credibility (*Commonwealth v. Gallagher*, 1988; *State v. Hutchens*, 1993; *State v. Saldana*, 1982; *United States v. Whitted*, 1993).

The battered-woman syndrome has the most interesting history. Initially women who introduced the syndrome in self-defense cases were rebuffed. But today many jurisdictions permit testimony about battered-woman syndrome (*State v. Allery*, Washington, 1984; *State v. Anaya*, Maine, 1981; *State v. Hickson*, Florida, 1993; *State v. Hill*, South Carolina, 1986; *State v. Kelly*, New Jersey, 1984), and at least 11 states have a specific statutory authorization mandating admissibility of battered-woman syndrome evidence (Mosteller, 1996, p. 484 n. 77). The syndrome met initial resistance because acquitting a woman for killing her batterer when he was not attacking her at the time struck courts as antithetical to the traditional requirement that threats be imminent before they justify retaliation (Moenssens et al., 1995, p. 56). But more recently, as Mosteller observed, the groundswell of support for battered women has led courts and legislatures, implicitly or explicitly, to subjectify self-defense law in this type of case. In other words, substantive law has been changed in response to political pressures, and thus the syndrome no longer pushes the doctrinal envelope.

In summary, courts spend very little effort evaluating scientific methodology in connection with psychiatric testimony offered in criminal cases. Instead, judges are often influenced by concerns tangential to validity, such as the generality of the testimony and its implications for the substantive law. Although these issues are not irrelevant, their role in the analysis, as well as the precise role of reliability assessment itself, needs to be more clearly conceptualized.

TOWARD A MORE NUANCED APPROACH
TO EVIDENTIARY ANALYSIS

The courts' often chaotic approach to the admissibility of psychiatric evidence in criminal trials could benefit from a coherent analytical framework. One such framework—embodied in Rules 401, 403, and 702 of the *Federal Rules of Evidence*—already exists. Under the 401/403 balancing analysis, any evidence, expert or otherwise, must be evaluated in terms of how its relevance to the facts at issue weighs against countervailing factors. When the evidence is meant to be expert, it must further assist the fact finder, as Rule 702 requires. Using these rules, the last part of this chapter fleshes out a step-by-step approach to evaluating the admissibility of psychiatric evidence. The first step involves gauging the relevance of the evidence, an inquiry that itself has traditionally been broken down into two components: an assessment of materiality and an assessment of probative value. The next step involves assessing the helpfulness of the evidence. The final step focuses on whether significant countervailing reasons for excluding the testimony exist.

Relevance–Materiality

Assessing the materiality of evidence requires an understanding of the governing substantive law. The previous section discussed the tendency of courts to exclude evidence that stretches traditional doctrinal boundaries. Unfortunately, this tendency is not always explicit; as already noted, one often gets the sense that the exclusion of evidence on lack of helpfulness or acceptance grounds is a smokescreen that hides a more pressing concern about substantive impact. At the other extreme, as Wilson (1997, p. 90) documented, some courts at both the trial and appellate level seem willing to admit almost any kind of testimony proffered by a mental health professional, without regard to its logical connection to the law of the jurisdiction. Neither approach is appropriate. Courts need to address the materiality issue directly. By doing so, they might not have to worry about reliability and helpfulness issues.

For instance, testimony that people with an extra Y chromosome are statistically more likely to commit crime is clearly not material to any defense based on cognitive impairment (i.e., lack of *mens rea*, self-defense, or the cognitive prong of the insanity defense). People with more "maleness" still intend to commit the crimes they commit and know that it is wrong do so (compare *Millard v. State*, 1970, p. 231; *People v. Tanner*, 1970, p. 659; *People v. Yukl*, 1975, p. 318). Even in a jurisdiction with a volitional prong to the insanity defense, XYY testimony ought to be excluded on materiality grounds. That people with two Y chromosomes are more likely to commit crime than people with only one Y chromosome does not mean the former are compelled to do so; at most they may have a stronger or more frequent urge to commit crime than others. As Moore (1985) persuasively argued, because all behavior is caused by something (biology, environment, character, or situation), proof of causation, by itself, cannot be proof of compulsion, nor can it support an excuse. The fact that people with tempers, people who grew up in poverty-stricken conditions, or people with low intelligence are more likely to commit crime does not excuse them from such acts. As Moore contended, unless the causative agent renders one unable to rationally control one's actions, compulsion is not present.

The same analysis can be directed at any psychiatric evidence that consists merely of a correlation between criminal activity and a certain trait (e.g., antisocial personality disorder, a particular brain structure, excess testosterone, premenstrual anxiety). Nonetheless, not only courts, but many commentators as well, seem to believe that any evidence describing a link between criminal behavior and an "abnormality" is material (Falk, 1996; Skeen, 1983). That approach disregards and therefore undermines the substantive criminal law.

Courts have often been more attuned to materiality analysis in the self-defense context. As noted earlier, a number of courts have held that psychiatric evidence about learned helplessness in battered women is material only in cases where the woman was imminently threatened by death or serious bodily harm at the hands of her victim (compare LaFave & Scott, 1986, § 5.7). Also noted was the fact that many jurisdictions have abandoned this relatively objective approach and permitted acquittal on self-defense grounds even when the perceived threats are longer term. But few courts have fine-tuned the materiality analysis any further. One compromise option, at least in homicide cases, would be to hold the woman liable unless the objective facts indicate an imminent threat, but permit a reduction from murder to manslaughter or negligent homicide if a mistake as to imminence occurred and it was reckless or negligent, respectively. Under this regime, a battered woman who killed in response to an objectively nonimminent danger would be convicted of some form of homicide, rather than acquitted outright. The same sort of result might be reached through application of the provocation doctrine (*State v. Whitney-Biggs*, 1997).

This is not the place to debate the appropriate contours of these difficult political and moral issues. The important point for present purposes is that courts and legislatures need to think hard about the scope of the insanity defense, self-defense, and other defensive doctrines. They should not dodge these issues through suspect rulings about psychiatric evidence.

Relevance–Probative Value

Daubert is right. The *Federal Rules of Evidence* do, and should, require an assessment of reliability. Evidence that is unreliable has no probative value. The more difficult issue is how to measure reliability. *Daubert* provides a starting point by recognizing the various ways reliability can be gauged, including assessment of its basis using the scientific method, proof of its error rate, peer review, and, if all else fails, an assessment of whether its basis is generally accepted. The U.S. Supreme Court appeared to place general acceptance at the bottom of the measurement hierarchy, as it should have. The fact that professionals in the field routinely rely on particular theories or methodologies is useful information in determining admissibility, but it is no substitute for a straightforward assessment of accuracy, if such an assessment is possible.

Thus, contrary to *Daubert*'s suggestion, the test developed in that case under Rule 702 is not always more liberal than the *Frye* test. Indeed, in the psychiatric context, the latter test is likely to produce more generous results. Testimony based on traditional psychiatric nosology is, almost by definition, generally accepted, yet much of it is not very reliable. For example, testimony about personality disorders such as schizoid personality disorder and antisocial personality disorder has played a prominent (and unchallenged) role in many trials, yet both laboratory and field trials show that the reliability of these diagnoses is well below 50% (Lieberman & Baker, 1985; Mellsop, 1982). Only psychiatric evidence based on research and new to the field is likely to fail the general acceptance test yet have a chance under *Daubert*.

So how does one decide when, if ever, psychiatric evidence must be subject to hard scientific scrutiny and when, if ever, it need pass only a less-rigorous general acceptance test? I propose that meeting the latter test is sufficient for evidence that is material to past mental states, but that *Daubert*'s test must be met when psychiatric evidence is used to prove any other type of issue (usually involving whether a particular act occurred).

The rationale for this approach is necessity: Whereas the phenomenology of physical acts can be subjected to the scientific method—that is, use of controlled populations, adequate samples, and meaningful criterion variables—past mental states cannot be. This is so for two reasons. First, past mental states are not objective facts whose existence can be proved in the same way the occurrence of an act can be proved. Second, even if they are, obtaining useful empirical information about legally relevant past mental states is virtually impossible, or at least much more difficult than studying the psychological correlates of actions.

The first assertion is based on the ideas of Taslitz (1998), who, drawing on feminist literature and other sources, argued that one can never discover objective truth about past mental states in the same way one can know whether an event, such as a death or a robbery, occurred. One can "know" such mental states only through acts of interpretation that inevitably differ depending on a host of factors, including the identity of the observer and the time at which the mental state is observed. Thus, even the person whose mental state is in question, if asked to report what it was at a particular point in time (which is the type of report on which psychiatric evidence usually relies), engages in interpretation. As Taslitz stated,

> Memory itself is an assertion, a self-report, which we play an active role in constructing. Our memories never involve solely historical truths, for we seek to create an account of the past consistent with a preconceived cognitive or moral scheme. Memory is thus at least partly a created narrative (pp. 19–20).

The difficulty of ascertaining past mental state is exacerbated by the possibility that an actor may not know his or her mental state even at the time it is occurring. Taslitz (1998) noted, "We may be ambivalent, desiring and spurning simultaneously, leaving us confused, and we may deceive ourselves out of fear, guilt, or self-protection" (p. 24). This result may be particularly true in criminal situations of the type normally the subject of psychiatric testimony, where motivations, thoughts, and urges are likely to be jumbled together rather than straightforward and logical.

When the fact finder is a third party rather than the subject, the truth about mental states becomes even more contingent. Members of the jury or the judge trying to discern the person's mental state add their own interpretive gloss. As Taslitz (1998) observed, "When jurors name a mental state as 'premeditation,' 'heat of passion,' or 'belief in the imminent need to use deadly force in self defense,' they are crafting an interpretation that partly embodies their own assumptions, attitudes and beliefs" (p. 26).

In short, whereas acts are objective facts that, in theory, can be ascertained, "narrative thinking" dominates attempts to reconstruct mental state. Any description of mental state resembles a story more than a depiction of an observable event. Science cannot tell us the truth about past mental states because science is meant to identify objective reality, not interpretations of reality. At most, science can help us decide whether acts and other types of objectively discernable facts have occurred.

Even if, in theory, the existence of a particular mental state can be scientifically proved, as a practical matter science often will not be up to that task. This point can be illustrated through the explication of another recent work, by Lyon and Koehler (1996). They argued that the probative value of a given type of expert evidence often can be gauged by what they call the "relevance ratio" (pp. 46–50). The relevance ratio is simply the ratio between the proportion of cases in which a symptom is observed in the population of interest and the proportion of cases in which the same symptom is observed in the rest of the population. For instance, assume that 60% of children who are abused suffer from symptoms X, Y, and Z, and that 30% of children who are not abused suffer from symptoms X, Y, and Z. The relevance ratio in this case is 2:1 (60%/30%), which means that proof that a child has these three symptoms has significant probative value on the issue of whether the child was abused.

Lyon and Koehler (1996) argued that the relevance ratio is "the most efficient way to think about evidentiary relevance" (p. 47). Assuming that methodological problems do not render invalid the information relied on (compare pp. 67–74), this assessment seems to be on target: The ratio is an eminently sensible way of evaluating the probative value of evidence. If the subject population is no more likely to have the symptoms than the general population (i.e., the relevance ratio is 1 or less), the evidence has no probative value concerning the relationship of the symptoms to the subject population. If the ratio is greater than 1, the evidence has some tendency to prove a fact at issue, which is the definition of relevance under Rule 401. Relevance ratio analysis might prove very useful in conducting the reliability assessment demanded by *Daubert* and Rule 401.

Consider, however, the difficulty of gathering information necessary to calculate the relevance ratio when psychiatric evidence about past mental state is involved. For instance, in a battered-woman case in which self-defense is asserted, one would need to determine the proportion of battered women who kill their spouses believing they have no alternatives and the proportion of nonbattered women who kill their spouses believing they have no alternatives. Without any other information, the most plausible conclusion is that, of the two groups, the battered women are more likely to feel they have no options. But that kind of thinking is not science; the scientific method requires large enough samples of both groups being compared and the development of reliable methods of obtaining the relevant information about them.

In conducting such research, one significant problem would be ensuring that no third variables taint the comparison; that is, the two groups should be similar in all significant ways except the battering variable. This problem, however, confronts any attempt to use the relevance ratio. A second problem, and one more likely to afflict the study of past mental state phenomena, is measuring the dependent variable. Even assuming that past mental state is an objective fact rather than an interpretive story, how does one accurately tell whether a female killer believed she had no alternative way of avoiding serious physical harm at the time she killed? The researcher can of course ask the woman whether she felt the killing was necessary. But leaving aside problems with self-serving statements made about an event that may have occurred months ago, gauging the all-important variable—the intensity of the woman's belief in the necessity of her action—and then comparing it to the beliefs of other women is all but impossible. Morse (1978) observed in a related context, "there is no scientific measure of the strength of urges" (p. 584; see also Morse, chapter 7, this volume). Likewise, there is no scientific measure of the strength of beliefs that occurred at a specific point of time in the past.

Another example of the difficulty of calculating the relevance ratio in a past mental state case comes from *People v. Gorshen* (1959). In this case, the psychiatrist testified that the defendant killed his employer, with whom he had had an argument, to avoid psychic disintegration and insanity. A *Daubert* relevance ratio calculation in this case would require the impossible task of determining the proportion of people on the verge of psychic disintegration who kill someone they dislike to the proportion of those who choose to (or allow themselves to) disintegrate instead of killing the disliked person. Even if one could meaningfully define "psychic disintegration," trying to find people who refrained from aggressive action while on the verge of such disintegration would be a fruitless endeavor. If through some magical methodology such people were found, one would still need to measure the strength of the psychic pressure they experienced, which, as Morse (1978) noted, is not possible.[1]

In summary, even if research relevant to past mental state can be characterized as science, it is science that is so likely to be tainted by methodological flaws that in effect it does not differ from interpretation and storytelling. In contrast, research conducted to assist in proof of acts would not need to determine the strength or existence of slippery phenomena like beliefs, emotions, or urges in the past. In the child abuse example, the task would be to locate abused and nonabused children and to catalogue their present symptoms. This task is not easy (Lyon & Koehler, 1996, p. 70), but it is certainly easier than ascertaining whether spouse killers felt they had alternatives or whether people on the verge of psychic disintegration felt the need to kill.

Because of the theoretical and practical difficulties in scientifically proving past mental state, a *Daubert* analysis—involving a relevance ratio calculation or some other scientifically based technique—should not be required in assessing the probative value of psychiatric evidence on that issue. Instead, a general acceptance test should suffice. This test, as I would formulate it, would still require psychiatric evidence on past mental state to be based on a plausible theory or methodology accepted by a significant number of professionals in the field. Furthermore, the logic underlying the relevance ratio could still play a role by framing the plausibility inquiry. For instance, testimony on the battered-woman syndrome should probably be admissible because a sizeable number of professionals now believe— although they have not "scientifically" proven—that battered women who kill their spouses feel they have fewer options than those spouse killers who are not battered. In contrast, the theory that urban Black youths who kill other urban Black youths fear their victims more than other killers of Black youths is less plausible and, probably for that reason, not well accepted among professionals. In the words of Rule 702, even if it cannot be called scientific knowledge, psychiatric evidence directed toward proving past mental state must at least be "specialized" knowledge.[2]

---

[1] Compare the statement of Sir Karl Popper, the progenitor of the "falsifiability" concept given so much play in the Supreme Court's *Daubert* opinion, that one of the "best examples" of unfalsifiable theories is Freudian thought (Underwager & Wakefield, 1993, pp. 158–159). The point is only that relevance ratio analysis cannot profitably be carried out in this situation. I am not arguing that the psychiatric testimony in *Gorshen* should have been admissible. For one thing, there is a good argument that it was immaterial; the testimony was proffered to show lack of *mens rea*, to which volitional impairment is irrelevant. Second, it is not clear that the psychiatrist's theory of "psychic disintegration" is one that is generally accepted among other professionals, a test that, it is argued below, must be met by any psychiatric evidence.

[2] Although *Daubert* (1993) left open the possibility that "specialized knowledge" was not subject to its scientific validity test (p. 580 n. 8), the Court has since made clear that all

Helpfulness

Even if material and probative, evidence is not and should not be admissible as expert opinion unless it assists the fact finder. In theory, the easiest way to find out whether expert evidence helps the jury is to compare the accuracy of jury decision making with and without the expert testimony. Indeed, studies comparing lay and expert decision making on questions like the accuracy of eyewitnesses or determinations of abuse might be quite useful in this regard. Unfortunately, not much of this type of research has been done (Borum, 1998; Frazier & Borgida, 1988). Furthermore, a distinction may again exist between evidence about acts, as in the eyewitness and abuse examples just given, and evidence about past mental states. Assessing the helpfulness of expert testimony about the latter issue could be virtually impossible in some cases, not because of the elusiveness of past mental states (the problem discussed in the previous section), but because of the elusiveness of the doctrines to which they are relevant. For instance, if a jury and an expert disagree on who is insane, how does one decide who is right?

Accordingly, assessments of helpfulness today must usually be based on more of a seat-of-the-pants assessment. Testimony that merely repeats what "everyone knows" is a waste of time. On the other hand, testimony about acts or mental states that is meant to rebut presumptions, overcome statements or innuendo from the opposing side, or provide counterintuitive or corrective information should be considered helpful. A few examples of these three situations should illustrate the point.

The criminal law presumes sanity (*Davis v. United States*, 1895; LaFave & Scott, 1986, § 4.5(e)) and permits an inference that one intends the natural and probable consequences of one's acts (LaFave & Scott, 1986, § 3.5). These legal rules are based in part on normative and procedural considerations but rely primarily on empirical assumptions that are probably right: Most criminal defendants are sane, and most intend the natural and probable consequences of their acts. More importantly, these assumptions are undoubtedly shared by most people, including the majority of jurors and judges. Thus, any past mental state evidence offered to the contrary ought to be considered helpful. Specifically, probative testimony tending to support an insanity, provocation, or lack of *mens rea* defense ought to be admissible because it rebuts legal and lay preconceptions about mental state.

In other situations, it is a party, rather than the law itself, that relies on commonly held assumptions. For instance, in a battered-woman case in

---

expert testimony must meet *Daubert* (*Kuhmo Tire v. Carmichael*, 1999). At the same time, *Kuhmo* emphasized that *Daubert* announced a "flexible" test and that its "list of specific factors neither necessarily nor exclusively applies to all experts or in every case" (p. 1171), an approach that is not inconsistent with the above proposal.

which self-defense is the issue, the prosecution might make much of the defendant's failure to leave a battering husband despite several apparent opportunities to leave. In a child abuse or rape case, the defense might emphasize the victim's failure to report the alleged offense immediately after it supposedly occurred. In these situations, probative psychiatric evidence—respectively, about battered-woman syndrome, child sexual abuse accommodation syndrome, and rape trauma syndrome—would be helpful, because it would disabuse jurors of the notions that most battered spouses leave and that abuse and rape victims usually report the assault immediately. Even courts that are resistant to this type of testimony as a general matter often permit it as rebuttal evidence in such cases (Askowitz & Graham, 1994, p. 2040; Fischer, 1989, pp. 713–717; Mosteller, 1996, p. 479).

Finally, situations exist in which neither the law nor the parties make explicit statements about behavior or mental state, yet psychiatric evidence can help by providing counterintuitive information. Determining when such a situation exists can be difficult. Ideally, there would be empirical information indicating people's preconceptions about various issues (compare Deffenbacher & Loftus, 1982; Frazier & Borgida, 1988; Goodman, Golding, & Haith, 1984), but even that can be misleading because stereotypes constantly change and may differ between jurisdictions or even juries. When in doubt, the court should err on the side of admissibility, if the other evidentiary prerequisites are met.

For example, psychiatric evidence that the defendant has a "passive" character may be proffered to show that the defendant did not commit the act charged. Such evidence does not involve proof of mental state and thus would first have to pass the *Daubert* relevance ratio hurdle. If it does, it should be considered helpful as well, because most jurors are likely to assume that people who are charged committed the act. This assumption may seem to run afoul of the presumption of innocence, but unlike the presumption of sanity or the inference regarding intent, the presumption of innocence is not supported empirically (most people charged are guilty) and is probably not believed by most laypeople. By the same token, unless offered in rebuttal of such evidence, proof that a person is not passive should not be admissible because it would merely reinforce the widespread assumption that a person charged with a crime did it. This outcome is consistent with the traditional character evidence rule barring proof of propensity by the prosecution unless the defense opens the door (*Federal Rules of Evidence*, 1997, Rule 404).

Psychiatric evidence about the credibility of a witness might be analyzed the same way. Because most people probably assume that witnesses who testify under oath and under threat of perjury will tell the truth, testimony suggesting otherwise would be helpful, whereas testimony supporting truthfulness, unless offered in rebuttal, would not be (compare *Fed-*

eral Rules of Evidence, 1997, Rule 608(b)). The more significant hurdle for this type of testimony is whether it is probative under the *Daubert* relevance ratio test (because testimony about credibility usually concerns whether an act, such as abuse, occurred).

A harder case is testimony about "repressed memories" designed to bolster or attack testimony from an alleged abuse victim about incidents often decades old. Although jurors probably believe that witnesses tell the truth, they might also assume that an account of something that occurred so long ago, the memory of which was just recently discovered, is not likely to be accurate. Accordingly, evidence about the repressed memory phenomenon should probably be considered helpful regardless of which side seeks to offer it, although its ultimate admissibility would still depend on whether it meets the *Daubert* relevance ratio test (again, because it is being used to prove that an act occurred).

Helpfulness analysis is also important in determining the form that psychiatric evidence may take. Such evidence can be conceptualized as having several layers (Melton et al., pp. 16–17), including

1. behavioral observations (e.g., the person hears voices when no one is talking)
2. inferences or symptoms (e.g., the person has hallucinations)
3. diagnosis (e.g., the person has schizophrenia)
4. application of the clinical information to the legal issue (e.g., the person was cognitively impaired at the time of the offense)
5. application of the clinical information to the ultimate legal issue (e.g., the person was insane).

Morse (1978) has argued that only the first level of information is helpful to laypeople, because they do not need clinical labels or expert speculations about degrees of impairment to reach the moral judgments demanded by the law (pp. 554–560). Bonnie and I countered that, with the exception of ultimate issue testimony, informed speculation by mental health professionals can be of assistance on some occasions (Bonnie & Slobogin, 1981, pp. 452–466). That debate will not be revisited here.

Where Morse and we clearly agreed is that, given its moral content, ultimate issue testimony is not helpful and should be proscribed. That position should be amended to recognize, once again, the distinction between psychiatric evidence on mental states and psychiatric evidence used to prove an act. Ultimate testimony as to whether someone is likely to have committed a particular act may be helpful to the jury in the sense that the expert will know more about the correlation between certain symptoms and acts. Furthermore, such testimony is not a moral judgment, but a statement of probabilities about an objective fact. On the other hand, expert testimony that someone is insane or acted reasonably in response to perceived provocation is not only a value judgment but also something that cannot be objectively verified; thus, it cannot be said that an expert's view on this matter is any better than that of a layperson who has been instructed on and follows the law.[3]

Countervailing Factors in Excluding Evidence

If expert evidence is material, probative, and helpful, it should usually be admissible. However, as Rule 403 recognizes, even evidence that meets these prerequisites might be so time consuming relative to its importance, so confusing, or so likely to prejudice unfairly a party that it should be excluded. Generally, psychiatric evidence should not be excluded on these grounds. It is likely to be important enough in a given case to avoid exclusion on waste-of-time grounds, although redundant or peripheral testimony might be censored. Further, at least when compared to other types of expert evidence, psychiatric testimony is unlikely to befuddle the average jury. Testimony about human behavior, even when put in psychiatric terminology or expressed in terms of syndromes and relevance ratios, is far more understandable than discussions of physics, DNA analysis, and economic principles. For much the same reason, psychiatric testimony is relatively unlikely to awe the jury or carry undue weight. Laypeople appear to understand that psychiatric evidence is very fallible (Slater & Hans, 1984; Vidmar & Schuller, 1989).

However, a few recurring scenarios might pose a Rule 403 risk. First, testimony that merely bolsters strong preconceptions might unduly prejudice the party fighting the preconception. For instance, evidence that a person charged with rape fits a "rapist profile" reinforces the assumption of guilt and should be excluded. Of course, such evidence should be excluded on character evidence and unhelpfulness grounds as well (and perhaps also as lacking in probative value). However, some wily prosecutors may be able to evade the character evidence prohibition by characterizing the testimony as proof of intent or motive (compare *Federal Rules of Evidence*, 1997, 404(b)) and might also be able to make a colorable argument that any probative scientific evidence adds to the jury's knowledge. If so, they should still not be able to get past the Rule 403 hurdle.

A second situation in which Rule 403 analysis should play a role, likely to be more frequent, is when the psychiatric evidence is minimally relevant, either in the sense of being of low materiality or of low probative

---

[3] The relevant federal rule prohibits ultimate issue testimony only as to "mental state or condition" (*Federal Rules of Evidence*, 1997, Rule 704(b)). Although such testimony is not helpful, it might be allowed for other practical reasons, principal among them that it is so hard to avoid, at least in paraphrase. As I have noted elsewhere, in a truly adversarial proceeding ultimate issue testimony is probably harmless, even if it is not technically "expert" (Slobogin, 1989).

value. For instance, general testimony about the inaccuracy of eyewitness identification might be of relatively low materiality because of its lack of fit with the case at hand. Yet jurors, impressed by the probative value of the evidence (which, given the strong research on the subject, is very high), might nonetheless rely on the testimony as proof that no eyewitnesses can be trusted, a result some courts have admitted they fear (*People v. Enis*, 1990, p. 1165). This type of problem is likely to occur often with social framework evidence, where an almost inverse relationship between probative value (i.e., reliability) and case-specific materiality may exist. In such situations, the court may need to evaluate the impact of the psychiatric evidence not only by itself but also in conjunction with other evidence. For instance, a judge might decide to exclude generalized testimony about eyewitnesses if it is the only defense evidence, but permit it if the defense also has a colorable alibi claim.

Psychiatric evidence that is clearly material but that has only minimal probative value might require similarly delicate balancing. Imagine evidence of past mental state based on a barely plausible theory that is accepted by a sizeable group of professionals but also rejected by many professionals, or suppose that syndrome evidence tending to show an act occurred exhibits a positive, but very weak, relevance ratio. Such evidence might justifiably be excluded despite passing the official threshold test for probative value because of its potentially untoward impact on the jury (see Lyon & Koehler, 1996, p. 70). Unlike judges who have heard many cases involving expert evidence, juries do not have a comparison sample. Although jurors are not incapable of understanding that theories are arcane or that a given relevance ratio is weak, they may have trouble putting that information in context or gauging its relative helpfulness.

Of course, a functioning adversarial system may be able to expose the flaws in psychiatric evidence. Through cross-examination and rebuttal experts, lawyers can uncover the relative implausibility of a theory or its lack of acceptance among other professionals and can explain a syndrome's weak probative value. Accordingly, a third situation that merits close consideration under Rule 403 occurs when the psychiatric evidence is not subjected to adequate adversarial testing. Unchallenged, the usually minimal risk that psychiatric theories, relevance ratios, and ultimate issue testimony will overwhelm the jury's capacity to think for itself may increase significantly. As one study concluded, "nonadversarial expert testimony causes less systematic processing of . . . expert testimony" (Brekke, 1991, p. 471).

Another reason for ensuring that psychiatric evidence is subjected to adversarial testing is to prod the research community to do better. This point is similar to, but ultimately in conflict with, Faigman's (1995) argument that strict admissibility rules are needed to provide an incentive to improve the psychiatric product. Faigman contended that relaxed admissibility rules of the type advocated in this chapter for past mental state are detrimental to scientific progress because they put the courts' imprimatur on the status quo (pp. 972–977). But gaining admission of evidence is only winning the initial battle; the evidence must sway the fact finder to win the war. Not surprisingly, many of the novel defenses that have received press attention, although presented in court using psychiatric evidence, did not prevail and are consequently seldom raised (Arenella, 1996, pp. 703–705, 709; Bonnie, 1995, pp. 3–4, 15; Goldberg, 1994, p. 42). To the lawyer-consumers of psychiatric evidence, unfavorable verdicts, brought about by adversarial testing, should provide as much incentive to push for better research as would outright exclusion.

The difficulty comes in implementing the preference for adversarial testing of psychiatric evidence. Judges normally cannot foresee the adequacy of a lawyer's preparation or his or her skill during trial. Even if they could, a rule that evidence should be excluded because the opposing side is too incompetent to combat it is paradoxical to say the least. However, some steps are possible. Judges can conduct hearings *in limine* to get a sense of whether evidence will be effectively explored; if not, they can appoint their own expert to flesh out the issues. Indeed, the court might routinely appoint "expert experts" to point out the weaknesses (and strengths) of evaluation procedures and research methodologies (Elliot, 1989; Sanders, 1994). The jury can be authorized to ask questions to make up for attorney oversights (compare Samborn, 1997, p. 22) and can be provided with briefs on the scientific issues as well. Ethical rules governing both mental health professionals (e.g., American Psychological Association, 1990, § 1.04, "Boundaries of Competence"; § 1.05, "Maintaining Expertise"; § 7.02(c) "Forensic Assessments") and attorneys (e.g., American Bar Association, 1992, Rule 1.1) can be enforced more vigorously against incompetent, lazy, or pretentious individuals. In short, the judicial system can develop effective ways of ensuring that the fact finder is not presented a one-sided or confused picture of the evidence.

One might argue that if good adversarial presentation of the evidence could be guaranteed through these or other methods, then courts should welcome even psychiatric opinions that have little or no demonstrable probative value; after all, the reasoning might go, the weaknesses of such opinions can be uncovered by the process. Adversariness that clarifies rather than obfuscates cannot be guaranteed on a routine basis, however, and even if it could be, knowingly giving the fact finder information that lacks any indicia of reliability is antithetical to the ideal of a system that purports to do justice. Thus, although a well-functioning adversarial process may allow courts to be more flexible in their admission of evidence than they would otherwise be, it should not nullify the threshold requirements of professional plausibility for past mental state evidence and scientific validity for other types of psychiatric evidence.

CONCLUSION

The courts are suspicious of psychiatric evidence that is nomothetic in nature, departs from the traditional medical model, and seeks to support doctrinally novel theories. This suspicion often exists without regard to or in spite of the evidence's reliability. At the same time, courts accept unquestioningly traditional psychiatric evidence that may be just as unreliable, if not more so. Furthermore, the judiciary on the whole has yet to devise a coherent framework for evaluating the admissibility of suspect psychiatric evidence.

The foregoing discussion has provided such a framework. All psychiatric evidence, both traditional and nontraditional, ought to be subject to admissibility thresholds using the four-step analysis provided by the *Federal Rules of Evidence*. The evidence must be material, a requirement that may often necessitate a hard look at the substantive law. It must be probative, a maxim that should require that it meet a general acceptance test, if the evidence seeks to prove past mental state, and more rigorous scientific testing using relevance ratio analysis or other scientific methods if it does not. It must be helpful, which means it should combat legal presumptions, common preconceptions, or claims by the opposing party. Finally, it must be fairly presented as the tentative information it is, a result that can usually be ensured through adequate adversarial testing.

The end result of this approach is that defendants' psychiatric evidence will typically be subjected to less judicial scrutiny than evidence proffered by the prosecution.[4] The rationale for this stance is a combination of necessity, given the difficulty of proving past mental state, and helpfulness, given the natural assumptions about past mental state that most laypeople make. Some might object that psychiatric evidence is never necessary if it is of low probative value and that it can never be helpful, even when counterintuitive, if it leads to questionable findings (e.g., Faigman, 1995; Morse, 1978). The better approach, in this view, is simply to rely on lay rather than expert testimony and fact rather than opinion when the issue is past mental state.

A deeper reason for nonetheless adhering to the framework outlined in this chapter is based on democratic principles and the appearance of fairness (Slobogin, 1999). Our individualistic, pluralistic society espouses a preference for allowing everyone to voice his or her point of view. On issues about which competing versions of truth exist, as with past mental state, litigants in criminal trials should be able to describe their stories. We

---

[4]This is not always the case, however. For instance, prosecution evidence of rape trauma syndrome, which focuses on the past mental state of consent, would be evaluated under a general acceptance standard, whereas defense evidence that repressed memories are manufactured, which focuses on whether an act occurred, would be evaluated under a *Daubert* relevance ratio analysis.

would never prevent a defendant from taking the stand and telling his or her version of the facts so long as it stays within the bounds of the substantive law.[5] We should likewise be reluctant to prevent an expert retained by the defendant from doing so.

A utilitarian side to this argument can be made as well. The viability of the criminal justice system depends in part on the perception that it is willing to ascertain the truth (Lind & Tyler, 1988). If the system prevents litigants from telling plausible stories based on theories accepted by the relevant professionals, it may well undermine the trust both of litigants and of society at large. Such a result, to the extent it stems from the desire to enhance reliability, would be ironic at best.

REFERENCES

American Bar Association. (1992). *Model rules of professional conduct*. Chicago: Author.

American Law Institute. (1962). *Model penal code*. Philadelphia, PA: Author.

American Psychiatric Association. (1994). *Diagnostic and statistical manual of mental disorders* (4th ed.). Washington, DC: Author.

American Psychological Association. (1990). *Ethical principles of psychologists*. Washington, DC: Author.

Anspacher, C. (1965). *The trial of Dr. DeKaplany*. New York: New American Library.

Arenella, P. (1996). Demystifying the abuse excuse: Is there one? *Harvard Journal Law and Public Policy, 19*, 703–709.

Askowitz, L. R., & Graham, M. H. (1994). The reliability of expert psychological testimony in child sexual abuse prosecutions. *Cardozo Law Review, 20*, 2027–2101.

Berger, M. A. (1987). A relevancy approach to novel scientific evidence. *Federal Rules Decisions, 115*, 89–91.

Bonnie, R. (1984). Compulsive gambling and the insanity defense. *Newsletter of the American Academy of Psychiatry and Law, 9*, 6.

Bonnie, R. (1995). Excusing and punishing in criminal adjudication: A reality check. *Cornell Journal of Law and Public Policy, 5*, 1–17.

---

[5] Indeed, the U.S. Supreme Court has held unconstitutional a per se rule barring the defendant from offering hypnotically induced testimony unless the state can show that such testimony "is always so untrustworthy and so immune to the traditional means of evaluating credibility that it should disable a defendant from presenting her version of the events for which she is on trial" (*Rock v. Arkansas*, 1987, p. 61). The Court's subsequent decision in *United States v. Scheffer* (1998) permitting an absolute prohibition on polygraph evidence presented by the defendant, does not undercut this point. The Court distinguished *Rock* by noting that a ban on polygraph evidence did not prevent the defendant from telling his story about the crime, but merely barred the defendant "from introducing expert testimony to bolster his own credibility" (pp. 1268–1269). For further discussion of this point, see Slobogin (1999).

Bonnie, R., & Slobogin, C. (1980). The role of mental health professionals in the criminal process: The case for informed speculation. *Virginia Law Review, 66,* 427–522.

Borum, R. (1998, March). *The incremental validity of social framework evidence: Does expert testimony improve decisionmaking accuracy?* Paper presented at the annual meeting of the American Psychology–Law Society (Div. 41, American Psychological Association), Redondo Beach, CA.

Brekke, N. J. (1991). Of juries and court-appointed experts: The impact of non-adversarial versus adversarial expert testimony. *Law and Human Behavior, 15,* 451–475.

Burgess, A., & Holmstrom, L. (1974). Rape trauma syndrome. *American Journal of Psychiatry, 31,* 981–986.

Commonwealth v. Crawford, 682 A.2d 323 (Pa. 1996).

Commonwealth v. Fatalo, 191 N.E.2d 479 (Mass. 1963).

Commonwealth v. Gallagher, 547 A.2d 355 (Pa. 1988).

Commonwealth v. Seese, 517 A.2d 920 (Pa. 1986).

Coppolino v. State, 223 So.2d 68 (Fla. Dist. Ct. App. 1969).

Daubert v. Merrell Dow Pharmaceuticals, 509 U.S. 579 (1993).

Davis v. United States, 160 U.S. 469 (1895).

Deffenbacher, K. A., & Loftus, E. (1982). Do jurors share a common understanding concerning eyewitness behavior? *Law and Human Behavior, 6,* 15–30.

Dershowitz, A. (1994). *The abuse excuse and other cop-outs, sob stories and evasions of responsibility.* Boston: Little Brown.

Dutton, M. A. (1992). Understanding women's responses to domestic violence: A redefinition of battered woman syndrome. *Hofstra Law Review, 21,* 1191–2042.

Elliot, E. D. (1989). Toward incentive-based procedure: Three approaches for regulating scientific evidence. *Boston University Law Review, 69,* 485–511.

Erlinder, C. P. (1984). Paying the price for Vietnam: Post-traumatic stress disorder and criminal behavior. *Boston College Law Review, 25,* 305–347.

Ernsdorff, G. M., & Loftus, E. (1993). Let sleeping memories lie? Words of caution about tolling the statute of limitations in cases of memory repression. *Journal of Criminal Law and Criminology, 84,* 129–174.

Ex parte Williams, 594 So.2d 1225 (Ala. 1993).

Faigman, D. (1995). The evidentiary status of social science under Daubert: Is it "scientific," "technical," or "other" knowledge? *Psychology, Public Policy, and Law, 4,* 960–979.

Falk, P. (1996). Novel theories of criminal defense based upon the toxicity of the social environment: Urban psychosis, television intoxication, and black rage. *North Carolina Law Review, 74,* 731–811.

Federal Rules of Evidence. (1997). St. Paul, MN: Westgroup.

Fischer, K. (1989). Defining the boundaries of admissible expert psychological testimony on rape trauma syndrome. *Illinois Law Review, 1989,* 691–734.

Flanagan v. State, 625 So.2d 827, 829 n. 2 (Fla. 1993).

Frazier, P., & Borgida, E. (1988). Juror common understanding and the admissibility of rape trauma syndrome evidence in court. *Law and Human Behavior, 12,* 101–122.

Frye v. United States, 293 F. 1013 (D.C. Cir. 1923).

Goldberg, S. (1994). Fault lines: Has a talk-show mentality softened jurors to accept any excuse? *American Bar Association Journal, 80,* 40–44.

Goodman, G. S., Golding, J. M., & Haith, M. M. (1984). Jurors' reactions to child witnesses. *Journal of Social Issues, 40,* 139–156.

Hagen, M. A. (1997). *Whores of the court: The fraud of psychiatric testimony and the rape of American justice.* New York: Regan Books.

Handberg, R. B. (1995). Expert testimony on eyewitness identification: A new pair of glasses for the jury. *American Criminal Law Review, 32,* 1013–1064.

Ibn-Tamas v. United States, 407 A.2d 626 (D.C. 1979).

Ibn-Tamas v. United States, 455 A.2d 893 (D.C. Ct. App. 1983).

Imwinkelreid, E. J. (1983). The standard for admitting scientific evidence: A critique from the perspective of juror psychology. *Villanova Law Review, 28,* 554–592.

Isely v. Capuchin Province, 877 F. Supp. 1055, 1067 (E.D. Mich. 1995).

Jahnke v. State, 682 P.2d 991 (Wyo. 1984).

Jones v. State, 862 S.W.2d 242 (Ark. 1993).

Kanaras v. State, 460 A.2d 61 (Md. 1983).

Kuhmo Tire v. Carmichael, 119 S. Ct. 1167 (1999).

LaFave, W., & Scott, A. (1986). *Criminal law* (3rd ed.). St. Paul, MN: West.

Lewin, T. (1975). Psychiatric evidence in criminal cases for purposes other than the insanity defense. *Syracuse Law Review, 26,* 1051–1115.

Lewis v. State, 572 So.2d 908 (Fla. 1990).

Lieberman, P., & Baker, F. M. (1985). The reliability of psychiatric diagnosis in the emergency room. *Hospital and Community Psychiatry, 36,* 291–293.

Lind, E. A., & Tyler, T. R. (1988). *The social psychology of procedural justice.* New York: Plenum Press.

Loftus, E. (1979). *Eyewitness testimony.* Cambridge, MA: Harvard University Press.

Louisell, D. W., & Mueller, C. B. (1977). *Federal evidence* (Vol. 1). Rochester, NY: Lawyers Co-op.

Lyon, T. D., & Koehler, J. J. (1996). The relevance ratio: Evaluating the probative value of expert testimony in child sexual abuse cases. *Cornell Law Review, 82,* 43–78.

McCord, D. (1987). Syndromes, profiles and other mental exotica: A new approach to the admissibility of nontraditional psychological evidence in criminal cases. *Oregon Law Review, 66,* 19–108.

Mellsop, G. (1982). The reliability of Axis II of DSM-III. *American Journal of Psychiatry, 139*, 1360–1361.

Melton, G. B., Petrila, J., Poythress, N., & Slobogin, C. (1997). *Psychological evaluations for the courts: A handbook for mental health professionals and lawyers.* New York: Guilford.

Millard v. State, 261 A.2d 227 (Md. 1970).

Moenssens, A. A., Starrs, J. E., Henderson, C. E., & Inbau, F. E. (1995). *Scientific evidence in civil and criminal cases* (4th ed.). Westbury, NY: Foundation Press.

Montgomery, L. (1994, November 12). Teen guilty of murder; urban theory not allowed. *Detroit Free Press*, p. 6A.

Moore, M. (1985). Causation and the excuses. *California Law Review, 73*, 1091–1149.

Morse, S. (1978). Crazy behavior, morals and science: An analysis of mental health law. *Southern California Law Review, 51*, 527–654.

Mosteller, R. P. (1996). Syndromes and politics in criminal trials and evidence law. *Duke Law Journal, 46*, 461–516.

New Hampshire v. Morahan, W.L. 378571 (N.H. Super. May 23, 1995).

North Dakota Century Code. (1998).

Note. The XYY chromosomal abnormality: Use and misuse in the legal process. (1972). *Harvard Journal of Legislation, 9*, 469–493.

Owens, W. (1995). State v. Osby, the urban survival defense. *American Journal of Criminal Law, 22*, 809–821.

Penrod, S. D. (1995). Expert psychological testimony on eyewitness reliability before and after Daubert: The state of the law and the science. *Behavioral Sciences and the Law, 13*, 229–259.

People v. Enis, 564 N.E.2d 1155 (Ill. 1990).

People v. Gorshen, 336 P.2d 492 (Cal. 1959).

People v. Jones, 266 P.2d 38 (Cal. 1954).

People v. Leahy, 883 P.2d 321 (Cal. 1994).

People v. Medina, 47 Cal. Rptr.2d 165 (1995).

People v. Poddar, 26 Cal. App.3d 438, 103 Cal. Rptr. 84 (1972).

People v. Santos, No. 1K046229 (Crim. Ct. N.Y. Nov. 3, 1982).

People v. Shelton, 385 N.Y.S. 708 (1986).

People v. Stoll, 783 P.2d 698 (Cal. 1989).

People v. Tanner, 91 Cal. Rptr. 656 (Ct. App. 1970).

People v. Taylor, 75 N.Y.2d 277, 552 N.E.2d 131 (N.Y. 1990).

People v. Yukl, 372 N.Y.S.2d 313 (1975).

Price, N. (1994, May 31). The "abuse excuse": A threat to justice? More and more lawyers using trauma as defense to crimes. *Legal Intelligencer*, pp. 3–4.

Reisner, R., & Slobogin, C. (1990). *Law and the mental health system: Civil and criminal aspects* (2nd. ed.). St. Paul, MN: West.

Richardson, J. T., Dobbin, S., Gatowski, S., Ginsburg, G., Merlino, M. L., Dahir, V., & Colton, C. (1995). The problems of applying Daubert to psychological syndrome evidence. *Judicature, 79*, 10–16.

Richardson, J. T., Dobbin, S. A., Gatowski, S., Ginsburg, G. P., Merlino, M. L., Dahir, V., & Colton, C. (1998, March). *A case law survey of social and behavioral science evidence after Daubert*. Paper presented at the annual meeting of the American Psychology–Law Society (Div. 41, American Psychological Association), Redondo Beach, CA.

Rock v. Arkansas, 483 U.S. 44 (1987).

Saltzburg, S., & Redden, K. (1982). *Federal rules of evidence manual* (3rd ed.). Charlottesville, VA: Michie.

Samborn, H. V. (1997). Changing the jury tool box. *American Bar Association Journal, 83*, 22–23.

Sanders, J. (1994). Scientific validity, admissibility and mass torts after Daubert. *Minnesota Law Review, 78*, 1387–1441.

Shatan, C. (1973). Soldiers in and after Vietnam. *Journal of Social Science, 31*, 25–29.

Skeen, D. (1983). The genetically defective offender. *William Mitchell Law Review, 9*, 217–265.

Slade, M. (1994, May 21). I am a victim of (fill in the blank) and couldn't help myself: Legal defenses put blame on syndromes. *Star Tribune* [Minneapolis–St. Paul], pp. 4A–5A.

Slater, D., & Hans, V. P. (1984). Public opinion of forensic psychiatry following the Hinckley verdict. *American Journal of Psychiatry, 141*, 675–679.

Slobogin, C. (1989). The "ultimate issue" issue. *Behavioral Science and the Law, 7*, 259–266.

Slobogin, C. (1999). The admissibility of behavioral science information in criminal trials: From primitivism to Daubert to voice. *Psychology, Public Policy, and Law, 5*, 110–119.

State v. Allery, 682 P.2d 312 (Wash. 1984).

State v. Anaya, 438 A.2d 892 (Me. 1981).

State v. Bednarz, 507 N.W.2d 168 (Wisc. Ct. App. 1993).

State v. Bible, 858 P.2d 1152 (Ariz. 1993).

State v. Black, 745 P.2d 12 (Wash. 1987).

State v. Cephas, 637 A.2d 20 (Del. Super. 1994).

State v. Foret, 628 So.2d 1116 (La. 1993).

State v. Gardiner, 636 A.2d 710 (R.I. 1994).

State v. Hickson, 630 So.2d 172 (Fla. 1993).

State v. Hill, 339 S.E.2d 121 (S.C. 1986).

State v. Hutchens, 429 S.E.2d 755 (N.C. 1993).

State v. Kelly, 478 A.2d 364 (N.J. 1984).

State v. Kim, 645 P.2d 1330 (Haw. 1982).

State v. Ott, 686 P.2d 1001 (Or. 1984).

State v. Roberts, 544 P.2d 754 (Wash. 1976).

State v. Saldana, 324 N.W.2d 227 (Minn. 1982).

State v. Treadaway, 568 P.2d 1061 (Ariz. 1977).

State v. Whitney-Briggs, 936 A.2d 1047 (Ct. App. Ore. 1997).

State v. Wilson, 456 N.E.2d 1287 (Ohio 1982).

Strong, J. W. (1970). Questions affecting the admissibility of scientific evidence. *University of Illinois Law Forum, 1970,* 1–22.

Strong, J. W. (Ed.). (1992). *McCormick on evidence.* St. Paul, MN: West.

Summit, R. C. (1983). The child sexual abuse accommodation syndrome. *Child Abuse and Neglect, 7,* 177–191.

Taslitz, A. E. (1993). Myself alone: Individualizing justice through psychological character evidence. *Maryland Law Review, 52,* 1–121.

Taslitz, A. E. (1998). A feminist approach to social scientific evidence: Foundations. *Michigan Journal of Gender and Law, 1,* 1–80.

Underwager, R., & Wakefield, H. (1993). A paradigm shift for expert witnesses. *Issues in Child Sex Abuse Accusations, 5,* 158–163.

United States v. Alexander and Murdock, 471 F.2d 923 (D.C. Cir. 1973), cert. denied 409 U.S. 1044 (1973).

United States v. Azure, 801 F.2d 336 (8th Cir. 1986).

United States v. Christopher, 833 F.2d 1296 (9th Cir. 1987).

United States v. Davis, 835 F.2d 274 (11th Cir. 1988).

United States v. Downing, 753 F.2d 1224 (3d Cir. 1985).

United States v. Fosher, 590 F.2d 381 (1st Cir. 1979).

United States v. Gillis, 773 F.2d 549 (4th Cir. 1985).

United States v. Hearst, 412 F. Supp. 889 (N.D. Cal. 1976).

United States v. Hiss, 88 F. Supp. 559 (S.D. N.Y. 1950).

United States v. Kime, 99 F.2d 870 (8th Cir. 1996).

United States v. Lewellyn, 723 F.2d 615 (8th Cir. 1983).

United States v. MacDonald, 688 F.2d 224 (4th Cir. 1981).

United States v. Pollard, 282 F.2d 450 (6th Cir. 1960), mandate clarified, 285 F.2d 81 (6th Cir. 1960).

United States v. Powers, 59 F.3d 1460 (7th Cir. 1994).

United States v. Salamanca, 990 F.2d 629 (D.C. Cir. 1993).

United States v. Scheffer, 118 S. Ct. 1261 (1998).

United States v. Two Bulls, 918 F.2d 56 (8th Cir. 1990).

United States v. Whitted, 994 F.2d 444 (8th Cir. 1993).

Van Poyck v. State, 694 So.2d 686 (Fla. 1997).

Vidmar, N. J., & Schuller, R. A. (1989). Juries and expert evidence: Social framework testimony. *Law and Contemporary Problems, 1989*, 133–176.

Walker, L. (1979). *The battered woman*. New York: Harper & Row.

Walker, L., & Monahan, J. (1987). Social frameworks: A new use of social science in law. *Virginia Law Review, 73*, 559–598.

Weinstein, J., & Berger, M. (1986). *Weinstein's evidence* (Vol. 3). Westbury, NY: Foundation Press.

Wilson, J. Q. (1997). *Moral judgement: Does the abuse excuse threaten our legal system?* New York: Basic Books.

Zamora v. State, 361 So.2d 776, 779 (3d D.C.A. 1978).

V

THERAPEUTIC JURISPRUDENCE

14

THE DEVELOPMENT OF THERAPEUTIC JURISPRUDENCE: FROM THEORY TO PRACTICE

DAVID B. WEXLER

The past quarter century has witnessed an explosion of research and scholarship falling under the rubric of mental health and the law, as well as the emergence of new perspectives that enrich our understanding of the law as a whole. Therapeutic jurisprudence, the study of the role of the law as a therapeutic agent, is one such development. This chapter is an exercise in forward reflection, reassessment, and reformulation; my goal is to trace the development of therapeutic jurisprudence, examine where it is today, and point the way toward its most profitable paths for the future.

A PRACTITIONER'S AND FIELD'S COMING OF AGE

I began my work in the field of mental health and the law during the early 1970s. Initially, my research focused on a wide variety of specific substantive areas within this discipline: an empirical study of Arizona's civil commitment system (Wexler & Scoville, 1971), a conceptual critique of a psychosurgery case (Wexler, 1981), a constitutional and behavioral look at token economies (Wexler, 1973), an analysis of the links between the civil commitment and the criminal commitment systems, and a warning against subordinating justice concerns to therapeutic ones (Wexler, 1972).

Other portions of my research throughout that initial period were driven by a more distinctive perspective. Examples of this approach include an article that focused on how the contingencies operative in the legal system encouraged or discouraged certain behaviors and activities in either a therapeutic or an antitherapeutic way (Wexler, 1977); an analysis of the *Tarasoff* case that concluded that the decision might prompt therapists to think in terms of couple or conjoint therapy (Wexler, 1979); a review essay of Robert Burt's book *Taking Care of Strangers* (Wexler, 1980); and an article that speculated that the evidence-gathering requirements of civil libertarian commitment codes might induce parents to act in therapeutically appropriate ways with disturbed young adult children and thus might ironically render commitment unnecessary (Wexler, 1986).

A common thread running through many of these articles inspired me to find that same unifying concept cropping up in the works of others. Winick's (1977) critique, on grounds of its antitherapeutic impact, of the rule in certain jurisdictions barring the trial of those rendered "artificially" competent (i.e., by virtue of taking psychotropic medications) was a case in point, as was the article by Ensminger and Liguori (1978) entitled "The Therapeutic Significance of the Civil Commitment Hearing: An Unexplored Potential." It was not until the summer of 1987, however, while working on a paper for a National Institute of Mental Health (NIMH) workshop, that I finally understood that these other academics and I were on the brink of a provocative new area of study; it was at this point that I clarified my own research aspirations and objectives. I had been asked to write something in the more general area of law and therapy. It quickly became clear to me, however, that my particular interests were not synonymous with the general rubric of law and therapy. I did not want to review the psychosurgery case, nor did I want to rehearse the arguments for or against a right to treatment or a right to refuse treatment. My interest was not so much in law *and* therapy as it was in law *as* therapy. And it had been this very concept, the law as therapy, that had formed the common thread in my own work and in that of others. I therefore seized the opportunity of writing the paper for the NIMH workshop to explicitly lay out a perspective of law as therapy—of therapy through law—and it is that perspective that is now known as therapeutic jurisprudence.

The original draft, however, did not refer to the law-as-therapy approach as "therapeutic jurisprudence." The original term used was *juridical psychotherapy* (Poythress & Brodsky, 1992), but its tenure was short lived. When I revised the draft, I struggled with many alternatives and ultimately settled on "therapeutic jurisprudence," a designation that had merely been an "also-ran" when I wrote the original paper. The term *therapeutic juris-*

prudence has itself often been criticized. As one commentator correctly noted, "the words 'therapeutic jurisprudence' roll uneasily off the tongue" (Acker, 1992, p. 273). Additionally, the word *therapeutic* has been criticized ("too vague; too medical-sounding"), as has *jurisprudence* ("where's the comprehensive theory?"). These are valid concerns and criticisms. Yet, although commentators claim that therapeutic jurisprudence "in retrospect may not have been the wisest of titles to adopt" (Carson, 1995, p. 463), it is difficult to posit a term that perfectly captures the general notion and the primary focus of this perspective. In any event, for better or for worse, the term has now stuck.

My workshop paper (Wexler, 1990) was published under the title "An Introduction to Therapeutic Jurisprudence" as the introductory chapter to an anthology I edited entitled *Therapeutic Jurisprudence: The Law as a Therapeutic Agent*. Apart from the NIMH workshop paper explicating the therapeutic jurisprudence perspective, the other works in the anthology fell implicitly within the newly named perspective. Substantively, the chapters related to core mental health law topics—incompetence, insanity, involuntary civil commitment, and the like.

Following on the heels of that book, Winick and I published a volume entitled *Essays in Therapeutic Jurisprudence* (Wexler & Winick, 1991). In *Essays*, all of the chapters explicitly used the therapeutic jurisprudence perspective. Like the predecessor volume, the substantive thrust of the book was in mental health law. We recognized, however, the much broader potential of the framework. As the introduction states,

> It seems only natural (at least to those of us who specialize in mental health law) that initial forays into therapeutic jurisprudence take place within the core content areas of mental health law. Obviously, however, therapeutic jurisprudence will also have applications in forensic psychiatry generally, in health law, in a variety of allied legal fields (criminal law, juvenile law, family law), and probably across the entire legal spectrum. (p. x)

The *Essays* book included a chapter addressed principally to trial courts—a chapter relating how judges holding insanity acquittee release hearings might use psychological principles to increase the probability that acquittees will comply with the imposed conditions of release. *Essays* also called for empirical inquiry to ascertain the therapeutic consequences of various legal arrangements (p. 303) and advocated a more comparative law approach to therapeutic jurisprudence. More specifically, it urged the release of legal scholarship from the confines of U.S. constitutional construction in favor of an understanding of law as something more than a domestic discipline; it promoted studying and discussing, in a truly international context, the relationship between legal arrangements and therapeutic outcomes (p. 517).

Five years after the publication of *Essays*, Winick and I edited an anthology entitled *Law in a Therapeutic Key: Developments in Therapeutic Jurisprudence* (Wexler & Winick, 1996), which included scholarship consistent with the recommendations made in *Essays*. *Law in a Therapeutic Key* contained work by more than 50 authors, all expressly falling within the realm of therapeutic jurisprudence. The anthology included some of the empirical work that had begun, and it was different from its predecessors in terms of its substantive coverage. Although the subject matter of traditional mental health law was again included, so too were correctional law, criminal law, criminal procedure, sentencing, family and juvenile law, sexual orientation law, disability law, health law, personal injury and tort law, the law of evidence, labor arbitration law, contracts and commercial law, and professional responsibility.

THERAPEUTIC JURISPRUDENCE: THE CURRENT STATE OF AFFAIRS

Therapeutic jurisprudence is thus no longer merely a special way of looking at mental health law. Instead, it is now a therapeutic perspective on the law in general. Moreover, this explicit approach has raised many interesting questions and has generated important research and writing that might otherwise not have occurred. Significantly, therapeutic jurisprudence brings together under a single conceptual umbrella a number of areas that, at first glance, do not seem to be particularly related: how the criminal justice system might traumatize victims of sexual battery, how workers' compensation laws might create the moral hazard of prolonging work-related injury, how a fault-based (rather than a no-fault) tort compensation scheme might enhance recovery from personal injury, and how the current law of contracts might operate to perpetuate the low self-esteem of disadvantaged contracting parties.

Therapeutic jurisprudence is an optimistic perspective. It searches for recent developments in the clinical behavioral sciences and seeks opportunities to import this new work into the legal arena (Wexler, 1997). One particularly promising avenue looks not so much to the reform of law as to the reform of practice, concentrating on how existing law, whatever its content, may be therapeutically applied (Wexler, 1996b). Furthermore, therapeutic jurisprudence scholarship is now being enriched by efforts to explore intellectual links with related perspectives such as procedural justice (Tyler, 1996), restorative justice (Scheff, 1998), the ecology of human development (Babb, 1997), alternative dispute resolution (Abrams, Abrams, & Nolan, 1996), and preventive law (Stolle, 1996).

The International Network on Therapeutic Jurisprudence at the University of Puerto Rico School of Law, of which I serve as director, was established to encourage work in therapeutic jurisprudence by serving as a global clearinghouse and resource center. The network supports conferences and maintains a Web site (http://www.law.arizona.edu/upr-intj) with an up-to-date bibliography. In July 1998, it cosponsored the First International Conference on Therapeutic Jurisprudence in Winchester, England, principally organized by the Behavioural Science and Law Network at the University of Southampton. Some of the conference papers have been published in the "Therapeutic Jurisprudence Forum," now a regular feature of the University of Puerto Rico's law journal *Revista Jurídica UPR*. The forum publishes therapeutic jurisprudence scholarship by academics, professionals, and students in numerous relevant fields (e.g., law, psychology, psychiatry, social work, criminal justice and corrections, and public health). The inaugural feature carried an article by University of California sociologist Thomas Scheff (1998) on community conferences and offender–victim mediation, an article by Eilis Magner (1998), dean of an Australian law school, about the problems and prospects of adapting the therapeutic jurisprudence approach to Australia, and an article by University of Arizona law student Kathryn Maxwell (1998) on preventive law strategies for minimizing psychological trauma to the children of divorcing couples.

It appears, then, that therapeutic jurisprudence now has a rather firm footing in the world of academia. But for an approach developed largely in the universities, what sort of movement will occur "from the top down" (Finkelman & Grisso, 1996), from the towers to the trenches?

A VISION FOR THE FUTURE: THERAPEUTIC JURISPRUDENCE AND PREVENTIVE LAW

Fortunately, the movement of therapeutic jurisprudence from the academy to real-world practice is now beginning to occur, particularly with respect to the therapeutic application of the law by trial judges and in the context of legal counseling by attorneys. It should come as no surprise that some members of the judiciary will balk at considering the therapeutic consequences of their behavior and rulings. They will resist the suggestion that, knowingly or unknowingly, willingly or unwillingly, they inevitably play a role akin to that of a social worker and, therefore, ought at least to try to become better in that capacity (Wexler, 1996a). Nor, however, should it come as a surprise that some judges will naturally gravitate toward the therapeutic jurisprudence approach. Many of them have engaged in a form of therapeutic jurisprudence judging implicitly and intuitively, if unsystematically—much like my own involvement in therapeutic jurisprudence scholarship in the years before 1987.

This consonance with therapeutic jurisprudence may be especially true of family and juvenile court judges, of special "treatment court" judges

—such as drug court professionals (Hora, Schma, & Rosenthal, 1999), and of a number of general jurisdiction judges (Kane, 1996). The National Association of Women Judges (NAWJ), for example, chose therapeutic jurisprudence as the theme for its September 1997 Annual Convention in Salt Lake City and invited two drug court professionals—Judge Peggy Hora and Judge William Schma—along with Bruce Winick and myself to address the opening plenary session. Judges Hora and Schma, major contributors to the therapeutic jurisprudence literature (Hora et al., 1999), discussed with attendees certain practices and situations such as how the acceptance of no contest pleas may frustrate later attempts at rehabilitation and elicited from participants instances where trials or hearings were shaped, within legal limits, in such a manner as to promote healing or to reduce trauma for those involved in the legal proceedings.

At the meeting, participants proposed a collaborative effort for research and judicial education. It was recommended that judges sensitive to the therapeutic jurisprudence approach make notes of circumstances relevant to therapeutic jurisprudence—and the strategies used to deal with such situations. The judges' accounts could then be collected, shared, discussed, and critiqued, just like other traditional topics of judicial interest. In that way, therapeutic jurisprudence scholarship might enjoy greater practical application, and routine judicial education in therapeutic jurisprudence might simultaneously be encouraged. Importantly, such a collaborative effort might lead to the explicit use of a therapeutic jurisprudence perspective in day-to-day judging.

And what of therapeutic jurisprudence and lawyering? Of course, if judges—who help create the legal culture in their courtrooms and often in their communities—begin to care about this psychological dimension, lawyers will almost certainly follow suit. In fact, Judge Schma regularly meets with a group of lawyers in his own community to speak with them about therapeutic jurisprudence and related practice issues. With lawyering, however, judicial influence and persuasion has its limits. Judges sensitive to the therapeutic jurisprudence approach can act accordingly in their courtrooms, or during pretrial or settlement conferences, when presented with what Winick termed a "therapeutic moment," such as a hearing to accept a plea. For lawyers, however, the most crucial therapeutic moment may not occur in a judicial setting at all, but instead in the office during a client consultation. If lawyers are to be effective in advising clients to handle legal situations in therapeutically beneficial ways, they must develop sensitivity to these situations. Furthermore, clients must be persuaded to come for a consultation in the first place.

For all of this to occur, the perspective of therapeutic jurisprudence should be integrated with the perspective of preventive law, an integration first proposed by Stolle (1996) in the context of elder law. Preventive law involves careful client interviewing and counseling, as well as thoughtful planning and thorough drafting to avoid legal conflicts. The practice of preventive law emphasizes the importance of "periodic legal checkups" (Hardaway, 1997, p. 189). Moreover, it seeks to identify "legal soft spots"— potential points of dispute—and to fashion strategies for avoiding or minimizing the anticipated legal trouble (p. 192). In law school teaching, preventive law proponents suggest a "rewind" technique as a pedagogical device (p. xlii). After discussing an appellate decision in a contract case, for example, an instructor might "rewind" the situation back to the stage of drafting and ask what might have been done differently to avoid this type of problem.

When integrated with preventive law, therapeutic jurisprudence would suggest that during these "legal checkups" and counseling sessions, lawyers look not only to "legal soft spots," or areas that can lead to future legal disputes, but also to "psycholegal soft spots" (Stolle, Wexler, Winick, & Dauer, 1997), areas where a legal intervention or procedure may lead not to a lawsuit but, instead, to anxiety, distress, depression, or resentment. At these moments, the lawyer should raise such issues with the client and discuss possible strategies for avoiding harmful scenarios. Consider, for example, the situation of elderly parents with two adult children, one of whom functions marginally because of a history of drug and alcohol problems. If, in drafting a will, the parents leave funds outright to one child but specify that money for the troubled child must be held in trust, the troubled child will likely develop hard feelings toward the parents and the sibling with unconditioned funds. A lawyer combining the perspectives of therapeutic jurisprudence and preventive law will anticipate such a situation, regard the proposed testamentary disposition as a psycholegal soft spot (although not necessarily as a legal soft spot vulnerable to legal attack), and discuss with the clients possible strategies for coping with, as well as minimizing, the law-related psychological distress. For example, the clients might speak to the adult children before taking such an action, or they might specify in the will—or in a separate letter—why they opted for the course they chose.

Preventive law gives therapeutic jurisprudence a set of practical procedures whereby lawyers may counsel clients to deal with legal problems in a more therapeutic manner; therapeutic jurisprudence gives to preventive law a humanistic, psychological dimension, while adding structure and substance to the lawyer's role as counselor. Stolle's proposed integration of these two perspectives has sparked the interest of the therapeutic jurisprudence and preventive law communities (Stolle & Wexler, 1997). Most recently, Stolle, Winick, and I collaborated with Professor Edward Dauer, president of the National Center of Preventive Law, on an article proposing, among other things, systematic research into psycholegal soft spots and effective strategies for handling these kinds of situations (Stolle et al., 1997). The article also called on interested practitioners to develop a combined concentration in therapeutic jurisprudence and preventive law. In seeking to develop a psychology and law-based model of lawyering, we referred to such lawyers as "TJ preventive lawyers."

The University of Puerto Rico School of Law is already at work on implementing such an approach. Students working in the legal clinic are currently keeping journals of psycholegal soft spots that they encounter, parallel to the judicial journals of psychojudicial soft spots discussed at the conference of the NAWJ. Indeed, the two projects are mutually beneficial. Consider, for example, a therapeutic moment discussed by Judge Peggy Hora at the NAWJ plenary session. Judge Hora was once called on to hear a case between siblings involving a contested will. The brother sought to overturn, on the grounds of undue influence, a disposition of the mother's dilapidated house to the sister, who had cared for the mother in her later years. Unlike his sister, the brother had a decent income and a home of his own. Finding no undue influence, Judge Hora upheld the will. She sensed, however, that the case had little to do with money and had to do, instead, with the brother's hurt feelings. At the close of the hearing, she remarked to him that, given the differing financial situations of the siblings, the disposition seemed understandable, and it did not seem to her to suggest that the mother loved him any less. The brother broke down in tears.

Judge Hora's case is itself the kind of vignette that should be collected, disseminated, discussed, and debated, for it showcases the psychojudicial soft spots and therapeutic moments that can form the basis of research and judicial education. But with the preventive law "rewind" technique, these cases can also be used as a database for educating TJ preventive lawyers. In fact, Judge Hora's case can be rewound twice.

First, an instructor could rewind to the lawyer's office when the brother and his lawyer are contemplating challenging the will. If, after ascertaining the relevant facts, the lawyer had given the brother a legal and psychological assessment of the case similar to the one that Judge Hora gave at trial, perhaps the brother would not have brought the case at all. Of course, this raises numerous questions regarding the lawyer's role and potential conflicts of interest and about professional responsibility more generally. These questions are matters for further discussion in shaping a TJ preventive lawyer.

The second rewind of Judge Hora's case could take students to the law office of the mother's attorney at the time of the drafting of her will. In that setting, a TJ preventive lawyer might recognize the proposed disposition as a "psycholegal soft spot" and could then discuss with the client possible preventive strategies: perhaps talking to her son now, or stating in the will, or in a separate letter, or on an audiotape or videotape, that despite her love for her son, the disparate financial situations necessitated such action.

Just as many judges have intuitively used a therapeutic jurisprudence perspective, there are obviously many lawyers who have implicitly practiced as TJ preventive lawyers. We hope, however, that by making this approach explicit—by giving it a name—receptive lawyers will begin to practice as TJ preventive lawyers openly, regularly, and systematically. As with the therapeutic jurisprudence perspective itself, specific recognition of TJ preventive lawyering may lead to substantially greater activity among practitioners. Furthermore, as therapeutic jurisprudence continues to influence legal and judicial practice, the stories that emerge will constitute more than part of the stock in trade of TJ preventive lawyers and of judges interested in a therapeutic jurisprudence approach. These practice vignettes will also provide fodder for academics, who will in turn categorize, discuss, and critique them. Accordingly, the theory–practice relationship, in this context, can become the two-way street that it most certainly ought to be.

REFERENCES

Abrams, R. I., Abrams, F. E., & Nolan, D. R. (1996). Arbitral theory. In D. B. Wexler & B. J. Winick (Eds.), *Law in a therapeutic key: Developments in therapeutic jurisprudence* (pp. 499–523). Durham, NC: Carolina Academic Press.

Acker, J. (1992). Review of essays in therapeutic jurisprudence. *Journal of Psychiatry and Law, 20,* 273–278.

Babb, B. A. (1997). An interdisciplinary approach to family law jurisprudence: Application of an ecological and therapeutic perspective. *Indiana Law Journal, 72,* 775–808.

Carson, D. (1995). Therapeutic jurisprudence for the United Kingdom? *Journal of Forensic Psychiatry, 6,* 463–466.

Ensminger, J., & Liguori, T. (1978). The therapeutic significance of the civil commitment hearing: An unexplored potential. *Journal of Psychiatry and Law, 6,* 5–44.

Finkelman, D., & Grisso, T. (1996). Therapeutic jurisprudence: From idea to application. In D. B. Wexler & B. J. Winick (Eds.), *Law in a therapeutic key: Developments in therapeutic jurisprudence* (pp. 587–595). Durham, NC: Carolina Academic Press.

Hardaway, R. M. (1997). *Preventive law: Materials on a nonadversarial legal process.* Cincinnati, OH: Anderson.

Hora, P. F., Schma, W. G., & Rosenthal, J. (1999). Therapeutic jurisprudence and the drug treatment court movement: Revolutionizing the criminal justice system's response to drug abuse and crime in America. *Notre Dame Law Review, 74,* 439–537.

Kane, R. J. (1996). A sentencing model for the 21st century. In D. B. Wexler & B. J. Winick (Eds.), *Law in a therapeutic key: Developments in therapeutic jurisprudence* (pp. 203–212). Durham, NC: Carolina Academic Press.

Magner, E. S. (1998). Therapeutic jurisprudence: Its potential in Australia. *Revista Jurídica UPR, 67*, 121–135.

Maxwell, K. E. (1998). Preventive law strategies to mitigate the detrimental effects of clients' divorces on their children. *Revista Jurídica UPR, 67*, 137–164.

Poythress, N., & Brodsky, S. L. (1992). In the wake of a negligent release law suit: An investigation of professional consequences and institutional impact on a state psychiatric hospital. *Law and Human Behavior, 16*, 155–173.

Scheff, T. J. (1998). Community conferences: Shame and anger in therapeutic jurisprudence. *Revista Jurídica UPR, 67*, 97–119.

Stolle, D. P. (1996). Professional responsibility in elder law: A synthesis of preventive law and therapeutic jurisprudence. *Behavioral Sciences and the Law, 14*, 459–478.

Stolle, D. P., & Wexler, D. B. (1997). Therapeutic jurisprudence and preventive law: A combined concentration to invigorate the everyday practice of law. *Arizona Law Review, 25*, 25–33.

Stolle, D. P., Wexler, D. B., Winick, B. J., & Dauer, E. (1997). Integrating preventive law and therapeutic jurisprudence: A law and psychology based approach to lawyering. *California West Law Review, 34*, 15–51.

Tyler, T. R. (1996). The psychological consequences of judicial procedures: Implications for civil commitment hearings. In D. B. Wexler & B. J. Winick (Eds.), *Law in a therapeutic key: Developments in therapeutic jurisprudence* (pp. 3–15). Durham, NC: Carolina Academic Press.

Wexler, D. B. (1972). Therapeutic justice. *Minnesota Law Review, 57*, 289–338.

Wexler, D. B. (1973). Token and taboo: Behavior modification, token economies, and the law. *California Law Review, 61*, 81–109.

Wexler, D. B. (1977). Criminal commitment contingency structures. In B. D. Sales (Ed.), *Perspectives in law and psychology: Vol. 1. The criminal justice system* (pp. 121–138). New York: Plenum.

Wexler, D. B. (1979). Patients, therapists, and third parties: The victimological virtues of Tarasoff. *International Journal of Law and Psychiatry, 2*, 1–28.

Wexler, D. B. (1980). Doctor–patient dialogue: A second opinion on talk therapy through law. *Yale Law Journal, 90*, 458–472.

Wexler, D. B. (1981). *Mental health law: Major issues.* New York: Plenum Press.

Wexler, D. B. (1986). Grave disability and family therapy: The therapeutic potential of civil libertarian commitment codes. *International Journal of Law and Psychiatry, 9*, 39–56.

Wexler, D. B. (1990). An introduction to therapeutic jurisprudence. In D. B. Wexler (Ed.), *Therapeutic jurisprudence: The law as a therapeutic agent* (pp. 3–20). Durham, NC: Carolina Academic Press.

Wexler, D. B. (1996a). Therapeutic jurisprudence and the criminal courts. In D. B. Wexler & B. J. Winick (Eds.), *Law in a therapeutic key: Developments in therapeutic jurisprudence* (pp. 157–170). Durham, NC: Carolina Academic Press.

Wexler, D. B. (1996b). Therapeutic jurisprudence in clinical practice. *American Journal of Psychiatry, 153,* 453–455.

Wexler, D. B. (1997). How the law can use *what works*: A therapeutic jurisprudence look at recent research in rehabilitation. *Behavioral Sciences and the Law, 15,* 365–370.

Wexler, D. B., & Scoville, S. E. (1971). The administration of psychiatric justice: Theory and practice in Arizona. *Arizona Law Review, 13,* 1–25.

Wexler, D. B., & Winick, B. J. (1991). *Essays in therapeutic jurisprudence.* Durham, NC: Carolina Academic Press.

Wexler, D. B., & Winick, B. J. (1996). *Law in a therapeutic key: Developments in therapeutic jurisprudence.* Durham, NC: Carolina Academic Press.

Winick, B. J. (1977). Psychotropic medication and competence to stand trial. *American Bar Foundation Research Journal, 1977,* 769–816.

15

THE CIVIL COMMITMENT HEARING: APPLYING THE LAW THERAPEUTICALLY

BRUCE J. WINICK

Procedural due process requires an adversarial judicial hearing before an individual may be subjected to involuntary mental hospitalization. In practice, however, the hearing most patients receive is a brief episode in which patients' attorneys often relax their advocacy role and appear to act in concert with clinical evaluators and the judge to facilitate commitment. The hearing frequently seems to be a mere formality, lasting only minutes, in which the judge rubber-stamps the conclusions of the clinical experts.

Attorneys and judges act as they do based on the paternalistic assumption that the patient is ill and needs hospitalization. The sham nature of the hearing may, however, actually have antitherapeutic consequences for the patient, frustrating what could be the important participatory or dignitary value of the hearing and reducing the effectiveness of the hospitalization and treatment that typically are ordered. This chapter presents an analysis of civil commitment hearing practices based on *therapeutic jurisprudence*, the study of law's healing potential (Wexler & Winick, 1996; see Wexler, chapter 14, this volume). Legal rules and the way various legal actors play their roles have inevitable consequences for the mental health and psychological functioning of those affected. What are those consequences in the context of civil commitment hearings, and how can judges, attorneys, and expert witnesses play their roles so as to minimize antitherapeutic consequences for the patient and maximize the therapeutic potential of the hearing? This chapter criticizes existing practices in the civil commitment hearing as antitherapeutic and makes suggestions for restructuring hearing practices in ways that will effectuate the participatory interests of patients, producing increased satisfaction on their part and increasing the therapeutic potential of hospitalization.

The chapter begins with an examination of the due process requirement as it applies in the context of civil commitment hearings. It then examines how civil commitment hearings actually occur in practice and the antitherapeutic consequences of those hearings for patients. The chapter then analyzes the psychology of procedural justice and its applicability to the commitment hearing before exploring the psychological impact of coercion and choice for the patient. Although some have argued that these psychological principles may be inapplicable to patients facing commitment hearings, the next section argues that such patients can experience the psychological value of the hearing and that existing practices in the conduct of such hearings should therefore be restructured. The final section contains specific recommendations for how attorneys, judges, and clinical expert witnesses should play their roles at the hearing.

DUE PROCESS AND CIVIL COMMITMENT

Civil commitment in any form involves a substantial curtailment of liberty (*Addington v. Texas*, 1979). The interest in being free from external restraint—the core of the liberty protected by the due process clause—has recently been described by the Supreme Court as a "fundamental" liberty interest (*Foucha v. Louisiana*, 1992). When the state seeks to impose civil commitment on an involuntary basis, this liberty interest is directly infringed. In the early period of civil commitment in America, dating back to the late 19th century, involuntary hospitalization was based simply on a physician's certification of need (Sydeman, Cascardi, Poythress, & Rittenband, 1997). Commitment under early statutory provisions was based on a necessity for care and treatment in a hospital, and considerable deference was accorded to the expertise of psychiatrists in these matters. In the late 1960s and early 1970s, however, this model of commitment was challenged.

The civil rights struggle in the early 1960s had produced a new generation of lawyers committed to protecting and promoting the rights of a variety of minority groups and other disadvantaged populations, and these lawyers soon turned their attention to the civil commitment process (Brooks & Winick, 1987; Wald & Friedman, 1978). In the late 1960s, state institutions were overcrowded, underfunded, and understaffed. Media exposure of the abysmal conditions in state institutions coupled with a challenge to psychiatric expertise and to the wisdom and legitimacy of involuntary hospitalization set the stage for legal change. Law reform litigation on behalf of mental patients was brought by such organizations as the New York Civil Liberties Union and the Washington-based Mental Health Law Project, as well as by legal services programs and pro bono lawyers and law firms. This litigation effort succeeded in producing judicial decrees and statutory changes that tightened the criteria for commitment and created the right to a hearing on whether those criteria were satisfied. An influential case was the three-judge federal district court decision in *Lessard v. Schmidt* (1972), which required various procedural formalities at the involuntary hospitalization hearing.

It is now widely accepted that the procedural due process guarantee of the Fourteenth Amendment requires notice and a formal hearing before civil commitment may occur (or shortly thereafter when commitment is sought on an emergency basis) (*Addington v. Texas*, 1979; Brakel, Parry, & Weiner, 1985; "Developments," 1974; Perlin, 1989; compare *Vitek v. Jones*, 1980). Such a hearing requires the rights to counsel (which will be given if the individual is indigent), to notice of the proceedings, to a hearing presided over by a fair and impartial judge or hearing examiner, to cross-examine adverse witnesses and to present evidence, and to allocation of the burden of proof to the state by clear and convincing evidence (Brakel et al., 1985; Perlin, 1989; Stransky, 1996). Some jurisdictions also include the right to the assistance of a court-appointed clinical evaluator in the defense process (Perlin, 1989). In short, due process requires a fairly formal adversarial judicial hearing at which the state must carry the burden of proof.

THE CIVIL COMMITMENT HEARING IN PRACTICE

Although due process theory may require a formal adversarial judicial hearing, a large gulf exists between law on the books and law in action in this context. The formal due process model is often undermined by the way many attorneys representing individuals in civil commitment hearings play their roles. Although the law's commitment to an adversarial model in this and most other contexts contemplates competent attorneys who represent their clients' interests zealously, in fact counsel in civil commitment cases act in ways that often do not satisfy this model (Andalman & Chambers, 1974; Cohen, 1966; Costello, 1996; Perlin, 1992; "The role of counsel," 1975). Many attorneys relax their advocacy role and adopt a "paternalistic" or "best interests" approach, in which they seek to implement what they may perceive as their clients' best interests (Abisch, 1995;

Perlin, 1992; Perlin & Sadoff, 1982). Some commentators have even suggested that lawyers should play a nonadversarial role in order to function in a way that is more consonant with the paternalistic aims of the civil commitment system (Appelbaum, 1983; Brakel, 1981). One study showed that even when lawyers are trained in adversarial practice, they nonetheless continue to play a paternalistic role in civil commitment, seeking their clients' best interests as they perceive them to be rather than as their clients may articulate them (Poythress, 1978).

To some extent, this paternalistic role represents what Perlin called "sanism," a deeply ingrained prejudice against those with mental illness reinforced by stereotypes, pretextuality, and a basic dishonesty in the civil commitment process shared by judges, lawyers, and clinicians (Perlin, 1996; Perlin, in press; Perlin & Dorfman, 1996). This practice has turned the adversarial model into a farce and a mockery in which procedural rights are accorded in only a formal way so as to achieve what judges, lawyers, and clinicians perceive to be the best interests of the patient. In practice, commitment hearings tend to be brief and nonadversarial episodes in which judges appear to rubber-stamp the recommendations of clinical expert witnesses (Poythress, 1977). Indeed, studies show that judicial agreement with expert witnesses in this area ranges from 79% to 100% and most frequently exceeds 95% (Poythress, 1977). From the patient's perspective, the hearing may resemble the one presided over by the Queen of Hearts in *Alice in Wonderland:* "First the sentence, then the verdict" (Carroll, 1992, p. 96).

The paternalistic role played by some counsel in the civil commitment process, as well as the role often played by the judge, thus frustrates the goals of the procedural protections mandated by the due process clause. Accuracy is undermined because the system assumes that the individual is a legitimate subject of paternalism when he or she in fact may not satisfy this condition. Moreover, the practice undercuts the participatory or dignitary value of the procedure (Mashaw, 1976; Michelman, 1977; Tribe, 1988, p. 666; Winick, 1989; see *Goldberg v. Kelly*, 1970; *Marshall v. Jerricho*, 1980; *Morrissey v. Brewer*, 1972). The basic dishonesty of the process can have severe antitherapeutic consequences for the patient, who may lose trust and confidence in the judges, lawyers, and clinicians involved and in the genuineness of their purportedly benevolent intentions. As a result, many feel coerced by civil commitment, with potentially negative consequences for the efficacy of the commitment process (Tyler, 1992; Winick, 1997a).

PSYCHOLOGY OF PROCEDURAL JUSTICE AND THE COMMITMENT HEARING

Scholarship on the psychology of procedural justice suggests that people are more satisfied with and comply more with the outcome of legal proceedings when those proceedings are perceived to be fair and when they have an opportunity to participate in them (Lind & Tyler, 1988; Thibault & Walker, 1978; Tyler, 1990). Applying these principles to the civil commitment hearing, Tyler (1992) argued that increasing the patient's sense of participation, dignity, and trust during the commitment proceedings is likely to increase the patient's acceptance of the outcome of the hearing and to lead to a greater willingness to accept hospitalization and treatment —and, thus, to enhanced treatment efficacy. In a recent critical analysis of Tyler's work, Sydeman et al. (1997) suggested that Tyler's conclusion is also supported by principles derived from both the social cognition and the consumerism literature.

The social cognition literature emphasizes "information control," the perception of control that results when an individual obtains information relating to a stressful situation or event (Fiske & Taylor, 1984; Sydeman et al., 1997). Such information provides the individual with an opportunity to understand what is happening to him or her. Properly administered, the civil commitment hearing may be an opportunity to provide patients with a degree of information control, enabling them to understand the reasons for commitment and the positive expectations that the judge and clinicians testifying at the hearing have concerning the outcome of hospitalization. The commitment hearing can thus be seen as an opportunity to provide information to patients that might relieve their stress, increase their acceptance of the commitment determination, and set up expectancies of positive treatment results that might, in turn, help to bring about the desired outcomes.

Participation, dignity, and trust, as well as the opportunity to "tell their story," are themes often voiced in the mental health consumer (or survivor) literature (Sydeman et al., 1997). The consumer's desire for an opportunity to tell his or her side of the story suggests the applicability in the civil commitment context of the "voice" effect described in the procedural justice literature. Allowing patients at the commitment hearing an opportunity to tell their story, therefore, might be an important mechanism for increasing patient perceptions of fairness, respect, and dignity in the process, with a resulting increase in their receptivity to treatment.

PSYCHOLOGICAL EFFECTS OF COERCION AND VOLUNTARY CHOICE

Tyler's (1992) conclusion is also supported by recent research by the MacArthur Research Network on Mental Health and the Law on patient perceptions of coercion (Bennett et al., 1993: Gardner et al., 1993; Hoge et al., 1997; Lidz et al., 1995; Monahan et al., 1995; Monahan et al., 1996; see Winick, 1997a; and Monahan and Steadman, chapter 10, this volume).

This research found that people feel noncoerced—even in coercive situations like civil commitment—when they perceive the intentions of state actors to be benevolent and when they are treated with dignity and respect, rather than in bad faith, and given a voice and validation.

The MacArthur work on coercion is significant when considered in connection with a body of theoretical work on the psychology of choice that suggests that people perform more effectively and with greater motivation when they choose voluntarily to do something and perform less effectively, with poor motivation and sometimes with psychological reactance, than when they are coerced into doing it (Winick, 1997c, chap. 17; see also Brehem & Brehem, 1981; Winick, 1991a, 1991b, 1992, 1994). Principles of cognitive and social psychology, including the goal setting effect, expectancy theory, intrinsic motivation, the psychology of commitment, and cognitive dissonance in general, support the positive value of choice and the negative effects of coercion (Winick, 1997c, chap. 17; see also Winick, 1991a; 1991b; 1994). Empirical investigation is needed, however, to determine the extent to which these general principles apply to people with severe mental illness (Sydeman et al., 1997; Winick, 1994, 1997c).

Sydeman et al. (1997) noted that widespread cynicism on the part of patients with mental illnesses and the severe symptoms of their psychopathology might interfere with their ability to perceive accurately the commitment process and the motivation of others. They suggested that these factors may diminish the ability of such patients to experience the procedural justice value of the commitment hearing that Tyler (1992) posited. At least some people suffering the acute symptoms of schizophrenia at the time of the hearing may not realize these benefits. Many patients, however, including some with schizophrenia, are not so cognitively disorganized or impaired.

The MacArthur Treatment Competence Study (Appelbaum & Grisso, 1995; Grisso & Appelbaum, 1995) provided important data that may shed light on these questions (see Grisso, chapter 8, this volume). The study compared a group of patients hospitalized for mental illnesses with a group of patients hospitalized for heart disease and with a group of community controls matched on various demographic factors. The groups were provided with information concerning treatment options and were rated on their ability to engage in rational treatment decision making. Although the group of mental patients performed significantly less well, this result was attributable to a small minority in the schizophrenia subgroup. Nearly half of the schizophrenia subgroup and 76% of the depression subgroup were found to perform in the adequate range across all decision-making measures, and a significant portion performed at or above the mean for people without mental illness (Grisso & Appelbaum, 1995; see Winick, 1996b). A high percentage of recently hospitalized patients with mental illnesses, including schizophrenia, the most seriously disturbing of the major mental illnesses, were thus found to perform in a relatively unimpaired range. Moreover, the findings revealed significant variability among patients within each diagnostic category.

The MacArthur Treatment Competence Study examined the ability to engage in rational treatment decision making, including the ability to understand treatment information, to appreciate it, to think rationally about treatment, and to express a choice. These abilities may not equate with the ability of patients at a commitment hearing to follow the proceedings, to understand the information conveyed, or to make accurate attributions concerning the motivation of the various actors in the commitment process. The general findings of the MacArthur work, however, concerning the high degree of variability among patients and the ability of a significant percentage of the group with severe mental illness to perform in a normal range strongly suggest that although some patients at the commitment hearing will be so impaired as to be unable to realize the procedural justice benefits of the hearing, many, and perhaps most, will not be so impaired.

That many patients are able to respond to the procedural justice effects of the commitment hearing also was suggested by Susman's (1994) research on dispute resolution mechanisms for hospitalized psychiatric patients seeking to refuse treatment. Susman found that patients who felt that their argument had been listened to and given serious consideration were more likely to feel that the procedure was fair and to accept the outcome as just. Although the patients in Susman's study may not have been so seriously disturbed as some patients at the point of commitment, his findings supported Tyler's (1992) conclusion that many patients will receive procedural justice benefits from properly conducted commitment hearings. Although more empirical work is needed to investigate the ability of patients in civil commitment hearings to experience these procedural justice benefits and to probe the relationship between such benefits and the treatment outcome, good reason exists to conclude that many patients will experience these benefits and, as a result, will be more receptive to hospital treatment and respond more favorably to it.

As Sydeman et al. (1997) correctly observed, many patients facing an involuntary commitment hearing are cynical about the judicial and hospitalization process. The impact of patient cynicism on the ability to realize the procedural justice benefits of the hearing also deserves empirical investigation. Predictably, cynicism born of mistreatment in society or at prior commitment hearings that seemed unfair will have a corrosive effect on trust and confidence in the benevolent motives of the legal actors in the commitment process. The remedy for such cynicism, however, would be more procedural justice, not less. To break down such cynicism, much of it justified, patients should be treated with fairness, dignity, respect, and genuine tolerance. To the extent that such cynicism may be an impediment to a positive treatment response, the civil commitment hearing constitutes an opportunity to remove this barrier to effective treatment.

Sydeman et al. (1997) also pointed out that Tyler's (1992) analysis is subject to the criticism that the civil commitment hearing itself is merely one phase of the commitment process and, from the patient's perspective, perhaps an insignificant one. They suggested that the commitment process can more realistically be viewed as a series of decision points between the patient and the physician, including whether to detain the patient for an evaluation, whether to petition for commitment, how to treat the patient in the hospital, and so forth. These decisions, they noted, as well as the way in which other disputes between the patient and physician are resolved, "could facilitate or undermine procedural justice effects during the hearing" or significantly dilute them (Sydeman et al., 1997, 219). Polite and respectful treatment of the patient during the hearing, they suggested, might not therefore have much of an impact if the patient is treated unfairly and disrespectfully both before and after the hearing by the psychiatrist and the hospital staff.

It may be that how the committing psychiatrist and hospital staff treat patients is more important than how patients are treated at the commitment hearing. This observation, however, does not argue against conducting the hearing so as to convey respect and a sense of fair treatment to the individual. To the contrary, it argues that the actions of the committing psychiatrist before, during, and after the hearing, as well as those of hospital staff, should also be restructured along these lines. Clinicians conducting evaluations concerning the need for commitment, testifying at commitment hearings, and participating in the treatment process, no less than judges and attorneys, need to recognize the importance of treating patients with dignity and respect, affording them voice and validation, and ensuring that they perceive their actions as benevolently motivated (Winick, 1997a). If anything, the work of Sydeman and her colleagues (1997) therefore suggests not only that the commitment hearing should be reformed in line with Tyler's (1992) analysis, but also that the entire commitment process be changed in this way.

RESTRUCTURING THE ROLE OF THE ACTORS IN THE COMMITMENT PROCESS

Therapeutic jurisprudence is the study of law's therapeutic consequences (Wexler & Winick, 1996; Winick, 1997d, 1997b). The rules of law and procedure, as well as how the actors in the legal system apply them, pose inevitable consequences for the mental health and psychological functioning of those affected. An important new direction in this approach focuses attention on how laws are applied and calls for a heightened sensitivity on the part of legal actors to the way they act in applying the law (Stolle et al., 1997; Wexler, 1996; Winick, 1997a, 1997b). In the context of the civil commitment process, judges, lawyers, and clinicians need to understand the potential they have for applying the law therapeutically and should restructure their behavior to realize this potential.

Judges, lawyers, and clinicians need to understand that the way they play their roles in the civil commitment process has inevitable therapeutic implications for the patient. They need to heed the admonitions of the MacArthur work on coercion and reframe their roles and practices in ways that produce in the patient feelings of noncoercion. They need to make patients feel that they are being treated fairly, with respect and dignity, and to accord them a greater sense of voice and validation. Civil commitment proceedings need to be restructured along this dimension to increase the potential therapeutic value of such hearings and decrease their antitherapeutic consequences.

Role of Counsel

The role of counsel in particular needs restructuring. In addition to teaching counsel adversarial methods and arming them with more information about the clinical aspects of the commitment and treatment process, which Poythress (1978) found insufficient to change behavior, lawyers need to be provided with information about the psychology of procedural justice and the recent MacArthur work on coercion. In addition, they need to be armed with information concerning the recent MacArthur work on competence, which demonstrates that many people with mental illness, even schizophrenia, are capable of performing within a relatively normal range with regard to decision making about mental health treatment.

The need also exists for a more detailed specification concerning the law's expectations about the role of counsel in civil commitment. Existing codes of ethics for attorneys do not define the role of counsel in the representation of clients with mental illness (Abisch, 1995; Costello, 1996). In the absence of such guidance, attorneys predictably will play their roles in different ways. Some play the traditional adversarial role, but some relax their advocacy and play a more paternalistic role (Abisch, 1995). More guidance is needed concerning how lawyers should reconcile the interest in protecting their clients' legal rights with that of promoting their therapeutic needs.

Attorney–Client Relationship

The attorney–client relationship in this context needs to be reconceptualized in ways that augment its potential therapeutic effects. Although the primary role of counsel is not to promote the mental health of the client but rather to protect the client's legal interests, the two roles need not be seen as conflicting. In many ways, acting to promote the client's interest in a fair hearing on commitment can have positive therapeutic value. Indeed, attorneys who relax their adversarial role in the commitment process based on a paternalistic motive to help the client who they perceive as mentally ill and in need of hospitalization may do more therapeutic harm than good.

Clients' legal rights can be promoted in ways that are good for their mental health. Attorneys in civil commitment cases should communicate and consult more with their clients, thereby providing them with an increased sense of information control (Fiske & Taylor, 1984) and empowering them in ways that can increase their mental health and psychological functioning. The attorney is a primary vehicle for effectuating the client's participatory interests and therefore should never act in ways that suggest betrayal of the client. The attorney is also in an excellent position to diminish the potential for real and perceived coercion in the admission process (Winick, 1991b). By effectuating rather than compromising the client's participatory interests in the commitment process, the attorney can contribute to the client's sense that he or she was treated fairly, to his or her ability to accept an adverse outcome of the proceeding, and to his or her willingness to comply with the court's decision in ways that can better achieve the goals of hospitalization.

The tendency of attorneys to be uncertain of the role they should play in the civil commitment hearing, particularly when they think that the client is incompetent, can be diminished by increasing their awareness of their ethical responsibilities and by providing them with additional information concerning the notion of competence. For purposes of civil commitment, competence is a legal rather than a clinical concept (Winick, 1991a). The standard, however, has been poorly defined in the case law, resulting in a predictable uncertainty concerning its application. At a minimum, the concept of competence requires the ability on the part of the individual to evidence a reasonably consistent choice. In addition, it requires some degree of ability to appreciate information and to engage in rational decision making. How much appreciation and rationality are required? Attorneys in the civil commitment process should understand that all clients, even those in other areas of practice, have diminished abilities to appreciate information and to engage in rational decision making. Too high a degree of appreciation and rationality should not be insisted on as a condition for competence (Winick, 1997c, chap. 18; see also Winick, 1991a, 1991b).

It is likely that many attorneys in the civil commitment process tend to apply too demanding a standard of competence. As a result, they conclude that their clients are incompetent and therefore that they should not advocate against a seemingly paternalistic intervention like mental hospitalization. If the client can evidence a consistent choice concerning hospitalization and can justify that choice in ways that are not obviously irrational or otherwise the product of mental illness, the attorney should consider the client to be competent and should respect his or her decision either to accept voluntary admission or to oppose hospitalization.

When an attorney believes that commitment is likely and would be appropriate for a client in a given set of circumstances, he or she should recommend that course to the client. When the client assents to voluntary admission or wishes to choose voluntary admission and the attorney concurs, the attorney should negotiate with the state the terms under which voluntary admission should occur, including an agreed-on treatment plan. In this context, counsel can play what has been described as a mediational role (Abisch, 1995). This is not unlike the role played by criminal defense lawyers in negotiating guilty pleas for clients who seem likely to be convicted and in attempting to convince them that such a plea may be more advantageous than a guilty verdict and resulting sentence.

When the client opposes admission, the attorney should play the adversarial role contemplated in the due process model, putting the state to its proof and helping the client to achieve full participatory value from the hearing process. The analogy to the role of defense counsel in criminal cases is again apt: Even if the defense lawyer believes that a plea bargain would be more advantageous, the client might disagree. In such cases counsel should then mount a vigorous defense.

What should the lawyer do when the client appears to be incompetent based on the attorney's discussions and consultations with him or her? If the client is unable to express a consistent choice, the client should be considered incompetent. Where the client's expression of choice seems to the attorney to be irrational or otherwise based primarily on mental illness, the client again should be deemed incompetent. In such instances, however, the attorney may need to have clinical consultation to make the judgment of competence, and such consultation should be available at state expense when the client is indigent (see *Ake v. Oklahoma*, 1985). When the attorney is convinced that the client is incompetent, voluntary admission should not be possible (see *Zinermon v. Burch*, 1990). Instead, the adversarial process should go forward, and counsel should put the state to its proof. In these cases, incompetence should not be difficult for the state to demonstrate by the requisite clear and convincing evidence standard; competence, however, is not the only issue. Counsel can play a constructive and important role in insisting and ensuring that commitment is in the client's best interests and is the least restrictive alternative for protecting the client's needs. If the attorney is unsuccessful and the client is committed, counsel should attempt to enable the patient to reframe the commitment experience in a positive way.

This more defined role for counsel can enhance the therapeutic potential of the commitment process while fulfilling its accuracy, fairness, and participatory goals. Moreover, it is more likely that counsel trained to play this role and to understand its therapeutic value will adhere to rather than subvert it out of paternalistic motives. Lawyers who relax their adversarial role to achieve what they think will be a paternalistic outcome probably do so because they feel an inner sense of conflict concerning their obligations to promote their client's best interests as well as their legal rights. However, a client who perceives a commitment as coerced and unfair and who believes that the attorney's actions are a betrayal of his or her real interests may experience the commitment as less therapeutic than a client who feels that the attorney was a genuine ally who assisted in effectuating his or her participatory and dignitary interests.

When the attorney plays this adversarial role, he or she can gain the client's trust and confidence in ways that might enable the attorney to help the client achieve whatever benefits hospitalization may offer. Such an attorney can also play an important role in helping the client avoid future problems. In this connection, the lawyer should consider having clients execute advance directive instruments dealing with future instances of mental health treatment or hospitalization (Winick, 1996a).

ROLE OF JUDGES AND CLINICIANS

Judges and clinicians also need training to sensitize them to the therapeutic potential of the roles that they play so their conduct may enhance the therapeutic potential of the commitment hearing; they require education in the psychology of procedural justice and in the psychological value of choice and harmfulness of coercion. Judges play an important symbolic role. The literature on the psychology of procedural justice demonstrates that people place a high value on how they are treated by legal authorities (Tyler, 1990). They value the affirmation of their legal status as competent citizens and human beings entitled to be treated with dignity. Judges who conduct commitment hearings in ways that seem to assume that the patient is an incompetent subject of paternalism and that deny him or her worth and respect frustrate the dignitary value of the hearing. In furthering this goal, patients should be permitted to dress appropriately for the hearing, rather than being required to appear in hospital garb, as sometimes occurs. Through his or her actions, the judge should affirm the patient's dignity and humanity. The manner in which the judge conducts the proceedings can convey to the patient that it is a process designed for his or her welfare and that he or she is valued and will be treated with fairness and dignity.

Both the judge and the expert witness can play an important role in providing the patient with a sense of information control (Fiske & Taylor, 1984). The patient, facing the uncertainties of a hospital commitment to which he or she is objecting, will predictably experience a high degree of stress and anxiety at the hearing. The judge and clinical experts, by reassuring the patient and by demonstrating concern for his or her welfare, can help to relieve at least some of that stress. By carefully and coherently conveying information to the patient about the hearing process and about what will occur at the hospital if commitment is ordered, the judge can diffuse much of the stress that the commitment process itself might produce.

The patient should not be treated as invisible at the hearing. Rather, the judge and expert witnesses should address the patient and attempt to communicate in everyday language rather than in professional jargon. If the expert witness recommends commitment, the reasons why this would be beneficial should be explained in ways that are designed to be convincing to the patient. Moreover, a sense of optimism should be conveyed. The patient should be told that although he or she suffers from a mental illness, such illness is very likely to respond to hospital treatment within a reasonably brief period. The benefits of psychotropic medication and other forms of treatment should be explained to the patient in ways that are calculated to persuade the patient as to their value.

The judge should listen attentively to the patient and convey the impression that what the patient has to say is important and will be given full consideration. According voice and validation in this way can considerably enhance the patient's feeling of participation and can inspire trust in the judge. Too often, the judge does not convey the sense that what the patient has to say will be considered and instead conveys the impression that the results of the hearing are a foregone conclusion. Such an impression can inspire distrust by the patient in the judge and the feeling that he or she is not being treated fairly and in good faith. In addition to paying close attention to the patient's testimony, the judge should ask questions of the expert witness in a way that shows that the judge will make an independent decision rather than merely rubber-stamp the witness's recommendation.

At appropriate points in the proceedings, recesses should be taken to give the attorney and client an opportunity to consider whether, in light of the testimony, the client might wish to explore the possibility of a negotiated voluntary admission in order to avoid what might appear to be the inevitable and more restrictive and stigmatizing involuntary commitment. If commitment seems to the attorney to be the likely outcome, counsel can explain the legal and other advantages of accepting voluntary admission and recommend this option to the client. Counsel should, however, assure the client that the decision is ultimately up to him or her and that if he or she continues to resist hospitalization, counsel will do all he or she can to achieve that result, even if success is unlikely. A choice by the client in favor of voluntary admission at this point, as long as the client experiences it as voluntary, may increase the potential that hospital treatment will be efficacious (Winick, 1991b). If a negotiated settlement in favor of voluntary admission is not possible, and if the judge concludes that commitment is warranted, the judge may consider giving the respondent a final opportunity before judgment is issued to accept voluntary admission in view of the decision that the judge feels compelled to make as a result of the testimony. If this final opportunity is not accepted, the judge should seek to explain the commitment decision to the respondent, addressing the respondent directly, and offer to provide any information concerning questions that the respondent may have.

Not only at the hearing, but also throughout the commitment and hospitalization process, clinicians should treat the patient with dignity and respect and should demonstrate the genuineness of their benevolent motives. The clinician should always attempt to persuade rather than coerce, to involve the patient in the decision-making process rather than dictate treatment decisions unilaterally, and to treat the patient as a person rather than as an object (Winick, 1997a). In this way, clinicians can inspire trust and confidence in the patient and the formation of a caring therapeutic alliance, both of which may be essential to a positive therapeutic outcome (Winick, 1997c, chap. 17; see also Winick, 1994).

CONCLUSION

Under basic notions of procedural due process, patients facing involuntary commitment should be given hearings to protect against inaccurate deprivations of liberty. Hearings in this context also serve an important participatory or dignitary function that should not be neglected. Restructuring the civil commitment process in the ways suggested in this chapter can significantly increase patients' perceptions of fairness, thereby increasing the likelihood that they will accept the outcome of the hearing, will view it as being in their best interests, and will participate in the treatment process in ways that will bring about better treatment results. Not only must the legal rules governing the civil commitment hearing seek to accomplish these values, but lawyers, judges, and clinicians should learn how to play their roles so as to apply the law therapeutically rather than antitherapeutically.

REFERENCES

Abisch, J. B. (1995). Mediational lawyering in the civil commitment context: A therapeutic jurisprudence solution to the counsel role dilemma. *Psychology, Public Policy, and Law, 1,* 120–141.

Addington v. Texas, 441 U.S. 418 (1979).

Ake v. Oklahoma, 470 U.S. 68 (1985).

Andalman, E., & Chambers, D. L. (1974). Effective counsel for persons facing civil commitment: A survey, a polemic and a proposal. *Mississippi Law Journal, 45*, 43–91.

Appelbaum, P. S. (1983). Paternalism and the role of the mental health lawyer. *Hospital and Community Psychiatry, 34*, 211–214.

Appelbaum, P. S., & Grisso, T. (1995). The MacArthur treatment competence study: I. Mental illness and competency to consent to treatment. *Law and Human Behavior, 19*, 105–126.

Bennett, N. S., Lidz, C. W., Monahan, J., Mulvey, E. P., Hoge, S. K., Roth, L. H., & Gardner, W. S. (1993). Inclusion, motivation, and good faith: The morality of coercion in mental hospital admission. *Behavioral Sciences and the Law, 11*, 295–306.

Brakel, S. J. (1981). Legal aid in mental hospitals. *American Bar Foundation Research Journal, 1981*, 26–93.

Brakel, S. J., Parry, J., & Weiner, B. (1985). *The mentally disabled and the law* (3rd ed.). Chicago, IL: American Bar Association.

Brehem, S. S., & Brehem, J. W. (1981). *Psychological reactance: A theory of freedom and control.* New York: Academic Press.

Brooks, A. D., & Winick, B. J. (1987). Forward: Mental disability law comes of age. *Rutgers Law Review, 39*, 235–242.

Carroll, L. (1992). *Alice's adventure in wonderland.* New York: W.W. Norton.

Cohen, F. (1966). The function of the attorney and the commitment of the mentally ill. *Texas Law Review, 44*, 424–469.

Costello, J. (1996). Why would I need a lawyer? Legal counsel and advocacy for people with mental disabilities. In B. D. Sales & D. W. Shuman (Eds.), *Law, mental health, and mental disorder* (pp. 15–39). Pacific Grove, CA: Brooks/Cole.

Developments in the law: Civil commitment of the mentally ill [Note]. (1974). *Harvard Law Review, 87*, 1190–1206.

Fiske, S. T., & Taylor, S. E. (1984). *Social cognition.* Reading, MA: Addison-Wesley.

Foucha v. Louisiana, 504 U.S. 71 (1992).

Gardner, W. P., Hoge, S. K., Bennett, N. S., Roth, L. H., Lidz, C. W., Monahan, J., & Mulvey, E. P. (1993). Two scales for measuring patient perceptions for coercion during mental hospital admission. *Behavioral Sciences and the Law, 11*, 307–321.

Goldberg v. Kelly, 397 U.S. 254 (1970).

Grisso, T., & Appelbaum, P. S. (1995). The MacArthur treatment competence study: III. Abilities of patients to consent to psychiatric and medical treatment. *Law and Human Behavior, 19*, 149–174.

Hoge, S. K., Lidz, C. W., Eisenberg, M. M., Gardner, W. S., Monahan, J., Mulvey,

E. P., Roth, L. H., & Bennett, N. S. (1997). Perceptions of coercion in the admission of voluntary and involuntary psychiatric patients. *International Journal of Law and Psychiatry, 20*, 167–181.

Lessard v. Schmidt, 349 F. Supp. 1078 (E.D. Wis. 1972).

Lidz, C. W., Hoge, S. K., Gardner, W. P., Bennett, N. S., Monahan, J., Mulvey, E. P., & Roth, L. H. (1995). Perceived coercion in mental hospital admission: Pressures and process. *Archives of General Psychiatry, 52*, 1034–1039.

Lind, E. A., & Tyler, T. R. (1988). *The social psychology of procedural justice.* New York: Plenum Press.

Marshall v. Jerricho, Inc., 446 U.S. 624 (1980).

Mashaw, J. L. (1976). The Supreme Court's due process calculus for administrative adjudication in Matthews v. Eldridge: Three factors in search of a theory of value. *University of Chicago Law Review, 44*, 28–59.

Michelman, F. I. (1977). Formal and associational aims in procedural due process. *Nomos, 18*, 126–171.

Monahan, J., Hoge, S. K., Lidz, C. W., Eisenberg, M. M., Bennett, N. S., Gardner, W. P., Mulvey, E. P., & Roth, L. H. (1996). Coercion to inpatient treatment: Initial results and implications for assertive treatment in the community. In D. L. Dennis & J. Monahan (Eds.), *Coercion and aggressive community treatment: A new frontier in mental health law* (pp. 13–28). New York: Plenum Press.

Monahan, J., Hoge, S. K., Lidz, C. W., Roth, L. H., Bennett, N. S., Gardner, W. P., & Mulvey, E. P. (1995). Coercion and commitment: Understanding involuntary mental hospital admission. *International Journal of Law and Psychiatry, 18*, 249–263.

Morrissey v. Brewer, 408 U.S. 471 (1972).

Perlin, M. L. (1989). *Mental disability law* (Vol. 3). Charlottesville, VA: Michie.

Perlin, M. L. (1992). Fatal assumption: A critical evaluation of the role of counsel in mental disability cases. *Law and Human Behavior, 16*, 39–59.

Perlin, M. L. (1996). The voluntary delivery of mental health services in the community. In B. D. Sales & D. W. Shuman (Eds.), *Law, mental health, and mental disorder* (pp. 150–177). Pacific Grove, CA: Brooks/Cole.

Perlin, M. L. (in press). *On the waters of oblivion: Sanism, pretextuality, and mental disability law.* Washington, DC: American Psychological Association.

Perlin, M. L., & Dorfman, D. A. (1996). Is it more than "dodging lions and wastin' time"? Adequacy of counsel, questions of competence, and the judicial process in individual right to refuse treatment cases. *Psychology, Public Policy, and Law, 2*, 114–136.

Perlin, M. L., & Sadoff, R. L. (1982). Ethical issues in the representation of individuals in the commitment process. *Law and Contemporary Problems, 45*, 161–192.

Poythress, N. G. (1977). Mental health expert testimony: Current problems. *Journal of Psychiatry and Law, 5*, 201–227.

Poythress, N. G. (1978). Psychiatric expertise in civil commitment: Training attorneys to cope with expert testimony. *Law and Human Behavior, 2,* 1–23.

The role of counsel in the civil commitment process: A theoretical framework [Note]. (1975). *Yale Law Journal, 84,* 1540–1563.

Stolle, D. P., Wexler, D. B., Winick, B. J., & Dauer, E. A. (1997). Integrating preventive law and therapeutic jurisprudence: A law and psychology based approach to lawyering. *California Western Law Review, 34,* 15–51.

Stransky, D. S. (1996). Civil commitment and the right to refuse treatment: Resolving disputes from a due process perspective [Comment]. *University of Miami Law Review, 50,* 413–433.

Susman, J. (1994). Resolving hospital conflicts: A study on therapeutic jurisprudence. *Journal of Psychiatry and Law, 22,* 107–133.

Sydeman, S. J., Cascardi, M., Poythress, N. G., & Rittenband, L. M. (1997). Procedural justice in the context of civil commitment: A critique of Tyler's analysis. *Psychology, Public Policy, and Law, 3,* 207–221.

Thibault, J., & Walker, L. (1978). A theory of procedure. *California Law Review, 66,* 541–566.

Tribe, L. (1988). *American constitutional law* (2nd ed.). Minneola, NY: Foundation Press.

Tyler, T. R. (1990). *Why people obey the law.* New Haven, CT: Yale University.

Tyler, T. R. (1992). The psychological consequences of judicial procedures: Implications for civil commitment hearings. *Southern Methodist University Law Review, 46,* 433–445.

Vitek v. Jones, 445 U.S. 480 (1980).

Wald, P. M., & Friedman, P. R. (1978). The politics of mental health advocacy in the United States. *International Journal of Law and Psychiatry, 1,* 137–152.

Wexler, D. B. (1996). Applying the law therapeutically. *Applied and Preventive Psychology, 5,* 179–187.

Wexler, D. B., & Winick, B. J. (Eds.). (1996). *Law in a therapeutic key: Developments in therapeutic jurisprudence.* Durham, NC: Carolina Academic Press.

Winick, B. J. (1989). Forfeiture of attorney's fees under RICO and CCE and the right to counsel of choice: The constitutional dilemma and how to avoid it. *University of Miami Law Review, 43,* 765–869.

Winick, B. J. (1991a). Competency to consent to treatment: The distinction between assent and objection. *Houston Law Review, 28,* 15–61.

Winick, B. J. (1991b). Competency to consent to voluntary hospitalization: A therapeutic jurisprudence analysis of Zinermon v. Burch. *International Journal of Law and Psychiatry, 14,* 169–214.

Winick, B. J. (1992). On autonomy: Legal and psychological perspectives. *Villanova Law Review, 37,* 1705–1777.

Winick, B. J. (1994). The right to refuse mental health treatment: A therapeutic jurisprudence analysis. *International Journal of Law and Psychiatry, 17,* 99–118.

Winick, B. J. (1996a). Advance directive instruments for those with mental illness. *University of Miami Law Review, 51,* 57–95.

Winick, B. J. (1996b). The MacArthur treatment competence study: Legal and therapeutic implications. *Psychology, Public Policy, and Law, 2,* 137–166.

Winick, B. J. (1997a). Coercion and mental health treatment. *Denver Law Review, 74,* 1145–1168.

Winick, B. J. (1997b). The jurisprudence of therapeutic jurisprudence. *Psychology, Public Policy, and Law, 3,* 184–206.

Winick, B. J. (1997c). *The right to refuse mental health treatment.* Washington, DC: American Psychological Association.

Winick, B. J. (1997d). *Therapeutic jurisprudence applied: Essays on mental health law.* Durham, NC: Carolina Academic Press.

Zinermon v. Burch, 494 U.S. 113 (1990).

AFTERWORD: THE EVOLUTION OF MENTAL HEALTH LAW: A RETROSPECTIVE ASSESSMENT

RICHARD J. BONNIE

The chapters of this book expose three sources of ambivalence at the center of mental health law. One is a deep and fundamental tension between the ethics of caring and the ethics of autonomy, which surfaces in all contexts of mental health treatment. The second is the shifting focus between offense and offender that pervades all theories of responsibility and punishment. The third is the methodological tension between scientific and moralized approaches to competence, dangerousness, and other fundamental concepts that frame mental health law. Notwithstanding these centrifugal forces of the field, researchers and practitioners in mental health law share a common bond—a commitment to humanitarian values—that draws together the diverse strands of the field and sets the agenda for its future development. This afterword briefly explores each of these points.

CARE AND RESPECT

Therapeutic ethics and mental health law reflect two sometimes divergent impulses—to care for and protect vulnerable individuals and to respect their autonomy. A normative account of mental health law over the past quarter century would trace the ascendancy of respect for dignity and autonomy as a counterpoint to unthinking paternalism. The protective impulse must often yield to the imperative of respecting the wishes of patients who resist intervention. This development is epitomized by the right to refuse treatment. Simultaneously, however, there have also been strong, though yet unfulfilled, efforts to establish a legal right to treatment, a positive right to receive mental health services grounded in a felt obligation to care for vulnerable individuals.

Chapter 1, by Burt, digs beneath these legal and ethical abstractions to explain the evolution of this nation's social policies relating to people with mental illness. In his account, legal protection of a right to treatment for people with mental illness can be seen as an expression of common humanity, whereas retreat from a social responsibility to protect and serve reflects a strong countervailing impulse to exclude or ignore such people that leads to ostracism and social invisibility. From this standpoint, the legal protection of autonomy can serve either as an instrument of respect (equal status as persons) or as an instrument of abandonment. There is evidence of both in the recent history of mental health law and policy.

OFFENSE AND OFFENDER

The intersections between mental health and criminal justice represent occasions for individualized decision making. One such intersection involves attributions of responsibility. How deeply should the offender's beliefs, motivations, and emotions be probed in a just system of punishment? Even within an entirely retributive frame of reference, what aspects of mental and emotional life have a just bearing on culpability? The more subjective the inquiry, the greater the need for participation by mental health professionals in the adjudicatory process. The need for clinical information (and services) is also enhanced wherever courts rest their judgments on assessments of amenability to treatment or on the likelihood of future offending.

The formative era of mental health law in the 1960s and early 1970s corresponded to a period of utilitarian dominance in sentencing. Assessments of amenability to rehabilitation and risk of recidivism were made every day by judges, correctional authorities, and parole boards. This was also a period of professional outreach by psychologists (community psychology) and psychiatrists (social psychiatry), as evidenced by the growth of the community mental health movement and the explosion of training in these fields. Soon thereafter, however, in the late 1970s and early 1980s, loss of faith in rehabilitation, together with a pervasive dissatisfaction with "lawlessness" in sentencing and parole, resulted in a hard turn toward offense-oriented sentencing and, in recent years, toward mandatory sentences of increasing severity. The emphasis on offense and harm has also reached the juvenile court, the last bastion of the rehabilitative ideal, leading to a curtailment of juvenile court jurisdiction over youths who commit serious offenses and to enhanced punishment of offenders who remain in juvenile court.

Individualized judgments are being squeezed out of criminal and juvenile justice in every sphere except capital sentencing (where it is constitutionally mandated). Many specialists in mental health law, especially forensic psychologists and psychiatrists, are viewing this trend with great concern. Chapter 8 by Grisso (on juvenile justice) and chapter 9 by Halleck (on capital mitigation evidence) are illustrative.

In the moral vocabulary of responsibility and punishment, these trends in the law and the practice of criminal justice reflect ongoing debates regarding the characteristics of individual offenders that are morally relevant to punishment for criminal conduct. The observations of Morse in chapter 7 and Saks in chapter 12 reflect these debates. However, from a criminological standpoint, these same trends may be better understood as a transition to an actuarial model of penology based on aggregate classification and risk management. In this view, the social practice of punishment in the 1990s reflects a clear emphasis on efficient social protection through the incapacitation of criminal populations or groups. The current tools of punishment are actuarial aggregation rather than clinical (or even moral) differentiation. Rehabilitation has no place in a statistical order organized around sentencing matrices that dictate long terms of confinement determined by severity of current offense and extent of prior record. Ironically, the civil commitment of violent sex offenders—on its face, the exemplar of individualized decision making—can be seen as the end point of this trend. It represents offense-based incapacitation packaged as if it were therapeutic intervention linked to clinical differentiation.

In short, the prevailing social practice of punishment is categorical and statistical; it is rooted either in a vengeful form of retribution or a sweeping form of incapacitation. Whatever the explanation for the trend (or whatever its moral justification, if there is one), values associated with individual dignity have been suppressed. There is little room for psychiatry and psychology in a system of criminal justice that makes no pretense of understanding the offender as a person or of making individualized judgments about the offender's future behavior. To use Burt's vocabulary, criminal offenders are extruded and isolated as a form of environmental protection and thus denied their very identity as members of the moral community.

SCIENCE AND MORALITY

Another fundamental challenge at the very center of mental health law lies in drawing and policing the boundaries between science and morals. Everyone in the field recognizes that attributions of responsibility, incompetence, and dangerousness require value judgments shaped by the normative context of the decision (e.g., the societal and individual interests at stake). They all accept, in principle, the idea that these judgments should be informed, as much as possible, by science and that intuition and supposition should not be mistaken for science.

Within this framework, however, the development of the field has been shaped by shifting intellectual currents in epistemology (e.g., degrees of skepticism about science), by specific advances in behavioral science, and by developments in the law of evidence. Morse's work has represented one pole of the debate, emphasizing that all legally relevant decisions in mental health law require moral judgment, that science often has little to offer, and that courts should be reluctant to admit clinical testimony (Morse, 1978, 1982; compare Bonnie & Slobogin, 1980). During the same period, Monahan (1981) exposed the scientific frailty of testimony on clinical predictions of violence and emphasized the value-laden nature of attribution of dangerousness.

The challenges by Morse, Monahan, and others in the late 1970s and early 1980s signaled the beginning of a continuing effort to refine expectations regarding the scientific integrity and quality of behavioral science in the courtroom. The development of specialized education and training in forensic mental health described by Hawk and Fitch in chapter 11 can be seen as the primary professional response to this challenge. Meanwhile, as Slobogin notes in chapter 13, the courts have struggled to define suitable conditions for admitting mental health testimony into evidence, taking into account the diverse values at stake.

During the past two decades, extraordinary advances have been made in neuroscience and in our understanding of the biological substrates of severe mental disorder. It appears that many psychiatric diagnoses may now satisfy even the most demanding test for scientific evidence, and that could not be said 25 years ago. It is quite revealing that in the 1990s, Morse joined hands with Monahan, me, and other members of the MacArthur Foundation's Research Network on Mental Health and the Law to invest in strengthening the scientific foundation of mental health law. (The MacArthur research is summarized on the Network's Web site at http://macarthur.virginia.edu) As a result, the empirical basis for competence assessment has been improved, although all MacArthur Networkers are quick to emphasize that the new instruments assess performance on competence-related abilities and that ultimate judgments about competence are inevitably evaluative (for example, Grisso & Appelbaum, 1998; Poythress, Nicholson, et al., 1999). In perhaps the most striking development of all, Monahan and colleagues (2000) have strengthened the scientific foundation for assessing the risk of violence among people with mental disorders. Whether and how these advances in research will affect clinical practice and legal decisions remain to be seen.

HUMANITARIAN VALUES

Another important theme emerges from the chapters in this book— the grounding of mental health law in an aspiration to promote human well-being. This idea surfaces in several different ways. In therapeutic ethics, the idea is beneficence. As Dresser shows in chapter 3, continuing concerns about the exploitation of research participants with mental illness emphasize the need to promote and preserve the trust of potential participants, their advocates, and their surrogates in the ethical integrity of the research enterprise. Polubinskaya shows in chapter 6 that human rights are at grave risk when psychiatric power is aligned with the agents of social control and when psychiatrists have lost their footing in therapeutic ethics. It will take several generations to nurture public trust in post-Soviet psychiatry. The changing financial structure of mental health services, described by Petrila in chapter 4 and Bevilacqua in chapter 5, present more subtle threats to patient well-being, endangering the spirit of trust that must underlie mental health care. Ways must be found to preserve the fiduciary obligation of providers in a financing system in which interests of providers and clients are not perfectly aligned.

Students of therapeutic jurisprudence converge on a similar point from a different angle—they are interested in promoting the well-being of all individuals who interact with the legal system. Obviously, benevolence is not a pre-eminent value in legal settings, but Wexler in chapter 14 and Winick in chapter 15 encourage scholars and investigators to investigate the effects of legal rules and procedures on the individuals whose lives are affected by them.

These convergent ideas suggest that one of the distinguishing characteristics of mental health law, despite its diverse components and disciplines, is a fundamental concern about human dignity and well-being. Whatever the context and whatever the person's perspective on the fundamental ethical puzzles that organize the discourse of the field, the work of scholars and researchers in mental health law is bound together by an underlying basic commitment to humanitarian values. This commitment has inspired the advances of the field and has defined its causes and disappointments over the past 25 years. It also defines the agenda for the future.

REFERENCES

Bonnie, R., & Slobogin, C. (1980). The role of mental health professionals in the criminal process: The case for informed speculation. *Virginia Law Review, 66,* 427–522.

Grisso, T., & Appelbaum, P. (1998). *Assessing competence to consent to treatment.* New York: Oxford University Press.

Monahan, J. (1981). *The clinical prediction of violent behavior.* Washington, DC: U.S. Government Printing Office.

Monahan, J., Steadman, H., Appelbaum, P., Robbins, P., Mulvey, E., Silver, E., Roth, L., & Grisso, T. (2000). Developing a clinically useful actuarial tool for assessing violence risk. *British Journal of Psychiatry, 176,* 312–319.

Morse, S. (1978). Crazy behavior, morals and science: An analysis of mental health law. *Southern California Law Review, 51,* 527–654.

Morse, S. (1982). Failed explanations and criminal responsibility. *Virginia Law Review, 68,* 971–1084.

Poythress, N. G., Nicholson, R., Otto, R. K., Edens, J. F., Bonnie, R. J., Monahan, J., & Hoge, S. K. (1999). *Professional manual for the MacArthur Competence Assessment Tool—Professional Adjudication—MacCAT-CA.* Odessa, FL: Psychological Assessment Resources, Inc.

AUTHOR INDEX

Numbers in italics refer to listings in the reference sections.

Broder, D. S., 110, *111*
Brodsky, S. L., 280, *288*
Bromley, D. L., 218, *226*
Brooks, A. D., 292, *305*
Brown, P., 196, *208*
Buck, J. A., 81, *97*
Buck v. Bell, 16, 24, *29*
Bulatao, E. Q., 40, *54*
Bureau of Justice Statistics, 26, *29*
Burgess, A., 246, *271*
Burt, R., 14, 15, 19–22, 25, 26, *29*, 231, *242*
Butterfield, F., 26, *29*

California Alliance for the Mentally Ill, 69, *72*
Campbell, J., 40, *53*
Capron, A. M., 69, 71, *72*
Carroll, L., 294, *305*
Carson, D., 281, *287*
Cascardi, M., 292, *307*
Caudill, D., 232, *242, 243*
Chamberlin, J., 79n2, *97*
Chambers, D. L., 293, *305*
Childress, J. F., 60, *72*
Choate, P. A., 218, *226*
Churchland, P., 142, *164*
Cicourel, A., 169, *178*
City of Cleburne v. Cleburne Living Center, 35–37, *53*
Civil Rights for Institutionalized Persons Act, 85, *97*
Clarke, R., 146, *164*
Cocozza, J. J., 195, 200, *210*, 218, *225*
Code of Virginia, 184, *192*
Coelho, T., 38, *53*
Cohen, F., 293, *305*
Colton, C., *274*
Commonwealth v. Crawford, 246, *271*
Commonwealth v. Fatalo, 250, *271*
Commonwealth v. Gallagher, 256, *271*
Commonwealth v. Seese, 255, *271*
Coppolino v. State, 250, *271*
Cormier, C., 202, 203, *210, 211*
Corporate Health Insurers, Inc. v. Texas Department of Insurance, 91, *97*
Costello, J., 293, 299, *305*
Coughlin, K., 80, *97*
Crocco v. Xerox, 89, *97*

Dahir, V., *274*
Darley, J. M., 160, *166*
Daubert v. Merrell Dow Pharmaceuticals, 251, 252, 258, 259, 261, 262, 264, 265, *271*
Dauer, E. A., 285, *288, 307*
Davis v. United States, 263, *271*
Decree No. 2171 of the President of the Russian Federation, 119, *125*
Deegan, P., 79n2, *97*
Deffenbacher, K. A., 264, *271*
Dennis, D., 44, *53*
Department of Health, Education, and Welfare, 63, *72*
Department of Mental Health Law and Policy, 83, *97*
Dershowitz, A., 227, *244*, 248, *271*
DeSimone, P. A., 153, 154, 161, *165*
Dickman, S., 154, *164*
Diller, M., 38, *53*
DiNatale, L., 176, *178*
Dobbin, S. A., *274*
Dorfman, D. A., 294, *306*
Dresser, R., 65, *72*
Dukes v. U.S. Healthcare, Inc., 88, *97*
Durham, M. L., 85, *99*
Dutton, M. A., 246, *271*

Edens, J. F., *314*
Education for all Handicapped Children Act, *29*
Ehrmann, J. C., 182, *192*
Eisenberg, M. M., *305, 306*
Elliot, E. D., 268, *271*
Ellis, R. P., 80, *97*
Ellison, R., 17, 22, *30*
Employee Retirement Income Security Act (ERISA), 86, 88, *97*
Ensminger, J., 280, *287*
Epstein, S., 65, *72*
Erlinder, C. P., 255, *271*
Ernsdorff, G. M., 246, *271*
Estelle v. Smith, 216, *225*
Ex parte Williams, 253, *271*

Faigman, D., 267, 269, *271*
Fair Housing Act Amendments, *53*
Falk, P., 258, *271*

Farnsworth, E. A., 239n2, *243*

Federal Policy for the Protection of Human Subjects, 64, *73*

Federal Rules of Evidence, 246, 250, 252, 256, 258, 264–266, 269, *271*

Feld, B., 171–173, *178*

Findlay, S., 80, *97*

Fingarette, H., 145, *164*

Finkelman, D., 283, *287*

Fischer, K., 264, *272*

Fischhoff, B., 206, *210*

Fisher, W. H., 218, *225*

Fiske, S. T., 295, 300, 303, *305*

Fitch, W. L., 215, 217, 218, *225, 226*

Flanagan v. State, 252, *272*

Foner, R., 22, *30*

Food and Drug Administration (FDA), 65, *73*

Foucha v. Louisiana, 41–43, *53*, 217, *225*, 292, *305*

Frank, J., 232, *243*

Frank, R. G., 79, 80, 93, *97, 98*

Frankfurt, H., 146, 147, *164*

Frazier, P., 263, 264, *272*

Freud, A., 228, *243*

Friedman, P. R., 292, *307*

Frost, R., 29, *30*

Frye v. United States, 250, 253, 255, 259, *272*

Furrow, B. R., 93, *98*

Gabbard, G., 231, *243*

Gable, R., *179*

Gardner, J., 147, *164*

Gardner, W. P., 200, 203, *208, 209*, 295, *305, 305, 306*

Garofalo, R., 200, *209*

Gatowski, S., *274*

Gaylin, W., 26, *30*

Genden, J., 170, *179*

General Accounting Office, 84, 90, *98*

Gerbasi, J., 45, *53*

Giles, J. P., 59, *73*

Ginet, C., 145, *164*

Ginsburg, G. P, *274*

Glover, R., 75, *98*

Goldberg, S., 245, 268, *272*

Goldberg v. Kelly, 294, *305*

Golding, J. M., 264, *272*

Golding, S., 219, *226*

Goldman, W., 105, *111*

Goldstein, J., 227, 228, 230, 234, 235, 239, *243, 244*

Goldstein, S., 228, *243*

Golland, V. B., 121, *125*

Goodman, G. S., 264, *272*

Goodrich, P., 232, *243*

Gottfredson, M., 153, *164*

Graham, M. H., 264, *270*

Greaney, T. L., *98*

Greene, J., 82, *98*

Greer, A., 218, *225*

Gregg v. Georgia, 184, *192*

Grijalva v. Shalala, 90, *98*

Grisso, T., 95, *98*, 160, *164*, 169, 170, 178, *179*, 201, *208–211*, 214, 215, 218, *225*, 283, *287*, 296, *305, 314*

Group for the Advancement of Psychiatry, 183, *192*

Gurovich, I. Y., 121–123, *125*

Hagen, M. A., 246, *272*

Haith, M. M., 264, *272*

Hall, L. L., 38, *53*

Hall, M. A., 94, *98*

Halleck, S. L., 182, *192*, 196, *208*

Handberg, R. B., 253, *272*

Hans, V. P., 266, *274*

Hansen, M., 15, *30*

Hardaway, R. M., 285, *287*

Hare, R., 202, 204, *208*

Harris, G., 200, 202, 203, *208, 210, 211*

Hart, H. L. A., 137, *165*, 241, *243*

Hart, S., 200, *208*

Harvard Law Review, 293, *305*

Hasse, A. F., 145, *164*

Hawk, G., 215, *225*

Heatherton, T. F., 161, *164*

Heilbrun, K., 205, *209*, 215, 218, *225, 226*

Henderson, C. E., 250, *273*

Henry, G., 176, *179*

Hernandez, T. K., 232, *243*

Higham, J., 21, *30*

Hilts, P. J., 69, *73*

Hirschi, T., 153, *164*

Hogan, P., 232, *243*

Wolf, S., 133, *166*
World Medical Association, 59, *74*
Wyatt v. Stickney, 3, 4, *7,* 14, 30, 107, *111*

Yakovlev, A. M., 116, *125*
Yale Law Journal, 293, 308

Youngberg v. Romeo, 46, 47, 49, *54,* 96, *100*

Zakheim, M. H., *100*
Zamora v. State, 247, *254, 276*
Zimring, F., 172, *180*
Zinermon v. Burch, 301, 308

SUBJECT INDEX

Fact judgments, 236–238
Fair Housing Act Amendments of 1988, 37
False memory syndrome, 246
Family and Medical Leave Act of 1993, 33
Family law, 228–230
Family movement, 79
FDA (U.S. Food and Drug Administration), 65
Federal Rules of Evidence, 250–251, 256–258, 261, 264–267
Fifth Amendment, 216
Florida, 83, 174
Forensic consulting, relevance of capacity for normative competence to, 157–163
Forensic mental health evaluation services, 213–224
   capital mitigation evaluations, 186–188
   compensation for, 223–224
   and competence to stand trial, 214
   and designation of forensically trained clinicians, 223
   education/training related to, 220–222
   evolution of, 213–214, 218
   and facility capacity, 219–220
   high demand for, 214–216
   interviews with defendants, 188–190
   and rights of the defendant, 216–218
   specialized clinicians, utilization of, 224
   system flexibility in delivery of, 220–221
   team approach to, 222
   in Virginia, 219–224
Foucha v. Louisiana, 41–43, 217, 292
Fourteenth Amendment, 34, 235, 293
Frank, Jerome, 227
Frankfurt, Harry, 147
"Freedom and Resentment" (Sir Peter Strawson), 129–130
Free will, 139, 145–148, 241–242
Freud, Anna, 228
Frye test, 250–253, 255
Fundamental psycholegal error, 142

Gaylin, Willard, 26
Gender discrimination law, 33

General Motors, 87
Georgia, 50–52
Georgia Regional Hospital (GRH), 50
"Get-tough" laws, 175–176
Goldman, Bill, 105
Goldstein, Joseph, 228–230, 235, 239, 240
Goodell, Charles, 25
Goodell Commission, 25–26
Gorbachev, Mikhail, 114–116
Gregg v. Georgia, 184
GRH. *See* Georgia Regional Hospital
Grigson, James P., 184
Grijalva v. Shalala, 90–91
Guilt, unconscious, 234

Hard choice model, 137
Hare Psychopathy Checklist, 204
Harsh punishment approach, 175–176
Health Care Financing Administration (HCFA), 103–104
Health maintenance organizations (HMOs), 76, 83–84, 89–91
Helsinki Declaration, 59, 62
Hepatitis, 59–60
HEW. *See* U.S. Department of Health, Education and Welfare
HHS. *See* U.S. Department of Health and Human Services
Hiss, Alger, 249
HMOs. *See* Health maintenance organizations
Holmes, Oliver Wendell, Jr., 16, 20, 24, 28, 31, 52
Homeless people, 26
Humanitarian values, 313–314
Human radiation experiments, 67

Impulses, 153–155
Indeterminate sentencing, 182–183
In re Gault, 39, 169, 170
Insane asylums, 19
Institute of Judicial Administration and American Bar Association Joint Commission on Juvenile Justice Standards, 171
Institute of Law, Psychiatry and Public Policy (University of Virginia), xiii

National Association of Forensic Social
   Work, 214
National Association of Women Judges
   (NAWJ), 284, 286
National Bioethics Advisory Commission
   (NBAC), 70, 71
National Center for State Courts, 199,
   205
National Coalition on Health Care, 110
National Commission for the Protection
   of Human Subjects of Biomedical
   and Behavioral Research, 61–64
National Institute of Mental Health
   (NIMH), 206–207, 280, 281
National Institutes of Health (NIH), 65,
   207
National Mental Health Association
   (NMHA), 106
National Research Council, 205
National standards, 108–110
NAWJ. *See* National Association of
   Women Judges
Nazism, 22, 58
NBAC. *See* National Bioethics Advisory
   Commission
New England Journal of Medicine, 59, 60
New Jersey, 129
New York, 67–70, 175, 218
*New York State Association for Retarded
   Children v. Carey*, 196
*New York State Conference of Blue Cross
   and Blue Shield Plans v. Travelers
   Insurance*, 88
New York State Office of Mental Health
   (OMH), 67, 68
New York Times, The, 68–69
NGRI. *See* Not guilty by reason of
   insanity
NIH. *See* National Institutes of Health
NIMH. *See* National Institute of Mental
   Health
1984 (George Orwell), 101
NMHA. *See* National Mental Health As-
   sociation
Nomothetic framework testimony, 247
Normative competence, 131–135
North Carolina, 47–48, 86–87, 186
North Dakota, 249
Not guilty by reason of insanity (NGRI),
   41–43
Nuremberg Code, 58–59, 62

O'Brian, Eddie, 176
Occupational Safety and Health Admin-
   istration (OSHA), 40
Oklahoma City bombing, 185
Olmstead v. L.C., 49–51
OMH. *See* New York State Office of
   Mental Health
OPRR. *See* U.S. Office for Protection
   from Research Risks
Oregon, 215
Organic findings, 159
Organization Man, The (William Whyte),
   18
Orphanages, 19
Orwell, George, 101
OSHA. *See* Occupational Safety and
   Health Administration
Outpatient treatment, 44–45

PACT. *See* Program in Assertive Com-
   munity Treatment
Parens patriae, 39, 44
Parents of children with mental retarda-
   tion, 15–17
Patient bill of rights, 92–93
Payer liability, 87–90
Pedophiles, 134–135
Penitentiaries, 19
Pennsylvania, 14
*Pennsylvania Association of Retarded Chil-
   dren (P.A.R.C.) v. Pennsylvania*,
   14
Perlin, Michael L., 294
Plessy v. Ferguson, 23
Police power, 39–43
Posttraumatic stress disorder (PTSD),
   246, 255
Preventive law, 283–287
Primary consumer movement, 79
Principle of offense, 171
Principles for the Protection of Persons
   with Mental Illness and the Im-
   provement of Mental Health
   Care, 117, 118, 121
Privatization of human services, 81–82
Procedural justice, psychology of, 294–
   295
Program in Assertive Community Treat-
   ment (PACT), 107

Willowbrook State School for the Retarded, 59–60
Wisconsin, 3, 4, 183
Witnesses, credibility/accuracy of, 249–250
Workers' compensation laws, 51–52
Workplace, violence in the, 40–41
World Health Organization (WHO), 123

World Medical Association, 59
World Psychiatric Association (WPA), 113, 115, 118
Wyatt v. Stickney, 3, 4, 14

Youngberg v. Romeo, 46–47, 49, 96

Zamora v. States, 254

ABOUT THE EDITORS

Lynda E. Frost, PhD, JD, is assistant professor of medical education and director of the Forensic Evaluation Training and Research Center at the University of Virginia's Institute of Law, Psychiatry, and Public Policy. Through the institute, she trains clinicians in laws relevant to forensic evaluation and provides consultation to various state agencies regarding forensic practice and policy.

Prior to her current position, Professor Frost worked as a law professor, teaching criminal law, international law, and mental health law courses at the law schools of the University of Richmond, the University of Iowa, and the University of Virginia. As part of her work in the field of international human rights, she has lived and worked on four continents and has recently participated in a fact-finding mission investigating conditions in Mexico's mental health system under the auspices of Mental Disability Rights International.

Richard J. Bonnie, LLB, is John S. Battle Professor of Law at the University of Virginia (UVA) School of Law and director of UVA's Institute of Law, Psychiatry, and Public Policy. He writes and teaches in the fields of criminal law and procedure, mental health law, bioethics, and public health law.

He served as associate director of the National Commission on Marihuana and Drug Abuse, has been a member of the National Advisory Council on Drug Abuse, served as advisor for the American Bar Association's Criminal Justice Mental Health Standards Project, and was a member of the John D. and Catherine T. MacArthur Foundation Research Network on Mental Health and the Law. As former chair of Virginia's State Human Rights Committee, he was responsible for protecting rights of persons with mental disabilities. In 1991, Professor Bonnie was elected to the Institute of

Medicine (IOM) of the National Academy of Sciences, and currently serves on the IOM Board on Neuroscience and Behavioral Health.

Professor Bonnie has served as an advisor to the American Psychiatric Association's Council on Psychiatry and Law since 1979, and has received the American Psychiatric Association's Isaac Ray Award in 1998 for contributions to forensic psychiatry and the psychiatric aspects of jurisprudence.